PRENTICE–HALL, INC.
Englewood Cliffs, New Jersey 07632

DON A. BROWN

University of Northern Colorado

READING DIAGNOSIS
AND REMEDIATION

Library of Congress Cataloging in Publication Data

BROWN, DON A.
  Reading diagnosis and remediation.

  Includes biographies and index.
    1. Reading—Ability testing.   2. Reading—Remedial
teaching.   I. Title.
LB1050.46.B76   428.4′2   81–15777
ISBN 0-13-754952-0   AACR2

Editorial/production supervision
    and interior design by Anne Armeny
Cover design by Tony Ferrara Studio
Manufacturing buyer: Edmund W. Leone

Printed in the United States of America

10 9 8 7 6 5 4 3 2 1

ISBN 0-13-754952-0

Prentice-Hall International, Inc., *London*
Prentice-Hall of Australia Pty. Limited, *Sydney*
Prentice-Hall of Canada, Ltd., *Toronto*
Prentice-Hall of India Private Limited, *New Delhi*
Prentice-Hall of Japan, Inc., *Tokyo*
Prentice-Hall of Southeast Asia Pte. Ltd., *Singapore*
Whitehall Books Limited, *Wellington, New Zealand*

To Beth

CONTENTS

It is possible that, in literate society, inability to read is second only to loss of sight or hearing as a handicap to learning. A reading disability is a life-blighting condition that severely limits an individual's efforts to become all that he is otherwise capable of becoming.

Yet how we learn to read and the factors that block or impede that learning process are often poorly understood. That *anyone* learns to read may be one of life's greatest miracles, a miracle we are only beginning to understand. This text discusses recent research concerning the mind and its functions of memory and learning as they relate to reading. In addition, it looks at the changes seen in our society that have produced parallel changes in factors contributing to the development of reading problems. For example, never before has a text on reading difficulties had to be concerned about the effects of alcohol and drug abuse, but it has become a part of our contemporary culture and has become a concern for those involved with reading instruction for our children and young people.

Recent changes in both the concepts behind assessment and the instruments of diagnosis have necessitated an updating of information in this area. More emphasis has been given to specific suggestions for diagnosis by classroom teachers, the use of criterion-referenced tests, and familiarity with the most recent editions of individual diagnostic reading tests. Reflecting a need this writer felt when first becoming a reading teacher, this text includes a number of reproduceable diagnostic instruments in the appendix that make it possible to diagnose most reading difficulties without reference to additional materials.

This text includes several new approaches to remediation for the seriously disabled reader together with older approaches that have become favorites over the years. Descriptions of the various approaches are sufficiently specific for the user to understand and implement any of them without having to go to more detailed sources.

In addition to general approaches, numerous specific well-tested activities for teaching reading are included in the text. Although most of these have been tried by the author, he is indebted to the many teachers who have shared with him some of their best teaching ideas for inclusion here. A special word of gratitude should go to the late Lucille Andrews, one of this writer's first graduate students, for the willingness with which she taught me, her professor, so much about the use of activities in teaching reading.

It would be impossible to express appreciation to all who deserve it for their contribution to my learning and, therefore, to this book. I want to acknowledge and thank the hundreds of poor readers—every one important—with whom I have had the chance to work. They were *my* most important teachers. I also want

PREFACE

to thank the teacher/students in my graduate classes for all I have learned from them. In addition, I want to express my appreciation to Nick Glaser, Carol Ann Moore, Jean Waldron, and Shirley Broderius for their comments and suggestions. My sister, Phyllis, deserves special appreciation for her help and continuous interest. Doug Burron and Bob Pavlik gave support and encouragement. And to those who kept the writing of this text so much in their prayers—Jackie Daugherty, Sherry Derr, Bob and Janie Wiley, and other friends—God's blessing.

There is one more set of special acknowledgements that are most important of all. I owe my family more than I can say for their continual support, patience, and encouragement. This book is the result of my wife, Beth's, belief that what I had to say was worth the effort involved in putting it on paper. My daughters Amy and April were patient and loving in the face of deadlines and commitments. David, Sharon, and Kayleen's interest was a support to me.

And finally to you who are readers, I deliver my thoughts on paper. I hope it is as worthwhile for you to read them as it was for me to write them.

Don A. Brown

Chapter One examines the importance of reading ability in today's highly literate society and the consequences—both to ourselves and to our world—of poor reading ability. The chapter then examines current psycholinguistic research related to the reading process. Although what is known is far less than what is yet to be learned, new discoveries promise improved insights into the problems of disabled readers.

THE NATURE OF READING

When Bill Klein* completed high school, he was given a "certificate of attendance" instead of a high school diploma. Although he possessed normal intelligence, Bill's school achievement was poor. Scores on a standardized reading test taken during his last year in school indicated that he had only third-grade reading ability. Later individual testing confirmed his parents' fears that his reading level was even lower than that.

Three years after high school, Bill decided to do something about his poor reading ability. He located an adult learning center and told a counselor his problem. An initial placement test indicated that he read about as well as a beginning second-grader.

The counselor reviewed Bill's school records. His scores on reading readiness tests taken during first grade indicated that he had not been ready for beginning reading instruction at that time. Nevertheless, his teacher had moved him through all the reading levels expected of a normally successful first-grade pupil, including three pre-primers, a primer, and a first-grade reader.

His second-grade teacher had noted on Bill's cumulative record that he had arrived in her class as a "nonreader" and had made no progress in reading during second grade. His third-grade progress also was poor, and the decision was made to retain him for another year at that level. His retention apparently did little to improve his reading ability.

During the middle grades, he received special instruction with a small group of other students, but instruction, even in this special group, was offered at a level much too difficult for him. At the end of sixth grade, his special teacher noted laconically, "Bill has made little progress."

Bill's secondary-school experience was, if anything, even worse than his years spent in elementary school. Although an attempt was made to place him in a special program for the mentally retarded, Bill was found to be "too bright." He was then placed in a special class for one period per day; this offered instruction in reading and math for students with learning disabilities. Much use was apparently made of programmed materials and workbooks designed to be used by students working independently. Again, the material was considerably beyond his ability.

Most of his high school career was spent in courses created for students with low ability. Unfortunately, no attempt was made to meet Bill's need for individualized reading instruction. He completed high school with an instructional reading level of low second-grade ability.

On the basis of Bill's past performance, it might be assumed that it was simply not possible for him to learn to read effectively. But fortunately, that is not the end of the story for Bill. At age 21, he began a new learning experience. Having been unable to read well enough to obtain and hold a satisfying job, he applied himself in an adult learning center. With materials available at his instructional

* All persons described in this book are real, but the names and descriptions have been changed.

reading level, with individualized instruction, and with time and patience, Bill eventually passed a high school equivalency test and received a diploma. His reading is still somewhat slow, but he reads with good comprehension. He enjoys reading. He is now planning to enroll in a trade school to prepare to become a trained auto mechanic.

If it had not been possible to help Bill—if there had been something "wrong" with him, as his parents, teachers, and even Bill himself firmly believed—then his early educational failure would simply have been an unavoidable tragedy. The evidence that he could indeed be helped points up the necessity that teachers, reading specialists, learning-disability teachers, administrators, and professors of reading do their best to help students avoid the crippling effects of poor reading ability. That is the purpose of this book—to help teachers and specialists assist students to overcome their reading difficulties.

READING ABILITY

The ability to read is crucial to the success of students in school and important for a satisfying life for adults. There is little question that many people—both children and adults—read more poorly than their potential would indicate. Harmon (1970) reported that 50 million American adults were unable to read well enough to function independently in today's society. Surveys by Louis Harris & Associates (1970, 1971) indicated that approximately 30 million had low, questionable, or marginal literacy skills. Fifteen million were found to lack the reading ability necessary to make correct responses when confronted with common printed materials. The Adult Performance Level Project (1975) found profound illiteracy problems among 39 million American adults and significant illiteracy problems among still another 35 million.

Gadway and Wilson (1975) reported that when they administered the *Mini-Assessment of Functional Literacy* to 17-year-olds still in school—not dropouts—54 percent could not identify the last day a fine could be paid when given a traffic ticket, 56 percent could not determine the amount to return with an application to a book club, and 83 percent could not find the maximum amount an insurance policy would pay.

The National Center for Health Statistics (Vogt, 1973) estimated that approximately 1 million young people aged 12 to 17 years could not read at the beginning fourth-grade level.

In 1980, a nine-month study by a task force under the direction of Vice President Mondale was reported by the Associated Press (*Greeley Tribune*, 1980) as having found little improvement in general literacy among youths aged 14 to 21. The report noted that the problem of joblessness among the young was related to the degree of literacy, and that it could be expected to remain a serious problem in the 1980s.

Such findings would seem to lend credence to the belief that something has suddenly gone wrong with the American system of education and, more specifically, with reading instruction. In actuality, the most recent reports of the National Assessment of Educational Progress in 1977 indicate that schools appear to be producing slightly better readers on the whole than they did a few years ago. These reports are corroborated by Fisher's publication for the National Institute of Education (1978) and the research and writings of Farr (Farr, Fay, and Negley, 1978; Farr, 1978). It seems apparent the answer is not to return to the instruction and methods of the past, since they appear to be less productive than those of today. Neither can anyone be satisfied with what is being done today. Reading instruction is too far short of achieving what needs to be accomplished. Instead, teachers and educators must work to improve instruction in reading beyond anything in the past.

The effects of good—or poor—reading ability may be seen in many ways. The ability to read affects students' success or failure in school. It has a profound effect on how much he* is able to learn in his classes, how he feels about himself as a student, the courses he will be able to take in advanced grades and secondary school. To some extent it will influence the classmates with whom an individual will be placed and the friends he is likely to make. It will help determine whether to pursue further training or education after the completion of high school and, in fact, whether the student is even likely to finish high school. Reading ability plays a role in determining the occupations from which people may choose and, therefore, the salary they will be able to make, who their occupational associates and friends may be, and consequently, where they may live. Because reading ability has such an influence on the people one meets, it could even be said that reading ability may play a part in whom a person will marry and, therefore, who his children will be. And of course, in turn, the ability to read will influence the quantity and quality of reading materials likely to be in a person's own home, and because of this it will be likely to have an effect on how successful his children will be in learning to read!

PSYCHOLINGUISTICS AND THE NATURE OF READING

In simplest terms, reading is the product of the processes by which we gain understanding of the thoughts someone has communicated in writing. Few people would suggest that we have sufficient understanding of the brain and its functioning to speak with finality concerning those processes. The greatest difficulty in dealing with "Psycholinguistics and the Nature of Reading" lies in the dynamic growth of knowledge in this field. Although the contributions of many early researchers and theorists are quite valuable, the rapid advance of knowledge fre-

---

* The author recognizes the need for the equal treatment of males and females but, for the sake of improved readability, uses the convention of a masculine pronoun when both male and female may be implied.

quently antiquates accepted opinions dating back only a short time. Nevertheless, current research in psycholinguistics gives us a better understanding of the nature of reading, and promises greater insight into the reader/learner and his difficulties.

The Communication Chain   In order to understand the nature of reading, it is helpful to understand some of the basic principles of psycholinguistics and communication, including principles involving not only the person who *receives* communication (in this case the reader), but the one who *transmits* it as well.

The Transmitter.   Communication originates in the thoughts—the "mind" —of a person who wants to communicate something to someone else. We commonly say we "think in English" or we "think in language," but in actuality our thoughts are in existence before they are put into words, and most of them are never expressed in language at all, not even to ourselves in inner speech. The essence of each person's being might be said to exist in an "intentional consciousness" or "faculty of mind" which directs the programs of the brain (Young, 1978, p. 175; Chomsky, 1975, p. 23).

The mind uses language as it uses other programs of the brain—that is, to carry on its various activities. But thought or mind is *not limited to language* and *is not inseparable from language* (Young, 1978, p. 46).

The separation between thought and language can be demonstrated rather easily. A fact of language and brain function is that it is not possible to use inner speech to say one thing and oral speech to say another simultaneously. Since it is impossible to separate inner speech from oral speech in that fashion, we know that if we involve a person in oral language, that person's inner speech will be occupied concurrently with the same words we hear him speak orally. If, then, we have a subject recite something he has thoroughly memorized, something he can repeat orally without having to "think" about it, we know we can cause him to involve both inner and oral speech. By having a subject repeat the alphabet orally over and over again while working at a nonlanguage task or puzzle such as playing chess or solving a puzzle knot, we can demonstrate that speech is not an essential component of thought and that it can exist separately from thought.

Each time we have difficulty expressing our thoughts or, after having said something, find that what has been said does not express our thoughts well, we have proved again the difference between thought and the language used to express that thought. If thought existed only as it is embodied in language, what we say would be the same as what we think. There could be no difference between the two. One would have to be the same as the other. But since, in fact, there is often a difference between what we say and what we think, and since we often must search for the words to express our thoughts, it shows that (1) thought is different from language, (2) thought precedes language, and (3) thought does not always match language.

This *does not mean* that language is unimportant to thought. The thinker uses language to identify, categorize, and organize as an aid to cognitive structure, and for the facilitation of the processes of memory (storage) and retrieval. And, of course, language is vital to communication.

Communication, then, begins with thought. The transmitter frames some of his thoughts in inner speech and a more limited amount as expression to others. When communicating, the transmitter may be said to be sending signals to another person—signals that are designed to arouse associations in the mind of the person who hears them or sees them. The signals are more limited than the thought and, to be fully comprehended, the receiver must utilize his background of experiences, his stored memories, to relate to the words he is reading or hearing (Baddeley, 1976, pp. 273–99).

If we describe a person, a piece of music, and an abstract painting all as "beautiful," we do not mean that they resemble one another. We rely on the receiver's ability to relate to what we are saying, remembering beautiful people, or pieces of music, or paintings that he has encountered, to understand our meaning.

The Receiver   In many ways, reading parallels listening in the chain of communication. Just as an individual who *hears* but cannot understand is a poor listener, the person who recognizes and *pronounces* words in print but does not comprehend them is a poor reader. Neither one has developed the skills to be an effective receiver of communication. Reading is not completed until the reader understands what the writer has written. The ability to recognize and pronounce the words is not enough.

In reading, the person who receives the communication utilizes

1. Vision
2. Perception
3. Recognition
4. Comprehension
5. Reaction

An understanding of these elements is critical to understanding the nature of reading; consequently, we will discuss each in turn.

*Vision. The reader must be able to see the print with sufficient clarity to be able to read. In much the same way that a blind reader who uses braille may become unable to read if his or her fingers are calloused, making it impossible to sense the different letters clearly, the reader who uses print may not be able to read if his or her sight is impaired.

*Perception. The reader must have the ability to construct meaning from the information received through the visual senses. The reader experiences sensation when light strikes the nerve endings or receptors in the retina of the eye. The optic nerve delivers these impulses to the visual center of the brain, where "vision" becomes "perception." By experience, the brain learns to analyze correctly the impulses received through the optic nerve. In a sense, perception is "what the brain does with what the eye tells it." For instance, when light passes through the lens of the eye, the image appears on the retina of the eye in inverted position, as shown in Figure 1-1. But when the brain receives this information via the optic nerve, it interprets the signal in terms of the knowledge it has gained previously about the actual state of the field of vision, and the individual views the scene in his mind right side up (Restak, 1979; Young, 1978, pp. 117–31).

It is possible to "trick" the brain by putting lenses over the eyes which turn everything upside down. In a few days, if the lenses remain in place and totally cover the field of vision so that no other visual information is received other than that seen through the lenses, the brain will begin to reinterpret the information received through the optic nerve and turn everything back right side up, provided the individual actively interacts with the environment. Removal of the lenses results in the brain readjusting to the new information and again interpreting the optic nerve impulses so that they are an accurate picture of the field of vision (Smith, 1971).

Another illustration of the perceptual process relates to the "blind spot" in each person's field of vision. Although there is an area that is unseen by the eye, the brain "fills in" the blind spot so the viewer is unaware of the missing portion.

It should be reiterated that perception is based on experience—i.e., the brain interprets the impulses of the optic nerve in keeping with what it has learned about reality. Optical illusions test one's perception by posing ambiguous stimuli which, when received and reported to the brain, may be interpreted in more than one way. In Figure 1-2, for example, the viewer may perceive either a vase or two faces. Either perception is "correct"; that is, either interpretation will fit in with what the brain has learned about reality, but the brain will not make both inter-

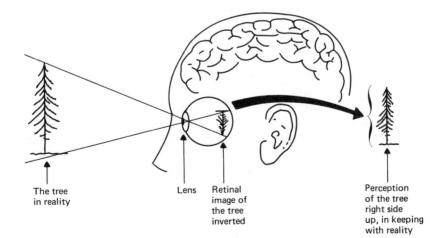

The tree in reality | Lens | Retinal image of the tree inverted | Perception of the tree right side up, in keeping with reality

Figure 1-1.   The Visual Perceptual Pathway

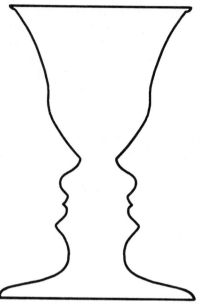

Figure 1-2. An Optical Illusion

pretations simultaneously. Reality does not readily permit the interpretation that two faces and a vase would be posed together in that fashion.

To press the illustration further, it is not possible to see something that is not in keeping with the brain's sense of reality. Everything seen is *relationally accurate*. It is not possible suddenly to perceive the vase upside down, for example, or to see the two faces looking away from each other. Even in an optical illusion, perception in the normal human brain is generally holistic. It does not invert or reverse some limited portion of what is seen.

*Recognition. The third element is often left out. People frequently describe the processes involved in reading as *vision, perception, comprehension,* and *reaction.* Although recognition involves a low level of comprehension, it is helpful to separate it from comprehension in order to differentiate it from either perception, which is a relatively mechanical process, or the more usual concept of comprehension, which involves somewhat higher thought processes. At the recognition level the reader associates the words with a surface level of meaning. Where vision and perception are beyond the power of conscious control in any substantial degree, recognition is more easily affected by the reader's thought.

We have all had the experience of writing a word we know very well but which suddenly, for some reason, does not "look right." We may write the word two or three different ways, trying to find a spelling that looks all right. In this situation, which is somewhat different from reading in the respect that we already know the concept we are trying to communicate, it is possible to reason

8

that we *see* the word, *perceive* it as a word, but have difficulty *recognizing* its correct form.

As mentioned, recognition involves a low level of comprehension. Perception is involuntary and generally quite stable. It takes several days for the visual field distorted by the lenses to be interpreted in correct perspective. By comparison, recognition may change quickly. It is unlikely, for example, that you will immediately recognize the words below:

```
b  o  d  s  e  o
o  y  g  c  a  r
t  si  a  r  e
h  a  r  n  n  a
b  nl  l  t  d
```

You can recognize the letters, of course, but even though you see both the words and the letters, it takes you several seconds before you notice that the words are written top to bottom and you are able to perceive and recognize them, and then understand the message "both boys and girls can learn to read."

Again, in reading, vision receives and reports the sensations from the field of vision; perception is the interpretation of those sensations in keeping with what the brain has learned from previous experience; and recognition takes place as the brain makes meaningful associations with the word forms it has perceived (Baddeley, 1976).

*Comprehension. A person must be able to understand what the author writes in order to be an effective reader. Of course, the fault in missed communication may be due to the author's poor writing. Even a capable reader may have difficulty understanding an ineffective writer. Or a person who is ordinarily a good reader may have difficulty reading a technical article outside his field of experience, even if the article has been written by a good writer.

The area of concern for the reading teacher, however, is the missed communication caused by poor reading ability. Inadequate comprehension may be due to the fact the reader cannot understand the vocabulary or has difficulty grasping the concepts discussed.

*Reaction. The reader must not only see, perceive, recognize, and comprehend the author's message; he must *react* to it as well. It is not enough simply to receive the author's message. The mature, effective reader must weigh the writer's words, evaluate them, appreciate them, enjoy them, and test them against personal knowledge and experience. Immature readers may accept whatever they see in print without questioning, without reference to what they already know about the subject.

Many poor readers never interact with what they read. The words they encounter are dead and lifeless. Nothing they read excites them. What they read fails to make them happy, sad, angry, pleased—in short, it fails to touch their emotions altogether. When this is the case, they have not experienced all that good reading can mean to them.

Levels of Processing   Everyone has the ability to process information at a conscious cognitive level while performing other activities at an "automatic" level. New readers begin learning to recognize words by thoughtfully considering the words. They compare them, learn to discriminate between them, and eventually learn to recognize them. As they become more capable readers, word recognition becomes almost completely automatic, freeing their higher cognitive "channels" to consider the author's meaning.

There is a limit to our conscious cognitive ability, however. We cannot handle two divergent thoughts at the same time. It is true that we can often "laminate" them, considering first one thought and then the other so we have the impression that we are able to think about two things simultaneously, but only one thought can occupy our minds at any specific moment. The reader who is using his conscious thought to analyze unfamiliar words will have difficulty understanding what the author has written at the same time. The greater the attention devoted to word attack, the less likely it will be that the reader will grasp the meaning of the passage (Young, 1978, pp. 192–204).

People are capable of performing a number of mental tasks simultaneously if they are automatic, however, and they can do so without making the tasks the focus of attention. We should note that if something goes wrong during automatic processing, the brain immediately "takes it out of automatic" and focuses conscious attention on the problem. Nevertheless, capable readers recognize the words on a page automatically, guide their eyes automatically, hold the book automatically, turn the pages automatically, and thereby are freed to concentrate on the ideas of the author (LaBerge and Samuels, 1976; Samuels, 1978).

The process is similar to learning to drive a car. When we are learning to drive, we must give attention to many things: how to accelerate, how to steer, how to brake, and so on. If a passenger tries to talk to us, we usually find it distracting. We have to give our full attention to driving. We find it almost impossible to listen to someone and drive at the same time.

Later, after we have mastered the skill of driving, we talk with people while driving, listen attentively to the radio, or perhaps think about our plans for the day—all while driving quite well. Our driving skills have become automatic, freeing our conscious thought for other matters.

In reading, it is much the same. At first, as beginners, we must give a great deal of attention to the task of word recognition, leaving us little time for comprehension. Later, as we become more proficient, we process words automatically, making it possible to consciously consider the thoughts of the author.

On occasion, everyone has had the experience of "reading" a passage only to realize that our mind has been occupied with other thoughts and we have gained nothing from our reading. What happens in such cases is that we have used automatic processing to go through the passage but have focused our thoughts on matters unrelated to the reading material. As a result, we do not process the *content* of the passage.

Learning and Memory   It seems peculiar that students so often forget things they have been taught. Most teachers can remember "teaching" a student to recognize a difficult word only to find that he has forgotten it the next day. Some reading systems provide student record cards with an array of skills to be punched as the student passes a test showing mastery of a skill. Teachers teach the skill, punch the card, and frequently find out later that the student has forgotten the skill. The administrators of one major metropolitan school district became so frustrated when students forgot skills after the tests had been passed and the cards had been punched that they ordered small patches to be distributed so teachers could fill in the holes in the record cards!

Recent memory theory has tended to define memory as "an integral part of other information-processing tasks," such as perception, recognition, comprehension, and reaction (Baddeley, 1976, p. 187). Although earlier separation of memory into short-term and long-term memory systems served as a useful hypothesis which resulted in increased research and better understanding of memory (Smith, 1971, pp. 77–78), such a dichotomy is an oversimplification (Baddeley, 1976, p. 169).

Current views of the operation of memory include an "executive" system which includes 1. conscious awareness or the "mind," 2. a primary or working memory involving most of the functions of short-term memory, and 3. probably an ancillary dependent rehearsal loop. The rehearsal loop allows the executive to hold a limited amount of language for use as it functions. Instead of allowing needed thoughts to drift away, the rehearsal loop maintains them by repeating them as long as it needs them. For example, when we write, we frequently rehearse the words we intend to use as we express our thoughts. Similarly, we may hold and consider a strictly limited number of words as we read, providing a small contextual base for the immediate word we are recognizing. In other words, the executive seems to use the rehearsal loop to repeat words in order to "keep track" of either what he is going to write or what he is reading (or hearing).

It is possible that long-term memory is divided into two highly interrelated systems: episodic and semantic memory. Tulving defines semantic memory as a system dealing with the "meaning of words, concepts and classification of concepts." He defines episodic memory as a system dealing with "personal experiences and their temporal relations" (Tulving, 1972, pp. 401–402). Baddeley (1976, p. 318) disagrees that they are separate systems, preferring to use semantic memory as the system comprising both personal experience and general knowledge. In either case, an attempt to recall information from one of the areas often triggers retrieval from the other. An attempt to recall factual content may often be enhanced by a person's ability to recall when he read the material, what the conditions were when the matter was discussed, or a personal experience directly related to the information to be retrieved. A visit to Niagara Falls (personal experience—episodic memory) would bring a probable greater ability to recall information read relating to the Falls (semantic memory).

There are a number of factors that may affect encoding in memory. Apparently the depth at which information is processed will affect the likelihood that the trace can be retrieved. If a student is asked to count each word on a page, or if he is asked to pronounce them as separate but unrelated words, he will do much more poorly later if he is asked to recall the meaning of the passage than a student who has been asked to read in order to discuss the relationships between the ideas contained in the passage. The latter instance is suggested as an illustration of deeper processing.

The richness of encoding also affects retrieval. Richness depends on the number of features associated with the memory when it is stored. Certain words have a natural richness to them as the student learns them. *Grandmother* would be likely to have far greater richness than *with*, for example. Other words may be enriched by the teacher or by the material the student is reading. The teacher may present the word *with* in such a manner that the student encodes it with uncommon richness.

Information is more easily accessible if it is organized around main ideas and interrelated with other information as it is stored. As we take in information from either reading or listening, we strip away nonessential portions and retain the important concepts. A good reader, asked to report on what he read two days ago, will seldom recall the exact words because they have not been stored. Instead, this person recalls the major concepts, and tells the listener the essence of what was read, expressing it in his own language.

We can improve learning and retrieval by encouraging students to focus primarily on main ideas and important concepts as they read, and to work actively to relate those concepts to other information in the passage and to other information already learned.

Another factor that can improve retrieval from memory is the attention to the task or the "set to learn" of the student. The student who suffers from low vitality or anxiety unrelated to the subject at hand may not learn well because he gives poor attention to the reading. This may be due to low arousal or outside concerns competing for the student's attention.

Encoding and retrieval are two sides of the same coin. If a word or an idea is encoded in keeping with the principles above, it is generally more easily retrievable. Retrieval involves both recall and recognition. Recognition might be defined as "cued identification" in which a person is able to identify a word or other bit of information even if he has only partially learned it (Baddeley, 1976, p. 285). There seem to be other differences between recall and recognition, however. Recognition of words in reading seems to involve the ability to process cues very quickly by skipping some of the steps that might ordinarily have been a part of recall. Recognition seems to be facilitated by the expectations of the reader. As we read, we anticipate the words just ahead of the spot where we are reading. When our anticipations are correct, reading flows quickly and easily, but when we are surprised by the words we identify, we must slow down and engage in a deeper level of processing.

As we add words to our immediate sight-recognition vocabulary, it is possible that we modify the manner in which the word is recognized from storage in a bundle of traces identifying the word to a single "gnostic neuron" accessed for recognition of the word (Young, 1978, p. 177). Whatever the process, we are able to recognize the word in rapid fashion, taking little thought concerning analysis and allowing our minds to consider the ideas being expressed.

Words are recognized on the basis of different characteristics: physical (configural) cues, phonemic cues, and semantic cues. In each of these domains, processing may vary in depth and richness.

As a word is being learned, the student must first realize that he does not know the word. Words that are unknown, uncommon, or unusual are better recalled than words that are more common because the reader gives them more attention and usually processes them at greater depth and with more attendant richness than for common words. This means that a person who is learning to read diverts attention from the author's message to the characteristics of an unknown or poorly recognized word, encoding the encounter with that word more deeply and more richly than for the well-known words adjacent to it. Well-known words are processed in automatic fashion, with reliance on the previous encodings to recognize them (Lockhart, Craik, and Jacoby, 1976, pp. 95–96).

If, as a word is being learned, the student encounters the same word a second time within a few seconds, his retrieval will generally be quite different during the second attempt than it was the first time. In the initial attempt, the student will go through a lengthy process of sounding out the word or using other cues to help in recognition. If, a few seconds later, he is asked to identify the same word, he generally will do so much more quickly. He is apparently able to go directly to the final result of his previous processing without going through all the steps involved in the first trial.

If, however, there is a significant delay between the two attempts, the final result of the reader's first attempt may no longer be retrievable by him, and he must reconstruct his initial processing in order to identify the word.

Even then, the second attempt will generally be faster than the first. Lockhart, Craik, and Jacoby suggest that this is because fewer processes are being performed (Lockhart, Craik, and Jacoby, 1976, pp. 78–79). Whether this is the case or not, greater familiarity tends to increase the speed with which an item is recognized. The eventual result in the case of good readers is that the word is recognized quickly and without requiring conscious analysis.

As we attempt to recognize an unfamiliar word, we go through a process of constructing a "probe" from our analysis of the printed word. If we encounter an unknown word in our reading, we study the word in print and attempt to identify, reproduce, and blend the sounds of the letters and letter combinations to approximate the stored trace of that word. With this approximation as a probe, we try to elicit a "match" from the phonemic domain of our memory. The closer the approximation of the probe to the word-in-memory, the easier it is to make a match and recognize the word. When the reading passage is conducive to it, we also may use cues to the unknown word from the contextual meaning of the passage.

Recognition is aided by the distinctiveness of a word, the richness of its encoding, the reader's set to recognize the word, and the reader's level of arousal and attention (Lockhart, Craik, and Jacoby, 1976, p. 84). The more features there are to set the word apart, the easier it will be to learn. The greater the number and strength of associations with the word and the deeper the level of processing used in learning the word, the more likely it is that the word will be retrievable. In addition, the reader's own anticipation or expectation of the word in reading helps him recognize the word more rapidly when it is encountered. Finally, the reader's level of active interaction with the reading material, the extent of focus on the task and effort toward meaning, will have an effect on how readily that person will process what he is reading.

Sylvia Ashton-Warner (1959) had success in teaching children to read "organic words," words of love and hate. Students who had little success remembering ordinary words were able to remember organic words easily. The word *kiss*, for example, is likely to be processed in greater depth and encoded more richly than the word *is*.

Any word related to an individual's personal needs seems to be encoded with greater richness. High school students intent on being able to pass the driving test are likely to master words such as *intersection, passing lane, pedestrian crossing*, and *speed limit* more easily than words having nothing to do with the driving test. Students in an adult learning center may find that words related to money or getting a better job are easier to learn than words that seem to have little to do with personal needs.

Even an ordinary word, however, may eventually be learned if it is encountered with sufficient frequency. Imagine a reader faced with learning the word *can*. Although it is not a particularly interesting word, and the reader has no great personal need to learn it, he probably will learn it because it will be encountered often. The cumulative effect of multiple exposures will eventually build a retrievable, recognizable trace. We are told that the ancient Chinese water torture was effective not because of the initial force of the drops of water on the forehead of the person being tortured but because of the cumulative impact of the constant dripping over a long period of time. Eventually, the continual tapping of the water drove the poor unfortunate mad.

Although it may be dangerous to liken the lively art of reading instruction to a method of torture, it is a good analogy in one respect. The effect of a number of meaningful repetitions can produce sufficient processing for the word to be learned.

It is important to remember that errors in word recognition are a natural part of learning. Before any learning takes place, people are just as likely to call a word in print one thing as another; the response would be almost completely un-predictable. When we start learning to identify a word, we go through a process which Frank Smith (1971), and Gibson and Levin (1975) refer to as the "reduction of uncertainty." Even if we miscall the word, the error or miscue will be limited to a very few possible responses. For example, we may see the word *farm* and call it "from," but it is not likely we will call it "Washington" or "apple" or "big" or any of the other vast majority of words that make up our total vocabulary. In general, we will make fewer and fewer errors in recognition as we continue to "reduce uncertainty" and learn to recognize the word correctly, matching the probe with the right word-in-memory.

Ineffective readers may be satisfied by a match based on too little information or incorrect information in constructing the probe. They may, for example, be satisfied with "bank" for the word *blank* because they did not include all the phonemic information in their probes.

Sometimes it is possible to make a mismatch on the basis of an incorrectly learned or stored word. A person may be satisfied with a match of "there" for *where* or "what" for *that* because he has learned, incorrectly, to match the probe with the wrong word. This person has developed a "learned confusion." He has learned something—developed a trace incorrectly elicited by a probe—that is not correct.

Learned confusions often are the result of a lack of consistent correction. No one has listened to the student while he was reading and made him aware of the error, following through with correction until he was able to get the confusion sorted out in his mind. This may sometimes occur because a teacher has too many students in the classroom to provide the attention needed to correct the student's persistent miscall. A teacher may hesitate to interrupt a student while he is reading, but fails to go back to the word when he has finished reading, or perhaps hopes that the student will eventually correct his own mistake. Whatever the reason, learned confusions result when correction is lacking or inconsistent and the student therefore continues to recognize the word incorrectly.

Although recognition and recall are closely related, possibly representing different functions in the same system, there are some differences that are important to an understanding of the nature of reading. Recall relies much more heavily on reconstruction to summon a memory to conscious awareness. If asked to recall where you were and what you did at noon on the third Monday in February, you might engage in something like the following:

Let's see. Last February I was teaching school in Brentwood on Monday, so I was probably in school. I don't think I was sick, and that snowstorm that closed school was a little earlier in the year. Parent conferences were held on Wednesdays and Thursdays last year, so Monday was likely to have been a regular school day. My lunch hour began at 11:30 last year, and I only had noon hall duty the first week of each month, so I wasn't likely to have been on hall duty, and by 12:00 I would probably have finished my lunch and stopped in the teacher's lounge for a few minutes before going back to my classroom.

Remembering information stored in semantic memory is somewhat different, but still tends to rely on a similar process of reconstruction. An exception is the retrieval of a recently stored item. In trying to recall a recent event, a person locates the desired item by quickly scanning and selecting it from among other recent items rather than by going through the longer process of reconstruction (Lockhart, Craik, and Jacoby, 1976, pp. 89, 95–96).

When someone is asked to recall an item from material he has read, it is generally easier for him to retrieve it if it has been semantically coded—that is, coded in terms of its meaning rather than in terms of its visual or phonemic features. This is especially true if there is significant delay between the time of reading and the time of recall.

As mentioned earlier, recall is seldom an exact reconstruction of the original item. Except in situations demanding rote memorization, storage in semantic memory will usually involve condensation and summarization of the original event or concept, together with the reorganization, personal interpretation, elaboration, and distortions that take place as new information is integrated into what the individual has already learned (Reed, 1979, p. 24).

It is easier for a person to read connected discourse than jumbled or isolated words. Prose presented one word at a time is identified more slowly and remembered more poorly (Epstein, 1961 and 1962; Kulhavy, Dyer, and Caterino, 1975). Syntax is an important contributor to good reading, aiding the reader in anticipating the upcoming words and thoughts.

However, syntax and semantics are closely related. Regarding them as separate entities is somewhat impractical, because a change in syntax almost inevitably is accompanied by and related to a change in meaning as well (Baddeley, 1976, pp. 310, 315–16).

We can read the following passage and "answer" the questions below without having satisfactory comprehension of its meaning because we are able to use the syntactic markers in the language.

The Gasconade

As the canole and his tingen spingled collog, he gant the spaddle over the munt. On the gleeb of the munt, the tingen flem a gasconade. Thomly, pree skog the canole. "Brome welmly," mir snashed. "Fleg flemt a gasconade."

1. Who spingled collog with the canole? (his tingen)
2. What did he gant? (the spaddle)
3. Where did he gant the spaddle? (over the munt)
4. What did the tingen flem? (a gasconade)
5. How did pree skog the canole? (thomly)
6. What did mir snash? ("Brome welmly, fleg flemt a gasconade.")

Although we can answer the questions, that does not mean we understand the passage. We cannot explain what is happening in the selection because we do not understand the vocabulary used. The answers to the questions are without meaning, even to ourselves—they are without depth in our semantic domain.

Although the words used in the paragraph are nonsense words composed to illustrate a principle, the vocabulary in some material is almost as difficult as "The Gasconade" for many students having difficulty with reading comprehension. "The sabre-toothed tiger was a carnivore" may lack meaning for some students unless they can understand the meaning of the word *carnivore.* If they learn that it means a "meat-eating animal," the passage becomes clearer. Still, they may not realize that sabre-toothed tigers are long since extinct, and the teacher may need to help them develop a sense of the distant past in order to fully appreciate the sentence.

Students who have no understanding of the functioning of government may have difficulty understanding a passage such as the following:

> There are three branches of government: the legislative, the executive, and the judicial. In passing a law, the legislative branch must draft it and approve it; the executive must sign it, veto it, or allow it to become law without his signature; and the judicial must pass on the constitutionality of the law if it is brought into question through the legal system. An exception to the process above is that when a law that has been vetoed is brought back through the legislative process and passes the legislative branch by a sufficient margin, it may become part of the law of the land.

It may be impossible for some students to relate the concepts in the passage to anything they already know. They may well be able to "answer" a question asking how many branches there are in government, and they may even be able to label each branch, but still not understand what they are or even what is meant by a "branch of government." Not knowing what they are, such students have little idea about the process being described. In short, learners must be able to relate new information to what they already know in order to process the learning in a meaningful way.

Although there is not unanimous agreement, a review of research suggests that concepts may be stored either as specific detailed information or information organized around main ideas. We learn, or store, more details than organized ideas, but isolated details appear to be more difficult to retrieve. Research underscores the importance of trying to relate details to main themes for better retrieval. "The evidence suggests (1) that organized material is easy to learn, (2) that subjects will impose their own organization on random material, and (3) that the requirement to organize the material leads to good retention." (Baddeley, 1976, p. 274)

SUMMARY

In our society, reading is one of the most important skills; it affects virtually every aspect of our lives. Although data seem to indicate that reading ability is no worse, and possibly better, than it has been in the recent past, literacy demands have continued to increase, and a significant proportion of our student and adult populations are unable to read well enough to meet those demands.

Reading is a part of communication, and a successful reader must see, perceive, recognize, comprehend, and react to the author's message. Beginning readers must use their higher cognitive abilities to analyze and recognize words in print. More capable readers recognize words at an automatic level, leaving their conscious cognitive thought free to consider the author's line of thought. The effectiveness with which a memory may be stored depends on the depth at which the word is processed, the richness of its encoding, how well it is condensed and interrelated, and the attention and arousal of the learner. These may be affected by the importance the student attaches to the word, the degree to which it meets the student's needs, the distinctiveness of the word, and repetition of the word. Learning to recognize a word involves the reduction of uncertainty, narrowing the range of possible miscalls until the correct identification of the word is made with acceptable consistency. Some students have "learned confusions," recognizing the word incorrectly much or all of the time, because of inconsistent correction. They *learn* to respond incorrectly to the word.

In order to learn a new concept, students should be able to interrelate the new learning with information already stored in their memories. Unless they are able to do so, the new information may be difficult to retrieve.

RECOMMENDED READINGS

BADDELEY, A. D. 1976. *The psychology of memory.* New York: Basic Books.

GIBSON, E. J.; and LEVIN, H. 1975. *The psychology of reading.* Cambridge: MIT Press.

ROBECK, M. C.; and WILSON, J. 1974. *Psychology of reading: Foundations of instruction.* New York: Wiley & Sons.

SAMUELS, S. J. 1976. "Modes of word recognition," in H. Singer and R. Ruddell (eds.), *Theoretical models and processes of reading* second edition. Newark, Delaware: International Reading Association.

SMITH, F. 1971. *Understanding reading.* New York: Holt, Rinehart & Winston.

WEAVER, P. 1978. *Research within reach.* Washington, D.C.: Research & Development Interpretation Service, Inc., and National Institution of Education.

REFERENCES

Adult Performance Level Project. 1975. *Adult functional competency: A summary.* Austin, Tex.: Univ. Texas, Div. of Extension.

Ashton-Warner, S. 1959. *Spinster.* New York: Simon & Schuster.

Baddeley, A. D. 1976. *The psychology of memory.* New York: Basic Books.

Brown, D. A. 1964. *The effect of selected purposes on the oculo-motor behavior and comprehension of third grade and seventh grade students of fifth grade reading ability.* Unpublished doctoral dissertation, Univ. Oregon.

Chomsky, N. 1972. *Language and mind.* New York: Harcourt Brace Jovanovich.

Chomsky, N. 1975. *Reflections on language.* New York: Pantheon Books.

Epstein, W. 1961. The influence of syntactical structure on learning. *American Journal of Psychology* 74: 80–85.

_____. 1962. A further study of the syntactical structure of learning. *American Journal of Psychology* 75: 121–26.

Farr, R. August 1978. Competency testing and reading performance. *Reporting on Reading* 4: 1–6.

Farr, R.; Fay, L.; and Negley, H. H. 1978. *Then and now: Reading achievement in Indiana (1944–45 and 1976).* Bloomington, Ind.: School of Education, Indiana Univ.

Fisher, D. L. 1978. *Functional literacy and the schools.* Washington, D.C.: National Institute of Education.

Gadway, C.; and Wilson, H. A. 1975. *Functional literacy: Basic reading performance.* Denver: National Assessment of Educational Progress.

Gibson, E. J.; and Levin, H. 1975. *The psychology of reading.* Cambridge: MIT Press.

Goodman, K. 1968. *The psycholinguistic nature of the reading process.* Detroit: Wayne State Univ. Press, pp. 23–25.

Greeley Tribune (Greeley, Col.), January 9, 1980, p. 7.

Harmon, D. 1970. Illiteracy: An overview. *Harvard Educational Review* 40: 226–43.

Harris, Louis, & Associates. 1970. *Survival literacy: Conducted for National Reading Council.* New York: Louis Harris & Associates.

Harris, Louis, & Associates. 1971. *The 1971 national reading difficulty index: A study of reading ability for the National Reading Center.* New York: Louis Harris & Associates.

Kulhavy, R. W.; Dyer, J. W.; and Caterino, L. C. 1975. On connecting connected discourse: A comment on methodology. *Bulletin of the Psychonomic Society* 5: 146–47.

LaBerge, D.; and Samuels, S. J. 1976. Toward a theory of automatic information processing in reading. In *Theoretical models and processes of reading,* ed. Singer and Ruddell. 2nd ed. Newark, Del.: International Reading Ass'n.

Lockhart, R. S.; Craik, F. I. M.; and Jacoby, L. 1976. Depth of processing, recognition and recall. In *Recall and recognition,* ed. J. Brown. London: Wiley.

National Assessment of Educational Progress. 1977. *Results of two national reading assessments.* Denver: National Assessment of Educational Progress.

Penfield, W. 1969. Consciousness, memory, and man's conditioned reflexes. In *On the Biology of Learning,* ed. K. H. Pribam. New York: Harcourt Brace Jovanovich, pp. 127–67.

Reed, G. 1979. Everyday anomalies of recall and recognition. In *Functional disorders of memory,* ed. J. F. Kihlstrom and F. J. Evans. Hillsdale, N.J.: Lawrence Erlbaum Associates.

Restak, R. M. 1979. *The brain: The last frontier.* Garden City, N.Y.: Doubleday.

Robeck, M. C.; and Wilson, J. 1974. *Psychology of reading: Foundations of instruction.* New York: Wiley & Sons, pp. 58–60, 196.

Samuels, S. J. 1978. The technology of reading: A current view. Technological Report No. 2. Univ. Minnesota: Minnesota Reading Research Project.

Smith, F. 1971. *Understanding reading.* New York: Holt, Rinehart & Winston, p. 89.

Tulving, E. 1972. Episodic and Semantic Memory, in E. Tulving and W. Donaldson (eds.), *Organization of Memory.* New York: Academic Press, pp. 381–403.

Vogt, D. 1973. *Literacy among youths 12–17.* Vital and Health Statistics, Series 11–131, Washington, D.C.: U. S. Government Printing Office.

Weaver, P. 1978. *Research within reach.* Washington, D.C.: National Institute of Education, pp. 57–59.

Young, J. Z. 1978. *Programs of the brain.* New York: Oxford Univ. Press.

In this chapter we turn to the various facets of normal reading ability. Reading, certainly not a unitary act, involves a number of operations culminating in understanding and reaction to what has been read. The different aspects of reading are combined into a figure to aid in diagnosis and remediation. The scope and sequence of reading skills at the end of the chapter provides a "map" of developmental reading growth from level to level.

READING ABILITY

It would be difficult for physicians to identify, diagnose, and treat coronary difficulties if they had no idea how a healthy heart normally functions. It would be equally difficult to diagnose and correct reading problems not knowing how students ordinarily learn to read. Unless they have a checkpoint or frame of reference, even the best reading teachers may tend to overlook various aspects of reading. In this chapter, we will look at the "Diagnostic Model of Reading Behavior" and a scope and sequence of reading-skill development, to gain a better understanding of how reading ability develops in students and to provide a standard by which the reading teacher can judge the performance of less successful students.

In looking at the Diagnostic Model or the scope and sequence, it should be remembered that even the most advanced skill may be introduced and taught at a rudimentary stage in kindergarten or first grade. For example, teaching critical evaluation in reading may be thought to be the domain of secondary reading instruction, but when kindergartners are asked whether or not *Jack and the Beanstalk* is a true story about real people, they are beginning to be taught critical reading skills.

This implies another truth that relates to the development of reading: that skills develop or grow in sophistication and complexity as a student learns to read. Although the identification of the initial consonant sound of the letter *b* is a word analysis skill, it is much less involved than learning to successfully attack the word *crochet*. This word includes a consonant blend, an uncommon digraph, and an unusual ending vowel sound; moreover, the student requires the skills needed to syllabify and blend the elements of the word in order to arrive at the point of word recognition.

Neither is there any set order to the development of skills. Some teach long vowel sounds before short vowel sounds, while others reverse the order. Some would postpone word attack skills until late in the sequence of skills, preferring to develop a sizable basic sight vocabulary before beginning the development of word attack. Others introduce word attack skills very early. Each school of thought has its champions, its research, and its disciples; and each can point to successes in teaching children to read. There seems to be no specific magical formula that dictates just when to teach what skill in order to be successful in teaching reading. Students have learned—and failed to learn—to read following many different sequences of skills.

DIAGNOSTIC MODEL OF READING BEHAVIOR

The Diagnostic Model of Reading Behavior is a mnemonic device to help the reading teacher or diagnostician keep the various elements of reading in mind while performing a diagnosis. The figure has eight major aspects; several of them contain more than one element of reading behavior. Picture a boy walking a rail. Let the boy represent reading, and let the rail represent the foundation of reading readiness on which successful reading instruction is built. Let one leg stand for sight recognition of vocabulary and the other for word analysis skills. A reader needs both "legs" to learn to read effectively, just as he needs two legs to walk effectively. The legs support the "body of comprehension." The arms represent the use of context clues, and they are attached to the body because a reader cannot make good use of context clues unless he understands the context. The body of comprehension is itself divided into four areas: understanding vocabulary, understanding details, understanding the main idea, and the ability to imply or infer. Let the fact that the boy is walking or moving represent rate and fluency. The boy is carrying a book which stands for locational and study skills. And, to illustrate the last of the eight aspects, let the head of the boy illustrate reaction, usually divided into three areas: critical evaluation, appreciation, and enjoyment. Although the various facets of reading may be represented as you see in Figure 2-1, the purpose of the figure is to enable the reading diagnostician to visualize the necessary skills, attributes, and abilities of a good reader without having to refer to an illustration.

READING READINESS

Reading readiness is the first area indicated in the figure. Readiness might be defined as the student's ability to profit from initial reading instruction as it is of-

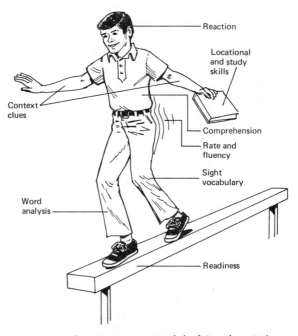

Figure 2-1.   The Diagnostic Model of Reading Behavior

fered to him. It might be possible for some students to learn to read effectively if reading instruction were offered to them in a different way, but readiness is that capability to learn to read under ordinary instructional conditions.

No one knows exactly how or why students develop reading readiness. There seems to be little doubt in anyone's mind that beginning readers vary in the degree to which they are ready for reading instruction, and there seems little doubt that given the opportunity, most students develop readiness. However, we are much less certain of the composition of that readiness (Gibson and Levin, 1975, p. 260). Nonetheless, several factors surface with regularity. Among these are visual discrimination, auditory discrimination, attention, and language base.

Visual Discrimination   Beginning readers must be able to recognize differences between letters before they can make good progress in learning to read (Richek, 1977–78). This is different from the ability to see clearly or accurately. Visual acuity, as that is usually called, is the ability to *see* the letters or words. Visual discrimination is the ability to distinguish one letter or word from another.

In the past, reading readiness tests attempting to measure visual discrimination often used gross forms and forms not directly related to words and letters. As illustrated in Figure 2-2, the task was to identify the form to the right of the line that was the same as the form on the left. The directions were sometimes difficult for a child to follow easily. Although not taken from any specific reading readiness test manual, the directions might have been similar to the following:

> "Look at the picture to the left of this line." (Point to the star and see that all the students know which figure is meant. Then indicate the line to them.) "Now I want you to look at each of the other figures to the right of the line." (Again point out the figures indicated.) "Look closely at each of them. Decide which of the four figures to the right is just like the figure to the left of the line. As soon as you find that figure, draw a circle around it."

Many students apparently became confused by such directions and performed poorly on the test. The conclusion that was drawn was that the students were unable to distinguish gross forms when, in actuality, what should have been concluded was that they had difficulty understanding the directions. A simple experiment was all that was necessary to prove the point. Researchers and teachers who gave the same tests to children on an individual basis, making certain that each

Figure 2-2.   An Example Item of the Kind Used in Early Reading Readiness Tests

student understood exactly what he or she was asked to do, found that even beginning readers had almost no difficulty in completing the tasks successfully. This seems to indicate that the children could tell the difference between a star and a square or between other gross forms (Heilman, 1977, p. 43). They simply were having difficulty understanding the directions.

Some letters do pose problems for the beginning reader, however. Probably the most difficult group of letters is that differentiated on the basis of the letters' position in space. Before a child goes to school, an object's position has almost nothing to do with its identification. A dog is a dog no matter where it is standing or where it is placed. As shown in Figure 2-3, a pan is a pan, whether it is facing right or left, upside down or right side up. It would be ridiculous to presume that a pan hung by its handle in an upside-down position would be a different object if it were placed on a table.

As soon as a child begins learning to read, however, a figure's position in space becomes important. As shown in Figure 2-3, although the letters *d*, *b*, *q*, and *p* resemble "pans" hung in different positions, the similarity is more apparent than real. Although the letter forms are quite similar, differing only in position, they each have distinctive values. Each spatially different letter represents a different sound. It is little wonder that children have difficulty with words such as *big* and *dig*. Based on their experience up to that point in their lives, *b* and *d* should be the same. Suddenly, when they begin learning to read, they must learn a new basis of visual discrimination, and they must learn to make the distinction between the two quickly and consistently.

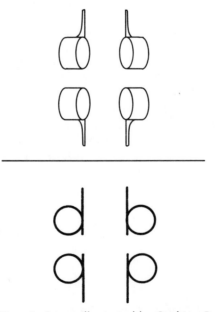

Figure 2-3.   Positions in Space Illustrated by Cooking Pans and Letters

Other letters also cause beginning readers difficulty. The letters *M* and *W, u* and *n*, and *t* and *f* are inversions of similar forms. The letters *L* and *J, O* and *Q, E* and *F*, and even *a* and *s* are confusingly alike for the beginning reader. The letters *m* and *n* seem almost purposely contrived to cause difficulty. Not only are the printed letters similar, the printed *n* has one "hump," the printed *m* has two "humps," the cursive *n* has two "humps," and the cursive *m* has three! Other letters that cause the novice reader problems are *l, j,* and *i* with their similar structures (Dunn-Rankin, 1978, pp. 122–30).

In summary, what we are asking the young readers to do is difficult. They must learn to discriminate visually between the various letters quickly and accurately. Most of us have forgotten just how difficult that is. To help refresh your memory, read through the passage below. A few hints have been added to help you out as you "learn to read" the following:

(#] /[[)   (The Book)

```
*[[)  − ( (#] /[[).
 +   = − %  &]] (#] /[[).
 +   = − %  ¢]−' (#] /[[).
 +   * +)] ([  ¢)−'.
```

_____

− is *a*, / is *b*, = is *c*, ' is *d*,] is *e*, # is *h*, + *is i*,) is *k*,
* is *l*, % *is n*, [is *o*, ¢ is *r*, & is *s*, (is *t*.

Even after years of practice with letters and letter forms, words and word forms, it takes time to understand the new system of markings for letter sounds and words in the illustrated selection. It is likely that the similarities between some of the letter marks caused you some difficulty, just as other letter similarities trouble beginning readers.

It is important to remember that discrimination is learned. Improper visual discrimination simply indicates that the student has not yet learned to differentiate between the two similar forms on the basis of position. It is common to suspect that poor visual discrimination is the result of poor vision. Although a minimal threshold level of vision is necessary in order to see the distinguishing positions, above that level there is no strong relationship between the two. Visual discrimination depends on learning to differentiate between letters and between word forms.

Auditory Discrimination   Another readiness skill is auditory discrimination. Students hear the word or the letter sound but have difficulty discriminating between the various sounds until they develop auditory discrimination. The short *i* and short *e* sounds frequently cause children difficulty. They often are hard pressed to distinguish between words such as "pin" and "pen," for example. Linguistic differences between Spanish and English make it difficult for some students who speak Spanish in their homes to distinguish between the "ch-" and "sh-" sounds. If a teacher emphasizes the recognition of certain letter sounds in the instructional program, and if he or she has some students who cannot distinguish between those sounds, those students are likely to have difficulty in reading. They will need further practice in discriminating between those sounds before being taught to use them as tools in analyzing words.

It is fortunate that many specific sounds are not essential for progress in reading. Look at the following example.

J__m's   D__g

J__m   h__d   w__nt__d   __   d__g   f__r   __   y____r.   Wh__n   h__s
b__st   fr__nd,   J__hn   g__t   __   l__ttl__   pupp__   f__r   h__s
b__rthd____,   J__m   d__c__d__d   h__   w__nt__d   a   p__p   m__r__   th__n
__n__th__ng   __ls__   __n   th__   wh__l__   w__rld!

If you were able to read the passage—from which all the vowels have been removed—you can see that specific vowel sounds are not so essential to reading that all progress in learning to read must be stopped until they are learned.

Attention   Another factor in reading readiness is attentiveness. In order for students to profit from reading instruction, they must be able to pay attention to what the teacher is trying to teach them. They must be able to maintain that attention long enough to learn. This requires more than just sitting still. To learn effectively, students must be able to focus their conscious consideration on the task to be learned in an active fashion. A student may be able to discriminate visually and auditorily but may not make gains in learning to read because he has not developed the ability to give the needed attention to instruction.

Language Base   Most reading instruction is based on the frequently erroneous assumption that before a child has begun to learn to read he or she has had five or six years of experience in dealing with the oral language in which reading will be taught. There are many students who come to school with limited exposure to English. Others may be native-born English speakers, but they speak a dialect that is sufficiently different from the English spoken in the classroom to handicap them in trying to understand the teacher. In such cases, a language enrichment program may help them become better learners. Such enrichment should not be limited to basic vocabulary study. Learners should be helped to build concepts and to develop broad understandings. Most people can eventually be taught to analyze and recognize words. It is equally important to begin building comprehension from the very earliest grades so students will be able to keep up with their classmates at later grade levels. Too often, reading programs for bilingual students or students who come from educationally disadvantaged homes tend to emphasize word recognition and do not provide for the development of informed, thinking young people. When such programs have run their course, producing students who can recognize words but often do not understand the author's message, it isn't surprising that they lag behind other students who have been developing a grasp of deeper concepts. The educationally disadvantaged students, instead of being helped to overcome a limited language background, have only fallen further behind.

Other Readiness Factors   There are many other social, cultural, economic, psychological, and educational factors that have been found to correlate with reading achievement. Exposure to reading in the home, availability of ample reading materials, family models who read, high levels of communication between parents and children, and the provision of educational toys and games have all been associated with reading readiness (TePoel, 1980). Many of these would seem to be related to the four factors discussed above. For example, children whose parents read to them tend to learn to pay attention and to develop a stronger language base.

SIGHT VOCABULARY

Students first begin to recognize words in print from the overall visual impact of the word. A first-grade student once explained with good logic that he knew the word *horse* because it *looked* like *horse* and it did not look like any other word. Beginning readers learn to identify words initially in the same way they identify other objects—by general visual appearance. They do not analyze letter-sound associations. They do not utilize skills of syllabication, slicing the word into smaller entities and blending these parts together again into a whole. They recognize a word by the way it *looks* to them.

The basic sight vocabulary is important because it forms a good foundation upon which word analysis skills may be developed. As soon as students can recognize a few words with similar letter-sound associations, they are ready to begin building word attack skills. Teachers use various techniques to help beginning readers develop a good basic sight vocabulary. Experience charts are widely used. The teachers may generate considerable cue force by using the words to make a story, pronouncing the words, discussing the words with the students, and repeating the words as they read the story—all making it easier for students to add the word to their immediate sight vocabulary.

When they approach reading through the development of initial sight vocabularies, learners go from things they know (words within their speaking vocabulary) to things with which they are less familiar (words represented in print). If reading were to be taught today by first teaching the letters and letter sounds, then teaching combinations of letters and letter sounds, and finally, by having the students learn words in print, they would have greater difficulty learning to read. It is generally less effective to go from an unknown (letters and letter sounds with little or no meaning for the novice reader) to another unknown (letter combinations) before arriving at words that have meaning for the new reader. It is more effective to start with what the reader knows and relate what he is trying to learn to what he already understands. This is as true for an older person who is just learning to read as it is for a first-grade child who is learning to read in a more usual developmental fashion.

There is an interesting relationship between basic sight vocabulary, word attack, and the broader immediate sight vocabulary that develops later. Mature readers have a vast number of words in their immediate sight vocabulary. They add words to their automatic-recognition vocabulary by a selective process which causes them to encode newer, less familiar words at a deeper level and with greater richness than words they already recognize (Lockhart, Craik, and Jacoby, 1976, p. 79). But students must have some means of recognizing an unknown word, or it remains unknown, making semantic or meaningful encoding impossible. Sometimes someone simply tells the student what the word is, but much more frequently he must attack the word on his own. This means that he must learn to analyze words. Word analysis, sometimes called "decoding skills," enables the student to recognize the word independently, which is necessary in order for him to discover the word's meaning or to have the meaningful repetitions needed to make the word a part of his immediate sight vocabulary.

In other words, without a basic sight vocabulary, most readers would have greater difficulty developing good word attack skills. But it is also true that without sufficient word attack skills, most readers would not be able to develop an adequate immediate sight vocabulary.

WORD ANALYSIS SKILLS

Word analysis instruction can be begun very early in the reading program; it usually starts with initial consonant sounds and progresses to ending consonants, vowel sounds, medial sounds, and then to more advanced word analysis skills. Aspects of word analysis are phonic analysis, structural analysis, syllabication, and blending.

Phonic Analysis   Usually the earliest instruction in word analysis deals with the sounds letters represent. As mentioned previously, no single element of phonic analysis is so essential that a student's reading progress should be halted until he masters that particular principle or rule. It is also true that instruction intended to lead to the memorization of phonic principles is less effective than instruction that leads the student to application of those principles when they apply. Most of us have had students who could recite phonic principles but could not use them in unlocking unknown words. For that reason, most reading programs try to lead students to functional application of phonic generalizations rather than rote memorization of principles (Heilman, 1977, p. 238; Harris and Smith, 1980, p. 148).

Most phonic principles are somewhat unreliable. Vowel sounds are more variable than consonants. A landmark study by Clymer (1963) examined 45 principles of phonic analysis and found that none of those that dealt with vowel sounds was always true. Only three of them were true at least 90 percent of the time, and 67 percent of them were *not true* one-third of the time *or more.* Nevertheless, most reading approaches spend a significant amount of time on phonic analysis. Despite the high degree of unreliability of most phonic generalizations, a sound instructional program in phonics can help a student make good use of some of the phonic principles. Three common precepts are helpful in teaching students to use phonic analysis of unknown words:

1. Students should be flexible in their application of phonic principles. If the application of a rule does not result in a meaningful word, students should be encouraged to substitute sounds—especially vowel sounds—for the unproductive ones. It is not necessary for them to sound out the word perfectly in order to be able to recognize it.
2. Good readers learn to combine phonic clues with other word recognition strategies, particularly context clues. The use of initial consonant sounds with the context is a much stronger word recognition strategy than either one alone.
3. Students should be encouraged to learn irregular words by sight recognition. Overemphasis on phonic analysis may cause a beginning reader to render the word *come* as "kō-mē" rather than "cum."

There are more irregular words among high-usage vocabulary than among words encountered less frequently. This is fortunate for the novice reader, because it means that words that are more difficult and unusual are more likely to conform to phonic principles. In other words, phonic analysis becomes somewhat more reliable when it is used with more troublesome words.

Structural Analysis   Structural analysis involves word recognition based on segmentation of words by meaning rather than strictly by letter-sound association. Although phonic analysis and structural analysis cannot be completely divorced from each other, structural analysis usually deals with larger units and emphasizes meaning as vested in roots, prefixes, suffixes, and inflectional endings. Structural analysis is generally taught later than phonics, but some aspects of it, particularly inflectional endings, are often introduced as early as the pre-primer level in first grade (Spache and Spache, 1977).

Syllabication   A syllable is a word or word part that can stand alone. Each syllable has one sounded vowel or vowel phoneme. It may be as small as one vowel or may consist of several consonants and vowels, although there can be only one vowel phoneme.

Students who have difficulty discovering the number of syllables in a word are often surprised to find that every syllable has a "beat" and that it is easy to count the number of syllables by tapping out the number of beats in a word—if the student pronounces the word correctly and distinctly.

Just as in phonic analysis, the memorization of principles or rules seems to be of limited value in syllabication. An approach that emphasizes *functional* syllabication is preferable and appears to be an important tool in advanced word recognition (Biggins and Uhler, 1978; Rubeck, 1977).

Blending   The ability to blend word parts to make a recognizable whole word is an important analysis skill. Most of us have worked with students who have greater difficulty with such synthesis than they do with sounding out the individual letters and syllables. A student may be able to pronounce the letter sounds, or phonemes, in *fatten*, for example, but not be able to synthesize the word; or be able to pronounce the separate syllables *con-duc-tor* but not be able to blend the syllables to recognize the word "conductor." To become an effective word analyzer, students need to develop the ability to (1) recognize the separate word parts, (2) hold them in their rehearsal loop in sequential order as they pronounce them, (3) increase the speed of pronunciation until it approaches normal fluency in pronunciation—all the while maintaining the correct pronunciation and order of the individual word parts.

CONTEXT CLUES

In the Diagnostic Model of Reading Behavior (Figure 2-1, p. 22), the ability to use the context to identify words and word meanings is represented by the arms attached to the body which symbolizes comprehension. This indicates that the use of context clues, or "syntax and structure," as many linguists prefer, depends on readers' ability to understand the bulk of what they are reading. Probably for this reason, mature readers, who read with greater comprehension and fluency, generally make better use of context clues than do beginning readers.

The use of context is not unlike a guidance system for a good reader. In much the same way that we can tell that a boy walking a rail has lost his balance and is about to slip off the track, by the way he waves his arms in trying to recover his balance, we can tell that a good reader has lost his comprehension and has "slipped off the track" by observing his use of context clues. When he reads a word that does not seem congruent with the rest of the passage, the good reader stops, goes back over the section, and corrects the error, if there has been one. For example, a good reader who reads, "The man leaped onto his house and rode away into the sunset" understands that the passage does not make sense. His "guidance system" stops his automatic word recognition, changes the focus of his attention from the meaning of the passage to the analysis and recognition of the incorrectly identified word where he discovers his error, changes *house* to *horse*, again picks up the chain of thought and reads on.

There are many careful analyses of the various kinds of context clues, but it is probably sufficient at this stage for us to note that they may be roughly divided into two categories: (1) those which enable readers to recognize words that are unknown to them in print but which are part of their speaking/thinking vocabulary, and (2) those clues which enable readers to understand the meaning of words whose *form* they recognize but which they don't understand.

An example of the first of these context clues is illustrated in the sentence,

> Joyce's cold had given her a bad *cough*.

If the reader did not recognize the word *cough* in print but understood its meaning, the context would probably enable the reader to identify the word.

The second use of context clues provides assistance in understanding a word whose meaning had not been previously understood even though its *form* was recognizable. The following sentence provides three possible examples:

> Smoke, noise, and the smell of diesel fuel filled the air as the *donkey's* pulleys and cables strained to *snake* the log up the mountain to the *landing*.

The words *donkey, snake,* and *landing* may all be *recognizable* to the reader but may not be understood without the context. The context helps him to understand that in this passage a *donkey* is an engine, *snake* is a verb meaning to drag, and a *landing* is a noun meaning a place where logs are loaded or unloaded.

Context clues become increasingly important as readers become more capable, even to the point that context frequently overrules analysis and sight vocabulary. In an interesting paper, Dunn-Rankin (1978) gives several examples of this. For instance, read the following sentence, which has been printed backward:

> .rat eht saw tac ehT

As most people read the sentence from right to left, they read either "The cat saw the rat." or "The cat was the rat." Their expectation, based on the context, rejects the correct reading, "The cat was the tar." because that does not make sense. Context overrules analysis. Dunn-Rankin cites another example, asking the reader to read the following:

The sense of the context causes many people to read "Paris in the spring," leaving out the extra *the* because it does not fit the meaning expected from the phrase. Although beginning readers tend to place greater reliance on word analysis, capable readers apparently place increasing emphasis on context clues and comprehension.

COMPREHENSION

In the Diagnostic Model of Reading Behavior, comprehension is symbolized by the body. No effective reader could be presumed to have completed the act of reading if he did not understand what he read. Readers who simply pronounce the words before them are not "reading" in any full sense of the word. Reading, like any other receptive communication skill such as listening or interpreting sign language, has many aspects, but certainly the most central aspect is the comprehension of the message.

Although there are many subskills, reading comprehension, as noted earlier, can be divided into four primary categories: understanding vocabulary, understanding details, understanding the main idea, and the ability to infer or imply. The other subskills can usually be related to one or another of these main divisions.

While understanding vocabulary and noting details need little additional comment at this point, reading to understand the main idea and reading inference may need some minor elaboration. The ability to understand the main idea and its relationship to other information seems more important in good comprehension and recall than had been thought in the past. Organized material is easier to learn, parallels a natural tendency to summarize and organize, and is more easily retrieved (Baddeley, 1979, p. 274). Ausubel (1960) demonstrated the effectiveness of having a student read a summary, called an "advance organizer," before reading a longer passage.

The main idea is not unlike a handle or stem by which many bits of information may be retrieved (Baddeley, 1976, p. 293). It is possible to compare the retrieval process to the ritual of Christmas-tree removal at the end of the holiday season. If you tried to remove the pine needles one at a time, it would take forever. But if you take the tree by the trunk, all the needles as well as the branches and trunk can be removed. If we try to retrieve separate details, it becomes an almost impossible job, but if we try to retrieve the main idea, we find that the details related to that idea become available, too.

The ability to infer is the ability to grasp meanings that are not concretely stated in the context of the reading material. Humor, poetry, and much of the material written in the realm of affective literature relies on the reader's ability to infer in order to achieve the author's intent. Many poor readers view reading as a rather cold, lifeless, and uninteresting activity. They often have difficulty with inference because what they read remains at a surface level for them, seldom leading them to look for the delight to be found in figures of speech, puns, imagery, and other figures clothed in print.

What teacher has not had a "Charles" in her class who complains that he cannot find the answer to a question. Although the teacher assures him that the answer is to be found on a certain page, he looks for it in vain. The teacher may finally even point out the specific paragraph, but still Charles searches without success. The passage might read something like this:

Archer glared at the letter, crumpled it in his hands, and tossed it on the secretary's desk. He stamped across the floor, slamming the door behind him. He kicked at a cat sleeping beside the path, barked his cycle into action and tore away in a cloud of gravel.

The question the teacher asks Charles to answer is, "How did Archer feel about having been fired?" and Charles cannot find the answer. All the passage says is that Archer glared at the letter, crumpled it in his hands, tossed it on the secretary's desk, stamped across the floor, and so on, but it does not *say* in so many words that Archer was angry. Charles has difficulty because he has not learned to *infer*. The emotions of reading do not "get inside" him. The words he reads do not make him *feel* what the author wants him to feel. All he understands is the surface level of the passage. Many poor readers never learn to enjoy what they read because they have not, first, learned to infer meanings.

FLUENCY AND RATE

The motion marks in the Diagnostic Model represent fluency and rate. These two are treated together, not because they are the same, but because they are so closely interrelated. It is possible for a good fluent reader never to become a good rapid reader, but a nonfluent reader seldom becomes a good rapid reader. Fluency is the foundation on which efficient reading rate is built. Some nonfluent readers may develop a "machine-gun" rapid reading approach, jamming one word after another without regard to fluency, but such an approach is not really effective. A fluent reader makes reading "sound like talk written down," at least to the extent that certain words are emphasized and others receive almost no attention at all. Read the following sentence fluently and notice that the words that are not underlined are touched very lightly:

The <u>boy</u> gave his <u>ball</u> to the <u>man</u>.

If the reading of the sentence were timed, it would be interesting to see that it would take longer to pronounce the word *ball* than the preceding two words, *gave* and *his*. A fluent reader spends very little time in pronouncing some words, making it possible for him to read faster as well as more fluently.

A by-product of fluent reading is added comprehension. Fluent reading communicates better, it sounds more interesting, and the ideas of the author are easier to follow than when the same words are read by a nonfluent reader. It is only necessary to remember the last time we listened to someone read something in a nonfluent monotone in order to recall how uncommunicative that sort of reading can be. Yet there are thousands upon thousands of nonfluent poor readers who have to endure the same uninteresting nonfluent reading every time they read to themselves. If we find it difficult to subject ourselves to just a few minutes of such boring reading, just think how nonfluent readers must dread an assignment to read a book.

It is important to begin to develop fluency at the earliest stages of learning to read. One young mother was dismayed when her first-grader, who had started school already able to read, seemed to be reading more and more poorly. Within two months his reading became a dull, word-by-word monotone. She seated her son and herself at a table and announced that she wanted to hear him read. He quite willingly opened the book she had given him and began to read in a nonfluent fashion. She stopped him, took the book, and demonstrated for him how she felt his reading should sound. He was quick to object. Resuming possession of the book, he said, "But that's not how we're supposed to read. In *school,* we learned to read like *this.*" And again he demonstrated how he had *learned* to read in school in a nonfluent, uncommunicative style. It is important that early readers learn that reading ought to sound interesting both to others and to themselves.

Rate is built on a foundation of fluency, but it goes far beyond that. Ordinary fluent oral reading seldom exceeds 200 words per minute and probably averages nearer 150 words per minute. It is possible for a *good* rapid reader to read *easy* narrative material silently with 75 percent comprehension at rates up to 600 words per minute. Depending on the difficulty of the material and his purpose in reading, the average adult reads at a rate of 200 to 400 words per minute. Rates above 600 words per minute are usually achieved by some degree of skimming or "surveying" the material.

Mature readers usually have the ability to read at different speeds for different purposes, their rate always modified by the difficulty of the material. Good readers usually read faster than poor readers, but sometimes they read *more slowly* (Brown, 1964). In other words, a good reader is a flexible reader. Maturity in reading ability leads readers to consider, and change, rate depending on the comprehension the readers demand. With these points in mind, Table 2-1 on page 35 may be taken as a guide for good mature readers.

While it is important to look at all behaviors that are a part of mature reading, the reading diagnostician will seldom find that poor readers need or should receive instruction in rate improvement. Generally, a poor reading rate indicates other more basic deficiencies in reading abilities.

LOCATIONAL AND STUDY SKILLS

In the Diagnostic Model of Reading Behavior, locational and study skills are represented by the book held by the boy (Figure 2-1, p. 22). The Adult Performance Level (APL) study undertaken at the University of Texas (1975) and supported by the United States Office of Education defined functional literacy competence as the "ability to *use* [literacy] skills and knowledge needed for meeting the requirements of adult living." (Italics added.) The study found that great dif-

Table 2-1.
Rates and Levels of Comprehension
for Various Reading Approaches

Reading Approach	Rate	Comprehension
Intensive, reflective	Rate unimportant, may be 50–125 WPM[a]	Approaching 100%
Study	125–300 WPM[a]	Generally above 90% necessary to satisfy the reader's purpose
Casual enjoyment	Rate unimportant, may be 125–300 WPM[a]	Comprehension of limited importance; only important in meeting reader's needs for enjoyment
Rapid	250–600 WPM[a]	60–80%
Rapid survey	400–4,500 WSPM[b]	35–45% overall comprehension (90–100% of main idea, 75–90% of supporting ideas, 30–40% of specific details)

[a] Words per minute.
[b] Words surveyed per minute. WPM would be deceiving used with this rate because usually the higher the rate the fewer the words actually recognized in skimming. Therefore the term "words surveyed per minute" is more accurate here.

ficulties were encountered by many adults in applying literacy skills in shopping and handling money, and in their occupations.

Before the APL study, it was common to speak of "in-book" and "out-of-book" locational skills, usually limited to a school setting. "In-book" locational skills included use of the index, table of contents, glossary, maps, and other aids to locate information. "Out-of-book" locational skills usually included the ability to use the dictionary, Atlas, library card file, *Reader's Guide to Periodical Literature*, and other tools to find necessary information outside the textbook.

After the APL findings received the attention of both the professional and popular press, "out-of-book" locational skills were broadened to include locational literacy survival skills. Many states now require that schools teach how to use shopping advertisements in newspapers, want ads, the yellow pages in the telephone directory, catalogues, menus, and other sources of information needed in a literate society.

Originally the term "study skills" was more ambiguous than "locational skills," including such things as attitudes, evaluation of information once located, and the use of any written information. It has taken on more structure and added a new dimension in recent years. "Study skills" tend to be limited reading activities aimed at mastery of content. That includes the ability to use the information found through the use of good locational skills, but also any information that may be viewed as part of content reading. The added dimension of study skills came about with the growth and the use of study formulae such as SQ3R, in which readers were taught to organize their approach to their reading material in order to improve their reading efficiency. The steps in SQ3R are: (1) Survey the material before reading, (2) raise Questions concerning the material you are to read, (3) Read to understand the passage and answer your questions, (4) Recite or report what you have read, and (5) Review to find information you have missed or confirm information you have gained (Robinson, 1961).

REACTION

Reaction is represented by the head of the boy in the Diagnostic Model. It may be defined as the interaction of the reader with the author's message. Reaction includes *evaluation, appreciation,* and *enjoyment* of reading.

Evaluation   Sometimes called critical reading or critical evaluation, evaluation is the ability of the reader to accept or reject either wholly or in part the reasoning and writing of the author. It may involve questioning the writer's background and knowledge, his bias in presentation of arguments, and the logic with which the arguments are offered. This implies the ability on the part of the reader to analyze the author's writing, examining it for propaganda techniques, soundness of data, and the ability to discriminate between the author's use of fact and opinion. A free society relies heavily on the ability of its citizens to evaluate what they read.

Appreciation   Appreciation of good writing is more than evaluation and differs from enjoyment, although it is intertwined with both. In order to appreciate what they read, readers must become aware of the style the author uses and the facility with which he or she writes. But awareness should not be mistaken for dissection, segmentation, and analysis in literature any more than the appreciation of a beautiful gown relies on the viewer's ability to take it apart and analyze it button for button and thread by thread. The inch-by-inch analysis of a painting masterpiece often defeats the impact of the whole painting.

There must be a feeling to appreciation. A student once said, "When I began to really enjoy good reading, I found I was not only reacting with my head but with my heart as well."

Can appreciation be taught? It can certainly be *learned*, and it is probable that effective instruction can guide the student to see and appreciate the differences between the satin of Pearl Buck, the rugged calculus of Hemingway, the mysticism of Emily Dickinson, and the bittersweet of Langston Hughes more quickly than if the student simply read on his own.

Enjoyment   More people read for pleasure than for any other reason. An old adage says, "To learn to read, you must read, then read some more, then keep on reading." "Practice makes perfect," but few people want to read just for "practice." Enjoyment draws them to reading. Most of you reading this book are good readers who enjoy reading. Some of you might even be called "reading addicts." With a few minutes on your hands, you always try to find something to read. At the breakfast table you read the backs of cereal boxes, at the dentist's office you read antique editions of magazines, while waiting for the repairperson you reread yesterday's newspaper. You enjoy reading.

A 17-year-old student in the Cherry Creek (Colorado) School District "I-Team Project" was admitted to the program aimed at dropouts and potential dropouts with only a 3.5-grade instructional reading level. He had never read a book or even any sizable portion of a book.

After a month or so in the project, he picked out Jack London's short story *To Build a Fire*. He worked with it laboriously. After two-and-one-half hours he still had not been able to finish it. He took it to the reading specialist working with the program and asked her if she would read the rest of it to him aloud. She suggested that he just put the booklet on a shelf and finish it the next day; that way, he would be able to say he had finished it himself. "I can't," he said. "I've got to find out how it turns out *today*."

The specialist, Marilyn Blevins, read the rest of the story, only three or four pages, to him, and he thanked her, got up, and started for the door. About halfway across the room, he stopped, turned, and came back. "Mrs. Blevins," he said, "do you have any other books like that?" She did. From that point on this young man began to read. He had found that reading could be interesting, and as a result he read everything within his range of ability. Needless to say, his reading gains during the year were excellent.

No one wants to learn to read so he can sound out a word. People want to read because reading is interesting. Fader's *The New Hooked on Books* (1977) propounds an approach to teaching reluctant readers, encouraging them to *want* to read. Enjoyment can be the key to the success of a reading program.

SCOPE AND SEQUENCE OF READING SKILLS

The Diagnostic Model of Reading Behavior may be helpful as an easily remembered reference in diagnosing general areas of reading skill weakness, but it is not sufficiently specific either in terms of the differentiation of subskills or in identifying at what level a specific subskill will be introduced, emphasized, or reinforced. Many excellent scope and sequence charts are available through the various basal reader publishers. These provide specific information on the placement and development of each reading skill within that particular series. As was pointed out at the beginning of this chapter, basal series often differ to some extent on the point at which a skill should be taught. Still, these variations are not usually of major proportions, and a teacher can learn much about the development of reading skills by reviewing the scope and sequence charts from two or three basal series.

A study of six basal reader series plus four remedial and adult reading-skill development charts resulted in the reading-skill scope and sequence on the following pages (Brown, 1973). It should be mentioned that this scope and sequence is useful only to give a general indication of when the different skills may be taught; various respected authorities differ on one or more points. Nevertheless, the following outline is useful for gaining a general overview of the progression of skills through which students may pass on their way to becoming capable readers. Except for the first step, initial reading readiness, reading skills are categorized according to the eight basic reading aspects listed in the Diagnostic Model of Reading Behavior.

SKILLS PROGRESSION

I.   Initial reading readiness
     Visual discrimination
       Discrimination of letter forms, both capitals and lowercase
       Recognize own written name
     Auditory discrimination
       Discrimination of the initial sound in a word
       Discrimination of final and rhyming word sounds
     Language base
       Building oral vocabulary
       Associating words and pictures
       Listening
       Following directions
       Learning that reading communicates, that it is "talk written down"
     Attention
       Listening
       Following directions
       Ability to focus attention on what the teacher is trying to teach
       Ability to work in a classroom situation
     General
       Ability to use a pencil, hold a book, turn pages correctly
       Learning left-to-right sequence
II. Beginning reading instruction, Level 1 (First pre-primer)
     Readiness continued
     Initial sight vocabulary
       Identifying students' names
       Identifying labels
       Learning to recognize an initial reading vocabulary at sight
     Word analysis
       Recognition of initial consonants *g* (hard), *m, h, s, f,* and *b*
       Recognition of *pl* and *sl* as beginning word parts
       Recognition of *-at, -nd,* and *-all* as ending word parts
       Recognition of *-s* ending

Context clues
Ability to fill in a word missing in oral context
Ability to fill in a word missing in printed context
III.   Beginning reading instruction, Level 2 (Second pre-primer)
Readiness, continued
Initial sight vocabulary, continued
Adding to initial sight vocabulary from reading
Identifying labels
Word analysis
Recognition of initial consonants *c* (hard), *g* (hard), *s* (both "s" and "z" sound), and all other consonants
Recognition of *ch, sh, th* (both as in that and thin), and *wh* digraphs
Recognition of *pl* and *sl* blends as word beginnings
Recognition of word endings *-all, -an, -and,* and *-ed*
Context clues together with word analysis
Identification of missing word using oral context and initial consonant
Identification of missing word using printed context and initial consonant
Fluency
Reading with natural expression
Comprehension
Reading to determine whether or not a statement is true
Reading to select the right answer
Rereading to note specific facts
IV.   Beginning reading instruction, Level 3 (Third pre-primer)
Initial sight vocabulary, continued
Word analysis
Recognition of all initial consonants (hard *c* and *g*)
Recognition of *ch, sh, th,* and *wh* digraphs
Recognition of *pl* and *sl* blends as word beginnings
Recognition of word endings *-ad, -all, -am, -and, -at, -ay, -ed, -en, -et, -id, -ig, -ill, -in, -it,* and *-ot*
Context clues with word analysis
Using context to identify vowel sounds (sit, sat; fall, fell)
Fluency
Reading with natural expression
Comprehension
Reading to choose the best answer
Reading to complete a statement
Reaction, evaluation, and enjoyment
Ability to distinguish between written material that could be true and material that could not be true
Understanding the feelings of characters in stories
V.   Beginning reading instruction, Level 4 (Primer)
Word analysis
Recognition of *bl, cr, fl, st, str,* and *tr* blends as word beginnings
Recognition of word endings *-ade, -ake, -ame, -ane, -ank, -ard, -ark, -ask, -ast, -ave, -eat, -ed, -ee, -end, -ent, -ew, -ight, -ike, -ile, -ine, -ing, -ist, -ite, -oat, -old, -ook, -oon, -ould, -ound, -out, -owe, -s, -ug, -ump, -un, -up,* and *-ust*
Use of final silent *e* rule of phonics
Context clues with word analysis
Using printed context with initial vowel to identify a deleted word
Using printed context to identify a vowel sound in a word

Broad sight vocabulary
  Developing a broad immediate sight vocabulary through wide reading
  Recognition of irregular words through reading and flash cards
Fluency, continued
Comprehension
  Listening to and remembering details
  Listening to a story and expressing the main idea
  Expressing the inferred ending of a story
  Understanding pronouns and descriptive words
  Reading to answer specific questions
Reaction, evaluation, and enjoyment
  Reading to appreciate humor

VI. Beginning reading instruction, Level 5 (First Reader)
  Word analysis
    Recognition of soft *c*, soft *g*, and *ph* digraph
    Use of final silent *e* phonics rule, continued
    Recognition of *br, cl, gr, pr, thr* blends as word beginnings
    Recognition of *a-* and *be-* as word beginnings
    Recognition of word endings *-ace, -ag, -age, -ail, -ain, -aint, -air, -ait, -alk, -ar, -arm, -art, -ate, -ell, -ice, -ide, -ime, -ink, -ize, -or, -ore, -oss, -other, -our, -ouse, -own* (grown)
    Recognition of words through analysis of compound words
    Recognition of contractions
    Understanding the use of apostrophes to show possession
  Context clues with word analysis
    Using the context to identify missing vowel sound in a word
  Context clues with comprehension
    Using context to determine the intended meaning of homonyms used in a sentence
    Using the context to determine the meaning of a word having more than one meaning
  Broad sight vocabulary, continued
  Comprehension, continued
  Fluency, continued
  Reaction, evaluation, and enjoyment, continued

VII. Beginning reading instruction, Level 6 (2¹ Reader)
  Word analysis
    Recognition of hard and soft *c* and *g* as well as *ph, gh,* and *qu*
    Recognition of final silent *e*
    Recognition of *br, cl, dr, gl, pr, thr, bl, cr, fl, fr, pl, sk, sl, sm, sn, st, str, tr,* and *tw* blends as word beginnings
    Recognition of word endings *-able, -ange, -ass, -aze, -eam, -ean, -ed, -eg, -en, -ense,-er, -ess, -ful, -ie, -ies, -ife, -le, -ly, -nd, -ng, -nk, -nt, -oast, -old, -ony, -ope,-ought, -ove, -owl, -udge, -urn, -x, -y*
    Recognition of long and short vowels *a, e, i, o,* and *u;* and the vowel digraphs *ai, ay, ea, ee, ie, oa, oo, ou,* and *ow* (the latter two as in *cow* and *snow*)
    Recognition of silent letters in the combinations *pn, kn,* and *gn*
    Recognition of the "sh" sound in *tion*
  Context clues with word analysis
    Using context to recognize words when the word is missing and (1) an initial consonant is given as a clue or (2) an initial vowel is given as a clue
    Using context to recognize a word when a medial vowel has been deleted from a word

Context clues with comprehension
　Using context to determine the meanings of homonyms and words having more than one meaning
Broad sight vocabulary, continued
Comprehension
　Interpreting commas
Locational and study skills
　Alphabetizing
　Using a dictionary
Reaction, evaluation, and enjoyment
　Making judgments based on facts gained from a story
　Evaluating a story
　Enjoying poetry

VIII.　Beginning reading instruction, Level 7 (2² Reader)
Word analysis
　Recognition of *r*-affected vowels
　Recognition of *ou, ow, oi,* and *oy* diphthongs
　Recognition of the silent letters *b, gh, h, k, p,* and *w*
　Recognition of *re, un,* and *be* as word beginnings
　Recognition of word endings *-aid, -airy, -amp, -ance, -aper, -are, -eal, -eck, -eel, -eer, -est, -ift, -iss, -oint, -oke, -oth, -ud, -uff, -ung, -unk, -utter*
　Using syllabication for word recognition, understanding that there are as many syllables in a word as there are "beats," or sounded vowels
Context clues with word analysis
　Using the context to recognize words when given an initial consonant or vowel
Context clues and comprehension
　Using context to determine word meanings
Broad sight vocabulary, continued
Comprehension
　Understanding the main idea
　Noting details
　Understanding the use of pronouns
　Interpreting commas
Locational and study skills, continued
Reaction, evaluation, and enjoyment
　Enjoying poetry
　Enjoying plays

IX.　Intermediate reading, Level 8 (3¹ Reader)
Word analysis
　Recognition of structural word beginnings *com, de, dis, en, ex, im, in*
　Recognition of consonant blends *scr, sp, squ,* and *sw*
　Recognition of word endings *-ale, -ang, -ape, -eak, -elf, -elt, -ie, -oft, -oin, -oof, -orn, -ost, -ule, -ush*
　Recognition of compound words
　Recognition of contractions
　Recognition of certain suffix structures in which the *y* is changed to *i*
　Using syllabication in recognizing unknown words
Context clues
　Using context to recognize words
　Using context to understand word meanings
Broad sight vocabulary, continued
Comprehension
　Understanding figurative language

Locational and study skills
  Using the index and table of contents of a book to locate information
  Using study helps such as advance organizers to increase comprehension
Fluency
  Oral interpretation of poetry, prose, and plays
Reaction, evaluation, and enjoyment
  Appreciation of figurative language

X.   Intermediate reading, Level 9 (3^2 Reader)
  Word analysis
    Recognition of structural word beginnings *con*, *for*, *per*, and *pre*
    Recognition of the *shr* blend as a word beginning
    Recognition of word endings *-ant*, *-asp*, *-irt*, *-oak*, *-oil*, *-ote*, *-umb*, *-unt*, and *-ure*
    Using syllabication to recognize unknown words by learning to *apply* the rules of syllabication
    Learning to blend syllables to recognize words
  Context clues, continued
  Broad sight vocabulary, continued
  Comprehension
    Recognition of similes
    Understanding the use of commas to indicate the person addressed and to set off items in a series
  Locational and study skills
    Ability to alphabetize through the second and third letter
    Ability to use the dictionary to pronounce and define words, including the use of diacritical marks and the selection of the appropriate definition for words having more than one meaning
    Ability to use the library, including the use of the card catalogue
    Ability to use a book index, including the use of key words, the interpretation of listings, and the use of symbols and abbreviations used to direct the reader
  Fluency
    Recognition of thought units
    Ability to read in thought units
  Reaction, evaluation, and enjoyment
    Differentiating between fact and opinion
    Ability to weigh different sets of facts and opinions bearing on the same subject

XI.   Intermediate reading, Level 10 (Fourth Reader)
  Word analysis
    Ability to recognize prefixes, suffixes, and roots in structurally analyzing words
  Context clues, maintenance
  Broad sight vocabulary, continued
  Comprehension
    Interpreting italics and other special type
    Identifying topic sentences and the main idea of passages
    Interpreting punctuation
    Understanding simple outline form
  Locational and study skills
    Ability to use an encyclopedia
    Ability to use an Atlas
    Ability to identify word derivations and inflected word forms, using a dictionary

                  Ability to alphabetize, using all the letters in the words
             Fluency and rate
                  Ability to identify the purpose for reading
                  Ability to adjust rate according to the level of comprehension required
                  Ability to read orally with expression
             Reaction, evaluation, and enjoyment
                  Understanding the author's use of humor
                  Broadening reading interests

XII.   Intermediate reading, Level 11 (Fifth Reader)
             Word analysis
                  Review and maintenance of syllabication and analysis skills
             Context clues, maintenance
             Broad sight vocabulary, continued and extended
             Comprehension
                  Making an outline
                  Identifying roles, story characters, and probable outcomes
                  Summarizing
             Locational and study skills
                  Taking notes
                  Using a reading study formula such as SQ3R (Survey before reading, Question before reading, Read, Recite, Review)
                  Using the library, understanding the different general classifications within the library (biographies, reference, fiction, etc.), the use of the *Reader's Guide to Periodical Literature*, and the use of bound periodicals
             Fluency and Rate
                  Oral interpretation
                  Variations of reading rate and comprehension according to the reader's purpose and the difficulty of the material
             Reaction, evaluation, and enjoyment
                  Reading to solve problems
                  Identification of the author's bias
                  Evaluation of the author's competency as an authority
                  Continued broadening and maturing of reading interests

XIII.   Intermediate reading, Level 12 (Sixth Reader)
             Word analysis, maintenance
             Context clues, maintenance
             Broad sight vocabulary, continued and extended
             Comprehension
                  Inferring meanings not explicitly stated
                  Review, maintenance, and extension of comprehension skills previously introduced and taught
             Locational and study skills
                  Refining reference skills used in library research
                  Locating information in the newspaper
                  Making effective use of study aids within texts—i.e., time lines, graphs, maps, and charts
                  Using advance organizers and refinement in the use of reading study formulas such as SQ3R
             Fluency and rate, extension of previous instruction in identifying purpose and matching rate and comprehension to accomplish the reader's purpose
             Reaction, evaluation, and enjoyment
                  Ability to cross-check contradictory points of view
                  Identification of a writer's bias

Applying logic in the analysis of biased writing
Continuing, extending, and broadening reading interests
XIV.   Advanced Reading, Level 13 (Secondary and Adult)
Word analysis
Ability to apply syllabication principles
Ability to use structural elements in analysis
Ability to use larger phonic letter combinations
Context clues
Ability to use context clues to determine word meaning
Ability to use context clues to recognize words
Broad sight vocabulary
Developing a broad general sight vocabulary
Developing a large sight vocabulary in several content fields
Comprehension
Ability to identify and evaluate propaganda techniques such as "home folks," "bandwagon," "straw man," "card stacking," "halo effect," "mud slinging" approaches
Ability to follow detailed directions
Ability to understand rules, regulations, and laws
Ability to gain mastery of written content materials
Ability to read for personal improvement
Ability to read for enjoyment; vicarious affection, excitement, beauty, and intellectual challenge and stimulation
Ability to summarize
Locational and study skills
Ability to locate, understand, organize, and utilize information from textbooks, reference materials, newspapers, telephone directories, library, television, and television guides, and such miscellaneous sources as public service pamphlets, road maps, menus, bus schedules, and catalogues
Fluency and rate
Ability to read orally with expression
Ability to use rates appropriate for the efficient accomplishment of the reader's purpose, including intensive reading, study reading, rapid reading, rapid survey reading, skimming, and scanning
Reaction, evaluation, appreciation, and enjoyment
Ability to identify and evaluate propaganda techniques such as "home folks," "bandwagon," "straw man," "card stacking," "halo effect," "mud slinging," and other approaches
Ability to read for enjoyment; including reading for excitement; suspense; the enjoyment of relationships, vicarious love, affection and romance; and intellectual challenge and stimulation
Ability to appreciate good literature, its structure and its beauty
Ability to identify with the characters in a story
Ability to analyze a piece of literature in terms of both structure and thrust
Ability to understand the motives behind the author's writing

SUMMARY

It is helpful for a reading teacher to have a framework against which poor readers may be measured. The Diagnostic Model of Reading Behavior and the scope and sequence of reading skills in this chapter provide such a guide, listing the reading skills of capable readers and outlining how they are commonly introduced and taught. The basic skills included in the Diagnostic Model include readiness for initial reading instruction, the development of sight vocabulary and work analysis skills, learning to use context clues to recognize and understand words and their meanings, building reading comprehension, developing fluency and rate, learning to employ locational and study skills, and building reaction to reading materials, including evaluation, appreciation, and enjoyment.

RECOMMENDED READINGS

DURKIN, D. 1976. *Teaching young children to read.* 2nd ed. Boston: Allyn & Bacon, Chapters 4, 10, 11, and 12.

HARRIS, A. J.; and SIPAY, E. R. 1980. *How to increase reading ability.* 7th ed. New York: Longman, Chapters 2, 3, and 4.

HARRIS, L. A.; and SMITH, C. B. 1980. *Reading instruction: Diagnostic teaching in the classroom.* 3rd ed. New York: Holt, Rinehart & Winston, Chapters 5, 6, 7, 8 and 9.

HEILMAN, A. W. 1977. *Principles and practices in teaching reading.* 4th ed. Columbus, Ohio: Charles E. Merrill, Chapters 2, 7, 8, 12, 13, and 14.

McKEE, P. 1966. *Reading: A program of instruction for the elementary school.* Boston: Houghton Mifflin, Chapters 2, 3, 4, and 7.

RANSOM, G. A. 1978. *Preparing to teach reading.* Boston: Little, Brown, Chapters 9, 11, 12, and 13.

SPACHE, G. D.; and SPACHE, E. B. 1977. *Reading in the elementary school.* 4th ed. Boston: Allyn & Bacon, Chapters 6, 11, 12, and 13.

REFERENCES

Adult Performance Level Project. 1975. *Adult functional competency: A summary.* Austin, Tex.: Univ. Texas, Division of Extension.

Ausubel, D. P. 1960. The use of advance organizers in the learning and retention of meaningful verbal material. *Journal of Educational Psychology* 51: 267–72.

Baddeley, A. D. *The psychology of memory.* New York: Basic Books.

Biggins, C. M.; and Uhler, S. Spring 1978. Is there a "workable" word decoding system? *Reading Improvement* 15: 47–55.

Brown, D. A. 1964. *The effect of selected purposes on the oculo-motor behavior and comprehension of third grade and seventh grade students of fifth grade reading ability.* Unpublished doctoral dissertation, Univ. Oregon.

_____. 1973. *Final report: Colorado penal reading project.* Report to Law Enforcement Assistance Agency.

Clymer, T. January 1963. The utility of phonic generalizations in the primary grades. *Reading Teacher* 16: 252–58.

Dunn-Rankin, P. January 1978. The visual characteristics of words. *Scientific American* Vol. 238 No. 1: 122–30.

Fader, D. 1977. *The new hooked on books.* New York: Berkeley Publishing.

Gibson, E. J.; and Levin, H. 1975. *The psychology of reading.* Cambridge: MIT Press, pp. 227–62.

Harris, L. A.; and Smith, C. B. 1980. *Reading instruction: Diagnostic teaching in the classroom.* 3rd ed. New York: Holt, Rinehart & Winston.

Heilman, A. W. 1977. *Principles and practices in teaching reading.* 4th ed. Columbus, Ohio: Charles E. Merrill.

Lockhart, R. S.; Craik, F. I. M; and Jacoby, L. 1976. Depth of processing, recognition and recall. In *Recall and recognition,* ed. J. Brown. New York: Wiley.

Nichols, R. 1967. The ten worst listening habits. Address to the Mid-year Conference at the University of Northern Colorado.

Richeck, M. A. 1977–78. Readiness skills that predict initial word learning using two different methods of instruction. *Reading Research Quarterly* 13: 200–222.

Robinson, F. P. 1961. *Effective study.* New York: Harper & Row.

Rubeck, P. Fall 1977. Decoding procedures: Pupil self-analysis and observed behaviors. *Reading Improvement* 14: 187–92.

Spache, G. D.; and Spache, E. B. 1977. *Reading in the elementary school.* 4th ed. Boston: Allyn & Bacon.

TePoel, D. 1980. *The investigation of parental roles during children's preschool development and reading achievement in the intermediate grades.* Published doctoral dissertation, University of Northern Colorado.

Why do some students have difficulty learning to read? Factors such as inappropriate instruction, low intelligence, dominance and obscured writing, learning disabilities and neurological dysfunctions, and emotional maladjustment are examined in this chapter as possible contributors to reading failure.

INSTRUCTIONAL, PSYCHOLOGICAL, AND NEUROLOGICAL FACTORS IN READING DIFFICULTY

Research findings dealing with the causes of reading difficulties are often confusing and conflicting. It is important to take the best evidence available and use it intelligently in trying to fathom the mysteries that surround the problems in learning to read.

Not everything that is correlated with reading difficulty is a *cause* of reading difficulty. For example, height and reading ability are quite highly *correlated*. If you measure the height of 100 first-grade children and of 100 sixth-grade children, then ascertain their reading achievement, it is easy to show that the tall children (the sixth-graders) read much better than the shorter children (the first-graders). The findings of such a study would show that height *correlates* highly with the ability to learn to read. But shortness is *not* a cause of reading difficulty despite that notable correlation. Parallel and coexisting circumstances have produced both gains in height and gains in reading. If a sixth-grade student had not grown because of some physical defect, he would, if otherwise normal and healthy, learn to read without difficulty.

Sometimes a factor is causally related to reading difficulty, sometimes there is only a correlation between the two, and at other times it is simply not possible to tell whether a factor is causative or only correlated with problems in learning to read. In the latter case it is usually wiser to be conservative unless logic dictates that, despite the inconclusiveness of the research, the factor would reasonably appear to be causative.

Two types of research studies need to be interpreted when we look at the research in this area. For survey studies, the data are easy to obtain in a relatively short period of time from a sizeable number of cases. Clinical studies take longer, their populations are usually much smaller, but they commonly are more intensive and thorough. A survey study of a large population may sometimes lose the significance of smaller groups within that population, where a clinical study might not. It is frequently to the advantage of the researcher interested in specific kinds of anomalies to pay closer attention to clinical studies in which those populations have received greater study than is possible in a survey study. In medical research, for example, it would hardly be worth an investigator's time and effort to peruse research dealing with the diets of 10,000 normal healthy subjects if he really only wanted to know the kinds of diets that had been most effective in treating peptic ulcers. Reading researchers often find that they are confronted with a similar situation when, for example, they want to study the effects of speech difficulties and learning to read. Clinical studies tend to find greater significance and survey studies tend to find lesser or no significance between the two. The inclusion of a number of subjects in the survey studies who are capable readers obscures the relationship for those where the association between speech problems and reading difficulties is interrelated.

In dealing with the causes of reading difficulty, it becomes too easy to look for *the* cause, as though there were only one. Most students who have reading difficulties have a constellation of causative factors. Owing to individual differences, a set of factors that may cause severe reading problems in one case may seem to have little effect in another. Certainly if anyone ever had visual problems of sufficient severity to cause reading difficulties, Aldous Huxley, author of *Brave New World*, did, but he learned to read, and he read omnivorously.

Neither is there any set formula a person should use to investigate the background causes for reading difficulties. Freud urged his students to observe everything without preconceived ideas regarding underlying causes. Although it is not possible to ignore preconceptions completely, Freud's advice is still generally good. Since there can be no complete guide to all possible causes of difficulty, the best safeguard is a diagnostician/teacher who is alert to observe indications that would otherwise go unnoticed.

INEFFECTIVE INSTRUCTION

A primary cause of reading difficulties is poor instruction. This may arise from various sources: improperly initiated instruction, inappropriately paced instruction, instruction that is not sequenced or programmed in areas in which students have difficulty, and instruction conducted under adverse circumstances.

Improperly Initiated Instruction   Jamie English knew no more than two or three dozen words when he arrived in the ninth grade. Withdrawn and passive, he had long since given up on the humiliating battle to learn in school. He now simply hoped to survive each day in the threatening environment of a secondary school.

His cumulative records showed that he had been given reading readiness tests twice during the first grade and had scored poorly both times. Nevertheless, he had begun to work in a first pre-primer by Thanksgiving, a second pre-primer after the Christmas break, a third pre-primer before spring vacation, and was working in a primer when he completed first grade.

He was promoted to second grade, where his teacher noted that he was a beginning reader when he entered. She formed three reading groups, and Jamie was placed in the lowest, reading at primer level—three levels higher than she had noted his ability. At the end of second grade, his records indicated that he had made "little progress in reading, language arts, or arithmetic."

It seems doubtful that Jamie was ready to successfully begin initial reading instruction until middle or late third grade, by which time he was receiving instruction at upper second-grade level along with six other pupils, mostly boys, in a low reading group.

Circumstances were not better during fourth, fifth, and sixth grades. Although he was never retained, neither his regular classroom instruction nor special instruction in reading were at a level at which he could profit from them. Usually he was placed in materials five or six levels beyond his instructional abilities, and his regular classroom content materials ranged even higher. Junior high school was a disaster. Teachers who faced 150 students each day had little time to work with Jamie. Although there was a special reading class, here again instruction was pitched at a level too high to be of any value for Jamie. He arrived in ninth grade able to recognize fewer than three dozen words. He had not learned to read, but he had learned a great deal *about* reading. He had learned that reading was hard, that it was embarrassing, and that even special programs were ineffective in helping him learn to read.

At first, the language experience approach was used with Jamie when, in ninth grade, he was selected for special reading help. Later, as he began to improve his reading ability, high-interest low-ability remedial reading materials were used with him at his instructional reading level. Although he was convinced he could not learn to read, he began to make slow progress. After three and a half years of individually prescribed instruction, he was functionally literate, reading at about seventh-grade level.

What can be learned from Jamie's case? Instruction had never truly been available at a level profitable to him. The previous reading instruction he had received was not only of little value, it actually created problems he had not had before. The results of ineffective reading instruction were frustration, poor self-concept, and avoidance of reading because it had become a painful and degrading activity. Jamie was not exactly excited to have been placed in "another" special reading class when he started ninth grade!

What was the cause of Jamie's reading difficulties? There was no lack of labels accompanying his cumulative records. According to them, the blame could easily be fixed on neurological problems, a perceptual communicative disorder, dyslexia, or a "too passive personality seeking attention through a maladjustive behavior pattern"—none of these explained why he made good gains as soon as he was given the benefit of a good "garden-variety" remedial program keyed to his level. A far more reasonable assessment of his problem would have been that he had had ineffective reading instruction. His first-grade teacher had been in too great a hurry to get him into beginning reading instruction before he was ready for it. To be fair to her, if she had not started Jamie in reading before the end of first grade, Jamie's parents and her principal would very likely have exerted pressure on her to start him. At any rate, Jamie had begun reading instruction before he was ready for it, and, in a chain reaction, each of Jamie's teachers had built on the previous one in continuing the error. No one had stopped the process begun in first grade, found the appropriate instructional reading level, and started Jamie at that level, not even in special instructional settings.

Jamie was like Paul Eley, and yet the outcome was quite different. Paul was the son of a school superintendent in Washington State. He also took reading readiness tests during first grade and scored poorly on them. But Paul's dad and the first-grade teacher decided to delay the start of formal initial reading instruction until they believed Paul would be ready to profit from it. This did not happen throughout first grade. In second grade, his teacher and his father again decided Paul was not yet ready. Finally, during the middle of his third-grade year, Paul began to be interested in reading. The administration of yet another readiness test added confirmation to the teacher's feelings that Paul was now able to profit from initial reading instruction. He began to read, and proved he was ready to learn, making steady progress. He became an above-average reader in less than two years. Paul's record from that point on lead through an excellent college career, where he served as the student body president in his senior year; later he became an outstanding teacher, then a creative elementary school principal, and he eventually developed a successful small business. Jamie had the intelligence to do the same thing. All he lacked was opportunity.

Inappropriately Paced Instruction   Gerald's clinician was pleased when she found that he was interested in one of the first remedial series readers she tried with him. Eleven years old the summer before going into sixth grade, Gerald had come to the university reading clinic to try to improve his low third-grade reading ability. He began the book he and his clinician had agreed upon, reading with enthusiasm. He moved through the book easily and went on to the next book in that series, then the next, and the next. But the enthusiasm he had expressed initially began to fade as he went through one book after another. His clinician was puzzled by his slow change in attitude. What had begun with high interest was now dragging dismally.

A brief reference to the teacher's manual for the series showed that the first book Gerald had read was posted at a readability of 2.5, the second was listed at 3.0, the third at 3.5, and the one he was currently reading was 4.0. In a period of five or six weeks, his clinician had moved Gerald from material he could read easily to materials that were too difficult for him. She had not paced the difficulty of the material to Gerald's learning ability.

A school district in New York State was having a problem with its reading program, as indicated by the test results given at the end of each school year. The sixth-grade achievement test results were adequate, but each year below that looked progressively worse, and the reading test scores at the end of the first grade showed that the students were averaging over a half-year behind. An investigation of the instructional program revealed an interesting problem. An influential district administrator had mandated that no first-grade child should be allowed to read anything above pre-primer level. As a result, even the most capable first-grade pupils were pinned to no more than middle first-grade reading materials. The second-grade teachers tried to make up some of the ground lost, the third-grade teachers continued the effort, and by the time the students were in sixth grade, they were only slightly behind the average for the state. The instructional program was not being paced to the abilities of the students.

Many students who have difficulty with reading are handicapped by reading instruction that moves ahead of them too quickly or lags behind them. In the cases described, an adjustment to bring instruction in line with student abilities resulted in increased gain, and incidentally, increased enjoyment from the students.

Improperly Programmed Instruction   Programmed instruction, as used here, means breaking a task or skill into its component parts and sequencing them in such a fashion that they are more easily learned.

When Bob's teacher asked the class to outline the chapter, his heart fell. He did not understand outlining. Now an eighth-grader, he had been trying to outline for two or three years. He always earned a low grade for his efforts. None of his teachers had ever taught him to outline, starting with the simplest steps and working up to more difficult aspects of the task. As a result, Bob did not even know how to begin.

This time, however, his teacher carefully sequenced a series of steps. First, she had him identify the main idea of some paragraphs by putting titles on them. Then they discussed whether the titles captured the sense of the paragraphs. Next, she had him do the same thing for a connected series of four or five paragraphs. After that she took one paragraph that contained a main idea and several supporting ideas, wrote out the main idea for Bob, added two of the supporting ideas, and asked him to find other ideas that supported or related to the main idea. After finding these, he did the same thing with several other paragraphs. As a last step before outlining, she gave Bob a partially filled-in outline of a short passage. Some of the main ideas were left blank, and in other places she left out supporting ideas. He filled in all the missing parts to the outline. By now he was ready to outline a passage.

When a student has difficulty with a skill, it is often possible to teach it by breaking it into easier steps. A student who cannot identify the number of syllables in a word may never have learned what a syllable is, or that there is a "beat" to each syllable in a word. Effective instruction often means finding the place in the sequence where a student can begin to learn successfully and planning a path by which he can learn.

Adverse Learning Circumstances   Ginny's parents were surprised that she was doing so poorly in first grade. By the middle of the year it became obvious that Ginny, a rather shy child, was afraid of school and afraid of her teacher. Her teacher, who had a good reputation in the community, was abrupt in talking with her pupils. Although Ginny was almost never the focus of her comments, Ginny reacted by withdrawing from the situation as much as possible. Eventually she would not even reply to the teacher when asked a direct question. Fearing emotional problems, her parents sought help for Ginny through counseling, but the counselor found nothing beyond her fear of the school situation. Although the teacher suggested retention in the first grade, the decision was made to promote her to second grade, placing her with a warm, accepting teacher. She adjusted to second grade well, and with remedial help was soon reading and performing at or above grade level.

Steve's mother was a reading teacher, and she became alarmed when her adopted son began to bring bad reports home from school. Unwilling to confront Steve's teacher, she let things go from bad to worse; finally, the teacher recommended that Steve be retained in second grade. A referral to a reading clinic showed that Steve had an IQ above 140, was energetic, had a good basic background in reading skills, and had no other significant problems except that he had apparently made little gain during his tenure in second grade. A visit to the classroom showed that he and his second-grade teacher did not get along well together. She believed he was lazy, that he would not do the work she had assigned (which was obviously true), and that he was a trouble-maker. The assignments Steve was failing to turn in consisted of literally dozens of pages of duplicated worksheets over skill work he had already mastered. His teacher had placed him in a reading group with children who were doing very poorly, and Steve found little challenge in the level of work assigned.

The "remedial" program for Steve consisted of moving him into more interesting and challenging material, and, since it was near the end of the school year, promoting him to third grade, where the change of teachers worked wonders for him.

George had a teacher who screamed at the children most of the time. Shirley's teacher had a "nervous breakdown" which eventually required her to be hospitalized, but while she remained with her class, the students accomplished very little. Bill's teacher resigned her position before Thanksgiving to have a baby, and Bill had four more teachers before the end of the year; the next year was almost as bad. Beth's teacher was so obsessed with her dog that discussion about the animal absorbed most of the time allotted for reading. Arlene's teacher had difficulty with her romantic life. When she was teaching she was upset and irritable, and much of the time substitute teachers directed the class.

But not all adverse circumstances are caused by the teacher. David did not learn very much in third grade because he had lost his mother the previous summer. Pam and Neal had a classroom that had to be repaired, and they spent the bulk of their second-grade year in a "classroom" at the end of a hallway. Overcrowding forced Kyle to attend a first-grade classroom with 43 children in it. An influx of children into Eric's school caused his class to be housed in the cafeteria for part of the day and the gymnasium (which also housed the school library at the other end) for the rest of the time. None of these children was incapable of learning. Adverse circumstances caused them to fall behind in their reading.

To what degree does ineffective instruction cause reading difficulties? It is virtually impossible to say. There can be no question that it is a major cause, perhaps the leading cause of reading difficulty, but the variability of possible factors and the impossibility of adequate measurement leave us without anything but estimations of the importance of ineffective instruction. Although Robinson's landmark study in 1946 listed "school methods" as causative in only 18.1 percent of the cases she studied, few authorities would agree with that figure today, judging from a review of those writing in the field of reading. Although Ekwall highlights Robinson's study, he disagrees with her, suggesting that the figure is much higher (Ekwall, 1976). Bond, Tinker, and Wasson (1979) say, "Among all the factors that are considered possible causes of reading disability, the group of conditions classed as educational stand out as tremendously important." Harris and Sipay (1980) write, " . . . it seems reasonable that teacher practices . . . must aggravate the learning problems of many children. . . ." Although there are some textbooks in the area that do not mention educational factors at all, it seems safe to say that the majority cite educational causes of reading difficulty as a crucial concern.

PSYCHOLOGICAL AND NEUROLOGICAL CONCERNS

Intelligence   Generally high correlations have been reported between success in learning to read and measurements of intelligence. As pointed out earlier in this chapter, however, it is important to look carefully at the reports of correlations before assuming that there is a strong causative relationship between the two variables, and further, that there is great significance to the reported findings. In a study of functionally illiterate adults, Brown (1970) found that intelligence measures were almost totally inadequate in predicting which members of the population would make the best progress in learning to read. Studies by Gerken (1978) and others have attempted to introduce variations on the results of intelligence measures to make them more usable in working with educationally disadvantaged students. The fact that a student is severely limited in reading ability often causes his intelligence test scores to be lower than his true abilities would indicate (Brown, 1970).

Nevertheless, if a range of intelligence test scores is wide enough, there is little question that those at the high end of the scale will generally do better in their reading than those at the lower end of the scale. Students averaging approximately 120 IQ will do significantly better than a group of students whose mean IQ is approximately 70. The limitation, however, is that there is little value in comparing two students whose scores are, respectively, 95 and 105. Both of them should be able to learn to read, and the student who has an IQ measured at 95 is not likely to be "handicapped" in comparison to the student who scores 105.

The task of assessing intelligence is a formidable one. For students from educationally disadvantaged homes, from homes where English is not the primary language, and for students who are significantly retarded in their reading ability, estimation of true intelligence, even with individual intelligence tests, is particularly subject to error. Group measures not only have the usual limitations of measurement when used with educationally disadvantaged students or those who have difficulty with English or reading; they have the additional disadvantage of unnoticed resignation by those students who become frustrated and stop trying. Unable to understand the test items because they cannot recognize many of the words even though they may have the intellectual ability to deal with the concepts, they either lay their pencil aside and stop wrestling with the test or they race through the test by simply marking random answers. Both actions produce low scores, which are inaccurate measures of intellectual ability.

Jensen (1969) interpreted a mass of intelligence test data as indicating racial differences in degree and type of intelligence. Brown (1970), however, found that a closer examination of individual intelligence test data showed no significant differences between the performances of functionally illiterate Black subjects on rote and higher cognitive tests. He further found that the *Wechsler Adult Intelligence Scale,* the most commonly used individual intelligence test for adults, was unable to identify good and poor learners in that population.

In attempting to estimate intelligence, one practice has been to add 10 points to the full-scale IQ score of students from homes in which English is not the primary language. Gerken (1978) found such a disparity, and Neville (1965) implied that the same addition, 10 points, would be a closer approximation of ability for retarded readers. Even though such adjustments may achieve closer approximations of intelligence, the IQ estimated by these additions are still only estimates. In fact, Kellaghan (1973) voiced the opinions of many when he concluded from his research that low intelligence-test scores were really better indicators of low achievement than of intelligence and that as disadvantaged students make gains in reading and achievement, their intelligence-test scores climb.

This is not to say that intelligence is unrelated to the ability to learn to read, nor that all measurement of intelligence is inaccurate. Tests of intelligence can be rather valid reflections of the mental ability of students within the dominant culture if they read well and if they have the physical ability to perform the tasks required by the tests.

Intelligence is as varied in its makeup as any other aspect of an individual. A student may have generally high intelligence and yet lack certain psycholinguistic abilities which relate to the development of good reading ability. On the other hand, a student may seem to be low in general intelligence and have normal abilities in the areas that relate most closely to reading ability. By age 15, Anne had had three individual intelligence tests, all of which had placed her in the 60 to 69 IQ range, but she was able to use her syntactic, phonemic, and visual domains well enough to process and "read" beginning high school level materials. Her semantic processing—*crucial* to truly effective reading—was severely limited, of course, but her oral reading performance was deceptively fluent and gave the appearance that she had nearly flawless reading ability.

Perhaps not unlike the *idiot savants* who have extraordinary mental abilities in certain limited areas while suffering from severe mental retardation in general, students like Anne help us to remember that artificial barriers based solely on intelligence-test scores are generally unwise, because of a number of individual exceptions. Generally speaking, those with IQ scores from 50 to 59 may learn to recognize a limited number of survival words, although long-term retention usually requires numerous repetitions. Students with IQ scores of 60 to 69 by age 16 may be able to read material of up to fifth-grade difficulty, although many such as Anne may have word recognition skills beyond that level. Those with IQ scores in the range of 70 to 79 usually have the ability to become functionally literate, reading at grades five, six, or seven. Those with 80 to 89 IQ can be expected to be able to read at grades seven to nine by the time they are 16. Of course, all such projections are based on the presumption that the students have good instruction paced to their rates of learning and to their instructional reading levels, and all such "standards" should be viewed as guidelines, rather than hard and fast rules. Students whose intelligence is estimated to be 90 or above should have no intellectual limitation to becoming fully literate adults.

One additional comment should be made relative to intelligence and ability to learn to read. Estimates, even within the dominant culture, of the correlation between the ability to learn to read and intelligence usually run in the area of +.45 to +.65, with high school correlations running somewhat higher (Harris and Sipay, 1980, pp. 146–7). This means that there is a large amount of unaccounted variability. In other words, even if a person were to accept a correlation of +.65 between intelligence and reading achievement, squaring the correlation would show that the relationship would only account for approximately 42 percent of the total, leaving nearly 59 percent of the success in learning to read related to other variables.

In summary, a certain degree of intelligence is undoubtedly necessary in order to learn to read. Problems arise in attempting to measure intelligence, particularly for students from educationally disadvantaged backgrounds and for those who do not have strong English-speaking backgrounds or who do not read well. Since approximately 50 percent of the population has intelligence estimated to be between 90 and 109 (Anastasi, 1968, p. 58), it is easy to see that intelligence is not likely to be a major factor in whether most students learn to read.

Lateral Dominance and Obscuring   Lateral dominance refers to the preference for using the right or left hand, eye, or foot. The relationship between lateral dominance and learning to read has been mystifying and often frustrating. It seems peculiar that anything so long observed in human behavior as handedness still leaves so many questions unanswered. Even the frequency of left-handedness is equivocal, with a range of from 4 to almost 15 percent being reported.

Early research by Dearborn (1933) found reading difficulties most likely to appear in children who had no preference for either hand in writing, followed by those who were left-handed. He suggested that those least likely to have difficulty learning to read were those who were both right-handed and right-eyed.

Early studies by Monroe (1932), Eames (1934), Crosland (1939), and Witty and Kopel (1936) generally supported the finding that reading problems were more frequently associated with children who had anomalies in laterality than with those who did not.

A study by Harris in 1957 (Harris and Sipay, 1980) found that 93 percent of unselected readers have definite handedness by the time they are 7 years old, as against only 70 percent of those having reading problems. By age 9 only 6 percent have not established dominance.

A number of studies have questioned the relationship between reading difficulties and laterality (Cohen and Glass, 1968; Douglas, Ross, and Cooper, 1967). In general, those studies which have tended to find no relationship have been survey studies, while clinical studies have tended to find a positive relationship.

Orton and Dearborn have developed the two most familiar theories related to lateral dominance as a possible cause of reading difficulty. Orton (1937) hypothesized that failure to establish dominance would lead to the exclusive use of memory traces in only one hemisphere and would result in interference and confusion, making it difficult to learn to read and write effectively. More recent medical and neurological research has tended not to substantiate his position, and at this time it does not seem to be a likely answer to the relationship between reading and laterality.

Dearborn (1933) believed that the difficulties experienced by left-dominant and confused-dominant students lay in the greater difficulty they have in moving their hands and eyes from left to right. Even if it is true that those who are left-dominant have more difficulty with those movements—and such a statement is somewhat questionable—it still would not account for the greater degree of difficulty among those with confused dominance over those who are left-dominant. If those who had not established dominance had greater difficulty than those who were left-dominant, it would not seem to support such a theory (Zangwill, 1962).

Shimrat (1970) studied the writing of children learning to write in English (left to right) and Hebrew (right to left). She found that right-handed children had an advantage when writing from left to right rather than right to left. Left-handed children wrote with equal speed in either direction but made fewer errors when writing from right to left.

Shimrat's research buttressed this writer's observations of a small number of clinical cases. A half-dozen extremely reading-disabled left-handed students were found who wrote with their wrists held straight, as though they were right-handed, and with the writing paper at an angle which was a left-hand image of a right-handed person writing. As a result, the students could not see the letters as they were written. They received no feedback at all. They did not grip higher up the pencil, look over the top of their hands, crook their wrists, or do any of the numerous things left-handed writers generally do to enable them to see what they are writing. Their hands simply obscured what they had written.

In a study by Brown (1981), 1139 third, fourth, and fifth graders in regular heterogenous classrooms were observed to determine whether or not they obscured. Thirty-three were found to obscure at least a portion of a seven-letter word as they wrote. Thirty-two of these were left-handed writers who wrote holding their wrists straight as seen in Figure 3.1.

The one right-handed student who obscured as he wrote held the pencil in a peculiar crabbed fashion as seen in Figure 3.2 with the pencil contacting the paper under the middle of the hand.

Of those who obscured, 16 students or 48.5 percent of the obscuring sample were identified by their teachers as falling within the lowest three stanines of

Figure 3-1.

readers within their classes. Stated another way, although only approximately twenty-three percent would have been expected to rank that poorly, over twice as many actually did. Even more striking was the finding that four times as many were ranked as extremely disabled readers than would have been expected.

Although further research is indicated, it appears that the likelihood that students will develop reading difficulties is significantly increased if students obscure as they write.

Neurological Causation and Learning Disability   Since the invention of printing by Gutenberg, people have grown to believe that everyone should be able to learn to read, and they have been puzzled by those who have not been able to do so. Hinshelwood, Critchley, Orton, and others have given us a legacy of terms

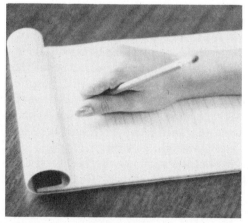

Figure 3-2.

such as "congenital word blindness," "strephosymbolia," and "dyslexia" to identify severe inability to learn to read presumably caused by some incapacity within the brain or nervous system. Although these particular terms have waned in favor, the desire to describe the condition, which we still do not understand, is as strong today as it ever was. Terms borrowed from medical science include one that appears frequently—"neurological dysfunction." Not to be confused with brain trauma, or "damage to the brain," a neurological dysfunction is a condition in which the normal neural mechanisms within the body do not function properly. The identification and definition of a neurological dysfunction as a root cause of a reading difficulty in any specific situation is extraordinarily difficult. Diagnosis through a neurological examination or through electroencephalography has not led to a satisfactory identification process. There tends to be no significant difference between good and poor learners on the basis of such examinations (Coles, 1978, pp. 325–26).

In search of a better term to describe what we do not understand, Kirk (1963) used "learning disabilities." Johnson and Myklebust (1967) preferred "psychoneurological learning disabilities," but "learning disabilities" seems to be more widely accepted (Lerner, 1979). Because of confusion regarding the meaning of the term, the United States Office of Education selected a committee to define "learning disabilities" (Lerner, 1971). Kass and Myklebust (1969) report the definition that resulted:

> Learning disability refers to one or more significant deficits in essential learning processes requiring special education techniques for remediation.
> Children with learning disability generally demonstrate a discrepancy between expected and actual achievement in one or more areas, such as spoken, read, or written language, mathematics, and spatial orientation.
> The learning disability referred to is not primarily the result of sensory, motor, intellectual, or emotional handicap, or lack of opportunity to learn.
> *Significant deficits* are defined in terms of accepted diagnostic procedures in education and psychology.
> *Essential learning processes* are those currently referred to in behavioral science as involving perception, integration, and expression either verbal or nonverbal.
> Special education techniques for remediation refers to educational planning based on the diagnostic procedures and results.

National legislation in 1969 used a somewhat different definition borrowed from the National Advisory Committee on Handicapped Children, which appeared in their report to Congress in 1968 as follows:

> Children with special learning disabilities exhibit a disorder in one or more of the basic psychological processes involved in understanding or using spoken or written languages. These may be manifested in disorders of listening, thinking, talking, reading, writing, spelling, or arithmetic. They include conditions which have been referred to as perceptual handicaps, brain injury, minimal brain dysfunction, dyslexia, developmental

aphasia, etc. They do not include learning problems which are due primarily to visual, hearing, or motor handicaps, to mental retardation, emotional disturbance, or to environmental disadvantage.

In 1975 Congress added legislation (Public Law 94–142) defining specific learning disabilities as *underachievement* in oral expression, listening, writing, basic reading skills, reading comprehension, mathematical calculation, or mathematical reasoning. Originally the total number of children who could be classified as learning-disabled was limited to 2 percent of the total school population. Operational portions of the act later eliminated this stipulation. An expansion of Public Law 94–142 added early childhood and adult populations to those covered by the law by widening the age limits to include those from age 3 through 21 (Lerner, 1979).

These definitions have added difficulty to attempts to clarify and delimit the conditions and causes classified under learning disability. Despite assurances that one or more of the definitions are "concise" (Lerner, 1971, p. 9), they seem so broad as to lend little direction to those trying to implement the existing legislation. In practice, attempts to identify those who are learning-disabled have of necessity been forced to emphasize those elements which are measurable within the definition(s). As a result, decreasing attention has been given to the measurement of processing skills, both because of the difficulty of measurement and because there seems to be little difference in processing between those who have been diagnosed as learning-disabled and remedial readers. Lerner (1971) points out that "the precise nature of the relationship between neurological abnormalities and learning disabilities is still not clear." Hartman and Hartman (1973) found little difference between children classified as learning-disabled and those who were classified as remedial readers. Carder (1974) came up with a similar finding.

With such confusion, it becomes necessary to go back to first principles and reexamine the area of learning disabilities in light of distinctive causation. Are there common elements to learning disability which set it apart from other causes of reading difficulty?

Lerner (1979) lists five qualifications used to distinguish learning-disabled students: first, those who have a disability caused by a neurological dysfunction; second, those who are disabled learners owing to an uneven growth pattern; third, those who have difficulty in academic and learning tasks; fourth, those who exhibit a discrepancy between their levels of achievement and their learning potential; those who exhibit a discrepancy between their levels of achievement and their potential; and fifth, those who do not learn and yet give no indication of other causes that would account for their difficulty.

An examination of these common elements is less than heartening to the reading diagnostician. "Neurological dysfunction" is difficult to identify, and even when it is presumed to exist, its relationship with reading difficulty is unclear. "Uneven growth patterns" among mental abilities is not measurable except through achievement testing, which allows the results to be contaminated by every other variable that can also affect achievement and achievement testing. "Those who have difficulty with academic and learning tasks" is too broad to be useful in examining causation, as is "those who exhibit a discrepancy between their levels of achievement and their potential." The last of those qualifications Lerner lists is really an exclusion of all other causes, "those who do not learn and yet give no indication of other causes which could account for their difficulty."

Virtually every student having difficulty in reading for whatever cause could be included under one or another of the identification criteria listed for learning disability. The broadness and the lack of precision in the term "learning disabilities" has made it difficult, if not impossible, to examine effectively in terms of causation. Nevertheless, "learning disabilities" has proved useful as a rallying cry for parents whose children are not learning as well as might be expected. It has been a vehicle through which parent groups have become involved in public education. Through these groups, strong lobbying action has been initiated which has proved to be an excellent means of procuring public funds through legislative action for the provision of special programs for improvement of instruction.

However, the term is not always helpful for the child. It has had the effect of focusing attention on the child as the source of his own difficulties. Although this certainly does not mean that a child is held personally responsible for his "condition" once identified as "learning-disabled," the fault is not then seen to lie with poor instruction, poor home background, uncorrected visual difficulties, or any of a myriad of other possible causes lying outside the individual's central nervous system. Since the difficulty is viewed as a central nervous system defect, little attention is given to changing conditions, circumstances, and programs to prevent the occurrence of disabled readers. This means that the great majority of causes of reading difficulty may be overlooked or discounted. Concerns about overcrowded classrooms, poor materials, inadequate instruction, or lack of reading materials in the home are more easily shrugged off or forgotten while greater efforts are invested in attempts to diagnose and remediate neurological dysfunctions or "processing deficits."

Another difficulty associated with identifying students as learning-disabled is that such students often come to believe that they are "different." They are "learning-disabled," and although no one really knows what that means, the students interpret it to mean that they are somehow not normal. They have something within them that makes them unlike others, something that causes them difficulty in learning. As such a student, his teachers, and his parents adjust to that label, they often come to treat the child differently. The classroom teacher, aware of his own limitations, is likely to feel he cannot teach the student because the student has a learning problem. The teacher expects little from the student and gives little to him because he does not understand what is meant by a "learning disability"—and who is to blame him for not understanding?

Because of its problems of definition and diagnosis, many have forecast a short tenure for "learning disabilities," but "LD" is likely to remain for the foreseeable future. It has been engraved on the laws of the land, funding is attached to it, parent groups are well organized and active. Although those concerned with causation and diagnosis might hope for clearer definitions of learning disabilities, the dedication of parents and others involved is something to be admired. Parents concerned about the learning problems of their children have succeeded in passing legislation to create and fund programs, and they have consistently maintained the strongest voice of support for those programs. It does not seem likely that the field of learning disabilities will soon disappear.

But it has and will continue to change in nature and structure. Instead of having its definitions refined, they have become broadened. Early concern with neurological dysfunction has been replaced with identification through a discrepancy between achievement and potential. A student now may be labeled as "learning-disabled" simply on the basis of test results indicating that he is reading more poorly than he should. It is no longer necessary to deal with the impossibilities of measuring processing skills or neurological dysfunction. All that is needed is that a student "manifest . . . imperfect ability to . . . read" (PL 94–142, 1975, Section 620 b 4A). If students do worse on a test of their achievement than a measure of their potential would indicate, they have the legal requirements of the federal regulations necessary to indicate learning disability.

Despite the difficulties associated with the definition and diagnosis of learning disabilities, the question remains, "Is there a psychoneural cause of reading disability?" Rabinovitch (1968) believes there is, and he labels the condition "primary reading retardation." Harris and Sipay (1980) and Vernon (1971) tend to agree. Smith and Carrigan (1959) hypothesize that biochemical imbalances within the synapses may cause difficulty resulting in reading disability. More recently, others have posited that factors affecting the ability of the brain to scan for retrieval (Young, 1978, pp. 130–31, 189), or defects in normal memory processing (Baddeley, 1976) may be causative factors inhibiting normal brain function required in learning to read. In sum, many authorities agree that there are students who do not learn to read for causes that elude us. They appear to have the mental and physical abilities necessary to learn to read. They have had the benefit of good developmental reading instruction and good remedial instruction, and yet they still have not learned to read. From the author's personal experience with hundreds of students in both public school and clinical settings, the number of such students is quite small, probably less than one in a hundred.

However, there are a few students who do not respond to ordinary remedial instruction for reasons that are difficult to identify. Pete was 14 years old and was unable to read beginning first-grade-level material without great difficulty. Careful examination of his records, interviews with Pete and his mother, and diagnostic testing revealed nothing of consequence. He began a remedial program at his instructional level which provided all the elements of a good remedial program, but he made no measurable gains in reading achievement. After ten weeks, the program was modified; further reinforcement was added, as was more individual instruction and more intensive work with basic sight vocabulary words. Still there was no significant change. It was not until he received intensive instructional remediation, such as that described in Chapter Ten, that he began to make progress, and even then his gains were slow. It is possible that Pete's diagnosis was faulty, failing to uncover external, sensory, or functional causes of his difficulty. However, it seems altogether likely that his problems may have been rooted in one or more psychoneural anomalies. No one can be certain. But Pete and others like him with whom the author has worked support the position that, however rare, there may be cases in which the student's reading disability may largely be caused by psychoneural factors.

Perceptual Disorders   *The American Heritage Dictionary of the English Language* (1969) defines *perception* as the act of perceiving, and defines *perceive* as "to become aware of directly through any of the senses; especially, to see or to hear." A reader utilizes (1) vision, (2) perception, (3) recognition, (4) comprehension, and (5) reaction. Vision is the physical act of visual sensing. Visual perception is the interpretation of those sensations received via the optic nerve. Restak (1979, p. 25) describes the perceptual process thus:

> . . . impulses are transferred along the optic nerve to visual analyzer cells located in the primary visual area at the back of the brain. Surrounding these cells are visual-association cells, which are important for organizing what is seen into meaningful visual patterns. As the final step in the hierarchy, a third group of cells, surrounding the first two, is responsible for coordinating what we see and hear into a single perception.

Perception is based on what the brain has learned about the world in which it lives, and in that sense perception is "learned." Although the perceptual centers in the brain invert the scene reported to it by the optic nerve (see Chapter One), they cannot invert some small portion of that scene. If, for example, a person looks out the window onto a beautiful panorama of mountains, trees, and greenery, it is not possible for him to see one tree in an inverted position while all the rest of the landscape is right side up. The perceptual centers of the brain interpret everything to the brain as right side up and relationally accurate to other elements in view.

This has importance in understanding perception as it relates to reading. Although the optic nerve reports everything to the perceptual centers upside down and backward to what is actually there, the entire scene is interpreted right side up and in proper left and right relationship based on the perceptual center's past experience of what is real. The perceptual center cannot interpret all of a page as right side up but leave one small word such as *was* or *saw* upside down and backward. It would be even further beyond belief to imagine that the perceptual center of the brain would interpret sensations received from the optic nerve right side up with the exception of the word *was* which it would interpret in reversed right-to-left order but not inverted. Such perception would be completely incredible.

The blame, then, for reversals (chiefly consisting of only two words, *was* and *saw*, although *on* and *no* and a few others occasionally occur), letter transpositions, and word transpositions is not a disorder in perception. The processing error lies at the next higher level, recognition.

Although some degree of semantic processing may be involved in visual perception, it is of very primary or shallow nature (Lockhart, Craik, and Jacoby, 1976).

As students learn to recognize a word, they must process that word at sufficient depth and richness to permit an easily retrievable memory trace. After having learned to recognize the word, they may use such minimal processing that we can term recognition as "automatic." Although initial learning may have involved processing from visual, phonemic, syntactic-semantic, and possibly even tactile domains, well-learned recognition tends to use only shallow processing within the visual and syntactic-semantic domains.

An exception to the latter occurs when the reader encounters difficulty in recognition. When he miscalls a word, and becomes aware of it, he diverts conscious thought from understanding the author's message to correctly identifying the missed word. This usually results in processing the word more deeply and richly. As we would expect, a reader who correctly identifies a word he has at first failed to recognize exhibits more learning in relation to that word than he does when encountering a word which he processes automatically (Lockhart, Craik, and Jacoby, 1976, p. 79).

When a reader recognizes words within his perceptual field, he is likely to recognize some of them inaccurately. He may recognize *was* for *saw* because he encoded both of those words on the basis of their visual configuration, received inconsistent guidance while learning them, and had not learned the cue value (in reading) to the visual and phonemic domains of memory in letter sequence (s-a-w/w-a-s being much the same to him as seeing himself in a mirror). He developed a "learned confusion." He will not "reverse" the vast majority of other words, including such words as *but* and *tub*, or *not* and *ton*, not because it is impossible to do so and make a word, but because the other factors that led to the confusion were not present when the words were being encoded.

It is not uncommon to find perception used in a manner that confuses its more precise technical definition with its lay use. In lay conversation, where scientific or technical accuracy is not a concern, many people use *perception* to include recognition. Although the lack of precision does not ordinarily pose problems, it does create difficulties when it invades a professional field. A student may be said to have a "perceptual problem" because he fails to recognize a word correctly. The misuse of the term *perception* in that case leads to the improper conclusion that the student does not accurately interpret the visual stimuli received through the optic nerve, when in actuality his perceptual processes and functions are quite normal, and the problem lies in the student's imperfect recognition of what he has perceived. This fact should be viewed with great relief. It is possible to remediate recognition difficulties. It is an understatement to say that perception is highly resistant to change by instruction.

Emotional Maladjustment   A wide range of emotional states has been treated under the heading of "emotional maladjustment" or "emotional disturbance." Positions have been taken by respected researchers and writers without sufficient concern for definition of terms. "Emotional maladjustment" relative to reading is seldom discussed in terms of severity either of the emotional disturbance or of the reading difficulty. Further, little discrimination seems to have been made between the different kinds of emotional disturbance.

Given the difficulties of definition, it is predictable that research results in this area have been so varied as to be almost useless at first glance. It is possible to choose almost any position dealing with emotional maladjustment as a cause or an effect of reading difficulties and find a reasonable amount of research to substantiate that position. Gann's (1945) classic treatment of the subject took the position that emotional maladjustment was not caused by poor reading. She found that when a child was both a poor reader and emotionally maladjusted, the emotional problem predated the problem with reading and frequently was causative of the problem. Fernald (1943), on the other hand, found in a study of 78 cases of extreme reading disability that only 4 could be identified as having had indications of emotional problems before they entered school. Robinson (1946) found that in approximately 41 percent of the cases that she studied, emotional difficulties were exhibited, and she believed that nearly 32 percent of those studied had emotional problems as a causative factor in the development of reading difficulties. The picture has not been clarified since that time; conclusions drawn from recent research studies are as varied as they were in the mid-1940s.

Perhaps a first step toward the clarification of the relationship between reading and emotional maladjustment is the establishment of at least some broad definitive boundaries demarcating the terms used. In this section we will use the terms *psychotic, neurotic,* and *maladjusted* to indicate the most global differentiations between categories of emotional difficulties. The first two of these are often referred to as classifications of "mental illness," reflecting the greater degree of severity generally associated with those bearing those descriptors. Each of these major categories has many subcategories, differing widely in the conditions they designate.

Psychoticism may be characterized by varying degrees of personality disintegration in which the individuals are unable to relate effectively to their environment or society. Although there are different classification systems in use emphasizing different criteria and different names of conditions, a common method of classification includes schizophrenia, childhood autism (often treated as a type of schizophrenia), depressive and manic-depressive states, and paranoid reactions. Psychopathic personalities—those people unable to give or receive affection and who are without morals, scruples, or who have no sense of guilt—are also sometimes classified as psychotic.

In those states that legislate educational opportunity for psychotic children not regarded as dangerous to themselves or society, reading instruction must be made available to them. It is quite possible to teach some psychotics to read, and the existence of a psychotic state does not, in and of itself, mean that the student will develop a reading problem. Schizophrenia may include hallucinations, delusions, disorientation, and disordered communication, all of which make it difficult for an individual to learn to read. Schizophrenic children tend to respond to words and letters in an unpredictable fashion. They also have difficulty using syntactic clues in helping them identify words (Robeck and Wilson, 1974, p. 92). The withdrawal of autistic children makes it difficult for them to learn, as does their impaired language development and sudden and severe emotional responses (Kisker, 1964, p. 359). Those suffering the affective states of depression and manic-depressive swings are often so turned in upon themselves that it is difficult to motivate them to try to learn to read. Their condition may possibly affect the limbic system which deals with the motivation, pleasure, and punishment. Paranoid states often cause individuals to be suspicious and withdrawn to the extent that they are difficult to involve in a learning situation. However, nonschizophrenic paranoids are intellectually capable, and able to function quite well in those areas which do not involve the delusional system. If, then, their delusions do not include the situation in which they are learning to read, they can be quite capable of learning.

Those who are classified as psychopaths also are capable of learning to read if they believe there is advantage in it for them. Though they can be particularly unpleasant to work with, they can make good progress if they decide they want to learn. Indeed, if they think there is some immediate value to them, they can be top students.

Many of the conditions included above are not common with younger students. Others, such as childhood autism, are of primary concern to the young. But no matter at what age the reading program is offered, individuals are able to learn to read if their condition leaves them with sufficient language capability and attention.

The use of drugs can often be effective in restoring the balance between the reticular (attention) system and the limbic (motivation) system needed to function effectively as a learner (Robeck and Wilson, 1974, p. 94). Robeck and Wilson point out a problem in using drugs, however. The knowledge gained while under the influence of a drug is sometimes not remembered after the effects of the drug wear off; however, the closely monitored use of drugs has generally been effective in helping those learn who are otherwise unable to do so.

It should also be mentioned that most of those who are psychotic change their condition over a period of time. Many of these are completely restored, others encapsulate their psychoticism so that they are normal most of the time, and, of course, others degenerate or become chronically incapacitated. Those who fall into the first two categories can be helped to learn to read if they have sufficient language capability and ability to give attention to the tasks to be learned.

Neuroticism is less serious than psychoticism. People who are neurotic are, unlike psychotics, in touch with reality. They are able to maintain their personality organization, and do not suffer from delusions, hallucinations, and other phenomena associated with psychoticism. Most neurotics—and it is estimated that in the United States one out of every twenty people is neurotic—are treated on an outpatient basis if they are treated at all. Their symptoms range from mild to severe, but in most cases reactions are relatively mild. It is altogether possible for a person to be neurotic under very limited circumstances and under all other circumstances to be able to get along very well.

The earmark of neuroticism appears to be anxiety. Neurotic students are those who have not developed effective means of anxiety control and/or expression. It is not surprising that students who have had difficulty learning to read often display neurotic behavior when they are placed in a position in which they must read. Their anxiety is aroused by having to read, and they have not been able to develop better adaptive behavior to handle their anxiety.

Under different neuroses, there may be varied effects on the person's ability to learn to read. It is conceivable that a student may have a phobia regarding going out in the dark which would cause him to stay at home and read books, helping him become a better reader, even though he had what might be classified as a mild neurosis. Other emotional disturbances listed may directly result in impaired learning. For example, although there seemed to be no physical cause for it, Paul became sleepy the minute his teachers began reading instruction. Within minutes he would be sound asleep. It did not seem to bother him that the other children laughed at him or teased him on the playground about being a "sleepyhead." When it was time for reading, for Paul it was time for a nap.

Greg was 14 years old, in the ninth grade, and able to read at middle fourth-grade level. His reading teacher found that Greg became extremely uncomfortable as soon as they opened a book to read. Magazines were not much better. His teacher tried to find some way of using print materials with him, but Greg's past experiences had apparently been so painful that almost anything in print made him get up from his chair, move around, chew his nails, and show other signs of intense anxiety.

The teacher eventually discovered a strategy that worked well. He took a roll of toilet tissue, fitted it onto a primary typewriter, and typed the material he wanted Greg to use on the tissue—one line on each sheet. Greg was so intrigued that he began to sit and read for the first time. Once started, he found that he *could* learn to read, and after a time moved on to more traditional materials.

It would not be very meaningful to say something like "neuroticism is associated with reading disability 50 percent of the time, and that it is causative 40 percent of the time." Such a statement, even if it were true, would be of little help to the reading diagnostician. Primarily, the only statement that is of any great value is that when neuroticism interferes with a student's ability to give attention to learning to read, it will lessen his chances of becoming a good reader. In some cases such interference is severe. In other cases it is mild, but still inhibiting to some degree. In many other cases, the student's neuroticism has no effect on whether or not he learns to read.

Can neuroticism cause a child to become a poor reader? Certainly. Can poor reading ability produce neuroticism? Yes. Reading is one of the most crucial skills learned in our society. Initial failure to learn to read can be traumatic for both child and parents. Sornson's study (1950) indicates the impact of such failure.

In summary, neurotic conditions that interfere with the attention necessary to learning to read can cause reading failure. Furthermore, unwise behavior by teachers and parents can cause sufficient anxiety to actually make a child neurotic, affecting his future chances of improving his reading.

Maladjustive behavior is exhibited by many students. Acceptance is a basic need; when people are unable to sense that they are acceptable (loved) by those from whom they want acceptance, their behavior is likely to change. When ordinary socially acceptable changes still do not produce the acceptance they want, their behavior is likely to become maladjustive.

Each child learns to function in his own environment. He learns how to belong and be accepted. He learns who he is, what his identification is, based on the reactions of those around him he feels are important. By experimenting with various behaviors until he finds those which give him the greatest degree of acceptance, he develops attitudes and eventually what Dreikurs calls a "lifestyle" (Dinkmeyer and Dreikurs, 1963). In that process he develops a private logic which supports his lifestyle. He accepts evidence which encourages his lifestyle and rejects that which does not.

Unfortunately, many children lack evidence that their parents love them just for themselves. Their behavior tends to become maladjustive as they attempt to gain the acceptance they need. Dreikurs (Dinkmeyer and Dreikurs, 1963, p. 28) lists four classifications of maladjustive behavior: attention-getting, power, revenge, and displaying inadequacy.

Attention-getting.   A diagnosis of Margaret's reading difficulties seemed to indicate no serious problems, yet she insisted that her poor reading really hampered her in her school work. Sensing the possibility that Margaret's poor reading ability might be related to her need to receive time and attention from her father, the teacher asked Margaret if she believed her father would still spend as much time with her if she were able to read quite well. Margaret's face immediately betrayed her serious doubts, although verbally she replied that she thought he probably would. It is likely that Margaret was controlling her father's time and attention in order to receive needed acceptance.

Power.   Power involves control and punishment. When a new principal took over the administration of an elementary school in the middle of the year, he quickly found out that one of his most pressing chores would be the socialization of a fifth-grade student named Joe. The principal's initiation came the first day when he was summoned to the resource room, where a teacher was working with a group of poor readers. When he arrived, Joe had already started a fight with one of the other boys and was now defying the teacher's attempts to restore order. Throughout the remainder of the week, Joe seemed to be involved in one difficulty after another. On his fourth visit to the office, Joe seemed as belligerent as ever. The principal took Joe to the school cafeteria to avoid Joe's feeling of being in "the principal's office." As they talked, Joe began to describe the problems he had with a new father in his home, three new brothers and a sister taking his mother's time, the belief that his new father didn't like him, and his feeling that his mother would be willing to get rid of him in order to keep the new family. Joe finished by saying he did not know anyone who liked him. He was not smart, he was not good looking, he could not read, he could not write, and he could not do arithmetic—enough to cause almost anyone to rebel!

A student may punish and control to gain power, as Joe did, or may use "silent" rebellion for the same purposes. The stubborn child may sulk, be uncooperative, and withdraw. The objectives are the same as those of the rebelling child. Only the behaviors are different.

Revenge   This type of maladjustive behavior is the earmark of children who gain satisfaction through violence, bullying, and other such means of making people sorry they have denied them acceptance.

Displaying inadequacy   Often, the student whose behavioral goal appears to be inadequacy "expects only failure. He uses inability or assumed disability to escape participation" (Dinkmeyer and Dreikurs, 1963, p. 28). Such a child tends to become seriously withdrawn, defeated, and discouraged.

At this point it is again time to pose the questions, "Can maladjustive behavior cause reading difficulties?" and "Can reading difficulty produce maladjustive behavior?" As with neuroticism, the answer to both questions is "yes." Maladjustive behavior is so varied that in some cases it results in poor reading ability; in others it may be produced by poor reading achievement; and in still other cases it has nothing to do with poor reading ability.

A more meaningful question would be, "What kinds of maladjustive behavior create the poor learning that produces reading difficulties?" When reading or learning to read is central to the student's maladjustment, the effect is likely to be harmful to his reading achievement. When the student is willing to sacrifice participation in reading to gain attention, or willing to disrupt the instructional setting in order to get revenge, his learning will generally suffer.

It is equally true that failure in reading can cause maladjustive behavior. Although it is not likely to be a sole cause, reading disability can result in the loss of acceptance, and anything that can do that can cause maladjustive behavior.

There are some words of caution regarding the discussion above. First, not all behavior can be neatly divided into the categories and classifications described. Human behavior is too complex for that. Second, student behavior is usually unconsciously motivated. Students do not consciously decide they are going to manipulate a situation to gain acceptance. They act in accordance with their unconscious desires, needs, attitudes, and lifestyle.

SUMMARY

Factors correlated with reading disability are not necessarily causative of reading disability. Many research studies have found significant correlations between various factors and reading difficulties but have not shown them to be the cause of the reading problem. In addition, disabled readers usually have several factors that contribute to their reading difficulty; those that are causative factors for one student will not necessarily prove to be causative for another student.

Ineffective instruction, which includes improperly initiated reading instruction, inappropriately paced reading instruction, inadequately sequenced reading instruction, and adverse learning conditions, seems likely to be the most frequent cause of reading difficulties. Low intelligence, though showing an overall strong correlation with poor reading achievement, owes most of the strength of that correlation to the extremes of the range. Most students, even those with low normal intelligence, appear to have all the ability necessary to learn the skills associated with reading. Only those at the lowest extremes seem to be unable to learn to read at all.

Although the relationship between lateral dominance and reading difficulties is not clear, it seems likely that the relatively low correlations found may be accounted for by the number of students who obscure what they have written as they write. Only a few students use this style, but where it exists, students tend to develop reading difficulties.

The term "learning disability" presently refers to a number of anomalies, most of which defy measurement. A current practice is to determine learning disabilities on the basis of a measured discrepancy between a student's learning potential and his reading achievement. This practice classifies the student as "learning-disabled," but does not attempt to specify the cause of his learning difficulty. It seems possible that the reading problems of some few students may be rooted in some sort of psychoneural dysfunction. Although some lay the blame on "perceptual disorders," perception limited to its technical definition does not seem likely to be the area of difficulty.

The conflicting research results relative to whether or not emotional difficulties may cause reading disability or vice versa can be clarified in part by an examination of the various emotional maladjustments. Psychotics can learn to read if their language facility is not seriously disturbed and if they have the ability to give their attention to the tasks associated with learning to read. There has been no serious indication that reading failure causes psychotic behavior. Neurotics are hampered in learning to read if their emotional condition interferes with their ability to focus their attention on learning to read. Reading failure can create sufficient anxiety within some students to produce neurotic behavior.

Common behavioral goals for maladjusted students include attention-getting, power, vengefulness, and the display of inadequacy. When the focus of the maladjustment affects learning to read, or when the student's behavior disrupts the learning situation even though reading is not a central issue, the student's ability to learn to read will be inhibited. Although not usually a singular cause, reading failure can contribute to maladjustive behavior.

RECOMMENDED READINGS

CHALL, J. S. 1978. A decade of research on reading and learning disabilities. In *What research has to say about reading instruction*, ed. S. J. Samuels. Newark, Del.: International Reading Assoc., pp. 31–42.

COLES, G. S. 1978. The learning-disabilities test battery: Empirical and social issues. *Harvard Educational Review* 48: 313–40.

HARRIS, A. J.; and SIPAY, E. R. 1980. *How to Increase Reading Ability*. 7th ed. New York: Longman, Inc., pp.300–309.

HARRIS, L. A.; and SMITH, C. B. 1980. *Reading Instruction: Diagnostic Teaching in the Classroom*. 3rd ed. New York: Holt, Rinehart & Winston, Chapter 15.

WEAVER, P. 1978. *Research within reach*. Washington, D.C.: National Institute of Education, pp. 39–42, 57–61, 111–15.

REFERENCES

American Heritage Dictionary of the English Language. 1969. Boston: American Heritage and Houghton Mifflin.

Anastasi, A. 1968. *Psychological testing*. 3rd. ed. New York: Macmillan.

Baddeley, A. D. 1976. *The psychology of memory*. New York: Basic Books.

Bond, G. L; Tinker, M. A.; and Wasson, B. B. 1979. *Reading difficulties: Their diagnosis and correction*. Englewood Cliffs, N.J.: Prentice-Hall.

Brown, D. A. 1970. Measuring the reading ability and potential of adult illiterates. In *Measurement and evaluation of reading*, ed. R. Farr. New York: Harcourt Brace Jovanovich, pp. 154–65.

———. 1970. Intelligence of adult illiterates. In *Reading: Process and pedagogy* Nineteenth Yearbook of the National Reading Conference, ed. G. B. Schick and M. M. May. Vol. 1. Milwaukee: The National Reading Conference, pp. 94–98.

Carder, M. E. 1974. *A comparison of oral reading miscues of poor readers assigned to learning disability classes with those assigned to remedial reading classes*. Unpublished doctoral dissertation, University of Northern Colorado.

Cohen, A.; and Glass, G. G. 1968. Lateral dominance and reading ability. *Reading Teacher* 21: 343–48.

Coles, G. S. 1978. The learning-disabilities test battery: Empirical and social issues. *Harvard Educational Review* 48: 313–40.

Crosland, H. R. 1939. Superior elementary-school readers contrasted with inferior readers, "range of attention" scores. *Journal of Educational Research* 32: 410–27.

Dearborn, W. F. 1933. Structural factors which condition special disability in reading. *Proceedings of the American Association for Mental Deficiency* 38: 266–83.

Dinkmeyer, D.; and Dreikurs, R. 1963. *Encouraging children to learn: The encouragement process.* Englewood Cliffs, N.J.: Prentice-Hall.

Douglas, J. W. B.; Ross, J. M.; and Cooper, J. E. 1967. The relationship between handedness, attainment and adjustment in a national sample of school children. *Educational Research* 9: 223–32.

Eames, T. H., 1934. The anatomical basis of lateral dominance anomalies. *American Journal of Orthopsychiatry* 4: 524–28.

Ekwall, E. E. 1976. *Diagnosis and remediation of the disabled reader.* Boston: Allyn & Bacon.

Fernald, G. M. 1943. *Remedial techniques in basic school subjects.* New York: McGraw-Hill.

Gann, E. 1945. *Reading difficulty and personality organization.* New York: King's Crown Press.

Gerken, K. C. March 1978. Performance of Mexican children on intelligence tests. *Exceptional Children* 44: 438–43.

Harris, A. J.; and Sipay, E. R. 1980. *How to increase reading ability.* 7th ed. New York: Longman, Inc.

Hartman, N. C.; and Hartman, R. K. April 1973. Perceptual handicap or reading disability? *The Reading Teacher* 26: 684–95.

Jensen, A. R. Winter 1969. How much can we boost IQ and scholastic achievement? *Harvard Educational Review* 39: 1–123.

Johnson, D.; and Myklebust, H. 1967. *Learning disabilities: Educational principles and practices.* New York: Grune & Stratton.

Kass, C.; and Myklebust, H. July 1969. Learning disabilities: An educational definition. *Journal of Learning Disabilities* 2: 377–79.

Kellaghan, T. Summer 1973. Intelligence and achievement in a disadvantaged population. *The Irish Journal of Education* Vol. 7, 23–28.

Kirk, S. A. 1963. Behavioral diagnosis and remediation of learning disabilities. *Conference on Exploration into the Problems of the Perceptually Handicapped Child.* Evanston, Ill.: Fund for Perceptually Handicapped Children, pp. 1–7.

Kisker, G. W. 1964. *The Disorganized Personality.* New York: McGraw-Hill, p. 359.

Lerner, J. 1971. *Children with learning disabilities: Theories, diagnosis, and teaching strategies.* Boston: Houghton Mifflin.

———. 1979. Working with learning-disabled children. The Eleventh Annual Reading and Learning Disabilities Conference at the University of Northern Colorado, Greeley, Col.

Lockhart, R. S.; Craik, F. I. M.; and Jacoby, L. 1976. Depth of processing, recognition, and recall. In *Recall and recognition,* ed. J. Brown. London: Wiley, pp. 75–102.

Monroe, M. 1932. *Children who cannot read.* Chicago: Univ. Chicago Press.

National Advisory Committee on Handicapped Children. January 31, 1968. Special Education for Handicapped Children. First Annual Report. Washington, D.C.: U. S. Department of Health, Education & Welfare.

Neville, D. January 1965. The relationship between reading skills and intelligence test scores. *The Reading Teacher* 18: 257–62.

Orton, S. T. 1937. *Reading, writing, and speech problems in children.* New York: W. W. Norton.

Public Law 94-142: The Education for All Handicapped Children Act of 1975. 1975. Washington, D.C.: U. S. Government Printing Office.

Rabinovich, R. D. 1968. Reading problems in children: Definitions and classifications. In *Dyslexia: Diagnosis and treatment of reading disorders,* ed. A. H. Keeney and V. T. Keeney. St. Louis: C. V. Mosby, pp. 4–6.

Restak, R. M. 1979. *The brain: The last frontier.* New York: Doubleday.

Robeck, M. C.; and Wilson, J. A. R. 1974. *Psychology of reading.* New York: Wiley & Sons.

Robinson, H. M. 1946. *Why pupils fail in reading.* Chicago: Univ. Chicago Press.

Shimrat, N. 1970. *Lateral dominance and directional orientation in the writing of American and Israeli children.* Unpublished doctoral dissertation, Columbia Univ.

Smith, D. E. P.; and Carrigan, P. M. 1959. *The nature of reading disability.* New York: Harcourt Brace, & World.

Sornson, H. H. 1950. *A longitudinal study of the relationship between various child behavior ratings and success in reading.* Unpublished doctoral dissertation, Univ. Minnesota.

Spache, G. D. 1976. *Investigating the issues of reading disabilities.* Boston: Allyn & Bacon.

Vernon, M. D. 1971. *Reading and its difficulties: A psychological study.* Cambridge: Cambridge Univ. Press.

Witty, P.; and Kopel, D. 1936. Factors associated with the etiology of reading disability. *Journal of Educational Research* 29: 449–59.

Young, J. Z. 1978. *Programs of the brain.* New York: Oxford Univ. Press.

Zangwill, O. L. 1962. Dyslexia in relation to cerebral dominance. In *Reading disability: Progress and research needs in dyslexia,* ed. J. Money, Baltimore: Johns Hopkins Press, pp. 103–14.

In addition to the instructional, psychological, and neurological correlates of reading difficulty discussed in the last chapter, there are a number of physical and social factors to consider. Visual, auditory, and speech anomalies are often cited as being related to poor reading. Some students appear to have reading problems rooted in low vitality, immaturity, or perhaps even genetically transmitted characteristics. Sociological factors correlated with reading difficulty may include the effects of poverty, and cultural and language differences.

No single factor usually is sufficient to account for poor reading ability. Generally, each student is likely to exhibit a constellation of interacting factors which, taken together, have resulted in his reading difficulties.

PHYSIOLOGICAL AND SOCIOLOGICAL CAUSES OF READING DIFFICULTIES

That reading is dependent on vision seems obvious. With the exception of those who read braille, every reader needs sufficient vision to see the printed or written letters and words.

Eye Movements   At one time it was thought that reading could be improved by changing the reader's eye movements. In reading, the eyes move across a page with the same stop-and-go movement of a typewriter. The pauses during which the eyes are stopped and the reader takes in what he sees are called *fixations*. The portion of the line that is seen during the fixation is called the *recognition span*. The movement between fixations is referred to as a *saccade* or a *saccadic movement*. At the end of each line the eyes move to the beginning of the next line in what is called a *return sweep*. Backward movements in which the reader rereads material are called *regressions*. Good readers tend to have a wider span of recognition, with college-level readers averaging slightly more than one word per fixation in comparison to only half a word at the first- and second-grade level (Taylor, Frackenpohl, and Pettee, 1960). However, faulty eye movements during reading are a symptom of poor reading and not a cause. Attempts to change ocular motor efficiency have generally been difficult and unproductive.

Visual Defects   Research relative to reading and visual problems often seems contradictory. Francis (1973), in a comprehensive review of research dealing with vision and reading achievement covering a span of 40 years, found that many factors were not controlled, the instrumentation and criteria used to identify and define visual anomalies varied widely, the severity of the visual defects was not taken into account, the identification of "reading difficulties" was often not defined or was poorly defined, and research design was frequently faulty.

A careful perusal of research indicates that there are three visual conditions frequently associated with poor reading. The first and generally most serious of these is farsightedness, or hyperopia, a condition in which the eyeball is too short, causing the farsighted reader to exert muscular effort in order to accommodate to materials seen at near-point. The muscular intensity tends to create discomfort, which in turn leads to avoidance of reading. The more severe the condition, the greater the tendency to avoid reading, although individual tolerances for discomfort vary.

First-grade children have a natural tendency toward farsightedness, although they soon develop "normal" vision as they progress through the first year or two of schooling. For those who continue to be farsighted, learning to read is frequently a problem. Students who are farsighted often try to change the shape of the eyeball—and thereby see better—by squinting. In a study of 3,500 students, Eames (1959) found that three and one-half times as many disabled readers were farsighted than among the control group of unselected students.

Farsighted students, finding it difficult to focus their attention on things near them, often tend to become disruptive in class. Laura is an example. She had had a history of talking and disturbing others during class. When she was transferred to a new school during her eighth-grade year, her new teacher timed her with a stop watch one day and found that she spent only a few seconds trying to read the assignment that had been given, spending the rest of the time talking, jabbing a pencil into another student, turning around in her seat looking at the student behind her, and being a general nuisance. Her teacher asked Laura if she had ever had her eyes checked. Laura had. The school nurse checked her eyes once each year, and Laura had never been notified that there was any cause for referral. She believed her eyes must be all right. Unfortunately, the school vision check was based on a Snellen Chart, in which vision is checked by having the student stand 20 feet away and read letters or indicate the position of *Es* on the chart. Eames (1942) found the Snellen to be effective in identifying visual defects in slightly less than half the cases he investigated.

Laura was referred for a complete visual examination by a qualified eye doctor who found that she was significantly farsighted. Corrective lenses were prescribed, and both her behavior and her schoolwork began to improve.

A second visual defect that seems to contribute to reading difficulties is lack of oculomotor coordination. There are three primary conditions affecting the ability to read—exophoria ("wall-eyedness"), in which the eyes turn outward, esophoria or "cross-eyedness," and hyperphoria, in which one of the eyes turns upward. Exophoria seems to have the most serious effect. It may pose an additional concern in that the individual may begin to overcome the confusion resulting from the two different images by suppressing the vision in one of the eyes. After a time, the eye may lose vision completely if the problem is not corrected.

A third problem, but one that is related to lack of oculomotor coordination, or "strabismus," as it is often called, is the lack of fusion. The brain, through the perceptual center, is able to accommodate some degree of imperfection in the two images reported to it. However, individuals differ in the amount of dissimilarity they can tolerate and still produce a clear picture of their field of vision. The perceptual process involved is called "fusion," and the degree of dissimilarity that can be accommodated is called the "amplitude of fusion." *Aniseikonia*, a somewhat uncommon condition in which the image seen with one eye is larger than that seen by the other eye, *astigmatism*, and *strabismus* may all contribute to dissimilar retinal images. When individuals cannot accommodate to such dissimilar images, they are said to have problems with fusion; such problems seem to be associated with the development of reading difficulties.

The existence of *nystagmus* or *nystagmatic* jerks in which the eyes jerk spasmodically and involuntarily, and *oculomotor spasms*, identified as being "very fine eye tremors occurring approximately at intervals of 18 seconds, with a duration of 1 to 3 seconds . . ." (Calvert and Cromes, 1966), have also been hypothesized as causing reading problems, but evidence is lacking as to the cause and the effect of these conditions (Francis, 1973).

Nearsightedness, or myopia, seems to be correlated with *good* reading ability.

Apparently, students who find it difficult to see things clearly at a distance may substitute activities such as reading in which they can see more comfortably. By spending more time reading, they tend to become better readers. Myopia makes it more difficult for the students to read from the chalkboard, bulletin board, or screen, but losses such as these are not as serious as the inability to read near at hand as is the case with the farsighted person.

Younger students often have the ocular flexibility to read comfortably at a distance of no more than 3 or 4 inches from the line of print. Although this looks abnormal to adults, there does not appear to be any harm in such close reading. As they grow older, however, they should naturally find it more difficult to read in that position, and they will move farther away from their material. A student in the middle grades who is still reading only 3 or 4 inches from his material should be referred for a vision screening. Reading too close will begin to hamper good reading progress in later years by making the student read more slowly than is otherwise possible. A student who reads too near reading material during middle or later grades may be seriously nearsighted, and even though mild or moderate nearsightedness tends not to interfere with learning to read, severe nearsightedness can cause difficulties with certain aspects of reading performance.

Severity of the condition is also the key to understanding the general relationship between reading achievement and *astigmatism*. Astigmatism is a lack of clear vision produced by an uneven surface on the lens of the eye. The rays are somewhat diffused instead of coming to a clear focus. In general, mild or moderate astigmatism does not correlate with reading difficulties, but more severe astigmatism does. Apparently the visual perceptual center can accommodate a certain amount of ambiguity in the image that is transmitted to it without causing the reader difficulty in learning. Beyond a certain point, different with each individual, the ability of the perceptual center to synthesize the images begins to break down, causing problems in learning to read. Astigmatism in a farsighted person causes more serious problems than simple astigmatism or astigmatism with nearsightedness.

Visual defects are not the major cause of reading difficulties, but where they are significant as an interfering factor, reading achievement may be seriously affected. When they are corrected, gains are also frequently gratifying.

HEARING

One of the most commonly misdiagnosed physical factors contributing to reading difficulty is hearing loss. Although Mackie (1969) estimates that the frequency of those having a hearing handicap is less than 1 percent, others such as Dahl (1949) and Bond, Tinker, and Wasson (1979) indicate that the incidence of those having serious hearing difficulties is more likely to be as high as 5 or even 10 percent. Even children with mild hearing losses show significant reading retardation (Embry, 1971), and those who are deaf and yet manage to graduate from high school, in at least one state school for the deaf, average only fifth-grade reading ability.

Students who have hearing difficulties frequently exhibit an interesting syndrome. The hard-of-hearing student is often identified as (1) inattentive, (2) mentally dull, and (3) good-natured. The first two descriptors seem more understandable than the third. It seems reasonable that students who do not hear much of what is going on in class would turn their thoughts to other things and, therefore, be regarded as a daydreamer. It also seems sensible that students who cannot hear comments or questions may be thought of as not very bright. But the third descriptor seems more difficult to understand until we realize that when people do not hear what is being said, they often use a smile as a defense. Someone joining a circle of friends just as they laugh may laugh with them even though he has no idea what has been said. The hard-of-hearing student who does not hear a question or comment does much the same thing—in a way, attempting to ward the teacher off with a smile and hoping she will go on to another student. Those students who do not use such a device but who instead continue to ask the teacher to repeat the questions or points in a discussion are frequently "punished" for their requests. The teacher, thinking such students simply are not paying attention, is apt to make comments that display irritation. Most students soon learn that it is better to smile and not ask questions.

In order to be considered a contributing factor to reading difficulties, a hearing loss should be (1) within the speech range, (2) a loss that affects both ears, and (3) a loss of 20 decibels or more. The loss is more critical when it is experienced during the years of early schooling. Some losses may be temporary, caused by a series of ear infections or colds, and, when the student is tested later, only a mild residual loss may be found. If the loss has been severe during early reading instruction, the student may develop reading problems. This is especially true if the instructional program has relied heavily on phonics. If the student's hearing is tested later to find the cause for his poor reading, his hearing may have improved to the extent that he may show no significant loss.

The speech range lies roughly between a low of 100 cycles per second, equivalent to a man's lower bass tones, to as high as 4,000 cycles per second, reached only by certain consonant sounds such as the fricatives *s, z, sh,* and *ch* when spoken by a woman with a high voice. For some reason, boys and men tend to have high-range losses more frequently than girls and women. This is particularly unfortunate for boys because the great majority of teachers during beginning reading instruction at the early grade levels are women.

Loudness is measured in terms of decibels. A loss of 20 decibels or more is quite likely to contribute to the development of a reading problem if, as mentioned above, the loss is permanent or if it is a temporary one that exists during the years of early reading instruction.

A hearing loss in only one ear is not likely to cause a reading problem. Although the incidence of reading difficulties is slightly greater for students with a hearing impairment in one ear than it is for those with normal hearing, it is possible that such a small difference may be due to earlier bilateral losses that have later disappeared.

Just as with other causes of reading difficulty, hearing losses may cause reading problems for one student but not for another. Certainly, the severity of the loss is important, but individual factors such as the loudness of speech of parents and teachers, motivation, intelligence, home environment, and the opportunity to learn, all affect whether or not the student becomes a disabled reader.

SPEECH

There are a number of speech defects which are commonly grouped together under a common heading of "speech problems." Research into the causation of reading difficulties has generally, although not always, noted that there seems to be a correlation between speech problems and reading difficulties (Robinson, 1946; Ingram, 1969; Lyle, 1970). Speech defects seem to be likely *causes* of reading difficulties when they interfere with speech production to the extent that they make it difficult for students to associate the phonemes they produce with the sounds made by the teacher and others involved in learning to read. The problem seems to be more serious when students are introduced to reading through a phonics-dependent approach. There appears to be little difficulty in learning to read if the speech defect is rather mild and limited to a few sounds. This probably accounts for the reason that survey studies generally find little relationship between speech problems and reading difficulties.

Speech defects may produce reading difficulties when they cause students to develop a poor self-image. Although evidence indicates that infantilism ("baby talk"), lisping, stuttering, and dialect are not usually associated with the development of reading problems, they may be a contributing factor if they cause the student to feel less acceptable and less capable in an academic setting. Although dialect should not be classified as a speech defect, it is frequently treated as such, and when a student's dialect is viewed as inferior, self-respect is likely to decline, and with it, level of achievement. In essence, the student's problem is not one of speech but of self-esteem.

A third relationship between reading and speech involves a speech difficulty known as "clutter." Cluttering affects the rhythm and clarity of speech. Cluttered speech is usually rapid, jumbled, and difficult to understand because of a "mushy" quality. The speaker often sounds as though he has marbles in his mouth, or his tongue is too thick. Cluttered speech is generally believed to be inherited or caused by some injury to the language centers of the brain. Although many portions of the brain are involved in reading, one of the areas most centrally concerned lies adjacent to the primary speech cortex. It appears likely that a major injury to that portion of the brain frequently results in damage to both the speech and reading centers. In such a case, the speech clutter and the reading disability would result from a common cause, and the speech defect would not be a cause of the reading problem.

It is important to remember that *most* of the time reading difficulties are neither caused by speech problems nor associated with them. It is also true that a speech defect that seems to be a cause of poor reading in one student frequently has little or no effect on the reading of another. The type of speech defect, its severity, the existence of other contributing factors, and the ability of the student all work to determine whether or not speech problems will produce a reading disability.

WRITING

Writing has usually been regarded as a skill related to reading but having little causal relationship with it. The research discussed in the previous chapter in relation to lateral dominance indicates that obscured writing, in which the writer does not see what he has written as he writes it, may be an infrequent but significant cause of reading disability. It may be inferred also that writing may produce deeper processing and richer encoding necessary for faster and more automatic word recognition, or, conversely, that the lack of writing experience may deprive a student of that processing, resulting in poorer word recognition. Writing demands interactive processing from visual, syntactic-semantic, phonemic, and kinesthetic or motor domains. It requires more attention given to more cues within a word than is required by simply looking at a word. Therefore, since writing involves processing from more domains, attention to more cues, and specifically makes use of the motor domain that is notable for the durability of its memory traces, it provides a valuable means for developing effective word recognition (Baddeley, 1976).

There are, of course, other means of developing word recognition, and if writing is replaced by other word analysis and word recognition techniques which produce the depth and richness of processing involved in writing, it should be presumed that the student would experience no loss in the development of good reading ability.

VITALITY

The reticular formation within the brainstem controls the level of functional alertness of the learner. The hypothalamus and the limbic system regulate anticipation, curiosity, pleasure, and the *desire* to learn (Restak, 1979). The student whose alertness and intensity to learn have not been excited will be a poor learner.

Unfortunately, there are a number of conditions and circumstances which tend to produce low vitality, depriving the student of an effective "set" for learning.

No list of factors could possibly be complete, but among those which should be considered are lack of sufficient sleep, anemia, malnutrition, prolonged poor health, and the use of both legal and illegal drugs.

Sleep   People differ in the amount of sleep they need, but many students do not get enough sleep to permit their bodies to eliminate the toxins and chemicals in their blood caused by fatigue. The student who usually watches television until midnight tends to lose the alertness needed in learning. Robert was a good example. Although he was in the eleventh grade, he had an instructional reading level of only the upper fourth grade. Within a few minutes of the time he arrived in the reading resource room, he would put his head down on his desk and go to sleep.

The school nurse found that Robert's father opposed his attendance at high school. He believed Robert had learned all that was necessary, and that he should quit school and work full-time on the family farm. He had told Robert that he could attend school only as long as he worked a full eight-hour day in addition to his attendance at high school. As a result, Robert's schedule began at four o'clock each morning and ended at nearly midnight each night.

An interesting "remedial" program was instituted. Since Robert was able to stay awake for the first two periods, third period was chosen for a nap. He reported to the nurse's office where he slept on a cot for 50 minutes. Before fourth period began, the nurse roused him, and he went through the rest of the day with sufficient energy to complete his work successfully. His "remedial program" began to make his reading instruction much more effective.

Anemia   When there are insufficient red blood cells or hemoglobin in the blood to supply oxygen to the cells within the body, the result is a condition called "anemia." Anemic students tend to tire easily and lack the energy to work or study.

Both of William's parents were professional people, his mother a teacher and his father a lawyer. He had had a good school record until he began junior high school. Then his teachers began to complain that he was not doing his assignments, his work was of poor quality, and he did not take part in class discussion. William complained to his parents that he was always tired. The family doctor had known William since birth, and after a cursory examination, suggested that there was nothing wrong with William that could not be explained by the fact that he was simply growing so rapidly.

His parents took William to a university reading center for help with his sagging school achievement. After looking at a number of factors, the reading clinician suggested another medical referral to check the possibility of sickle-cell anemia, a type of anemia peculiar to Blacks. His family physician ran tests which confirmed the hypothesis, and, although the prognosis for those with sickle-cell anemia is not highly favorable, newly advanced treatments were begun, and he has become more alert and able to profit from instruction.

Glandular Imbalance   Hypothyroidism of the most severe congenital nature produces *cretinism*, a type of mental retardation which includes a constellation of physical and behavioral peculiarities that usually bar the individual from classroom attendance. Less serious but of great importance to the reading teacher is the type of hypothyroidism that causes people to be overweight, lethargic, and lacking a degree of mental alertness. Individuals affected by this condition are not mentally retarded; rather they may be said to lack "mental energy." This makes it difficult for them to learn easily, and reading ability frequently suffers.

An abnormally high secretion of thyroid hormone tends to produce hyperactivity, restlessness, and inability to pay attention to instruction long enough to profit from it. This, of course, tends to contribute to the development of poor reading ability.

Dietary Deficiencies   In their so-called "Starvation Studies," Franklin, Schiele, Brozek, and Keys (1948) found that people on a restricted diet (six months on 1,570 calories per day) lost interest in work or study, became depressed and irritable, and became egocentric in their concerns, no longer interested in other people or events outside themselves. Lack of food, particularly protein, has been found to affect synaptic transmission in learning (Restak, 1979).

Specific dietary deficiencies also cause conditions that may produce poor learning. B complex deficiency, and especially thiamine, seems to produce restlessness, inattentiveness, and uncooperative behavior within the classroom. Lack of vitamin B_1 seems to lower learning speed (Blake and Ramsey, 1951). A number of questions have been raised in recent years regarding the effects of quantities of refined sugar, bleached white flour, red food dye, and the additives used to preserve foods. Although the research concerning these and other food contents has not yet been fully completed, it seems likely that excessive amounts tend to produce hyperactivity and poor learning in some people.

It is probably safe to say that poor diet can and does contribute to the learning problems of a number of children, and that in many cases improved diet can help students regain ability to learn more easily.

Prolonged Poor Health   Chronic poor health can have the effect discussed earlier related to anemia and some dietary deficiencies. Students who have had rheumatic fever, who suffer from serious allergies, or who have had long-term low-grade infections tend to be handicapped in their ability to learn. The student who endures one cold after another, or who suffers continuous attacks of asthma or other respiratory ailments, eventually becomes fatigued and loses the alertness necessary for good learning. Certain heart and circulatory problems can produce the same effect.

Brenda is 9 years old and in the fourth grade. She has a congenital heart defect which constricts the flow of blood to the head and other parts of the body. In order to function effectively in school, she needs to take frequent periods of rest. Otherwise, she becomes too tired and cannot learn effectively.

Drugs   Albert was sent to a university reading center for help with his reading because he was three years behind his sixth-grade placement. Although he was a bright student, he seemed to have great difficulty concentrating on his work. In order to improve his work in the reading center, his parents took him to their family physician for a prescription to calm him.

At the reading center the following week, his reading clinician found that he was almost completely passive. He hardly responded to anything she presented to him. After three or four days of such behavior, she called his mother and then the family physician. A tranquilizing drug had been prescribed for him to control his hyperactive behavior; unfortunately, its effect was much stronger than anticipated, and he became slow and apathetic. Reduced drug dosages produced greater alertness and better learning.

It is not uncommon to find that parents who are themselves on tranquilizers will occasionally "prescribe" the drug for their own children, and this can cause the children to lose the alertness needed for optimal learning.

The overuse or abuse of even patent medicines can cause a young person to become listless or hyperactive, depending on the drug. A number of cold remedies, for example, contain drugs which, although generally safe for adult use, may react more strongly on a child's system. Parents, concerned by, say, the cold symptoms of their child, are often moved to disregard the directions for administration of the drug and administer heavy dosages to alleviate the symptoms. Though occasional medication will not produce reading and learning difficulties, continual dosing by an overanxious parent or unsupervised drug use by a child can contribute to problems in learning.

Illicit drugs have become a serious problem reaching down into the middle grades in some parts of the country. There is no catalogue that can possibly recount all the effects and side effects of the illicit drugs available to young people, but at least two—alcohol and marijuana—are in common use everywhere, and research, although still somewhat sketchy in regard to marijuana, has given us a better understanding of their effects.

Evidence released in 1977 by the National Institute on Alcohol Abuse and Alcoholism, a part of the Public Health Service, states that

> . . . heavy use of alcohol by women during pregnancy may result in a pattern of abnormalities in the offspring, termed Fetal Alcohol Syndrome, which consists of specific congenital and behavioral abnormalities. . . While safe levels of drinking are unknown, it appears that a risk is established with ingestion above 3 ounces of absolute alcohol or six drinks a day. Between 1 ounce and 3 ounces, there is still uncertainty but caution is advised. (Noble, 1978, p. 39)

Further evidence indicates that "maternal alcohol use may be central to . . . abnormalities of attention, behavior, and learning . . ." (Noble, 1978, p. 43) One investigation found that eleven children who had been born to heavy-drinking mothers had normal intelligence but "reflected deficiencies in attention, concentration, memory, and learning. In addition, each was hyperactive, impulsive, and fidgety from early school years to adolescence." (Noble, 1978, p. 43) It appears likely that heavy maternal alcohol use could contribute to the development of reading and learning difficulties.

The synthesis of research contained in the National Institute of Alcohol Abuse and Alcoholism's *Third Special Report to Congress* concludes that memory and other intellectual capacities are affected by drinking, and that heavy and/or prolonged use of alcohol frequently results in cognitive and psychoneurological deficits (Noble, 1978, p. 55). Even though alcohol may not be the initial cause of a student's reading difficulties, its effects can diminish the learning abilities of poor readers who want to make up lost ground.

The seriousness of the problem among adolescents is reflected in statistics from the National Institute of Alcohol Abuse and Alcoholism, which reported in 1978 that 5 percent of seventh-grade boys and 4.4 percent of seventh-grade girls could be classified as problem drinkers, and nearly 40 percent of twelfth-grade boys and 21 percent of twelfth-grade girls were found to be problem drinkers. The greatest increase in problem drinking came between seventh and eighth grade for boys as the number rose from 5 to 15.6 percent, and eighth to ninth grade for girls saw an increase from 9.1 to 16.2 percent (Noble, 1978, p. 17).

Research into the relationship between marijuana and learning is far from complete, but on the basis of present evidence, marijuana appears to produce an immediate effect which makes it impossible for the user to learn. After the immediate intoxication has passed, it still may be several hours before the ability to learn returns to normal levels. For chronic users, the effects are more serious because of what appears to be a cumulative effect causing lower neurological functioning, poorer memory, and an attitude marked by lack of life goals, disinterest, and general apathy. These conditions tend to grow more pronounced with use and may not cease for several months after a student stops using the drug (National Institute of Drug Abuse, 1979, pp. 32–33).

Marijuana, or "pot," has become firmly entrenched in the habits of a sizable number of students at the secondary level and even below. There is a significant trend toward marijuana use at increasingly younger ages. Rates of usage are increasing so rapidly that data on the percentage of users are quickly outdated. Surveys of the high school graduating classes for 1975, 1976, and 1977, for example, showed that the number of students who had used pot by the end of ninth grade had increased from 16.9 percent for 1975 to 22.3 percent for 1976, and to 25.2 percent for 1977 (NIDA, 1979, p. 9). There is no reason to believe that current levels of use would not be even higher.

A special area of concern is the effect gained from combining marijuana and alcohol. According to the National Institute of Drug Abuse, "The combined use of marijuana and alcohol may result in greater skilled performance decrement than the use of either in similar amounts by itself" (NIDA, 1979, p. 31). Unfortunately, almost no research to date exists which outlines the consequences of such combined use.

The preponderance of boys classified as poor readers has been a continuing puzzle to educators. Heilman (1977, p. 76) points out that clinical referrals generally range from 65 to 90 percent male. Girls have greater success in reading and they learn to read at an earlier age despite male equality in intelligence.

Downing (1973) found that boys did more poorly in the United States, Japan, and France, contrasting with his earlier finding that in Nigeria, India, and Germany the boys were better readers than were the girls (1971). Preston (1962) had also found that German boys were better readers than German girls. Johnson (1972) noted that in four English-speaking countries—the United States, Canada, England, and Nigeria—girls were better readers in the first two and boys were better in the latter two. Cultural factors which place importance on reading for boys seem likely to be at least one of the factors involved in those countries in which the boys outperform the girls, and in the United States and other countries where boys do not learn to read as well as girls it seems likely that reading is viewed as more closely identified with being female. Downing (1977) found that when students in grades one, four, eight, and twelve were asked to indicate whether reading was more suitable as an activity for a 6-year-old boy or a 6-year-old girl, all but the first-grade group indicated that it was more suitable for girls.

In Stanchfield's research (1967, p. 60), a teacher is quoted as saying, "Boys are so overwhelmingly active, so frighteningly energetic, so terribly vigorous, so utterly strenuous!" According to McGuinness (1979, p. 82) nine times as many boys as girls are identified as "hyperactive." McGuinness further notes that the term "hyperactivity" does not usually refer to a high state of activity but to distractibility and behaviors considered "inappropriate" for the regular classroom. She cites evidence that from 8 to 10 percent of school children are taking Ritalin so they will be less of a "nuisance" in the classroom. She notes that

> . . . once diagnosed as hyperactive, they [mostly boys] are likely to develop social and psychiatric disorders such as depression and to fail in school far more often than normal children with the same IQ scores and ability. This effect lasts long after the hyperactive behavior has been outgrown; once a child is labeled a deviant, the distress caused by the stigma is difficult to erase. (McGuinness, 1979, p. 82)

McGuinness concludes that we will continue to have poor achievement in the language areas of school as long as we fail to recognize the reality of sex differences in our school programs. She warns:

> . . . we must avoid the tendency to ascribe all sex differences to some quirk of the environment or to some biological given. Both arguments are wrong and can harm us. . . . Biology initiates and sets limits, and within these limits culture plays an enormous role.
>
> We can intervene and influence these biological biases. We can stop forcing little boys to sit still, remain quiet, and learn to manipulate only verbal symbols, punishing those

who refuse with drugs and pejorative labels. We could instead rearrange primary classrooms to give boys an opportunity to move and explore in order to learn about their world and subsequently to develop certain higher-order skills. (1979, p. 88).

A number of studies have dealt with the possibility that severe reading disability may be inherited. Although there seems to be an undeniable familial pattern, it is not clear whether it is the influence of the child's environment or some genetic quality. The most recent studies, carried out by the Institute for Behavioral Genetics, seem clearly to rule out the possibility that reading disability is a simple sex-linked trait. The Institute's research still leaves open the possibility that there may be some sort of more complicated polygenic transmission possibly involving greater receptivity by males. It also points out that it is possible that reading disability may be the result of two or more hereditary factors interacting with environmental circumstances (Decker and DeFries, in press; DeFries et al., 1978; Foch et al., 1977).

In a most thorough treatment of the subject, Coles (1980) underlined flaws in the research dealing with the inheritance of reading difficulty and suggested that the research is not only questionable, but dangerous because it erroneously promotes the acceptance of low reading achievement based on inheritance. He cites the parents who worry that their children may have reading problems because the husband or wife is functionally illiterate, or who blame themselves for their child's poor reading because they also had difficulty learning to read.

PHYSICAL HANDICAPS

With the advent of mainstreaming, which has resulted from Public Law 94–142, more teachers are finding students with severe physical handicaps within their classrooms, and reading and learning disabilities teachers are confronted with the need to work with students who have not only reading decrements but also physical disabilities which limit the use of their limbs, skeletal structure, or musculature. Teachers in hospital schools and special educational facilities have long worked to create programs of instruction for the physically handicapped, but for many teachers and learning specialists working in the usual public school setting, Public Law 94–142 has presented a new challenge. Although much of the effect of the law, entitled The Education for all Handicapped Children Act, relates to learning disabilities, Section 618 specifies that handicapped children "receive special education and related services in the *least restrictive environment commensurate with their needs. . . .*" (Italics added.) This has allowed a number of children to receive instruction in a public school setting for the first time in their lives.

What is the relationship between the existence of a physical handicap and reading difficulties? While the effect of a visual or hearing impairment seems obvious, the impact of an orthopedic impairment is less apparent. If a person can see and hear, it may seem that he should have little trouble learning to read. Unfortunately, there are several physical factors that may prevent the student from becoming a good reader. For example, if the handicap involves the arms and hands, the student may not be able to hold a book or to turn the pages as he reads. Assistance of some sort, either in the form of a person or an expensive mechanical aid, will be necessary to help such a person manipulate the reading material.

If the disability is one affecting the legs, the student is likely to suffer experiential deprivation. It is often difficult to take such a child to places that will enable him to develop an experiential map or background necessary for good reading comprehension. Sometimes the handicap may affect bladder or bowel control, and the student is too embarrassed to go anywhere outside the home. Sometimes children are embarrassed by the crutches, braces, wheelchair, or what they see as their unusual or disfigured appearance, and they refuse to be seen in public. They are often at the mercy of others to take them places, and they may choose not to impose on the time of others. All these factors tend to produce a "closet child" effect; that is, behavior similar to that found in children who have been locked in closets or rooms for years as "punishment" by parents or elders who were themselves maladjusted. In addition, many handicapped students have spent long hours in hospitals or other therapeutic institutions, missing the schooling they otherwise would have had during that time. Sometimes handicapped children and their families suffer an increased financial burden because of the necessary special treatments and care; as a result, it may be difficult for the family to buy books, reading materials, and other educational toys normally used by children.

Even getting the disabled student to the doctor for additional medical help unrelated to his central handicap is often a chore. Handicapped children seem to have even more ailments and visual and auditory problems than physically capable children. Yet survey studies indicate that a far greater number of such disorders go untreated in the handicapped. It may be presumed that the person who is more difficult to move may go untreated simply because of the problems associated with getting him to the doctor or dentist. Low-grade infections such as those accompanying poor dental care and other untreated disorders create fatigue and produce poor learning.

There is a final effect of a handicapping condition. A number of children who suffer the effects of an orthopedic impairment go through long periods of discouragement and hopelessness. Such attitudes can sometimes lead the student to quit trying and to retreat into himself.

Although more research is needed regarding the effects of physical disability on reading and learning, there can be no doubt that the 1 or 2 percent of the school-age population that is orthopedically handicapped often find it unusually difficult to learn to read.

DEVELOPMENTAL IMMATURITY AND LACK OF MOTOR COORDINATION

Several researchers have hypothesized that reading difficulties can be caused by immaturity, especially immaturity associated with the central nervous system. Olson (1959) believed that reading development was a part of overall growth, that those who were generally immature at any specific age would eventually reach maturity, and that, in their own good time, they would arrive at reading maturity in the process, provided they had the opportunity to learn to read. Delacato (1966) theorized that students might develop poor reading ability because they lack certain experiences necessary to their neurological development. Kephart (1971) believed that the lack of motor coordination, especially hand–eye coordination, was a possible causative factor in learning disabilities.

The developmental factors involved include physical development, neurological development, and coordination. If the hypotheses are correct, it would seem that early maturation in these areas would be accompanied by some degree of superiority in reading ability, and immaturity would similarly be significantly correlated with reading retardation. Research in this area goes back to the turn of the century; in general, the vast number of studies have produced correlations so low that there is no predictive value in them. Although it is true that very bright students such as those studied by Terman and Oden (1947) tend to be slightly larger than their peers, children in the general population cannot be differentiated in reading achievement on the basis of their physical maturity (Stroud, 1956, pp. 250–53).

According to Kephart (1971), "The early motor or muscular responses of the child, which are the earliest behavioral responses of the human organism, represent the beginning of a long process of development and learning. . . .To a large extent, so-called higher forms of behavior develop out of and have their roots in motor learning."

Perceptual and motor skills, according to Kephart, should not be considered as separate activities because perception provides the feedback necessary for coordinating motor movement. Chalfant and Scheffelin (1969) point out:

> There are several assumptions which have been made about the interrelationship between visual perception and motor ability. The first assumption is that visual perception is dependent upon learning gross motor skills! This implies that disorders in gross motor skills should be corrected before training in visual perception is undertaken. Another assumption which has been made with respect to the development of perceptual-motor skills is that if a stage of the developmental sequence is not attained, failure will be experienced at the higher stages. There is little empirical evidence, however, that basic perceptual-motor training leads to improvement in p-m abilities or to better academic performance!

Many favor a remedial approach based on overcoming neurological deficits through exercises and work with nonalphabetic forms before beginning reading instruction. Such an approach is designed to "enhance cerebral maturation, to bring neurological functioning to the point where [the individual] is physiologically capable of learning to read" (Silver, Hagin, and Hersh, 1965).

Chall (1978), having summarized this research, rejects such a thesis, as does Weaver (1978), who says, "On the basis of research findings we do not recommend perceptual training using nonalphabetic shapes as a means of facilitating reading acquisition" (p. 40). The belief that exercise or practice work with nonalphabetic shapes will result in gains in neurological growth has few followers among researchers.

The question still remains whether neurological lag could lie at the root of the problem for some students who have reading difficulties. If it is so, such lag is too subtle to be measured as yet by research instrumentation, and attempts to relate neurological growth and development prerequisites to reading instruction do not appear to have been successful.

POVERTY

The affects of poverty on the learner are often quite subtle. Students who come from homes of severely limited economic means tend not to eat as well and to have poorer health care; are less likely to have a place to study or read alone; have fewer educational toys when they are very young and fewer reading materials when they are older; are more likely to have uncorrected physical defects such as visual problems, hearing problems, dental problems, and so on; tend not to have adult models in the home who read to them; are more oriented toward survival needs than long-range goals; tend to see a less optimistic future for themselves both in education and in career opportunities; usually have more family members and therefore less individual time with adults in the home; and, perhaps as important as any of the previous factors, tend to find that their teachers expect less of them than of children who come from homes above the poverty level (Harris and Sipay, 1980, pp. 311–15; Moran, 1980; Zintz, 1972, pp. 252–56; Horn, 1970).

Barton (1963, p. 249) found that economically advantaged children tended to perform about a year above level after first grade, while students from poorer families fell farther and farther back until they were about a year behind by fourth or fifth grade. Of the various factors reviewed, Barton found that "socio-economic class is still the most striking single feature." Even within minority groups, economic factors play a major role. When Takesian (1967, p. 103) compared Mexican-American dropouts with those who graduated from high school, he found that parental income was higher for those who had graduated.

The all-pervasive affects of poverty should be expected to have a harmful effect on a student's ability to learn to read. It is somewhat surprising that *all* students from poor homes do not have difficulty learning to read. The ability of many economically deprived students to do well in learning to read is a comment on the adaptability of young people and on the efforts of parents and teachers in helping them learn to read despite significant handicaps.

LANGUAGE AND DIALECT DIFFERENCES

There is a wide variety of dialects in this country which differ significantly from the dominant spoken English dialect. Labov (1967, p. 143) found that a speaker using Nonstandard English dialect 20 to 30 percent of the time will be perceived as using the dialect all the time. The larger the percentage of speech that is nonstandard and the greater the variance from Standard English, the more marked the dialect and the greater the chance of possible interference with learning.

A study by Melmed (1973, pp. 70–85) found that those students who used Nonstandard English had greater difficulty with sound–letter association and with silent reading. They were able to understand written word pairs even though they had difficulty auditorily discriminating the words and differentiating the combinations that were difficult for them. The Nonstandard English–speaking students made up to 34 percent more errors "in words contrasted by vowel variations" than students speaking Standard English. An important finding was that those who spoke Nonstandard-English made generally more comprehension errors in silent reading than in oral reading. In all, however, Melmed found that the students who spoke nonstandard English understood written Standard English very well, and that dialect was not a significant barrier to their comprehension.

Venezky and Chapman (1973, pp. 62–69) conclude from their research that "there is little direct interference of dialect with reading—but an enormous potential for indirect interference." They see indirect interference as lack of understanding on the part of the students' teachers and the failure of publishers to produce materials that are appropriate in terms of a commonly grasped vocabulary, syntax, and semantics.

Johnson (1971, p. 90), and Petty, Petty, Newman, and Skeen (1977, p. 82), in discussing dialects and literacy, agree that "persons who speak nonstandard varieties of English are socially handicapped." This handicap should be taken into account in planning reading instruction. The use of dialectic materials would appear not only to be unnecessary for Nonstandard English speakers but may serve to further "imprison" them within their dialect rather than lead them into full understanding of standard English and the accompanying improved educational, social, and economic opportunities.

Another area of concern is that of students for whom English is a second language. Some of these students speak little or no English. Others speak it fluently. Some speak their own primary language well, and others, who might be better called "alingual," do not even have a good command of their primary language. Some read and write in their primary language; others do not. All these variations have an effect on the ability of students to learn to read English well.

It is often difficult to separate culture from language. Zintz (1969, pp. 232–39) gives examples of the interaction of the Spanish language and the culture of Spanish-speaking students. When students for whom English is their primary language come to school late, they are apt to take the blame on themselves, saying, "I missed the bus"; Spanish-speaking students are likely to be more lenient on themselves through their language structure, reporting that "The bus left me." In an English-speaking society, where "time is money," the clock is said to "run." In

Spanish, a different attitude is apt to prevail in both the language and the culture—the clock is said to "walk."

Coleman (1966) investigated whether students from non–English-speaking homes entered school at an educational disadvantage. He concluded that such children are generally at "some disadvantage when they enter first grade," although the disadvantage is not "extremely large" (p. 524). Another study found that the achievement of students who speak only Spanish in their homes is significantly lower than for those who speak English in their homes: "Some 90 percent of both Mexican-Americans and Puerto Ricans who did not complete elementary school speak Spanish in their homes" (R J Associates, 1974, p. 59).

It seems apparent that unfamiliarity with the language in which reading will be taught is a handicap. There are over 5 million non–English-speaking school children in this country; over 80 percent of them speak Spanish (Modiano, 1973, p. 29). The Latin-American population in this country is growing at a rate that will soon make it the largest minority group. The implications for the reading and learning specialist are clear.

COMBINATIONS AND INTERACTIONS AMONG CAUSATIVE FACTORS

Throughout the discussion of causative factors, there is something of an artificiality in the separation of our consideration into seemingly distinctly different causal conditions. In actuality, there is seldom a single cause for a student's reading disability. In the real world, a student is more likely, for example, to have a visual problem compounded by missing important instruction in the early grades, compounded by lack of interest in reading in his home. Generally, the greater the number of causes, or the more severe the cause, the greater the chance that there will be reading difficulties. Even then there is no certainty in prediction. Individuals differ in their apparent susceptibility to reading difficulties. One student may develop a reading problem based on the existence of one or two rather mild causative factors, while another may learn to read well despite the existence of several factors that would seem to predict reading difficulties.

One further—but important—word. Our discussion of the causes of reading difficulties is by no means a total coverage of the subject. Although we probably have reviewed most of the major causative factors, the reasons for the development of poor reading ability can be as varied as the students themselves.

SUMMARY

A number of physical factors appear to contribute to the development of poor reading ability. Sensory defects such as farsightedness, lack of oculomotor coordination, and lack of fusion seem to be associated to some degree with difficulty in learning to read. A hearing problem in which there is a bilateral loss of at least 20 decibels within the speech range also may contribute to reading difficulties.

Expressive problems—speaking and writing—may also be factors in developing reading difficulty. In general, there is a low correlation between speech pathology and problems in learning to read, but "cluttering" or speech defects that make it difficult for the student to approximate the teacher's language are both correlated with poor reading ability. Lack of experience in writing or obscuring as one writes also seem to contribute to reading difficulties at the early stages of word recognition and word analysis.

Lack of physical vitality owing to chronic loss of sleep, anemia, glandular imbalance, dietary deficiencies, prolonged poor health, or the use of legal or illicit drugs and/or alcohol may affect the student's ability to learn. Heredity and sex differences are correlated with poor reading ability, but research into the bases for the correlation is not conclusive. Maturational and neurological lag seem to have low correlation with reading failure, perhaps in part because of the difficulty experienced in measurement.

Poverty and its effects contribute to the development of poor reading. The lack of reading materials, adequate health care, balanced diet, and other factors underscore the fact that economic deprivation is a significant causative factor in reading difficulties. Lack of a foundation in the language in which reading instruction is offered can limit the effectiveness of the reading program.

There is seldom a single cause of reading difficulty. Generally, the larger the number of causative factors or the more severe the condition, the greater the likelihood that there will be reading problems.

RECOMMENDED READINGS

HARRIS, A. J.; and SIPAY, E. R. 1980. *How to increase reading ability.* 7th ed. New York: Longman, Chapters 11 and 12.

HORN, THOMAS D., ed. 1970. *Reading for the disadvantaged: Problems of linguistically different learners.* New York: Harcourt Brace Jovanovich.

JOHNS, J. L., ed. 1974. *Literacy for diverse learners.* Newark, Del.: International Reading Assoc.

LAFFEY, J.; and SHUY, R. 1973. *Language differences: Do they interfere?* Newark, Del.: International Reading Assoc.

PETTY, W.; PETTY, D.; NEWMAN, A.; and SKEEN, E. 1977. Language competences essential for coping in our society. In *The teaching of English 1977.* Seventy-sixth yearbook of the National Society for the Study of Education. Chicago: National Society for the Study of Education, pp. 66–95.

REFERENCES

Baddeley, A. D. 1976. *The psychology of memory.* New York: Basic Books.

Barton, A. J. 1963. Reading research and its communication: The Columbia-Carnegie project in reading as an intellectual activity. *Proceedings.* Newark, Del.: International Reading Assoc. 8: 249.

Blake, R.; and Ramsey, G. 1951. *Perception: An approach to personality.* New York: The Ronald Press Company.

Bond, G. L.; Tinker, M. A.; and Wasson, B. B. 1979. *Reading Difficulties: Their diagnosis and correction.* 4th ed. Englewood Cliffs, N.J.: Prentice-Hall.

Calvert, J.; and Cromes, G. December 1966. Ocular spasms in handicapped readers. *The reading teacher* 20: 231–36.

Chalfant, J. C.; and Scheffelin, A. 1969. *Central processing dysfunctions in children.* Bethesda, Md.: National Institute of Neurological Diseases and Stroke.

Chall, J. S. 1978. A decade of research on reading and learning disabilities. In *What research has to say about reading instruction,* ed. S. J. Samuels. Newark, Del.: International Reading Assoc., pp. 31–42.

Coleman, J. S. et al. 1966. *Equality of educational opportunity.* Washington, D.C.: U. S. Office of Education, pp. 524–27.

Coles, G. S. Fall 1980. "Evaluation of genetic explanations of reading and learning problems" *Journal of Special Education.* 14: 365–83.

Dahl, L. A. 1949. *Public school audiometry: Principles and methods.* Danville, Ill.: Interstate Printers & Publishers.

Decker, S. N.; and DeFries, J. C. In press. Cognitive abilities in families of reading-disabled children. *Journal of Learning Disabilities.*

Defries, J. C. et al. 1978. Familial nature of reading disability. *British Journal of Psychiatry* 132: 361–67.

Delacato, C. H. 1966. *Neurological organization and reading.* Springfield, Ill.: Charles C. Thomas.

Downing, J. 1973. *Comparative reading.* New York: Macmillan.

Downing, J.; and Thackray, D. 1971. *Reading readiness.* London: Univ. London Press.

Downing, J.; and Thomson, D. Fall 1977. Sex role stereotypes in learning to read. *Research in the Teaching of English* 11: 149–55.

Eames, T. H. 1942. *Journal of Educational Research.* 36: 272–79.

Eames, T. H. February 1959. Visual handicaps in reading. *Journal of Education.* 141: 2–35.

Embry, J. 1971. *A study of the effects of mild hearing loss on educational achievement.* Unpublished doctoral dissertation, Univ. of Tulsa.

Foch, T. T. et al. 1977. Familial patterns of impairment in reading disability. *Journal of Educational Psychology.* 69: 316–29.

Francis, L. J. 1973. *The relationship of eye anomalies and reading ability, and an analysis of vision-screening programs.* Unpublished doctoral dissertation, Univ. Northern Colorado.

Franklin, J. C.; Schiele, B. C.; Brozek, J.; and Keys, A. 1948. Observations of human behavior in experimental semistarvation and rehabilitation. *Journal of Clinical Psychology.* 4: 28–45.

Harris, A. J.; and Sipay, E. R. 1980. *How to increase reading ability.* 7th ed. New York: Longman.

Horn, Thomas D., ed. 1970. *Reading for the disadvantaged: Problems of linguistically different learners.* New York: Harcourt Brace Jovanovich.

Ingram, T. T. S. 1969. The nature of dyslexia. *Bulletin of the Orton Society.* 19: 18–50.

Johnson, D. D. 1972. *An investigation of sex differences in reading in four English-speaking nations.* Technical Report No. 209. Madison: Wisconsin Research & Development Center.

Johnson, K. R. March 1971. Should Black children learn Standard English? In *Viewpoints: Bulletin of the School of Education.* Bloomington, Ind.: Indiana Univ. 47: 90.

Kephart, N. C. 1971. *The slow learner in the classroom.* 4th ed. Columbus, Ohio: Charles E. Merrill.

Labov, W. 1967. Some sources of reading problems for Negro speakers of Nonstandard English. In *New direction in elementary English,* ed. A. Frazier. Champaign, Ill.: National Council of Teachers of English, p. 143.

Lyle, J. G. 1970. Certain antenatal, perinatal, and developmental variables and reading retardation in middleclass boys. *Child Development.* 41: 481–91.

Mackie, R. P. 1969. *Special education in the United States: Statistics 1946–66.* New York: Teachers College Press.

Marijuana and Health. 1977. Seventh Annual Report to the U.S. Congress from the Secretary of Health, Education & Welfare. Rockville, Md.: National Institute on Drug Abuse.

McGuinness, D. February 1979. How schools discriminate against boys. *Human Nature.* 2: 82–88.

Melmed, P. J. 1973. Black English phonology: The question of reading interference. In *Language differences: Do they interfere?,* ed. J. Laffey and R. Shuy. Newark, Del.: International Reading Assoc., pp. 70–85.

Modiano, N. 1973. Juanito's reading problems: Foreign language interference and reading skill acquisition. In *Language differences: Do they interfere?,* ed. J. Laffey and R. Shuy. Newark, Del.: International Reading Assoc., pp. 29–39.

Moran, P. 1980. *Selected factors associated with low achievement among Mexican-American college students.* Published doctoral dissertation, Univ. Northern Colorado.

National Institute of Drug Abuse. 1979. *Marijuana and health: Seventh annual report to the U.S. Congress from the Secretary of Health, Education, and Welfare 1977.* Washington, D.C.: Government Printing Office.

Noble, E. P.; ed. 1978. *Third special report to the U.S. Congress on alcohol and health.* Rockville, Md.: National Institute of Alcohol Abuse and Alcoholism.

Olson, W. C. 1959. *Child development.* Boston: D. C. Heath.

Petty, W.; Petty, D.; Newman, A.; and Skeen, E. 1977. Language competencies essential for coping in our society. In *The teaching of English 1977.* Seventy-sixth Yearbook of the National Society for the Study of Education, pp. 66–95.

Preston, E. 1962. Reading achievement of German and American children. *School and Society.* XC: 350–54.

Restak, R. M. 1979. *The brain: The last frontier.* New York: Doubleday.

R J Associates. 1974. *A study of selected socio-economic characteristics of ethnic minorities based on the 1970 Census Volume I: Americans of Spanish origin.* Arlington, Va.: R J Associates.

Robinson, H. M. 1946. *Why pupils fail in reading.* Chicago: Univ. Chicago Press.

Silver, A. A.; Hagin, R.; and Hersh, M. F. 1965. *Reading disability: Teaching through stimulation of deficit perceptual areas.* New York: Dept. Psychiatry and Neurology, New York University Medical Center, mimeographed. Cited in A. J. Harris and E. Sipay. 1975. *How to increase reading ability.* 6th ed. New York: David McKay, p. 392.

Stanchfield, J. M. 1967. Do girls learn to read better than boys in the primary grades? In *New directions in reading,* ed. R. Staiger and D. Sohn. New York: Bantam Books.

Stroud, J. B. 1956. *Psychology in education.* New York: Longmans, Green.

Takesian, S. A. 1967. *A comparative study of the Mexican-American graduate and dropout.* Unpublished doctoral dissertation, Univ. Southern California.

Taylor, S. R.; Frackenpohl, H.; and Pettee, J. L. 1960. *Grade level norms for the components of the fundamental reading skill.* Research Bulletin No. 3. Huntington, N.Y.: Educational Developmental Laboratories, Inc., a Div. of McGraw-Hill.

Terman, L. M.; and Oden, M. H. *The gifted child grows up.* Stanford, Cal.: Stanford Univ. Press.

Venezky, R. L.; and Chapman, R. S. 1973. Is learning to read dialect bound? In *Language differences: Do they interfere?*, ed. J. L. Laffey and R. Shuy. Newark, Delaware: International Reading Association.

Weaver, P. 1978. *Research within reach: A research-guided response to concerns of reading educators.* St. Louis, Mo.: Research & Development Interpretation Service, Inc., and Washington, D.C.: National Institute of Education.

Zintz, M. V. 1969. *Education across cultures.* 2nd. ed. Dubuque, Ia.: Kendall/Hunt.

———. 1972. *Corrective reading.* 2nd. ed. Dubuque, Ia.: Wm. C. Brown.

In this chapter we turn from factors that may contribute to reading difficulties to a consideration of some basic principles of reading diagnosis. Diagnosis and instruction should be based on certain general differences among poor readers. Some need little intervention and others need major changes in their instructional programs if they are to make significant improvements in their reading ability. Placing an extremely disabled reader in an instructional setting with twenty other disabled readers and one teacher will almost invariably result in the failure of the student's program. On the other hand, a 1:1 student–teacher ratio for a corrective reader is generally a waste of time and money since such a child can usually be at least as easily helped in a small to regular-sized classroom setting.

Initial reading diagnosis should indicate the information necessary to initiate a successful reading program, but a complete case study is seldom needed before beginning students' instruction. Diagnostic measures should be used with an understanding of their strengths and their limitations in planning a good reading improvement program.

BASES FOR DIAGNOSIS

Alan was a high school senior. The son of an orthodontist, he and his parents both hoped he would go on to college and be successful there. The only problem was his ability to get through the reading material assigned in his classes. His word attack skills were excellent, his comprehension was good, but he simply did not read fast enough to complete the reading necessary in classes requiring large amounts of outside reading. He and his parents were afraid that if he attempted to go on to college, he would not be able to do the outside reading customarily assigned in college classes. He had enrolled in speed reading courses but without satisfactory results. Although he was not a "remedial reader," he went to a university reading center to see if anything could be done to help him overcome his difficulties.

At the center, it was discovered that during his high school career, Alan had taken courses in advanced math, advanced sciences, advanced Russian, and bookkeeping—all requiring intensive, reflective reading. Speed reading in any of those courses would have resulted in a lack of understanding and poor work. One decimal point misplaced in bookkeeping, or one sign missed in calculus, could mean a serious error. Therefore he had learned to read meticulously, and he had been uneasy when he tried to read more rapidly because he was "afraid he might miss something important." A test for reading rate and comprehension showed that he read easy narrative material at a rate of approximately 100 to 125 words per minute with perfect comprehension. The phrase "slow but sure" described him perfectly.

An individualized education program was developed to help him learn to read for the main idea. There were times when he read to note every minute detail, but through discussion and guidance, he came to learn that it is neither necessary nor wise to read *everything* in that manner. He learned that on occasion it was important to read just for the main idea. Within six weeks this new concept of reading, together with guided practice, resulted in the development of an added reading skill. When reading for the main idea, he was able to read twice as fast as ever before, and by the end of the year, he was able to finish most of his outside reading assignments. He went on to college and was generally able to handle his reading assignments there.

Alan is an example of a student who had a *specific skill deficiency*. A limited amount of instruction, often carried out under the direction of a classroom teacher, is usually sufficient to overcome most such difficulties. They are not so serious that they cause the student to be a disabled reader. Many developmental or even advanced readers may have such deficiencies. They simply limit the reader's effectiveness in one or two reading skill areas.

Developmental readers are those who are "on track" for their age and ability. They are making "normal" progress in learning to read. There is, of course, some degree of variation even in normal reading ability. A high school student would be classified as a developmental reader if he were within two years of his actual

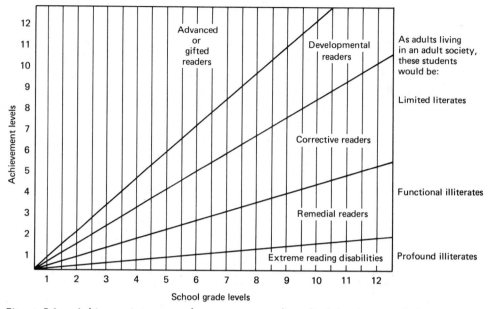

Figure 5-1. Achievement ranges for extreme reading disabilities, remedial, corrective, and advanced or gifted readers.

grade placement. If an eleventh-grade student were reading no lower than 9.0 nor higher than 13.0 grade equivalent, he would be classified as a developmental reader. The range of abilities classified as developmental is more narrow at the lower grade levels than in the upper grades and at the secondary levels (see Figure 5-1).

Students reading above the developmental track are classified as *advanced* or *gifted readers*, while those reading below that level are *corrective readers*. The term "corrective reader" tends to be used more frequently at the secondary than at the elementary level. In the early grades, it is difficult to differentiate between those who are remedial and corrective, and as a result, the two terms are often used interchangeably at that level. By the middle grades, however, it is usually possible to distinguish between those who are remedial and those who are not so seriously retarded in reading achievement (corrective) or between those who are remedial and those who have extreme reading disabilities, as indicated in Figure 5-1.

At the beginning of fourth grade, the corrective range is usually 2.0 to 3.0. By seventh grade, corrective readers would be those able to read at levels ranging from 3.0 to 5.5, and by the time a student is in eleventh grade the span is from 5.0 to 9.0.

Leona had never done well in reading, and when she was tested in eighth grade, she was found to be reading at a 5.0 level. She was of normal intelligence and seemed to have no physical disability that would account for her poor reading. Although she was generally familiar with the techniques of word analysis, her word recognition was not as yet automatic. Her reading comprehension and use of context clues were both poor. She was nonfluent, reading in a monotone with little expression or phrasing. She read everything at about the same rate and found little or no pleasure in reading. As a result, she did little reading outside her classes.

Leona could read—to some extent—but did not. Her lack of automatic word recognition skills made reading a chore for her, and, because she found it hard to read, she did not get the practice she needed to automatize her skills and become a good reader.

Leona exemplifies a typical corrective reader. Her reading was significantly below her potential, but she had developed some degree of reading ability. At her level of ability, she should have been able to work in a classroom of 16 to 20 other corrective reading students. Without the help of a corrective reading program, Leona would have become a "limited literate" as an adult. Harmon (1970) aptly describes the circumstances her lack of complete literacy would have prescribed: She would have been able to read well enough to handle her literacy needs most of the time, but she would have required help from others on a number of critical occasions. In addition, she would have been unlikely to read well enough to profit from most programs of advanced training beyond the high school level.

Remedial readers lie within a band of ability below the corrective range, although at the earliest stages, as noted previously, all poor readers tend to be grouped together as "remedial" or sometimes as "corrective" readers. By middle grade levels it is possible to note differences among them. Fourth-grade remedial readers range in ability from 1.5 to 2.0. By the time they are in seventh grade, the range is approximately 1.8 to 3.0, and by eleventh grade it becomes 2.2 to 5.0.

Remedial readers are not usually as independent as corrective readers in their work; they require more individual attention and assistance. Programs for remedial readers ordinarily must be individually planned to meet the specific needs of each student. This mandates that there be fewer students per instructional period for the teacher to work with at the remedial level than at the corrective.

Claude was a remedial reader. He was unable to read any of the textbooks used in his seventh-grade classes. His instructional reading level was found to be about the 2^1 level (lower second grade), and he had serious problems with word analysis skills, the use of context clues, and comprehension. His spelling and handwriting were very bad. Claude read in a word-by-word fashion, struggling with many of the words he found in second-grade material.

Although Claude had average intelligence, during diagnosis he told his teacher he thought he was "dumb." He believed he couldn't read and could not learn to read. Although he had already had special instruction in reading, writing, spelling, and arithmetic, it had not generally been effective, and, except for some improvement in handwriting, Claude saw no gains as a result of the time he had spent in "special classes."

In the reading resource room Claude was not only tested to identify his functional reading levels and reading skill deficits; he was also checked for underlying causes for his poor progress. A vision check showed chronic conjunctivitis, an inflammation of the membrane covering the inner surface of the eyelid and the front portion of the eyeball. Such a condition often produces a sensitivity to light and causes an individual to avoid reading. An audiogram indicated significant hearing losses within the speech range in both ears, apparently due to a history of ear infections which still continued to flare up. Although his school attendance had been good, he suffered from frequent colds, allergies, and hay fever. His family was quite poor and visits to the doctor had been rare.

Claude's "remedial" program began with a visit to the school nurse, who confirmed the possibility that the chronic upper respiratory infection was related to Claude's difficulties with hearing and with the conjunctivitis. Medical assistance was obtained, a chronic low-grade infection was controlled, diet supplements were suggested and made available through the school lunch program, and successful remedial reading instruction was begun.

The reading program for Claude included both independent and instructional reading at appropriate levels (see Chapter Six for the identification of those levels), the development of word analysis techniques, and help with the use of context clues. Progress charts were used to dramatize his gains, and he began to be encouraged by the evidence of his progress. He worked in a group with six other remedial students. Although his instruction was individualized, he was able to work without teacher assistance much of the time. His gains were good, and in the course of two years he moved from a *remedial* to a *corrective* classification and continued his progress.

Without instructional intervention, Claude would have become a functionally illiterate adult; he would have been unable to read and write well enough to handle his own concerns without the help of someone else to read and write for him. The chances are high that he would not have finished high school. Despite his normal intelligence, his functional literacy would probably have limited his vocational potential to entry-level positions throughout his career. As a result of his success in his remedial and corrective programs, however, Claude was able to prepare himself as an auto mechanic, a field he enjoyed and found rewarding.

Extremely disabled readers usually read no higher than beginning first-grade level while they are in second grade. Without specialized help, little growth is seen in such students, and even extremely disabled readers well into their high school years are unable to read better than at the early second-grade level. Group instruction is usually ineffective with students having extreme reading disabilities. They generally depend on a teacher to guide and direct them, especially requiring much individual attention during the initial stages of remediation. Interventive instruction for the extremely reading-disabled student may well be described as "intensive instruction."

Mike was a ninth-grade student who seemed bright and personable. He made friends easily, expressed himself reasonably well, and seemed to have no physical defects that would lead anyone to expect a serious reading disability. Yet Mike could not read the simplest first-grade-level material.

It was possible to trace his history of reading failure from first-grade level, where he had taken two reading readiness tests and had done poorly on both of them. His cumulative file folder showed the frustration of each of his teachers in trying to help a boy who was almost totally unable to read. They had been instrumental in having his eyes checked, his ears examined, and his hearing tested, and they had twice suggested physical checkups, which had been carried out with no pertinent findings. His folder showed that he had been diagnosed at different times as being "dyslexic," have a "pseudoneurological impairment," as being "minimally brain-damaged," and as having a "perceptual problem," yet no one really seemed to know the cause of his difficulties. He had received help in a special class for children with learning problems, he had attended summer school, and a special tutor had been hired by his parents to help with his reading. Nothing seemed to help.

When he first entered the reading center, he was started on an individualized educational program designed to help him develop a larger basic sight vocabulary through the use of flash cards and beginning reading materials. It was obvious almost immediately that he was not learning through such an approach. His program was changed to the Amplified Fernald Visual-Auditory-Kinesthetic-Tactile intensive instructional approach described in Chapter Ten, and he began to make significant progress for the first time in his life.

Mike had an extreme reading disability, and did not respond to ordinary remedial techniques. But with intensive instructional methods, it seems likely that instead of living his adult life as one who is profoundly illiterate, he will attain functional literacy. Instruction for extremely disabled readers is expensive. They need highly individualized help in a setting in which there are not usually more than one or two other such students, and they require significant amounts of personal teacher effort in the beginning. As they make progress, they can be moved to remedial programs in which somewhat less individual assistance is required, resulting in a saving in personal teacher effort and cost. However, attempts to overload instructional groups for such students results in greatly decreased gains, and the cost in wasted time and discouragement is worse than the high cost of effective programs.

At this point a word of caution should be raised concerning the interpretation of Figure 5-1. It should be used as a guide but not as a strict rule. Human behaviors are not always as easily delineated as the lines in the figure would seem to indicate. Some students who meet the quantitative criteria for being corrective readers may *behave* as though they were remedial; that is, they are too dependent on the teacher to work alone for any sizable period of time and find themselves "lost" without that direction. Others who would seem to be identifiable as remedial may well behave as though they were corrective and, with rather minimal direction, work effectively alone or within groups, provided that their materials are at an appropriate level for them. In such cases, they can often be placed with corrective students and can make good gains.

DIAGNOSTIC PRINCIPLES

One of the most precious and perishable commodities in the remediation of reading difficulties is student enthusiasm. It is precious because so much more can be accomplished with a highly motivated student. It is perishable because it can disappear like morning dew in the desert if the student begins to sense he is not making good progress. Diagnosis can be important in maintaining or creating a good attitude by helping the student get off to a good start as quickly as possible. Initial diagnosis should be sufficient to insure success without wasting time on unnecessary testing.

Initial diagnosis should provide information on (1) the functional reading levels, and (2) the reading skill deficits on which instruction should be focused. In order of importance for instruction, the functional reading levels are the instructional, the independent, and the frustration levels as identified by an informal reading inventory (see Chapter Six) or other suitable measure. The *independent reading level* is the highest level at which students can read easily, comfortably, and without noticeable difficulty. The *instructional reading level* is the highest level at which students can read successfully even though they find the material challenging. The *frustration level*, almost by definition, is the lowest level at which students encounter frustration. The ability to recognize these three levels is important to the reading teacher hoping to overcome a student's difficulties; ascertaining the instructional reading level is probably the most important step in helping a student become a better reader.

A good initial reading diagnosis should indicate the skills that are to receive top priority in the student's reading instructional program. Without it, valuable instructional time may be lost or wasted on skills that are either already known by the student or are too advanced for the student to learn. In either case, the student may fail to make progress and may become discouraged.

It is equally important to avoid unnecessary testing. No test should be given without a good reason, and in diagnosis the only good reason for giving a test is to help the student become a better learner and reader. Testing that does not assist the student in learning wastes instructional time and often contributes to development of a poor attitude on the part of the student being tested.

There are times, of course, when it is important to do testing that includes more than functional reading levels and reading skill deficits. Some extremely disabled readers have conditions that will not permit them to make good progress in learning to read, and until those conditions are discovered, interventive instruction may be inefficient. This was the case with Claude, discussed in the previous section in this chapter. If the interfering physical conditions had not

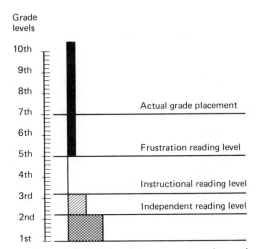

Figure 5-2. The functional reading levels of Sam, a seventh-grade boy, reading at 2^2 independently, 3^2 instructionally, and fifth-grade frustration reading level.

been rectified, it is unlikely that his remedial program would have been any more effective than the instruction he had had previously. In the case of Alan, who had a specific skills deficiency; Leona, who was a corrective reader; and— peculiarly— Mike, who had an extreme reading disability, the only diagnostic testing necessary was for the purpose of identifying functional reading levels and reading skill deficits. A diagnostician would ordinarily expect to look further in Mike's case, but as it turned out, placement in an intensive instructional program was all that was necessary. Initial diagnosis for extremely disabled readers ordinarily would include more than ascertaining levels and skills, because in such cases there are likely to be important inhibiting factors interfering with effective learning; in Mike's case, however, such additional testing was unnecessary.

There is often a temptation to place too much confidence in test results in diagnosis. It is important for a diagnostician to remember that tests have their limitations. A test is a measure of a student's ability at *one time* and in *one place*. At a different time or in a different place, the student might perform differently.

Carol was brought to a university reading center at the suggestion of her teacher, who believed that Carol was suffering from "mental degeneration." Carol had just moved to a new suburban school from her former urban residence, and on entering the fourth grade in the new setting, she had taken a form of the same achievement test she had had a few months earlier in her previous school. In comparing the results of the two tests, the teacher was alarmed to find that Carol's most recent scores were much worse.

Diagnosis, however, indicated no cause for concern; it showed, in fact, that Carol had made progress since the previous spring. Further investigation disclosed that Carol's fall achievement test had been a "makeup" test, since she had been ill when the rest of her class had taken it. Her teacher had placed her outside the room so she would not be disturbed by the rest of the class; unfortunately, every time another class was released for recess, all the students passed by Carol. They were, naturally, curious about what she was doing, and so stopped and talked with her, both before and after recess. Because Carol was continually disturbed, her test scores were low. When her teacher saw the low test scores, he believed them rather than Carol's classwork, which was good.

The teacher should have been more cautious in accepting the test results. If Carol had taken the test under different circumstances—a different time (the previous week with the rest of her class) or a different place (in some quiet place rather than a busy hallway)—she would have done much better, and her teacher would not have been concerned that Carol was a victim of "mental degeneration."

SUMMARY

Some readers have specific skill deficiencies that are nonlimiting in nature and that can be overcome through instruction in a regular classroom setting. Others have more serious problems. *Corrective readers* are usually able to work in normal-sized class groups. They are relatively independent and do not need the highly individualized instruction required by students whose reading retardation is more serious. With proper instruction, gains tend to be good in classes offering corrective reading instruction. *Remedial readers* have more serious learning problems than corrective readers; class sizes must be smaller, usually ranging from three to eight students. Remedial readers need an individualized educational program, and, though they are able to work independently to some degree, they require individualized, personal attention from a teacher to insure that headway is maintained and good progress is made. Students who have *extreme reading disabilities* must have highly individualized educational programs, particularly as they begin. A teacher is most effective working with from one to three extremely disabled students; larger groups are less effective.

Initial diagnosis should attempt to insure a successful beginning. Basic information in an initial diagnosis includes ascertaining the student's functional reading levels and reading-skill deficits. If that information is enough to plan a program that will enable the student to make good gains, no other diagnostic testing is necessary. If progress is not good or if knowledge of the student's functional reading levels and reading skill do not appear to be enough to ensure good gains, the diagnosis should include examination of other factors that may be inhibiting the student's progress.

RECOMMENDED READINGS

BOND, G. L.; TINKER, M. A.; and WASSON, B. 1979. *Reading difficulties: Their diagnosis and correction.* 4th ed. Englewood Cliffs, N.J.: Prentice-Hall, Chapters 2, 3, and 6.
HARRIS, A. J.; and SIPAY, E. R. 1980. *How to increase reading ability.* 7th ed. New York: Longman, Chapters 5 and 6.

HARRIS, L. A.; and SMITH, C. B. 1980. *Reading instruction: Diagnostic teaching in the classroom.* 3rd ed. New York: Holt, Rinehart & Winston, Chapter 14.

RUPLEY, W. H.; and BLAIR, T. R. 1979. *Reading diagnosis and remediation: A primer for classroom and clinic.* Chicago: Rand McNally, Chapter 6.

REFERENCE

Harmon, D. 1970. Illiteracy: An overview. *Harvard Educational Review* 40: 226–43.

Two major reasons for diagnostic testing are (1) to identify those students within the school who need special reading help, and having found them, (2) to identify their reading-ability levels. In this chapter, we address these two concerns, looking first at an effective testing and screening process, and then examining informal reading inventories and other means of estimating the most appropriate levels for students' reading instruction.

DIAGNOSTIC PRACTICES AND PROCEDURES: Special Reading Instruction and Functional Reading Levels

There are four major purposes for diagnostic testing: (1) to identify students who need special reading instruction, (2) to find students' functional reading levels, (3) to identify specific reading problems, and (4) to find any factors that make it more difficult for students to learn to read or to improve their reading ability. In this chapter, we address the first two of these concerns.

IDENTIFYING STUDENTS WHO NEED SPECIAL READING INSTRUCTION

The results of a standardized reading achievement test can provide a helpful first step in identifying poor readers within the student population. Test scores are often reported as grade placement scores, percentiles, or normalized standard scores reported as *stanines.* Standardized reading-test scores are more accurate for those students whose reading ability is at or above the levels the test was designed to measure. Lower scores are less reliable than scores within the central range of the test. To overcome this limitation, a cutoff point may be established; students falling below that point should be retested with an instrument designed to measure that lower range.

If the test scores are reported as grade equivalent scores, the cutoff point may be estimated by using the test's standard deviation (obtained from the test manual). If the test has been designed for use at seventh-, eighth-, and ninth-grade levels, and the standard deviation as reported in the test manual is 1.5 grade levels, the test should be reasonably accurate even 1.5 grade levels below seventh grade, the lowest level for which the test is designed. Subtracting the standard error, 1.5, from the lowest grade, 7.0, indicates that the test should measure reading ability as low as middle fifth-grade equivalent fairly reliably. Those students scoring below a 5.5 grade equivalent should be retested by means of a test designed to measure reading ability at, say, fourth- and early-fifth-grade level. Care should be taken in selecting a lower-level test to use a measure whose content is appropriate to the students.

If test results are reported in percentiles, the sixteenth percentile may be considered a usable cutoff point. Scores below that level would be sufficiently low to warrant retesting. If results are given in stanines, either the second or third stanine may be used as a cutoff point. If the second stanine is selected, only the poorest readers need be retested, since the second stanine falls lower on the normal curve of distribution than the third (see Figure 6-1). If the third stanine is used, approximately 23 percent of a normal population of students taking the test would be selected, whereas 11 percent would be selected if the second stanine is used.

After the cutoff point has been established and the students selected whose scores fall below that point, a second standardized reading achievement test should be administered. Those students whose scores fall below the levels for which the second test has been designed should be referred for remedial and

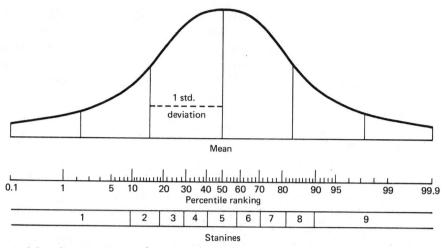

Figure 6-1. A comparison of percentile and stanine scores under a normal curve of distribution.

extreme-reading-disability diagnosis. Those indicated as reading at levels within the central range of the test should receive corrective instruction, and those who score above, as some will, generally do not need any reading assistance other than the developmental and content area reading instruction associated with ordinary good classroom teaching.

New students pose a special problem. Test results and other records are often unavailable, and poor readers may go unidentified for months. Midge was an eleventh-grade student who had attended many different schools. Although her reading ability was poor, she had never received special reading help because she was in each school for such a short period of time. The identification process worked so slowly that by the time her reading problems were recognized, her family had moved on. Her situation is not unusual. It frequently takes too long for a student to be identified and referred for needed remediation under normal circumstances. Schools should screen new students for reading difficulties as soon as possible after they enroll.

Identification at the lower grade levels and especially in self-contained classrooms tends to be easier than at the secondary level, where the larger numbers of students seen by the teacher every day makes it probable that individual student abilities will not be as well known.

How can a school or an individual teacher screen new students to find those who need reading help? If there are not too many students, a classroom teacher, reading teacher, or counselor may take a few minutes to administer an initial reading placement test. Initial placement guides from reading kits such as Science Research Associates' *Reading for Understanding* materials, word lists such as the *San Diego Quick Assessment List,* or the *Test That's Not a Test*(T-NAT) (explained later in this chapter and available for free use and duplication in the appendix) can be used for simple initial reading identification and placement.

If a large number of new students enter school every week, it may be necessary to set aside a regular time for testing, using the second step of the schoolwide program described earlier. Those scoring above the range for which the test has been designed may be considered developmental readers; those fitting within the range as corrective; and those below referred for remedial or extreme-reading-disability diagnosis.

IDENTIFICATION OF FUNCTIONAL READING LEVELS

It is likely that no other single item of information is as important to a student's success in reading as knowledge of his instructional reading level. The informal reading inventory (IRI), pioneered by Betts (1946) and Killgallon (1942), has become the standard means of measuring the independent, instructional, and frustration reading levels as well as a listening-capacity level that may be used as a measure of potential for younger students.

Informal Reading Inventory   An informal reading inventory is a series of sequentially more difficult reading passages, usually ranging from beginning to advanced reading levels, with one silent and one oral reading passage at each level of reading difficulty. Although there is no set length, passages are generally 100 to 200 words in length; lower-level passages are usually shorter.

An IRI is a basic diagnostic instrument, but it is not without fault, being heavily subject to the care with which it is constructed. It relies on the material it uses, and if the material is not representative of the levels it purports to measure, the IRI can yield misleading information. For this reason, it is important that any IRI likely to be used repeatedly be checked to determine that the levels are as accurate as possible.

Informal reading inventories are a type of criterion-referenced test (CRT)—that is, a test that measures a student's ability to perform against a predetermined standard or *criterion* of proficiency. An IRI uses dual criteria in establishing mastery or proficiency at each of two levels: independent and instructional reading. The two criteria are commonly 98 percent correct word call and 90 percent comprehension for independent reading, and 95 percent correct word call and 75 percent comprehension for the instructional reading level.

Other standards are preferred by some. Powell (1978) cited his own research supporting the acceptance of up to thirteen word-call errors at first- and second-grade levels, although he was much nearer the original Betts criteria for instructional levels at third through fifth grade (8 percent) and for sixth grade and above (6 percent). Cooper (1952) maintained that more than 5 percent errors at the instructional level resulted in decreased learning rates; this favored the Betts criteria. Pikulski (1974), in reviewing Powell's recommendations and the original

Betts criteria, reported contradictory findings. Ekwall (1976) and Woods and Moe (1977) argue for the continued use of the original criteria.

Informal reading inventories have had detractors (Spache, 1976, pp. 186–87), sometimes faulting IRIs for lacking normative data. However, IRIs, like other more common kinds of criterion-referenced tests, were not developed to compare one student's performance to that of other students. Instead, the IRI was designed to test student ability to perform competently at either of the two functional reading levels when presented with a series of reading materials. If a student is presented with a passage written at the fourth-grade level of difficulty, it is possible to determine whether or not he has independent-level mastery, instructional mastery, or lacks mastery at either level in fourth-grade material. This is accomplished by a comparison of his performance with the criteria established for mastery at the two functional levels.

For any criterion-referenced test, it is important that the material be as representative of the task as possible. In the case of an IRI, this means that the reading material for each level should be as representative as its author can find or produce of the various grade levels being tested. If the passages are accurate representations, then the research on which IRIs are based will allow the examiner to estimate the reader's functional reading levels. It is not necessary that normative data be gathered or that that specific IRI shall have been the instrument used in research to identify functional reading levels.

In the IRI included in the Diagnostic Reading Test Battery (see p. 316 in the appendix), for example, the passages were carefully written to correspond to the reading grade difficulty each passage represents. This process involved several steps. First, a core vocabulary of words included in at least three of the five most widely used basal reader series was developed for each reading level through grade six. Words that were deemed childish were deleted. This core vocabulary composed a minimum of 80 percent of the words in the reading selections at each level through sixth-grade difficulty. Second, all passages were tested for readability by means of the Fry Readability Graph. They were rewritten as necessary to conform to the appropriate levels, and effort was made to insure representative writing standards at the same time. Third, cloze tests were made from the passages and were administered to selected students. Their performance on the cloze passages was used to verify that the test passages had been properly identified in sequential order of difficulty.

Although the third step would not ordinarily seem necessary, it provides a further check to assure that the passages and questions increase in difficulty from one level to the next.

Oral fluency and silent-rate standards have been added to the IRI in the appendix. The standards are based on competence with interesting material. They seemed to discriminate in a pilot study with the passages, but it should be pointed out that reading rate is highly variable and subject to change even at the whim of the reader. Therefore, the standards are suggested only as a rough estimate of the student's ability.

It is possible for the teacher to build his own informal reading inventory by selecting passages, checking their reading difficulty level with a readability measure such as the Fry Readability Graph in the appendix, and writing his own questions. However, the Diagnostic Reading Test Battery in the appendix is for the teacher's use and may be duplicated and used freely.

As was defined earlier, the independent reading level is the highest level at which the student can read easily and comfortably with almost no errors in word call or comprehension. The instructional reading level is the highest level at which the reader is able to read challenging material successfully. At the frustration level, the reader is unable to cope with the material successfully (see Figure 6-1). The quantitative criteria favored by the author for use in identifying the three functional reading levels are as follows:

Functional Reading Level	Percent of Correct Word Call	Percent of Comprehension
Independent	98% or higher	90% or higher
Instructional	95% or higher	75% or higher
Frustration	90% or lower	50% or lower

For a level to be identified as independent or instructional, both word call and comprehension criteria must be met. In other words, the independent level is the highest level at which the reader can read with both 98 percent correct word call and 90 percent comprehension. Similarly, the instructional reading level is the highest level at which the student can read with both 95 percent correct word call and 75 percent comprehension. For example, look at the following eighth-grade student's IRI performance:

Grade Level	Percent of Correct Word Call	Percent of Comprehension	Functional Reading Level
4	85%	40%	
3^2	90%	70%	Frustration
3^1	92%	80%	
2^2	96%	80%	Instructional
2^1	95%	90%	
1^2	98%	100%	Independent
Primer	100%	100%	
Pre-primer	100%	100%	

Although this student met the comprehension criterion for the instructional reading level at the 3^1 level, it could not be identified as his instructional reading level because he had not met the criteria for both comprehension and word call.

The frustration level is identified differently; it is the *lowest* level at which the reader meets *either* of the two criteria. In the example, as soon as the reader met one criterion of frustration, that was identified as his frustration level. It was unnecessary for him to meet both criteria.

There are diverse opinions on the kinds of errors that should be marked in an oral IRI. Errors may be divided into those classified as "major" and "minor," major errors being those considered in identifying IRI levels. The following are suggested as major errors:

1. Omissions—words in the text that are left out by the reader.
   Example: *Text*   The older man smiled nervously.
   Reader   "The man smiled nervously."
2. Additions—words not found in the text but added by the reader.
   Example: *Text*   The horse broke into an easy lope.
   Reader   "The little horse broke into an easy lope.
3. Mispronunciations—errors that are similar phonetically to the word in the text.
   Example: *Text*   The man leaped onto the horse.
   Reader   "The man leaped onto the house."
4. Substitutions—errors that are not phonetically similar to the word in the text.
   Example: *Text*   She rode the horse with skill and grace.
   Reader   "She rode the colt with skill and grace."
5. Pronunciations—words on which the reader blocks and which must be pronounced for the reader. Unless the reader asks for help in pronouncing the word, the teacher should usually allow the reader about 5 seconds to recognize the word before pronouncing it.
6. Transpositions—the reader changes the order of words in the text. One error is counted for each time a student transposes word order.
   Example: *Text*   Was he invited to the party?
   Reader   "He was invited to the party."

If a student corrects an error before the teacher tells him the word, he should be given credit, and it should not be counted as an error.

Errors that do not count toward the determination of functional reading levels are called minor errors and include the following:

1. Repetitions—a word or series of words read correctly but repeated by the reader.
   Example: *Text*   He began to walk more slowly.
   Reader   "He began . . . He . . . He began to walk more slowly."
2. Dialectic pronunciations—a word pronounced in accordance with the student's own dialect.
   Example: *Text*   He couldn't see so he climbed the tree.
   Reader   "He cunt see so he clumb the tree."
3. Ignoring punctuation—the reader is unresponsive to the manner in which the sentence is punctuated.
   Example: *Text*   "Don't! Stop!" she screamed.
   Reader   "Don't stop," she screamed.
4. Lack of fluency—the reader reads without expression, in a word-by-word manner.
5. Hesitations—the reader pauses for less than 5 seconds before pronouncing a word.

Although it is obvious that some of the so-called "minor errors" can cause serious difficulty, they ought not to be counted in computing functional reading levels. They should be noted, however, and included in plans for remediation.

There are a number of different systems for marking, and the teacher should use one that makes sense to him. The following are common suggestions for marking major errors:

Error	Symbol	Example
Omissions	⟋	*Text* He left the (dirty) rag behind.
		Reader "He left the rag behind."
Additions	∧	*Text* She started to work ᵒⁿ the next day.
		Reader "She started to work on the next day."
Pronunciations	P	*Text* The big workhorse seemed hᴾuge.
		Reader "The big workhorse seemed . . . [blocked]"
Transpositions	∼	*Text* Was he afraid?
		Reader "He was afraid."
Mispronunciations	——	*Text* He ~~pulled~~ ᵖᵘᵗ the rope on the bell.
		Reader "He put the rope on the bell."
Substitutions	——	*Text* She tied her hair with a ~~string~~ ᵇᵒʷ.
(same as Mispronunciations)		*Reader* "She tied her hair with a bow."

Minor errors may be marked, though not counted as errors in the IRI, in the following manner:

Error	Symbol	Example
Repetition	⌣	*Text* He came home late at night.
		Reader "He. . .He came home late. . .late at night."
Ignoring punctuation	♂	*Text* He smiled at her "Sister I love you."
		Reader "He smiled at her sister I love you."
Lack of fluency	//	*Text* When/the/girl/opened/the/door,/it/was/gone.
		Reader "When. . .the. . .girl. . .opened. . .the door. . . it. . .was. . .gone."
Hesitations	h	*Text* The man ʰgrasped the doll.
		Reader "The man [pause] grasped the doll."

It takes time to learn a marking system, but it becomes easy with practice. The marking code may be attached to the teacher's clipboard with a masking-tape hinge, so it can be seen easily in the early stages of learning the code (see Figure 6-2).

Johnson and Kress (1965) strongly recommend that an individual IRI be timed with a stop watch. The timing of both the oral and silent reading passages allows for a comparison of performances at each level not only for comprehension but also for time. If the examiner decides to include time as a factor, he should be careful to equate the passages in length or to account for differences in passage length when comparing the time.

When a stop watch is used in test administration, it is important to counteract

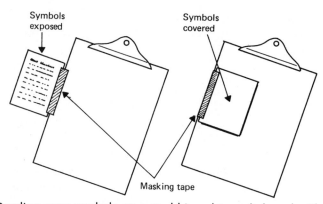

Figure 6-2. Reading-error symbols on a card hinged to a clipboard with masking tape.

the effect it may have on the student's performance. Seeing the stop watch, many students try to speed their reading, and, as a result, make an unusual number of errors. The examiner should either keep the stop watch out of sight or minimize its importance. Even then, students will sometimes try to read too quickly, and it becomes necessary to stop and reassure them that they should read at their normal rate.

ADMINISTRATION OF AN INFORMAL READING INVENTORY

The test administrator should endeavor to put the student at ease, establish a purpose for testing, and secure the cooperation of the student. It is good practice to clip the examiner's copy of the test to a clipboard and to use a ballpoint pen for marking. In this way, the examiner can hold the test out of the student's field of vision but still maintain an easy writing surface. A ballpoint pen allows the examiner to reduce the noise made in recording student errors and responses (a pencil tends to make enough noise to attract the attention of the reader, sometimes causing him to stop and ask whether or not he has made a mistake).

Before introducing the first passage of the IRI, it is helpful to use an initial placement guide such as a word list or the Test That's Not a Test (T–NAT) (described later in this chapter) to suggest a starting level. A word recognition list is included with the Diagnostic Reading Test Battery in the appendix, and may be duplicated freely. If a word list is used, it may be composed of groups of words representing each level of reading difficulty included in the IRI. (The word list included in the appendix with the IRI uses words selected as representative from pre-primer through the sixth-grade level.) The examiner should listen carefully as the student reads each word in isolation, noting difficulties the student has with word attack. When correct recognition falls below 90 percent, the examiner should test the next highest level to be sure the student has really reached his maximum and then terminate the word recognition test if that level, too, falls below

114

90 percent. The examiner should then drop one level below the highest passage on which the student had at least 90 percent correct word call to begin the IRI.

In initiating the informal reading inventory, the examiner should explain that he will begin by having the student read some passages that are relatively easy, but that some of the later passages will be more difficult. He should explain further that it is necessary to read the difficult passages in order to find out how the student handles words and concepts that are challenging.

There are two different methods for administering an IRI. Both usually involve identifying the starting level, as mentioned above. The teacher should introduce the starting-level passage to the student, asking him to "read this story about [insert the title of the selection] to me aloud." The student then reads the passage orally while the examiner records errors on another copy of the material from which the student is reading. In the first method, the examiner also times the student with a stop watch and notes on his copy how long it takes to read the passage. If the student begins to read silently, the examiner should stop the student and ask him to read aloud. If the student blocks in recognizing a word for more than 5 seconds, the examiner should tell the student the word and record a "pronunciation" on the examiner's copy. If the student tries to preread the test material silently before reading orally, the examiner should ask the student just to read it on sight. If the student begins to glance back through the material before finishing the selection, the examiner should ask him to finish reading the material before looking back.

Some of these points may seem contrary to good reading instruction, but they are necessary because the IRI is a test situation and the standards on which the reader's performance are measured require that the material be read in the fashion prescribed.

After the student finishes reading, the examiner should ask questions about the selection. Half or more of the questions test direct recall; the remainder test the student's comprehension of the main idea and inferences from the information contained in the selection. Questions that cannot be answered on the basis of reading the passage should not be included. For example, the examiner should not ask the meaning of a word if that word is not explained in the passage. When eight questions are used, one incorrect response results in an 87½ percent level of comprehension, and, although this is slightly below the 90 percent level that serves as the standard for independent-level reading comprehension, it may be accepted as satisfactory for independent reading. Half-credit is permissible if a student demonstrates a clear understanding of a major portion of the acceptable answer. The examiner should avoid the tendency to assume that the student understands material he has been unable to express. Neither should the examiner "teach" the test. If a student misses an answer, the teacher should simply go on to the next question and not try to coach the student to elicit a correct answer.

The examiner should try to record the student's answers as completely as possible. This will help later in analyzing the reader's comprehension difficulties.

In the first method of administering an IRI, the examiner times the student as he reads a passage at the same level silently; the examiner should observe carefully such behaviors as lip movements, pointing to words, saying the words aloud, and requested assistance with unknown words. The length of time it takes the reader to finish the selection should be recorded for comparison with the oral reading time on the same level of difficulty. If the passages are unequal in length, the time should be converted to seconds (1 minute and 43 seconds would be converted to 103 seconds, for example), and the number of words in the passage should be divided by the number of seconds. The number derived from this operation should then be multiplied by 60 to reconvert to the number of words read per minute. For example, if a student read a passage of 120 words in 103 seconds orally and had read another passage at the same level of difficulty which was 140 words in length in 115 seconds, comparable rates of reading could be calculated in words per minute as follows:

Oral Reading

$$\frac{120 \text{ words}}{103 \text{ secs}} = 120 \div 103 = 1.165 \times 60 \text{ secs} = 69.9 \text{ wpm}$$

Silent Reading

$$\frac{140 \text{ words}}{115 \text{ secs}} = 140 \div 115 = 1.217 \times 60 \text{ secs} = 73 \text{ wpm}$$

A hand calculator makes it possible to compute the figures needed in a few seconds.

In silent reading, some students reread all or a portion of the selection a second time before signaling that they have finished. Although this is acceptable under ordinary reading circumstances, it gives an inaccurate indication of the silent reading time for IRI test purposes. The examiner should ask the student to tell him as soon as he has finished and should note the time carefully.

As soon as the reader has finished his silent reading, the examiner should administer the comprehension check as he did for oral reading. Afterward, the examiner should ask the student to reread a portion of the silent reading selection orally, first establishing a purpose for the rereading. For example, he may ask the student to reread a section in order to find the answer to an inferential question dealt with in that portion of the passage. As the student rereads, the examiner should again record any errors exactly as he did for oral reading at sight, and the student's reading should be timed and his reading rate calculated. As soon as the reader has finished, the examiner should ask the student to answer the question or complete the action for which he had the student reread the section from the passage.

The IRI should be continued in this same fashion: oral reading at sight, silent reading at sight, and oral rereading of a section of the silent reading passage at each level, until a frustration level has been identified.

It is not uncommon for a student to read more poorly on some specific lower-level passage than he does on a more difficult level. The IRI is a maximum-effort instrument; that is, although it is never possible for a student to read better than he has the ability to read, it *is* possible for him to read *more poorly* than his ability level. Therefore, the examiner is counseled to always take the student's best performance as the most reliable estimate of reading ability. A student who reads more poorly on a beginning passage than on one read later does so for many different reasons. For instance, he may do so because of initial test anxiety or because he has not adjusted to the requirements of the test. If a student is anxious at first, the examiner may find that with relaxation, he will read better even though at a higher level. Again, the examiner should accept the student's best performance as more truly indicative of reading behavior.

As soon as the frustration level has been identified, the examiner may decide to continue on to find the listening-capacity level. As noted earlier, this level indicates the point at which the student has the ability to *understand* written material when it is read to him. This level is sometimes used as an indicator of the student's potential for reading improvement. It seems reasonable to assume that the student's listening-capacity level should be the level he could attain if he had the ability to read the material for himself. There are, however, several limitations to such an assumption. First, reading necessitates visual perception and visual recognition, while hearing requires auditory perception and recognition. The ability to perform well in one area does not necessarily predict ability to perform well in the other. In addition, listening and reading differ—in reading, a student has unlimited opportunity to reread anything he did not understand, whereas in listening, it is more difficult to have the speaker repeat comments. The limitations mean that a student's listening-capacity level may be used only as an *estimate* of potential. The older the student is, the less likely the estimate is to be useful.

The process for identifying the listening-capacity level begins at the next level after the frustration level has been identified. This time, instead of having the student read, the examiner reads it, at about 125 to 160 words per minute (about the rate most radio and television announcers use). He should use good expression and should ask the student to respond to a comprehension check just as for the earlier portions of the IRI. The listening-capacity level is the highest level at which the listener can understand at least 75 percent of the material on which he is questioned.

An IRI summary sheet such as that shown in Figure 6-3 may be used to gather the information gained from the IRI for easy reference.

The section headed "Analysis of Word Call Errors and Miscues" may be used for listing the words missed in each passage. The word as it appears in the text is written on the left and the error is written on the right. (Analysis of word call errors will be discussed in Chapter Seven.)

An Alternative Method of IRI Administration   A second approach used in administering an informal reading inventory differs from the method just described

Student's Name:

Reading Level:

Analysis of Word Call Errors and Miscues

	Percent of Correct Word Call	Percent of Comprehension	Rate in Words per Minute	Text	Reader	Text	Reader	Text	Reader
Oral Reading:									
Silent Reading:									
Oral Re-reading:									

Reading Level:

Analysis of Word Call Errors and Miscues

	Percent of Correct Word Call	Percent of Comprehension	Rate in Words per Minute	Text	Reader	Text	Reader	Text	Reader
Oral Reading:									
Silent Reading:									
Oral Re-reading:									

Reading Level:

Analysis of Word Call Errors and Miscues

	Percent of Correct Word Call	Percent of Comprehension	Rate in Words per Minute	Text	Reader	Text	Reader	Text	Reader
Oral Reading:									
Silent Reading:									
Oral Re-reading:									

Figure 6-3.   Informal reading inventory summary sheet

in that (1) the student is not timed as he reads, (2) the student is tested only on oral reading at sight, and is not asked to read silently or, of course, to reread a section of the silent passage orally, and, therefore, (3) no comparisons are made between the student's oral, silent, and rereading performances. Word call errors are still analyzed, and functional reading levels are identified in both methods.

The first method provides more information than the second, and provides more opportunity to observe the student's reading behavior under different reading circumstances. The second method is less time-consuming; when time is short, it can be used to garner important information within the restricted time limits facing the examiner.

Published Informal Reading Inventories   There are several published informal reading inventories. Among those in common use are the *Classroom Reading Inventory*, the *Reading Placement Inventory*, and the *Standard Reading Inventory*. Newer entries include the *Analytical Reading Inventory* and the *Contemporary Classroom Inventory*. The best way to make a determination regarding the value of a published inventory is to read the manual and administer the inventory two or three times. Each inventory reflects the thinking of its author in administration, scoring, and interpretation.

An informal reading inventory is a basic diagnostic reading instrument. It is useful in identifying a student's functional reading levels. In addition, it provides an opportunity for the diagnostician to identify and analyze word call errors, observe and record reading behaviors, check reading rate under three different conditions, note general fluency, test reading comprehension at various levels and for different purposes, and estimate potential for improvement. Commercially prepared standardized reading tests generally fall short of the benefits derived from the skilled administration of an informal reading inventory.

Briefly, the inventories mentioned may be described as follows:

The *Analytical Reading Inventory* (Woods and Moe, 1977) has three forms; each has a separate word recognition test and passages for testing grades two through nine. Summary sheets are included for use in analysis of errors and miscues.

The *Classroom Reading Inventory* (Silvaroli, 1976) has three sections: a word recognition test, oral reading passages, and a spelling test. There are three forms. It is possible to use the alternate forms to test silent reading and listening comprehension. The reading passages range from pre-primer through sixth-grade-level difficulty.

The *Contemporary Classroom Reading Inventory* (Rinsky and DeFossard, 1980) is an inventory designed for use in various content areas. Based on research such as that of Brazee (1976) and Wixson (1980) indicating that many students have different instructional levels in different content areas, this inventory provides passages for fiction, social studies, and science. The inventory includes supplemental tests for levels 4 to 9.

The *Reading Placement Inventory* (Sucher and Allred, 1973) has a word recognition section and oral reading passages which range from primer through ninth-grade reading difficulty. There is only one form of the test. The inventory includes a summary cover for error analysis.

The *Standard Reading Inventory* (McCracken, 1966) has two forms; each includes word lists and both oral and silent reading passages ranging from pre-primer through grade seven. The Standard Reading Inventory is unique in that it provides reliability and validity data, although their importance is a moot point.

Estimating Instructional Reading Levels   A limitation in the use of an informal reading inventory is the lengthy administration time. The benefits to be derived from knowing a student's functional reading levels must be balanced against the time involved in determining those levels by administering individual IRIs. If it takes 20 to 40 minutes to give an informal reading inventory to most intermediate-grade and secondary students, the investment in time and effort becomes a significant factor.

In an attempt to estimate reading levels more efficiently, it is not uncommon for teachers to turn to standardized reading-test scores. Unfortunately, even though they are usually readily available and even if they are reported in grade equivalent scores, they tend to rank students higher than an informal reading inventory (Sipay, 1964; Clement, 1980). Students placed in reading materials at the grade level indicated by standardized reading tests are often near their frustration levels. Brown (1965) found that very poor secondary readers may be placed several levels too high following this procedure.

When there is not time to administer a complete IRI, it is possible to turn to other measures which, although less accurate in identifying instructional reading levels than an IRI, are more accurate than standardized test scores and can provide a usable estimate. Included among these instruments are the initial placement tests mentioned earlier including word lists, placement guides borrowed from reading kits, and the Test That's Not a Test (T-NAT).

The T-NAT is patterned in part after the IRI but has the advantage of being much faster to give, usually less than 5 minutes. It is a special kind of criterion-referenced test, the criterion being 95 percent correct word call, indicating satisfactory instructional reading. The highest level at which the student can meet this criterion is identified as the student's instructional reading level.

The T-NAT is a series of reading passages of increasing difficulty developed for use without a stop watch, student record form, or other paraphernalia usually accompanying individual testing. Forms of the T-NAT printed on card stock and in a packet with directions are available through Basic Education Trade House. However, permission has been granted to include a T-NAT with directions in the appendix of this text. Copies may be duplicated freely by teachers wanting to use the test.

Group Reading Inventory   Teachers often need to identify the instructional reading levels of their students in the regular classroom. Although it is obviously of importance to identify student instructional reading levels to place them in materials at the proper level, a complete IRI takes too long to administer in a class of twenty-five or more students. A T-NAT, while an appropriate measure for estimating initial reading placement for a new student or for one who is about to be given an IRI, is inappropriate for use in this case, because it lacks an estimate of reading comprehension. As already noted, standardized reading tests usually overestimate the instructional reading level, making them a poor choice. Although word lists have been suggested, they, like the T-NAT, lack any measure of comprehension, and are therefore inappropriate for use in gauging the level of instruction for a classroom. A better approach is a group reading inventory.

The group reading inventory (GRI) described here is a teacher-made test for estimating student instructional reading levels in a classroom in a limited amount of time. It is based on the same general criteria as an IRI; that is, it identifies the instructional reading level as the highest point at which a student can read with approximately 95 percent correct word call and 75 percent comprehension. The GRI is divided into two parts: a test of word recognition and a separate test of reading comprehension. On the word call test, students take turns reading orally through the passages at three selected levels. In the comprehension test, each of three passages at the selected levels is read silently, with each student reading the same material at each level. Questions are then answered for each passage. Student performance is recorded for each test on a record sheet, and the instructional reading level is determined for each student.

In preparing a GRI, the first step is identification of a class *level*. This is usually the grade level of the class for which the test is to be used, but the teacher may want to vary the class level if student abilities are significantly higher or lower than would be expected or because the students who compose the class are not all from the same grade level. In the latter case, the teacher may use either the lowest grade level represented in the class or the level of the material commonly used for instruction in the class.

Once the class level has been identified, three levels of difficulty below that are chosen for testing. The first, called the *ceiling level*, is the level just below the class level. The intermediate is three levels below and the bottom is five levels below the class level. Identification of the various levels for a third-grade class and for a tenth-grade class is illustrated as follows:

Third-Grade Class	Levels	Tenth-Grade Class
3^1	Class	10
2^2	Ceiling	9
2^1	(skip)	8
1^2	Intermediate	7
Primer	(skip)	6
Pre-primer[3]	Bottom	5

Next, the teacher must find passages at the appropriate levels. It is possible to find materials that have already been identified in terms of grade-level readability, but frequently it is necessary to use a readability measure like the Fry

Readability Graph (see page 370 in appendix) to identify materials at the correct levels of readability. Although some variation in difficulty within passages is to be expected, it is best to select materials that are as consistent as possible by avoiding selections that obviously change style—and, therefore, level of difficulty—within the passage. Dialogue, insertions of poetry, quotations from other writers, and noticeable changes in the level of difficulty of the author's writing signal material likely to be too variable in technical readability to be usable for a GRI.

During the first test, word call, each student is asked to read a passage of fifty words plus whatever number of words remains beyond the fiftieth word to complete the sentence (see the example in Figure 6-4). Therefore, the teacher should find a selection or group of passages at each level which is long enough to provide material for each student to read without having to reread what another student has already read. A good rule of thumb in estimating passage length is to multiply 60 by the number of students at each level who may be asked to read. This allows fifty words for the portion of the reading over which the student will be evaluated and ten words, on the average, needed to complete the sentence beyond the test portion of the segment. Since many of the students may need to be tested at two or three levels, it is important to be sure there is enough material at each level.

It is unnecessary that all the reading material at one level be taken from the same source; moreover, all the passages need not deal with the same topic or subject. Neither is it necessary to select a passage that tells a complete story or follows a line of thought to its conclusion. Obviously, there is no objection to the selection of passages that *are* complete, but that ought not be a criterion for selection.

After the teacher has chosen reading material for the three word call levels, it is necessary to mark off the fifty-word segments which the students will read. Starting with the first word the first student will read, the teacher should count off fifty words, placing a slash mark after the fiftieth word. An "X" should be placed at the end of the sentence in which the fiftieth word appears. Beginning

Segment read by the first reader.

Georgie eyed the ski lift with more than a little concern. He wondered what would happen if he got into position just in front of it and then didn't sit down the way he was supposed to. What if it knocked him over, or worse yet, what if he wasn't/ able to really get on the chair? X

End of 50 words.

Stop.

Segment read by the second reader.

What if it dragged him across the snow and up into the air, dangling like a fool—a scared fool? He decided he'd better think about it for awhile.

Except there wasn't time. The line was moving quickly as the skiers in pairs each moved into position and were then/ swept away by the chair.X Georgie closed his eyes and tried to clear his brain.

End of 50 words.

Stop.

Third reader begins.

Figure 6-4. An illustration of the marking of two segments in the word call test of a group reading inventory.

with the next word, which starts the sentence the second reader will begin to read, the teacher should again count off fifty words, put a slash mark after the fiftieth word, and place an "X" at the end of the sentence. This process should be continued through the rest of the passage and through all three levels until all the segments have been marked off.

The teacher also needs to find material at the same three test levels for the comprehension portion of the GRI. Each passage should be long enough to provide a basis for eight open-ended or completion questions. A passage of 125 to 250 words at each level is usually enough. Selections of fewer than 100 words are generally not long enough to support eight good questions.

To prepare the passages for the comprehension test, the teacher should write eight open-ended or completion questions requiring short answers for each of the three selections. Four of those questions should deal with the main idea or general significance and inferences that may be drawn from the passage, and four should test direct recall of factual information. The answer for each question should be contained in the passage.

Enough copies of the GRI should be reproduced so that each student has a copy. When a teacher intends to test more than one class, enough copies should be made to accommodate the largest class, because the word call test can be re-used a number of times. On the comprehension test, however, there must be enough copies for the total number of students in all the classes to be tested because the questions are to be answered on the back of the sheet on which the passage is written. The teacher must make sure that the copies are clear and legible.

Before the administration of the GRI, the teacher should make a record sheet that lists the names of the students on the left side, with columns across the top, headed as indicated in Figure 6-5.

In administering and scoring a GRI, the appearance of a traditional test should be avoided. This is especially important for poor readers, who often feel threatened by reading tests. Before administering the group reading inventory, the teacher should ask the students for their help, and make it a point to assure the students that (1) they will not be graded on their performance, (2) the results of the inventory will help in selecting appropriate materials for use in the class (without knowing the instructional reading level of the students, it is impossible to match students and materials properly), and (3) if anyone has difficulty, the teacher will help. At that point, copies of the word call test should be distributed to each student. The ceiling-level passage should be on top of the packet, followed by the passage of intermediate difficulty, with the easiest passage last.

The teacher should explain that each student is to read a segment of the passage. Each segment is marked off by Xs at its beginning and ending (see Figure 6-4). The teacher should have every student read at the ceiling level if it seems possible that they could do so, taking turns until all have had a chance to read. The record sheet may be used as a guide to assure that no one has been missed. It is better not to follow a set pattern of selection because the students will begin to

Group Reading Inventory
Student Record Sheet

Students' Names	Word Call			Comprehension	Overall Instructional Reading Level
	Ceiling 9	Inter- mediate 7	Bottom 5		

Figure 6-5.   A sample Student Record Sheet for the group reading inventory.

anticipate their turn and read ahead, practicing the passage they will be asked to read. This will bias the test results, since the standards for performance on the test are based on the readers *not* having preread the material.

After all possible candidates at the ceiling level have had a chance to read, the teacher should direct the class to the passage at the intermediate level. Students asked to read at this level are (1) those who were not presumed to be able to read at the ceiling level but might be able to read at the intermediate level, and (2) those who were frustrated when they read at the ceiling level, indicating a need to be retested at the next lower passage level. Students should again be selected in random order. As soon as everyone conceivably able to read at the intermediate level has had a chance to do so, the teacher should have the students turn to the bottom passage. All students should read at this level who have not read previously or who have read poorly when they read at a higher level. The same random selection procedure should be followed at this level as at the higher level.

The word call portion of the GRI is similar to a three-level sifter, screening out those students able to read at the higher levels and only testing or retesting those students on the lower selections whose instructional reading levels have still not been found.

Occasionally a student who had not been presumed to be able to read at a higher level will do surprisingly well when tested on a lower passage, indicating ability to read instructionally at a higher level. When this happens, after the rest of the class has completed the test, the teacher should have the student return to the level above his independent performance, go to a segment the class has not read, and have the student read at this higher level.

After everyone has been tested at the three levels, some will be found to have reading ability below the bottom passage level. They should be tested on an individual informal reading inventory so their instructional reading level can be determined.

As each student reads, only the errors he makes in reading the first fifty words marked in his segment should be counted. Otherwise, the computational difficulties in identifying the instructional reading level become too great to make the process workable. Errors are the same as those counted for an informal reading inventory described earlier in this chapter.

As a student is reading, the teacher should make as few corrections as possible, only correcting errors essential to understanding the continuity of the passage. If a student makes four or more errors and appears to be upset by them, the teacher should take over the reading for the remainder of the segment. He should do so in a matter-of-fact way and without comment, if possible.

The criteria for performance on the word call test are as follows:

Number of Miscues/ Errors	Functional Reading Level Indicated	Suggested Symbol for Recording
0–1	Independent	+
2–3	Instructional	O
4 or more	Frustration	−

If a student reads with no more than one error, demonstrating independent-level reading ability, it shows that he can read instructionally *above* that level. Two or three errors indicates that the student is reading *on* the instructional level. In the case of four or more errors, the student is reading at his frustration level, indicating that his instructional reading level is *below* that level. Those reading on a frustration level should be retested on the next lower passage level. It is possible for a student to be tested once at the ceiling level, again at the intermediate level, and again at the bottom passage level. As soon as the teacher finds a student's instructional reading level for word call, an "o" is marked in that column on the record sheet, and the student does not need to be retested. If a student reading at the ceiling level demonstrates independent or instructional reading ability, there is no need to test that student later at a lower level. The appropriate symbol is entered after the student's name in the ceiling column of the word call portion of the record sheet. The teacher should mark the student's instructional reading level as base level or higher if he reads independently on the ceiling-passage level.

If a student demonstrates frustration-level ability at one level but shows independent-reading ability when tested at a lower level, his instructional reading level is interpolated between the two. If, for example, a student is frustrated in trying to read at seventh-grade level but, when retested at fifth-grade level, shows he is able to read independently, he is judged to be *below* seventh but *above* fifth. In other words, he is judged to be reading at a sixth-grade instructional reading level.

Occasionally, when students are reading at the bottom level, some of them begin to sense that only the poorer readers are still being tested, and they may feel denigrated. To protect them, the teacher can ask one or two good readers to read segments at the bottom level. By having a "red herring" drawn across their path in this fashion, poorer readers are less likely to become aware of the identification process that has left them at the bottom of the ability ranking and, therefore, less likely to feel self-conscious.

For the comprehension portion of the GRI, the three passages should be distributed to the class with the *easiest* passage on top, the intermediate passage next, and the ceiling passage on the bottom. The test is untimed. Each student is asked to read the top passage and then turn the sheet over and answer the questions on the back without looking at the selection again. After answering all the questions, the student should go on to the next passage, read it, and answer the questions on the back. Then, after answering the questions on the back of the third passage, the students should hand in the GRI without looking back over the passage to check answers.

As the students are working on the comprehension test, the teacher should again remind them not to look back at the passage in order to answer their questions. Because the questions are on the back, the teacher has an opportunity to notice whether some students are referring to the passage.

Because the comprehension section starts with the easiest passage first, good readers generally finish all three passages while very poor readers are completing the first one. The comprehension test should be terminated as soon as most of the students have completed the questions. Although the test has no set time limits, it has been found that delaying the completion of the test until the last student has finished does not provide any appreciably greater information.

In all, it usually takes less than 45 minutes to administer the word call portion of the GRI and less than 30 minutes to give the comprehension section.

After the comprehension test has been handed in, the teacher should check to determine the highest level at which each student has no more than three errors. The criteria are quite similar to those for the word call test:

Number of Incorrect Answers	Functional Reading Level Indicated
0–1	Independent
2–3	Instructional
4 or more	Frustration

Just as with the word call test, if a student reads at a frustration level on one passage but at an independent level on the next-lower passage, his scores are interpolated, and his instructional reading level is judged to lie between the two passages (see Figure 6-6).

After the results of both tests have been gathered and recorded on the record sheet, each student's instructional reading level is entered in the last column on the right, headed "Overall Instructional Reading Level." This is the highest level at which the student meets both the word call and comprehension criteria. In other words, the instructional reading level is always the lower of the two variables. If, for example, a student reads instructionally at the fifth-grade level for word call but at the fourth-grade level for comprehension, his overall instructional reading level is judged to be fourth-grade level, and fourth grade would be indicated in the column under "Overall Instructional Reading Level" (see Figure 6-6).

Note that in Figure 6-6, the teacher has used 6+ to indicate that the student was able to read independently on the ceiling-level passage for the comprehension test. The teacher noted that Lisa D. and Bill T. were above the 2^2 level but were frustrated by the 3^2 level, and wrote 3^1 between the two columns.

The group reading inventory provides an estimation of the instructional reading level for most students in a class, although the students who are reading above grade placement are only identified as able to read instructionally at that level or higher. On the sample in Figure 6-6, for example, the teacher simply notes that they are reading instructionally at sixth grade or above. Three students on the Student Record Sheet—David H., Amy O., and Jody S.— are all listed as reading below 2^2, and they await individual testing to find their instructional reading levels.

The group reading inventory is not as accurate, nor does it provide as much information, as an individually administered informal reading inventory, but it is

Group Reading Inventory
Student Record Sheet

Students' Names	Word Call			Comprehension	Overall Instructional Reading Level
	Ceiling 5	Intermediate 3^2	Bottom 2^2		
Heather A.	+			6^+	6 or higher
Jeremy A.	0			6^+	5
Toby A.	−	0		5	3^2
Jeffrey B.	+			5	5
Mark B.	0			3^2	3^2
Don C.		0		3^2	3^2
Lisa D.		−	+	2^2	2^2
Shawn E.	+			6^+	6 or higher
Kayleen H.	0			3^2	3^2
David H.	−	−	−	3^2	below 2^2
David J.			0	3^2	2^2
Joseph L.	+			5	5
Peter L.	0			6^+	5
Sharon N.	+			5	5
Amy O.	−	0		below 2^2	below 2^2
April O.	−	0		4 / 3^2	3^2
Beth S.			0	3^2	2^2
Jody S.			−	below 2^2	below 2^2
Kelly S.	+			5	5
Sam T.	−	+		4	4
George T.			0	3^2	2^2
Bill T.		−	+	4	3^1
Jean W.	+			6^+	6 or higher
Sue W.		0		3^2	3^2
Mike W.	0			5	5
Taylor W.	0	+		6^+	3^2
Allen Y.	0			5	5

Figure 6-6.   A sample Student Record Sheet for the group reading inventory filled in for a sixth-grade class.

usually accurate within a reading level, and it takes much less time than individual administration of an IRI to an entire class.

The cloze procedure and the use of placement guides from reading kits are also means of estimating the instructional reading level for students in a regular classroom or corrective-reading setting. Cloze is a technique in which the first sentence in a passage is left intact, but every *n*th word is removed after that. Although any pattern of deletions may be used with a cloze test, the most common is the deletion of every fifth word. The student taking the test receives credit only if the word he writes in the blank is the exact word that has been deleted. Passages should be approximately 250 words long. When the percentage of exact word replacements has been calculated, using an every-fifth-word deletion pattern, functional reading levels may be interpreted as follows:

58 percent or higher = independent reading level
44 through 57 percent = instructional reading level
43 percent or lower = frustration level.

Although Bormuth (1968) and Peterson and Carroll (1974), among others, report that the cloze is useful in the regular classroom for identifying the instructional reading levels of students, other researchers such as Hodges (1972) and Herron (1974) have found the technique to have significant limitations. The author has found that students have a tendency to become impatient with the process and frequently stop trying. This is especially true with poor readers. They satisfy themselves by simply filling in any word that comes to mind. This results in invalid test data.

It should be pointed out that any of the measures discussed are preferable to the common practice of disregarding the instructional reading level in planning students' educational program. Although all the methods delineated within this chapter are simply estimates, they usually provide information that is close enough to students' instructional levels to help in planning individualized instruction.

SUMMARY

Two of the major purposes for diagnostic testing are the identification of those students in a school who are in need of special reading instruction and the identification of functional reading levels. To meet the first of these two purposes, a "sifting" process may be used, begun by testing all students in the school with a standardized reading achievement test to find those significantly retarded in reading ability. Students scoring below the levels for which the test was designed should be retested with a lower-level instrument; those scoring below *this* test should be referred for individual diagnosis.

Although its uses extend beyond this purpose, the basic instrument for the identification of a student's functional reading levels is an informal reading inventory. Special adaptations of an informal reading inventory are useful for quick individual assessment of the instructional reading level and for identification of the instructional reading levels of students within the regular classroom.

RECOMMENDED READINGS

CHEEK, M. C.; and CHEEK, JR., E. H. 1980. *Diagnostic-prescriptive reading instruction: A guide for classroom teachers.* Dubuque, Ia.: Wm. C. Brown, Chapter 4.

EKWALL, E. E. 1976. *Diagnosis and remediation of the disabled reader.* Boston: Allyn & Bacon.

JOHNSON, M. S.; and KRESS, R. A. 1975. *Informal reading inventories.* Reading Aids Series, ed. I. Aaron. Newark, Del.: International Reading Assoc.

GOODMAN, Y. M.; and BURKE, C. 1980. *Reading strategies: Focus on comprehension.* New York: Holt, Rinehart & Winston.

PIKULSKI, J. November 1974. A critical review: Informal reading inventories. *The Reading Teacher* 28: 141–51.

POTTER, T. C.; and RAE, G. 1973. *Informal reading diagnosis: A practical guide for the classroom teacher.* Englewood Cliffs, N.J.: Prentice-Hall, Chapters 6, 7, and 10.

RUPLEY, W. H.; and BLAIR, T. R. 1979. *Reading diagnosis and remediation: A primer for classroom and clinic.* Chicago: Rand McNally, Chapter 7.

WOODS, M. L.; and MOE, A. J. 1977. *Analytic Reading Inventory.* Columbus, Ohio: Charles E. Merrill.

ZINTZ, M. V. 1972. *Corrective reading.* 2nd ed. Dubuque, Ia.: Wm. C. Brown, Chapter 2.

REFERENCES

Baddeley, A. D. 1976. *The Psychology of Memory.* New York: Basic Books.

Betts, E. 1946. *Foundations of reading instruction.* New York: American Book Co., pp. 443–81.

Bormuth, J. R. 1968. The Cloze readability procedure. In *Readability in 1968,* ed. J. R. Bormuth. Research bulletin prepared by a committee of the National Conference on Research in English, pp. 40–47.

Brown, D. A. Spring 1965. Testing poor readers in high school. *Reading Improvement.* 2: 65–66.

Clement, B. W. 1980. *A comparison of standardized group reading test and an informal reading inventory in estimating an instructional reading level.* Published doctoral dissertation, Univ. Northern Colorado.

Cooper, J. L. 1952. *The effect of adjustment of basal reading materials on reading achievement.* Unpublished doctoral dissertation, Boston University.

Ekwall, E. E. 1976. *Diagnosis and remediation of the disabled reader.* Boston: Allyn and Bacon.

Herron, M. J. 1974. *Relationship of scores obtained in two modified Cloze tests to functional reading scores as obtained from a silent IRI with second grade students.* Unpublished specialist practicum, Univ. Northern Colorado.

Hodges, E. J. 1972. *A comparison of the functional reading levels of selected third grade students of varying reading abilities.* Unpublished doctoral dissertation, Univ. Northern Colorado.

Johnson, M. S.; and Kress, R. A. 1965. *Informal reading inventories.* Reading Aid Series, ed. I. Aaron. Newark, Del.: International Reading Assoc.

Killgallon, P. A. 1942. *A study of relationships among certain pupil adjustments in reading situations.* Unpublished doctoral dissertation, Pennsylvania State College.

McCracken, R. A. 1966. *Standard Reading Inventory.* Bellingham, Wash.: Pioneer Printing.

Peterson, J; and Carroll, M. 1974. The Cloze procedure as an indicator of the instructional level for disabled readers. In *Interaction: Research and practice for college-adult reading,* ed. P. L. Nacke. Twenty-third Yearbook of the National Reading Conference, pp. 153–57.

Pikulski, J. J. 1974. A critical review: informal reading inventories. *The Reading Teacher.* 28: 141–51.

Powell, W. R. November 1978. *Measuring reading performance;* ERIC clearinghouse on reading and communication skills, National Council of Teachers of English. ED 155 589

Rinsky, L. A.; and de Fossard, E. 1980. *The Contemporary Classroom Reading Inventory.* Dubuque, Iowa: Gorsuch Scarisbreck Publishers.

Silvaroli, N. 1976. *Classroom reading inventory,* 3rd. ed. Dubuque, Iowa: Wm. C. Brown Co.

Sipay, E. R. January 1964. A comparison of standardized reading scores and functional reading levels. *The Reading Teacher.* 17: 265–68.

Spache, G. D. 1976. *Diagnosing and correcting reading disabilities.* Boston: Allyn and Bacon, Inc.

Sucher, F.; and Allred, R. A. 1973. *Reading placement inventory.* Oklahoma City: The Economy Company.

Woods, M. L.; and Moe, A. J. 1977. *Analytical reading inventory.* Columbus: Charles E. Merrill Publishing Company.

Effective reading diagnosis must include more than investigation of possible causes of reading and learning problems and more than identification of functional reading levels. It should define the reading skills students lack and indicate the skills that should receive topmost instructional priority. Chapter Seven deals with these concerns, reviewing processes of reading-skill diagnosis and measures frequently used for effective diagnosis of reading-skill difficulties.

DIAGNOSTIC PROCEDURES:
Diagnosis
of Reading-skill
Problems

Many poor readers exhibit a "Swiss-cheese effect" in their reading skill development, having some skills beyond their general level of ability and lacking others below that level. Therefore, remediation based simply on students' instructional reading level is ineffective and inefficient. For instruction to be most useful, reading-skill deficiencies need to be identified.

In diagnosing reading-skill difficulties, teachers may begin by looking at information already available. Frequently, much can be learned from scrutiny of students' cumulative file folders, which may include results of achievement tests and mastery tests, scores from criterion-referenced tests, records of daily schoolwork, and anecdotal records (from parents and/or teachers) suggesting areas in which individuals may be having difficulty. All test data and comments should be viewed with caution.

When Ben first came for remedial reading instruction, his mother, herself an experienced teacher, conferred with the clinician who would be working with Ben. She believed she knew Ben's reading skill deficiencies, and argued her view so forcefully that his teacher/clinician began instruction in those areas without doing additional checking. After about two weeks, it became apparent that Ben was not making good progress. His case was discussed in a staff meeting, and the decision was made to do a thorough diagnosis of his reading-skill difficulties. The results contradicted his mother's diagnostic assumptions and showed that Ben's instruction had been proceeding in the wrong direction. The clinician revised her plans and started Ben in different materials, with an almost immediate improvement in his progress.

By observing common-sense safeguards, a teacher can often save valuable time through using information already collected as a beginning step in diagnosis; it is important, however, to verify all such information.

In assessing test scores, a general rule of thumb holds that the longer a test, the more reliable the test scores will be (Ebel, 1965, p. 65). However, in working with poor readers, the opposite can be true. Longer tests tend to be discouraging to poor students, and they may give up without doing their best. For these students, shorter tests seem less forbidding, and disabled readers often give better effort for that reason. Therefore, in assessing the value of previous test scores, be aware that test length and test frustration sometimes produce lower scores than the abilities of the students would indicate.

Also keep in mind that the readability of the test should match the reading ability of the students. If an achievement test intended for students able to read at a tenth-grade equivalency or better is used for students whose instructional reading level is no higher than fourth grade, the results will likely be of little use.

Remember, too, that there is a temptation to record test scores even though they may not be valid. When Louis was tested in the reading center, his performance was surprisingly poor. His teacher was justified in her concern, and followed up the test results to find out why his scores had been so low. She found that Louis's grandmother had died during the week of the testing. Louis had been very fond of her and had spent a great deal of time with her. His poor test performance was closely related to her loss. Upon retesting two or three weeks later, his scores were significantly higher. His first scores would only have been misleading to those who might have used the information later.

Carmen had attended high school in Mexico City. Shortly after coming to this country, she enrolled in high school. Within a few days she was included with other new students in achievement testing. Although she had studied English in Mexico City, her English language mastery was hardly up to the requirements of advanced achievement testing, and understandably, she produced very poor scores. On the basis of those test results, she was referred for intelligence testing for possible placement in a class for mentally retarded students. The psychologist who conducted the mental test realized the reason for her difficulty and was helpful in securing English instruction for Carmen; if he had not recognized her language difficulties and had been unwilling to discount her test scores, Carmen might have been seriously misplaced. In two years—when she graduated from high school—she was doing honors work in mathematics and performing well in her other subjects.

The unquestioned use of standardized tests has always been dangerous. The first use of a "standardized test" is in the Bible in Judges 12:5-7:

> The Gileadites captured the fords of the Jordan leading to Ephraim, and whenever a survivor of Ephraim said, "Let me cross over," the men of Gilead asked him, "Are you an Ephraimite?" If he replied "No," they said, "All right, say 'Shibboleth.' " If he said, "Sibboleth," because he could not pronounce the word correctly, they seized him and killed him at the fords of the Jordan.

This might be called the ultimate in a "final exam"! Although we are not told anything about the test's "norming"or its "reliability" or "validity," it nonetheless had several strengths. It was objective, unbiased by inability to read, and short (meeting one of our previous criteria)—but unfortunately, the test had a high mortality rate!

The use of present-day achievement and intelligence tests without continued caution regarding how the results were produced and how they can properly be interpreted can be almost as disastrous as the test of the Gileadites.

DIAGNOSTIC QUESTIONS

After examining the information available, the teacher should formulate questions to guide the diagnosis of reading-skill problems. If these take the form of formal statements, they may be called "diagnostic hypotheses." However, they are more frequently stated as questions drawn from the background information concerning the student's reading difficulties.

It is possible that after consideration of the information at hand, the teacher/diagnostician may believe he knows all that is necessary to begin a productive corrective or remedial program; he may believe that available data show (1) that the student has no reading skill difficulties, or (2) that the difficulties have already been sufficiently well defined.

More frequently, however, more questions need to be answered. They may be of a relatively broad nature, designed to probe the general area of difficulty, or they may be more specific, used to pinpoint certain skill deficits within some larger, general area.

For example, when Ralph came into the reading center, his accompanying background information was minimal. The clinician's initial diagnostic question was broad: "Which general areas of the reading process cause Ralph the greatest difficulty?" The clinician decided to give an informal reading inventory, not just to identify Ralph's functional reading levels as described in Chapter Six, but to observe and listen to his reading performance and note possible areas of processing difficulties such as low recognition of sight vocabulary, difficulty with applied word analysis skills, poor use of context cues (both syntactic and semantic), inadequate comprehension, and lack of fluency (reflecting difficulties arising from slow word recognition and syntactic-semantic processing).

By contrast, before Jorge's reading teacher met him for the first time, she had already acquired a sizable store of information. First of all, she knew his instructional reading level. Other recorded observations and test results showed that Jorge's comprehension was much better than his attack skills and that he read in a slow word-by-word manner which limited his use of context clues. By the time she met Jorge, the teacher had decided to work on word attack and fluency. She believed that wide reading at the independent level would make his word recognition more automatic and aid his fluency. However, she was unsure which specific attack skills should receive initial priority. Her basic diagnostic question was, "Within the general area of word analysis, which specific word analysis skill does Jorge need to learn (next)?" To find the answer, she used a set of criterion-referenced tests like those in the appendix of this text to identify the areas of primary concentration.

Note that in both cases above, the questions preceded the testing. A good principle of diagnosis is that no test should be given unless it will help answer a question regarding instruction. Administering tests without regard to instructional questions leads to overtesting, creates a poor attitude toward testing on the part of the student, and is a waste of time for the examiner.

THE INFORMAL READING INVENTORY IN SKILLS DIAGNOSIS

In the first example above, Ralph's teacher used an informal reading inventory (IRI) to help identify his reading difficulties. An IRI is a basic diagnostic instrument.

In using the IRI to identify reading-skill difficulties, the diagnostician should be careful to record the student's word recognition performance. If a pretest of word recognition is used, the examiner should record the student's responses to each of the words, marking those called correctly with a check and writing miscalls as accurately as possible. When the student begins reading in the IRI, the examiner should again record reading performance as completely as possible. Although only major errors, as described in the preceding chapter, are used in identifying the functional reading levels, all errors are important in diagnosis and instruction and should be recorded.

INDIVIDUAL DIAGNOSTIC READING TESTS

Like informal reading inventories, individual diagnostic reading tests use reading passages as part of their battery but with notable differences in use and scoring. Such tests include the *Diagnostic Reading Scales, Durrell Analysis of Reading Difficulties, Gates-McKillop Reading Diagnostic Tests, Gilmore Oral Reading Test,* and *Gray Oral Reading Test.*

The *Diagnostic Reading Scales* (Spache, 1972) include word recognition tests, two parallel sets of reading passages ranging from primer through eighth-grade difficulty, and eight tests of word analysis skills. The passages have been well devised and standardized. This test lends itself easily to interpretation by means of informal reading inventory standards, but there is one major caution. Spache rejects the use of those standards and uses the term "instructional reading level" to mean the highest level at which a student can perform successfully while reading orally, and the "independent reading level" to represent the highest level he can read effectively while reading silently.

Certainly the rights of authorship allow a person to declare his position, but it is unfortunate that Spache did not choose to invent different terms for the levels indicated by his test. As it is, he has created confusion for those familiar with the terms as they are applied to an IRI. Many students read better orally than they do silently, and when that is the case, the *Diagnostic Reading Scale* results will, of course, indicate that their independent (silent) reading level is below their instructional (oral) reading level. This cannot happen with an IRI.

Spache's criteria for comprehension are also different from those used with an IRI. He suggests that comprehension for both the independent and instructional levels be a minimum of 60 percent. In short, the *Diagnostic Reading Scales* and its accompanying definitions and criteria provide a means of identifying independent and instructional reading levels only as defined by its author. The terms as used in the test not only pose problems for the test administrator; they also can create difficulties in communicating the results to teachers who are unfamiliar with their meaning.

The newly revised *Durrell Analysis of Reading Difficulty* (Durrell and Catterson, 1980) has eight oral and eight silent reading passages plus eight supplementary passages. Durrell and Catterson include four word lists for testing word recognition and word analysis. One of these lists is for first grade, and three progressively more difficult lists are for grades two through six. The student is given a brief exposure to each word by means of a somewhat awkward hand-held tachistoscope. If the student fails to identify a word correctly, the shutter of the tachistoscope is opened and he is allowed to study and analyze the word.

Additional subtests of the Durrell test include listening comprehension, listening vocabulary, pronunciation of word elements, primary and intermediate visual word memory, identification of sounds in words, phonic spelling, spelling, and two prereading phonics inventories.

The Durrell test has been a standby for years; it was first published in 1937. Although comprehension and word call errors are recorded, the norms for the oral reading selections are based on rate. For silent reading, the student is checked for unaided and prompted recall, but again the norms are based only on rate.

The 1980 revision attempts to equate oral reading (rate) performance with the instructional reading level, and silent reading (rate) performance with the independent reading level. The test manual reports no statistical basis substantiating such an interpretation.

The passages are somewhat short, and the reading difficulty of the selections does not increase evenly from passage to passage, a criticism also applied to earlier editions of the test (Eller and Attea, 1966). When difficulty is estimated by use of the Fry Readability Graph, the passages in the 1980 edition of the *Durrell* are ranked as follows:

Passage	Grade placement indicated in the Durrell manual	Fry Readibility Graph grade levels: Oral passages	Silent passages
1A	1	1.3	1.3
1B	2	1.9	1.4
2A	3	3.1	3.2
2B	4	2.4	2.6
3	5	6.7	6.7
A	6	6.9	6.9
B		7.2	7.2
C		9.2	9.2

Although it is possible for those who differ with Spache on the worth of IRI standards to superimpose those standards on the *Diagnostic Reading Scales* and identify a student's functional reading levels, this is impossible with the Durrell test. The irregularity of passage difficulty would produce inaccurate indications of the student's reading ability.

The test is particularly limited at first- and second-grade levels. The first- and second-grade levels usually include pre-primer[1], pre-primer[2], pre-primer[3], primer, 1^2, 2^1, and 2^2. Only two paragraphs are available to measure pre-primer through 2^2 reading levels and these are incorrectly identified as to their readability. This makes it difficult to estimate the placement of students who are seriously limited in their ability.

Throughout the *Durrell Analysis of Reading Difficulty* there are checklists which help guide the observations of the examiner. The checklists seem to be especially useful to teachers who are just beginning to work in diagnosis. Despite its limitations, the *Durrell* can be useful. It gives the most varied set of subtests of any instrument of this sort, and comparison between subtests can often provide insight regarding a student's reading performance.

No one is likely to use all the subtests of the Durrell test, and it is also likely that after some experience, a teacher will permanently discard several of them. Nevertheless, the author has used the test as often as any instrument and has gained much from its use.

The *Gates-McKillop Reading Diagnostic Tests* (1962) are published in parallel forms. They include an interesting oral reading test consisting of a continuous story which increases in difficulty as the student progresses through the levels. There is a word recognition test in which the words are first presented for one-half second each and later presented without a time limit. A second word list may be used for the untimed presentation, if preferred. Other tests involve phrase recognition, blending word parts, giving letter sounds, naming capitals, naming lowercase letters, association of sounds with nonsense words, association of initial letters with spoken words, association of ending letters with spoken words, association of medial vowels with a sound in a spoken word, auditory blending of word parts given orally, spelling ability, vocabulary (used to indicate reading capacity), syllabication, and auditory discrimination.

The nature of the continuous story for the oral reading test makes it necessary for everyone to begin at the lowest level. The story is somewhat brief and inappropriate for older students. Because the story is continuous, very poor readers are aware that they have been unable to complete the test owing to their poor performance. There are no questions over the material read, and performance is judged solely on the basis of the number of errors made. Neither is there any measure of silent reading ability.

A review of the test shows that some of the subtests do not appear to measure what they are said to measure, and the norms seem to be questionable or arbitrary. Nevertheless, the *Gates McKillop* is a usable test. As with the *Durrell*, no one is likely to use all parts of the test, but after becoming familiar with the instrument, the user will find several of the subtests valuable in providing insights into the reading difficulties of elementary students.

The *Gilmore Oral Reading Test* (1968) has four forms, each having ten passages ranging in difficulty from pre-primer through eighth grade. Reading performance is judged in terms of rate, word call accuracy, and comprehension. Peculiarities in marking and scoring limit the degree to which results on the *Gilmore* can be generalized. Rate is recorded as slow, average, or fast. Comprehension is based on the student's ability to recall details. Guidelines for marking word call accuracy differ from those commonly used by others. The differences are so significant they are likely to influence test results and make comparison of scores with other tests unwise.

The *Gilmore* is well standardized and, although the selections do not seem as carefully graded in terms of readability as are the *Diagnostic Reading Scales*, they are much more usable than other tests of this sort. This means it is possible to substitute other criteria for those of the authors if the examiner wishes to do so.

The *Gray Oral Reading Test* (1967) is available in four parallel forms, each one containing thirteen passages ranging in difficulty from first grade to college level. Reading grade placement is based on rate and word call errors. Although questions are included, comprehension is not used in judging grade level. As may be inferred from the title, silent reading is not tested. Separate norms are included for boys and girls.

The passages are brief, and reading difficulty appears to be increased by the use of a rather esoteric vocabulary. The lower levels are overly simple in nature, limiting the use of the test for older students at those levels. It is possible to use the paragraphs very well, however, for students who can read above the fifth selection. In using the test with older atypical populations in adult learning centers and in penitentiaries, the author has followed the practice of granting credit for the first four or five selections if the reader can read acceptably above that level and continue with the higher-level passages of the test. There is a distinct advantage to the test at the upper levels: The vocabulary is so advanced that readers do not feel denigrated by being asked to read from it, provided they have not been exposed to the first few passages. The author has found it necessary to prepare readers for the fact that the upper levels of the test will be difficult. Hearing that the upper portions of the test contain college-level materials does not seem to disturb older readers in particular. When the material begins to be too difficult for them to read easily, they accept their poorer performance with equanimity, realizing that they have been trying to read very difficult material.

Needless to say, extremely disabled readers do not reap this advantage. The test is not a good one for older students reading at first- or second-grade level.

The test includes a chart for classifying word call errors; types of errors listed are words aided, gross mispronunciations, partial mispronunciations, omissions, insertions, substitutions, repetitions, and word-order inversions.

Although the test lacks the subtests commonly included in some other inventories, the *Gray* is a good test. Its most serious limitations are the lack of a silent reading measure and the fact that comprehension is not figured into the reading grade scores.

MISCUE ANALYSIS

Diagnosis of word recognition errors has recently been aided by the techniques of "miscue analysis." As discussed earlier in this text, current theories tend to view reading as a process by which an individual utilizes language-represented-in-print as cues to obtain meaning.

Kenneth Goodman was one of the first to develop and study a psycholinguistic theory of reading. Oral reading errors were renamed "miscues" by Goodman (Goodman and Burke, 1968) to emphasize that readers use language-in-print as cues to help gain meaning.

Goodman views reading as the interaction of the reader with the text using strategies of *sampling, predicting, confirming,* and *correcting* in order to construct meaning. The reader, according to Goodman, processes "graphophonic," syntactic, and semantic cues simultaneously as he *predicts* meaning based on what he has already *sampled* from his reading, *confirms* that prediction, and *corrects* as necessary in order to accurately construct meaning (Goodman and Goodman, 1978; K. Goodman, 1976). He further suggests that "the reading process involves visual, perceptual, syntactic, and semantic cycles, each interlocking" (Goodman and Gollasch, 1980, p. 10).

The Goodman view, first given form in the 1960s, has added richly to our understanding of the nature of reading. The use of the term "miscue" rather than "error" seems justified in cases in which it is necessary to remind the reading teacher that not all errors interfere with the effort toward meaning; not all word call errors are of equal gravity. Surely it is less serious for a student to miscall the word *horse* as "pony" than "house," or, worse yet, as "bag."

Goodman developed a complex procedure for the analysis of different kinds of miscues (K. Goodman, 1969) which was later modified and simplified by Yetta Goodman and Carolyn Burke in the *Reading Miscue Inventory* (RMI) (1972). Basic procedures in miscue analysis outlined by K. Goodman (1973) may be summarized as follows:

1. A reading passage providing a continuity of meaning is selected for the reader. The selection must be somewhat difficult and long enough to generate a minimum of 25 miscues.
2. The selection is retyped and each line is numbered to correspond with the appropriate page and line from the original text, to be used as a code sheet for recording miscues.
3. The reader is informed that the reading will be unaided and that he will be asked to retell the story after he has finished reading. The code sheet is marked as the reader reads the selection. The reading and retelling are tape recorded for future reference.
4. The reader is permitted to retell the story without interruption. Following the unaided retelling, the reader is asked probing questions designed to explore areas omitted in the retelling.
5. The miscues are coded.
6. Miscue patterns are studied, interpreted, and translated into instruction.

(Wixson, 1979, p. 164)

The miscues are categorized on the basis of the following nine questions in the *Reading Miscue Inventory:*

1. Dialect. Is a dialect variation involved in the miscue?
2. Graphic Similarity. How much does the miscue look like what was expected?

3. Sound Similarity. How much does the miscue sound like what was expected?
4. Intonation. Is a shift in intonation involved?
5. Grammatical Function. Is the grammatical function of the miscue the same as the grammatical function of the word in the text?
6. Correction. Is the miscue corrected?
7. Grammatical Acceptability. Does the miscue occur in a structure which is grammatically acceptable?
8. Semantic Acceptability. Does the miscue occur in a structure which is semantically acceptable?
9. Meaning Change. Does the miscue result in a change of meaning?
(Y. Goodman and Burke, 1972, pp. 49–50)

The reader's comprehension is evaluated not only in terms of the analysis above but also through a retelling procedure. A "retelling score" is derived from an analysis of the student's retelling of the passage. After the reader initially reports what he has read, the examiner probes him with general questions concerning parts of the reading the reader may not have included in the initial retelling. The student's recall of the story is then analyzed, and points assigned to main ideas in the story are credited to the student if he has recalled them. Complete directions for the procedure are available in the manual for the *Reading Miscue Inventory* (Y. Goodman and Burke, 1972).

The Goodman psycholinguistic view faces several objections despite the significant contribution it has made to understanding the nature of reading. Recent theory and research (Baddeley, 1976) raises questions relative to the rationale for dividing semantic and syntactic domains. Cognitive psychologists have begun to favor a more unitary system with differentiation more likely due to depth of processing and richness of coding (Lockhart, Craik, and Jacobi, 1976). Other objections relate to the practice of having the reader read material for analysis that is "somewhat difficult." It seems likely that rather than providing "a window on the reading process" (Goodman and Goodman, 1977), it may provide an example of reading that is not likely to be typical for the student.

It also seems unfortunate that the miscue analysis procedure relies so heavily on the presumption that oral reading can disclose the reader's basic competence and provide a view of the psycholinguistic factors that have generated that competence. Silent reading would appear to provide more time for contemplation without interference from either oral production of the written material or from an examiner's interaction with the student regarding reading performance. Silent reading seems particularly suited for the deeper, more thoughtful reading involved in higher-level comprehension. It seems likely that oral reading cannot mirror inner cognitive processes without reference to silent reading.

A practical objection to the reading miscue analysis procedure lies in its length and complexity. Although the procedure may provide valuable insights into the reading behavior of some students, the fact that it is time-consuming limits its practicality for regular use as a diagnostic instrument in the classroom or school reading center. In addition, the complicated nature of the process makes it important for the potential user to obtain careful instruction in its application. Presently, analysis tends to vary significantly from examiner to examiner because interpretation is inconsistent.

Despite the fact that miscue analysis has created a greater awareness that reading is part of the communication process, (Wixson, 1979, p. 172) concludes that

> the exact nature of the relationship between oral reading errors, as analyzed by standard miscue analysis procedures, and the reading process remains unclear. Further, it is unknown whether miscue analysis succeeds in identifying the critical features of readers' oral reading performance which reveal their relative proficiency with the reading process.

It seems reasonable to assume that miscue analysis is more valuable as a research tool than as an instrument for reading teachers and reading specialists to use for the analysis of reading difficulties. Modifications of the procedure, based on additional empirical research, may make it more useful for teachers in the future.

THE DIAGNOSTIC READING TEST BATTERY

The author has attempted to create a reading test battery which combines the advantages of a complete informal reading inventory, criterion-referenced reading skills tests, and interpretation in line with current psycholinguistic research. (The *Diagnostic Reading Test Battery* is included in the appendix for free duplication and use.) Although it is probably as dangerous for an author to try to describe his own test as to objectively describe his own children, the attempt seems necessary. The *Diagnostic Reading Test Battery* (DRTB) is basically an informal reading inventory with an accompanying set of criterion-referenced tests. A cover sheet provides for easy collection of student identification data and for a diagnostic profile. The next page is for comments regarding the student's referral and significant areas of the student's background which the author has found useful in over twenty years of diagnosing and treating reading difficulties.

The next section of the test is a word recognition list containing words representing reading levels from pre-primer through college. This test provides the examiner with an opportunity to observe how well the student may recognize words in isolation—using only visual and phonemic areas of recognition. The list is also used to indicate a starting level for the oral reading portion of the DRTB.

Preceding the oral IRI is Table 1, used to identify functional reading levels as indicated by word call and comprehension errors in oral reading, and the DRTB Analysis of Errors and Miscues (Figure 7-1). Patterns of errors and miscues are more easily identified by using such a form. The first half of the analysis relates to common IRI word recognition errors. The second half provides an opportunity to

Did the reader self-correct?	
Did it sound much like the word in print?	
Did it resemble the word in print?	
Did it fit the sentence structure? Syntax	
Did it maintain meaning? Semantic	
Was it due to dialect?	
Was it a block, pronounced by examiner?	
Was it an addition?	
Was it an omission?	
Was it a transposition of words?	
Was it a mispronunciation?	
Was it a substitution?	

Informal reading inventory analysis of miscues and errors Name: _____	Reading level	Word in print	Error or miscue

Figure 7-1. Form for the Analysis of Errors and Miscues

analyze the errors or miscues from a psycholinguistic frame. The user should bear in mind that semantic and syntactic processing may well represent different levels of processing within the same domain of cognition.

It is generally more valuable to analyze the errors made at lower levels than at the frustration level, because material at the point of frustration is often read in a manner not typical of a reader's ordinary reading style.

The examiner should enter the reading level of the passage on the left in Figure 7-1. He should then list the words the student miscalled as they appear in print and then write the words as the student pronounced them under "Error or Miscue." To the right, the teacher should complete the analysis by answering the question at the top of each column. Areas of serious difficulty can be identified either through calculating the proportion of errors represented under each column, or by visual estimation.

The oral reading inventory passages range from pre-primer through college level. There are questions for each passage, and there is a place to record reading time, errors, and comprehension.

The passages were written for general interest, following a narrative style up to level 2^1. From level 2^2, they follow a social studies/science orientation. The questions were designed to mirror the increase in difficulty, with the upper levels requiring some ability to use inference. Although the vocabulary increases substantially in difficulty, an attempt was made to increase difficulty through concept difficulty as well.

A very brief silent reading checklist precedes the silent IRI. The same principles of construction were followed for the silent reading passages as for the oral. Reading difficulty was controlled through several steps. First, a core vocabulary was developed from words used at various levels in at least three of five leading basal readers, deleting words viewed as being childish. Various passages were written at each reading level, with an attempt to match the level of reading materials used at that level. Next, the Fry Readability Graph was used to evaluate the readability of each passage, and rewriting was done as necessary to match the reading levels. Students were then asked to read the passages and answer the questions to verify further that the selections increased in difficulty from passage to passage. The latter step was not an attempt to gather normative data but simply to provide further information as to whether the passages represented the anticipated levels by ranking them in overall difficulty. Four of the passages required additional work before they passed all tests.

Tables 2 and 3 present the levels of expected fluency for readers with ability between pre-primer and seventh grade (Table 2) and expected silent reading rate for students through the college level. Fluency and rate are highly variable, and the standards should be used only for a general indication of the student's ability.

At the end of the *Diagnostic Reading Test Battery* is a collection of criterion-referenced tests of word recognition skills. The nineteen subtests range in difficulty from readiness through approximately third grade in difficulty. Areas tested include visual discrimination of letters, visual discrimination of words, auditory discrimination of word beginnings, auditory discrimination of word endings, spoken context with initial letters, initial sight vocabulary, initial consonant sounds, final consonant sounds, final silent "e" rule, "r"-controlled vowels, "l"- and "w"-controlled vowels, vowel digraphs, hard and soft "c" and "g" diphthongs, open first-syllable rule, and closed first-syllable rule.

The tests included are certainly not all-inclusive, but they serve to test areas important in an analysis of phonic attack skills. Other tests may easily be added if a teacher believes they are necessary. A summary chart precedes the criterion-referenced tests and may be used to collect the data for a better look at the student's comparative strengths and weaknesses.

There are a number of other tests for use in individual skills diagnosis which do not include passages for the student to read. These include the *Botel Reading Inventory, Peabody Individual Achievement* Tests (PIAT), Roswell-Chall *Diagnostic Reading Test of Word Analysis Skills, Slosson Oral Reading Test* (SORT), *Wide Range Achievement Test* (WRAT), and the *Woodcock Reading Mastery Tests*. There is significant individual variability among the tests, and the potential user should review them carefully before choosing those compatible with his needs. In general, it seems unlikely that a complete and reliable diagnosis of reading ability can be made without having some knowledge of how the student may perform when reading running script. Nevertheless, some of the tests mentioned are widely used and can provide useful data on the ability of students within certain limitations.

The *Botel Reading Inventory* (1978) has two forms. It is basically a group test, but includes an individually administered word recognition test ranging in difficulty from pre-primer through fourth grade. The group test includes measures of phonics, word opposites (listening), and a phonemic inventory. The inventory is well made and is a useful test in estimating approximate instructional levels, although it should not be considered a thorough diagnostic instrument for individual work.

The *Peabody Individual Achievement Test* (PIAT) (1970) is an individual test of mathematics, reading recognition, reading comprehension, spelling, and general information. The reading recognition subtest is basically a test of letter and word recognition. It functions as a test of word attack only for those words students may not already have in their reading vocabulary. The authors suggest fourth-grade difficulty as the upper limit for its use. In the test of reading comprehension, the student reads a sentence and then selects one of four illustrations which represent that sentence. The test seems to provide reasonably reliable information about a student's reading comprehension, and a skillful teacher can usually gather more information than the authors intended by observing the student's word attack while reading the sentences.

The Roswell-Chall *Diagnostic Reading Test of Word Analysis Skills* (1959) is a quick test of word analysis skills. Five subtests are designed to measure recognition of consonants and consonant digraphs, short vowels, the final silent "e" rule, vowel combinations, and words with multiple syllables. The results may be somewhat questionable for students above third-grade level ability due to the likelihood that they have learned some of the words used in the test and do not need to employ the skills being tested in order to recognize the words.

The *Slosson Oral Reading Test* (SORT) (1963) is, despite its name, not a test of ordinary oral reading but is composed of word lists ranging in difficulty to the high school level. The total number of words read is converted into a grade placement score. There is no measure of comprehension. The best use of the test may be to indicate a starting level for more intensive reading tests.

The *Wide Range Achievement Test* (WRAT) (1978) contains measures of spelling and mathematical computation as well as reading. Level I is for ages 5 to 11 and Level II is for ages 12 to adult. The reading test, like that of the SORT, is basically a word recognition test. That the WRAT is a "wide-range" instrument is evident by the fact that the two levels attempt to measure abilities ranging from kindergarten through college. The inadequacy of the test to discriminate meaningfully between levels of college reading ability by testing word recognition seems obvious. Since the test only measures an individual's ability to pronounce multisyllabic words without any check on comprehension, it can easily misplace a good, fast word analyzer as an able college reader. The WRAT, like the SORT, is probably best used as a screening device and then only at lower levels.

The *Woodcock Reading Mastery Tests* (1974) consist of five subtests measuring letter knowledge, word recognition, word attack as measured by ability to handle nonsense words, vocabulary meaning and comprehension measured through a modified cloze technique. Harris and Sipay (1980, p. 188) report that although it has some limited value "Cloze tests do not closely approximate the functional reading levels. . ."

The *Woodcock-Johnson Psycho-Educational Battery* (1979) is described in the manual as able to identify the instructional reading level and to indicate student potential as well as to measure the areas tested by the *Woodcock Reading Mastery Tests* described above. Although the test is new, the reading cluster is much like that described in the previous test. Button's (1980) research indicates that this test fails to identify the instructional reading level in the majority of cases and that the upper levels of the test are more discrepant than the lower levels.

CRITERION-REFERENCED TESTS USED IN SKILLS DIAGNOSIS

As already discussed relative to informal reading inventories, criterion-referenced tests provide a specific and useful means for identifying reading difficulties. A skill is defined or an objective is identified, samples of reading requiring the exercise of that skill are gathered, and a criterion level is agreed upon as indicating a reader's mastery of that skill as he deals with the samples.

With CRTs for various skills such as word attack or use of context clues, criterion levels tend to be more arbitrary than with IRI levels because there is usually no research to indicate the level of mastery. In order to test a certain student's mastery, the examiner might present him with a sample of ten initial consonant blends and ask the student to identify them. If he does so with 90 percent accuracy, we would likely presume that he had mastered that particular skill, yet no one really knows on the basis of research that 90 percent accuracy represents mastery in the case of that particular reading skill. In fact, a stronger argument could be made logically for the position that only 100 percent would be an indication of mastery and then only if the items on the test were a perfect representation of the total possible number of consonant blends. Nevertheless, there is general agreement to accept a lower mark as representative of mastery—usually 90 percent.

Regardless of the difficulty in determining acceptable performance levels, criterion-referenced tests have proved to be more valuable to the teacher and diagnostician than norm-referenced measures. A norm-referenced test for word analysis skills would let a teacher know how a student may compare in ranking with other students in the norming sample and presumably with other students in general, but the teacher would not know which word analysis skills the student had mastered and which he still should be taught. A CRT, on the other hand, would allow the teacher to identify which word analysis skills had been mastered and which should still be the object of instruction. Obviously, the latter is of greater benefit to a teacher.

Criterion-referenced tests, such as those included in the appendix, may be made by a teacher or purchased from publishers. Many state departments of education also make them available.

Several publishers have developed reading management systems that make use of criterion-referenced tests. These include the *Wisconsin Design for Reading Skill Development, Individually Prescribed Instruction,* and *Fountain Valley Teacher Support System in Reading.* A management system usually involves (1) the division of reading into dozens or even hundreds of specific instructional objectives, (2) pretesting with CRTs to identify objectives students have not yet achieved, (3) instruction, most frequently through assigned skill work, to achieve mastery of the skill in order to achieve the objective, and (4) post-testing with a CRT to assess mastery.

Reading systems management approaches have been criticized as fractionating the act of reading into splinter skills not necessary for learning to read, and for making the teacher more of an examiner and recordkeeper than an instructor. When a student's total reading program is organized in such a fashion, it seems likely that comprehension and enjoyment of reading will be adversely affected. A better solution is likely to be the use of CRTs only to answer questions the teacher may raise when a student's reading progress begins to falter.

To summarize, in order to find reading-skill difficulties a teacher should begin by gathering enough background information to formulate questions to guide diagnostic testing. The information may already be available in the student's records or may be gained from the student, his teachers, or his parents.

Background information will often indicate general areas of weakness; occasionally, it will indicate specific problems. If background information is general—or specific but unreliable—the teacher may decide to administer an informal reading inventory to answer questions related to the student's functional reading levels and to help define general areas of skill difficulty.

By use of word recognition and miscue analysis, the teacher is able to "squeeze" the IRI for additional information. If greater specificity is needed, criterion-referenced tests can be used to pinpoint the areas of difficulty.

DIAGNOSIS THROUGH STUDENT OBSERVATION

Many teachers prefer to begin instruction as soon as possible after initial diagnosis has defined the scope of remediation within reasonable bounds. There are at least two distinct advantages to this. First, it gives the student a feeling of accomplishment to start his instructional program quickly.

A few years ago, a high school student who had just begun attending a summer reading clinic stopped by to see the author. He soon came to the point of his visit: "This is my fifth day in the reading center, and I've been wondering how long it will be before we start working on my reading." His clinician had been working to establish rapport and complete a thorough diagnosis. After five days, the student was eager to get started on what he saw as the purpose of his attendance, reading improvement. So far he had had nothing but testing and talking.

A second advantage to beginning instruction quickly is that it allows the teacher to observe—and diagnose—the student's reading difficulties in an actual instructional situation. Students sometimes behave differently when they are being tested than they do under instruction, and valuable insights can be gained from observation under instructional conditions. It is axiomatic to say that diagnostic observation should continue throughout the student's remedial program. In order to make best use of these observations, the teacher should use some sort of checklist or "accounting sheet" such as that shown in Figure 7-2.

The students' names for each period, class, or group should be listed down the left-hand side. Across the top are listed common reading difficulties that might be observed. Although the listing has been filled in on Figure 7-2, the teacher should replace the headings with those appropriate for the level of the group with which he is working. A lower-level group might include various aspects of reading readiness among the listings, while a more advanced group might not have any readiness factors listed.

A checklist such as that shown in Figure 7-2 permits a teacher to make quick diagnostic notations, and it is important to record observations at the time they are made. The palest ink is better than the brightest memory. When working with a student, there is a temptation to postpone recording insights into his difficulties, and when they are postponed, they are often forgotten.

To further the likelihood that observations will be recorded, the checklist

Areas of Needed Instruction

COMPREHENSION	Noting Details												
	Main Idea												
	Fact vs. Fiction												
	Evaluation of Stories												
	Making Judgments												
	Inferred Meanings												
CONTEXT	FLUENCY												
	W/Initial Vowel Cues												
	Words of Varied Meanings												
	Meaning of Homonyms												
WORD ANALYSIS	Word Families												
	Word Families												
	Word Families												
	Word Families												
	sh as in "tion"												
	ou, ow												
	ie, oa, oo												
	ee,ea												
	ai, ay												
	Two Vowels Together Rule												
	Silent e Rule												
	Short vowels												
	Long vowels												
	SIGHT VOCABULARY												

**Diagnostic-Prescriptive
Student Accounting
Record Sheet**

Don A. Brown

LEVEL III

Students' Names

Figure 7-2. Diagnostic-Prescriptive Accounting Sheet

should be kept readily at hand—perhaps on the back cover of the daily lesson plan book or on a clipboard used regularly in instruction.

Diagnosis during instruction helps to verify, alter, or sometimes completely redirect initial diagnostic findings. An example of this occurred when Buddy entered the Reading Center. He was 14 years old, small for his age, and ready to begin the eighth grade when his parents decided to bring him to the reading center from 200 miles away. They made arrangements for him to stay with friends while he attended the center to work on his primer-level reading abilities. His clinician, a man, gave Buddy an interest inventory during his first day of regular attendance. He wasn't surprised to find that despite Buddy's slight build, he seemed to be most interested in football and wrestling. Together they mapped out an interest unit capitalizing on these.

After two weeks, the absolute failure of the unit to arouse Buddy's interest baffled and frustrated his clinician. Laying his plans aside, the clinician took Buddy for a walk. As they walked and talked, Buddy picked up a leaf and pointed out its peculiar structure. The clinician grasped the clue and soon had Buddy talking freely about various trees, leaves, and flowers. They returned to the center and started work on a new interest unit built around this subject. Buddy became engrossed in the topic and began to make progress in his reading program.

Why had he not told his clinician his interest before? Buddy had left his home and familiar surroundings to be transplanted into an unknown city. He undoubtedly felt small and vulnerable. He had given the clinician signals of his manliness by declaring himself interested in wrestling and football, although his real interests lay in flowers and trees. It was a compliment to his clinician that Buddy soon found it unnecessary to maintain his facade and could allow his true interests to surface.

Faulty information is not limited to open-response inventories. Tests given in initial testing may contain misleading information, as mentioned in an earlier chapter. In the daily diagnosis that should accompany all regular instruction, it is likely that some elements of the initial diagnosis will be found to be incorrect. The teacher should always be willing to adjust to the findings.

SUMMARY

Reading diagnosis must consist of more than the identification of a student's functional reading levels. It should also indicate the reading skills that need instructional attention. Some clues to students' needs may be included in their records, although such information should never be assumed to be accurate unless it can be verified. Poor test records can be due to frustration with long tests, tests improperly matched to individual reading ability, and test results that have been recorded even though they should have been invalidated because of factors affecting ability to perform.

After receiving a student's background information, the diagnostician should form questions to direct the investigation of reading problems. An informal reading inventory or any of several diagnostic reading tests will usually provide answers concerning the general areas of difficulty. By analysis of the errors and miscues, a diagnostician is able to gain additional information concerning the types of mistakes the reader has made and the reasons he has made them. The use of criterion-referenced tests of specific reading skills can provide more specific identification where needed.

RECOMMENDED READINGS

BOND, G.; TINKER, M.; and WASSON, B. 1979. *Reading difficulties: Their diagnosis and correction.* Englewood Cliffs, N.J.: Prentice-Hall, Chapter 7.

CHEEK, M. C.; and CHEEK, E. H. 1980. *Diagnostic-prescriptive reading instruction: A guide for classroom teachers.* Dubuque, Ia.: Wm. C. Brown, Chapters 4 and 5.

EKWALL, E. E. 1976. *Diagnosis and remediation of the disabled reader.* Boston: Allyn & Bacon, Chapters 4a, 5a, and 9a.

RUPLEY, W. H.; and BLAIR, T. R. 1979. *Reading diagnosis and remediation: A primer for classroom and clinic.* Chicago: Rand McNally, Chapter 7.

SPACHE, G. D. 1976. *Diagnosing and correcting reading disabilities.* Boston: Allyn & Bacon, Chapter 7.

REFERENCES

Baddeley, A. D. 1976. *The psychology of memory.* New York: Basic Books.

Botel, M. 1978. *Botel Reading Inventory.* Chicago: Follett.

Button, L. 1980. *Standardized reading test scores and informal reading inventory results with modified miscue analysis for above and below average third grade students: A comparison.* Unpublished doctoral dissertation, Univ. Northern Colorado.

Dunn, L. M.; and Markwardt, F. C. 1970. *Peabody Individual Achievement Test.* Circle Pines, Minn.: American Guidance Service.

Durrell, D. D.; and Catterson, J. 1980. *Durrell analysis of reading difficulty.* New York: Harcourt Brace Jovanovich.

Ebel, T. L. 1965. *Measuring educational achievement.* Englewood Cliffs, N.J.: Prentice-Hall.

Eller, W.; and Attea, M. 1966. Three diagnostic tests: some comparisons in *Vistas in Reading* (ed.) J. Figurel. Newark, Delaware: International Reading Association.

Gates, A. I.; and McKillop, A. S. 1962. *Gates-McKillop Reading Diagnostic Tests.* New York: Teachers College Press.

Gilmore, J. V.; and Gilmore, E. C. 1965 *Gilmore Oral Reading Test.* New York: Harcourt Brace Jovanovich.

Goodman, K. S. 1969. Analysis of oral reading miscues: Applied psycholinguistics. *Reading Research Quarterly.* 5: 9-30.

Goodman, K. S. 1973. Miscues: Windows on the reading process. In *Miscue analysis: Applications to reading instruction,* ed. K. S. Goodman. Urbana, Ill.: ERIC Clearinghouse on Reading and Communication Skills, National Council of Teachers of English.

———. 1976. What we know about reading. In *Findings of Research in Miscue Analysis: Classroom Implications*, ed. P. D. Allen and D. J. Watson. Urbana, Ill.: ERIC Clearinghouse on Reading and Communication Skills, National Institute of Education.

Goodman, K. S.; and Burke, C. L. 1968. *Study of children's behavior while reading orally.* Final Report, Project No. S. 425. U.S. Dept. of Health, Education & Welfare.

Goodman, K. S.; and Gollasch, F. V. 1980. Word omissions: Deliberate and non-deliberate. *Reading Research Quarterly* 16: 6–31.

Goodman, K. S.; and Goodman, Y. M. 1977. Learning about psycholinguistic processes by analyzing oral reading. *Harvard Educational Review* 47: 317–33.

———. August 1978. *Reading of American children whose language is a stable rural dialect of English or a language other than English.* Final Report, Project NIE-C-00-3-0087. Washington, D.C.: U.S. Dept. of Health, Education & Welfare, National Institute of Education.

Goodman, Y. M.; and Burke, C. 1972. *Reading Miscue Inventory.* New York: Macmillan.

Gray, W. S.; and Robinson, H. M; eds. 1967. *Gray Oral Reading Test.* Indianapolis: Bobbs-Merrill.

Harris, A. J.; and Sipay, E. R. 1980. *How to increase reading ability.* 7th ed. New York: Longman.

Jastak, J. F.; and Jastak, S. R. 1978. *Wide Range Achievement Test.* Wilmington: Guidance Associates of Delaware.

Lockhart, R. S.; Craik, F. I. M.; and Jacobi, L. 1976. Depth of processing, recognition and recall. In *Recall and recognition*, ed. J. Brown. London: Wiley.

MacGinitie, W. H. 1973. An introduction to some measurement problems in reading. In *Assessment Problems in Reading*, ed. W. H. MacGinitie. Newark, Del.: International Reading Assoc.

McCracken, R. A. 1966. *Standard Reading Inventory.* Bellingham, Wash.: Pioneer Printing.

Roswell, F. G.; and Chall, J. S. 1959. *Roswell-Chall Diagnostic Test of Word Analysis Skills.* New York: Essay Press.

Silvaroli, N. J. 1973. *Classroom Reading Inventory.* Dubuque, Ia.: Wm. C. Brown.

Slosson, R. L. 1963. *Slosson Oral Reading Test.* East Aurora, N.Y.: Slosson Educational Publications.

Spache, G. D. 1972. *Diagnostic Reading Scales,* Monterey, Cal: California Test Bureau.

———. 1976. *Diagnosing and correcting reading disabilities.* Boston: Allyn & Bacon.

Sucher, F.; and Allred, F. 1973. *Reading Placement Inventory,* Oklahoma City: Economy Co.

Wixson, K. L. 1979. Miscue analysis: A critical review. *Journal of Reading Behavior* 11: 163–75.

Woodcock, R. W. 1974. *Woodcock Reading Mastery Tests.* Circle Pine, Minn: American Guidance Service.

Woodcock, R. W.; and Johnson, M. B. 1979. *Woodcock-Johnson Psycho-Educational Battery.* Circle Pine, Minn.: American Guidance Service.

The keystone to an effective diagnosis is the identification of a student's functional reading levels and reading-skill difficulties. For some students, however, a diagnosis limited to these two concerns is not enough to provide for a good remedial program. Some students have other factors to be considered—factors which interfere with their ability to make good progress in learning to read.

In this chapter we examine conditions that make it difficult for a student to make satisfactory gains in reading ability, and discuss how those conditions may be identified.

DIAGNOSTIC PROCEDURES:
Diagnosis
of
Inhibiting Factors

It is not important to investigate the cause of each student's reading difficulty. A diagnosis that indicates functional reading levels and identifies the reading skills the student needs to learn is usually all that is necessary to plan an effective program of instruction. Some students, however, have factors that inhibit their ability to improve their reading skills. Sometimes these are the same factors that caused their problems originally; sometimes they are new, different, or compounded factors.

As a teacher begins to work with a student, it may not be apparent at first that there are factors that impede reading improvement. At other times, the referral indicates a reading disability so severe that it seems likely from the first contact that the diagnosis should include the examination of possible inhibiting factors. Because unnecessary testing is wasteful, a teacher should look for inhibiting factors only if there is some indication that the student is unlikely to make good progress under ordinary well-planned instruction. There is no benefit in the identification of causative factors if they no longer limit the student's ability to improve reading.

Often, the only way to find out whether there are other elements in a student's situation that adversely affect his learning is by beginning a good instructional program and watching his response. It is usually possible within two or three weeks to determine whether the student appears to be making expected progress. If progress is good, the teacher has saved the time that otherwise would have been expended on diagnosis of inhibiting factors; if progress is poor, the teacher should begin to investigate possible influences affecting the student's learning.

STEP 1. REVIEWING BACKGROUND INFORMATION

After deciding that diagnosis of possible impeding factors is needed, the teacher should review what is known about the student. This should include an open-minded look at all possible pertinent information. Freud, in coaching his students in the art of diagnosis, suggested that they assume nothing as they began, thus avoiding the pitfall of predetermining the causes of patients' difficulties. The same advice applies to reading diagnosis. In looking at each new case, it is important that teachers not allow their perceptions to be colored by experiences or circumstances that are not applicable to the student under consideration. If, for example, the teacher has found three students in the last two days who have reading problems caused by cultural factors and poor first-grade instruction, there may be a natural tendency to look for evidence in the next diagnosis that would prove similar causes. Such a predisposition may cause the teacher to overlook important factors. The approach to each diagnosis should be as open and unbiased as it is thorough and well-organized.

Prenatal, Birth, and Early Childhood   In reviewing the available information, the teacher may want to examine prenatal, birth, and early childhood development factors. Recent research indicates that alcohol, caffeine, and nicotine taken into the system of expectant mothers may have the effect of slowing the child's ability to learn (Noble, 1978). Premature births, breech births, and anoxia at birth are among conditions that tend to be associated with reading difficulties during school years, although the precise reasons are not always clear. It seems possible that premature birth might cause a child to be less well-developed as he begins school, whereas breech births and oxygen starvation at birth may result in brain tissue loss in areas important in learning to read. Approximately 10 percent more reading-disabled students appear to have had difficulty with anoxia at birth (Kawi and Pasamanick, 1958).

In addition, seriously elevated temperatures maintained for a significant period of time may also produce injury to delicate tissues of the brain. Small children frequently run a fever up to 106 degrees F. without any apparent serious consequences, but the higher the fever and the longer its duration, the more likely that its effects may be harmful.

When a child falls and hits his head, the parent is usually greatly concerned and may report the occurrence to the reading diagnostician trying to locate the cause for later reading difficulties. Although, as with fevers, similar levels of severity often seem to produce different results, the best means of determining the seriousness of such an incident is through the family physician's reaction, if it is possible for the teacher to check this source.

There are hundreds of different circumstances that may be reported or available to a diagnostician. It may be impossible to determine whether a particular incident may have contributed to a student's reading difficulty. Depending on the severity of the student's difficulty, he may need to be referred for medical examination and possible treatment to maximize the ability to concentrate and learn. Sometimes no treatment is possible, but at other times carefully supervised medication can help to curb the effects of central nervous system damage so the student has an improved chance of being able to learn.

Medical History   The medical history of students may contain many suggestions for the cause of reading difficulties. Severe childhood diseases, rheumatic fever, surgery affecting the senses or the nervous system, medical conditions producing lowered vitality, and long illnesses or periods of recuperation that interfered with schooling may all contribute to the development of reading difficulties.

Sometimes the condition underlying a reading problem is unusual and surprising. Charles was 12 when he first came to the reading center. He brought a letter from an ophthalmologist saying that Charles' poor reading was not due to poor vision. His corrected vision, according to the ophthalmologist, was 20/30 at near point, sufficient for reading instruction to be successful.

A check of his functional reading levels showed that Charles was reading instructionally at pre-primer level. He seemed bright, his hearing was good, and he was apparently eager to learn, but he was a very poor reader.

Although his vision was apparently acceptable, the pupils of his eyes had a peculiar shape. A further check revealed that Charles had been totally blind until age 8, when an operation on his left eye had opened the pupil to allow light to enter. Two years later, a similar but even more successful operation had been performed on his right eye. For the first time in his life he had been able to see well enough with corrective lenses to approximate normal vision. His ophthalmologist had suggested his parents not discuss Charles' vision problems with the reading center staff for fear his reading difficulties would be attributed to his present mildly limited vision. If a reading clinician had not looked into Charles' medical background the real cause of his poor reading (which lay in his former blindness and resulting lack of visual learning) would not have been discovered.

Charles recalled, by way of illustrating the visual deficits he had to overcome after he had first gained his vision, how it had been necessary at first for him to close his eyes in order to make his way safely down a flight of stairs. All the things an infant has months to learn had been thrust upon Charles the moment the bandages were removed. He had not only missed a great deal of classroom instruction, he had also missed all the informal learning people ordinarily gain in finding out how to interpret and use visual cues. Even after the physical part of vision became possible, Charles' visual perception center had to learn how to use the information it was receiving.

Knowing his medical background helped in devising effective instruction. Top priority was given to helping Charles learn the visual discrimination skills needed in reading. Fortunately, he learned quickly and soon began to make progress.

No checklist exists that will raise questions needed to explore every possible inhibiting factor. The teacher must simply be as alert as possible to the clues that may be offered.

Family Factors   The earliest and longest-acting influence on most students is their family environment. This includes the student's place in the family group; the family's cultural, educational, and economic status and levels of aspiration; the primary language of the family; the nutritional adequacy of the family diet; and the relationships within the family structure. Any of these areas can provide a number of inhibiting factors.

Because Bernie believed he could never live up to his father's expectations, he became tired of trying, and stopped making any progress in reading. Clay was the bright 8-year-old son of a successful physician, an ideal child in many ways. But he refused to read the material used for reading instruction in his classrooms during the first, second, and third grades. He was referred to the reading center, where it was found that he was reflecting his father's attitude; the father refused to listen to his son read from basal readers because he found them "inane, silly, and childish." As a result, his son withdrew from reading instruction, and lacking other means by which he could practice and master his reading skills, he became a reading failure. Only by direct counseling with the father and an alternate approach for Clay was it possible to start him toward reading success.

Kristoph's parents spoke English in their home when talking to him, but frequently spoke Czechoslovakian to each other. They had few reading materials in the home and set little store in education. It is little wonder that Kris barely made it through the elementary grades, nearly failing to pass the eighth grade. His high school principal and coach saw hidden potential, and led Kris to discover the world of reading. Today Kris holds a doctorate and works as a reading consultant for a large city school system.

Educational History   Some of the most valuable clues to reading problems can be found in students' educational histories. Part of this may be in cumulative folders, recorded as yearly achievement results and as comments from former teachers. However, a student and his family are often able to add valuable elaborations to these records. Their recollections may shed light on teacher and classroom circumstances that may have prevented effective learning. Celia recalled how she had retreated from her first-grade teacher's actions because they were so threatening. Paul's parents recounted his attendance in a parochial school where the lack of funds had caused severe overcrowding during first, second, and third grade, adversely affecting his reading progress.

None of these original causative factors were still functioning to inhibit progress, but their residual effect was a poor start in reading and a bad attitude toward both school and reading.

Other Pertinent Information   Miscellaneous factors often figure in the picture of disabled readers. Usually the diagnostician's only tool in identification of these factors is keen observation. Hugh was a poor reader who didn't respond to instruction. There seemed no apparent reason for his difficulties, although his clinician noticed that he always held his head so that he read out of the corner of his eyes. Investigation revealed that Hugh had burned the retina of his eyes by looking at the sun during an eclipse. He had discovered that by holding his head to one side he could cause the point of focus to fall on an area of the retina that was unscarred. The accommodation he had made to his problem was the best "remediation" possible. The only improvement his clinician could suggest was the use of more light on the printed surface as he read to aid him in making faster discrimination. This suggestion was made because the areas away from the point of central focus on the retina have a somewhat lower sensitivity to light and, therefore, the brighter illumination made the image stronger and brighter.

STEP 2. RAISING DIAGNOSTIC QUESTIONS

In the process of reviewing background information, it is likely that the teacher will raise new questions concerning the existence of possible inhibiting factors. When Hugh was observed holding his head at a peculiar angle, the diagnostician asked himself (1) why Hugh was doing so, and (2) whether this had anything to do with his reading difficulties or was simply an affectation. These questions guided the direction of the diagnosis.

Although the teacher may often conduct a diagnosis without consciously formalizing questions, it helps to formulate them. Without guiding questions, it is easy to let the test or test battery guide the diagnosis, and time is wasted on the administration of possibly unnecessary tests. By raising questions based on the available evidence, the teacher is almost certain to make the diagnosis more direct and productive.

STEP 3. ASSESSING INHIBITING FACTORS

After formulating diagnostic questions, the teacher is ready to begin investigating factors that may be obstructing reading progress.

Intelligence   The measurement of intelligence is a difficult matter. As pointed out earlier, the overall correlation between mental test results and reading achievement is strong, but much of the strength lies in the extremes of the distribution because it is unlikely that a genius would be illiterate and even more unlikely that a person with an IQ of 50 would be a reader. Within the range of more normal variation, however, differences in intelligence are much less predictive of good or poor reading performance. Who can say what a difference of five or ten points in IQ will indicate in terms of reading ability?

In addition to the problem of what values may be placed on small variations in intelligence and reading, there are other problems the diagnostician must face in attempting to measure the intelligence of poor readers. Paper-and-pencil measures of intelligence usually are written somewhat below the reading level of the grades for which they are intended. Nevertheless, poor readers often have difficulty *reading* the tests. At the secondary level, this usually means that if students read more than two years below their grade placement, they will have some degree of difficulty reading an intelligence test. Poorer reading translates into lower test scores or, in other words, a reduction in their measured IQ. The greater a student's reading retardation, the greater the effect on mental test scores. Even individual mental tests such as the Wechsler or Stanford-Binet tests are dependent on reading ability to some extent (Brown, 1970).

The argument is often made that although mental measures are culturally biased and penalize those with poor reading and language skills, they *do* measure whatever skills seem to be necessary to academic success. When people make significant improvement in reading or language, or become more thoroughly familiar with the dominant culture, their IQ scores tend to climb. Since it seems unlikely that either improved reading or acculturation could significantly change a person's cognitive powers, the only reasonable conclusion is that under certain conditions mental tests have severe limitations in their ability to determine levels of intelligence. When dealing with students who have significant difficulties with reading or who lack language skills or knowledge of the culture on which the tests depend, it would be wiser not to consider them tests of intelligence. Under the conditions mentioned, they provide an indication, not of how ably the people can learn, but of the degree of handicap their reading, language, or culture may be for them *at the moment*. The more of their handicaps they overcome, the higher people's mental test scores will be.

When Buddy (Chapter Seven) began his special reading program, his full-scale WISC IQ was 83. Eighteen months later, he was retested and scored a full-scale IQ of 96. Neither test was likely to have been accurate. His reading retardation even at the time of the second test was still so significant that his performance was undoubtedly affected. However, the second test result was probably closer to his true intelligence than the first. What was actually indicated by the two test results was the effect of his improved reading on his test performance. There are a number of formulas in use today which attempt to use mental test scores, together with other factors, to indicate reading potential (Harris and Sipay, 1980, pp. 146–160); (Bond, Tinker, and Wasson, 1979, pp. 61–64). The use of such formulations to predict a student's ability to learn to read or to indicate his degree of retardation is not only misleading, it can be harmful and dangerous. Students who could well profit from remedial reading instruction may be shunted aside because their IQ scores seem to indicate poor learning ability, and yet those scores may well be depressed, not by limited intelligence, but by poor reading ability—the very thing that proves the students' need may deny their opportunity. All such formulas should be used with great care if they are used at all.

Is there never any value to tests of mental ability? Do they always provide faulty and misleading information? The answer, of course, is no. Mental tests are acceptably accurate when used to measure the ability of those within the dominant culture who have had an opportunity to master the media of school communication—reading, writing, listening, and speaking in the dominant dialect—and, therefore, have had an opportunity to gain the knowledge commonly expected of them. Students who do not fall within those bounds may have their IQ scores depressed 5 or 10 points or more.

When it is appropriate to estimate a student's intelligence, it is usually best to begin with an individual quick assessment rather than with a longer, though more reliable, instrument such as the Wechsler tests or the *Stanford-Binet Intelligence Scale* (1973). By using the *Slosson Intelligence Test* (1963) or the *Peabody Picture Vocabulary Test* (Dunn, 1965), or other such brief measures of general intelligence, a teacher is able to get a quick estimate of the student's present functioning ability. The *Slosson* is a shortened form of the *Revised Stanford-Binet Intelligence Scale* (Terman and Merrill, 1960). *The Peabody Picture Vocabulary Test* is easy to administer. It includes a book of plates, each containing four illustrations, one of which matches the word on the vocabulary list. *The Ammons Full-Range Picture Vocabulary Test* (1948) is an older alternative.

The reliability and validity of quick assessment measures is somewhat more questionable than full-scale measures. However, the shorter tests are useful as screening devices. Students indicated as having average or higher intelligence on such tests can usually be safely eliminated from further intelligence testing, saving the time that would be needed to take the much longer full-scale instruments. Only those students indicated as having significantly low intellectual abilities, then, need to be tested with one of the more comprehensive tests to address a diagnostic question of whether poor reading performance is due to low intelligence.

The *Stanford-Binet Intelligence Scale* (1973) is a "spiral" test, tapping various skills at progressively more difficult levels. It is begun at a level easy enough to allow students to pass all subtests. The highest level at which all subtests are passed is called the *basal age*. The test is continued until the student reaches the *ceiling age*, or the level at which he cannot pass any of the subtests.

The *Stanford-Binet* tends to be somewhat more verbally loaded than the Wechsler scales, which has caused them to be viewed from two interestingly different perspectives. Some authorities suggest that since the *Stanford-Binet* is more dependent on verbal skills, it is a better measure to use in relationship to reading because reading is a verbally related skill. Other experts have taken the position that those who do poorly in reading lag behind others in learning certain language skills and in the reading-related areas of language development. This, they believe, causes a spuriously low score on language-loaded tests such as the *Stanford-Binet*, and therefore yields an inaccurate picture of that individual's true learning ability.

The Wechsler scales, particularly the *Wechsler Intelligence Scale for Children* (WISC-R)—revised in 1974—have been used extensively in diagnosis. Rather than following the spiral design of the *Stanford-Binet*, WISC-R items are grouped into subtests and arranged in a sequentially more difficult order within each subtest. A full-scale IQ as well as separate verbal and performance IQs are obtained. This test is to be used with students aged 6 years to 16 years and 11 months.

By looking at the pattern of a student's subtest scores, a reading diagnostician can gather some general indications that may be useful in developing effective instructional programs. The twelve subtests of the WISC-R and some possible implications of each are listed below. The first six are verbal subtests, and the final six are designed to test performance.

1. *Information.* This subtest is basically a test of old learning, cultural background, and memory. The abilities tapped by this subtest are relatively stable. *Information* correlates .67 with the total score. It is an untimed test.
   Diagnostic implications: Low scores tend to indicate a limited background in the dominant culture. Highly weighted with academic material, a high score tends to indicate receptivity to classroom learning. A low score may indicate that the student resists authority or resists learning what he is told to learn. It may also indicate poor rote-memory ability.

2. *Comprehension.* This subtest draws on societal and judgmental skills. It includes the ability to generalize from past experience and apply that experience to the present

question. Comprehension correlates best with similarities and information. It is an untimed test.

Diagnostic implications: This subtest is a comparatively good indicator of social comprehension or good judgment. It may reflect what the child has been told rather than real ability to handle social problem situations properly. High scores may indicate strong home teaching.

3. *Arithmetic.* This subtest is a test of arithmetic reasoning rather than of computational skills, although the latter are included as necessary to arrive at logical and correct conclusions. It correlates with other subtests in relation to age. The older the student, the higher the correlation. It is a timed test.

Diagnostic implications: This test reflects vulnerability to anxiety and is a good test of the student's ability to concentrate on a task. Wechsler says that a good score is a sign of mental alertness.

4. *Similarities.* This subtest assesses the ability to discriminate between superficial and essential likenesses of the items presented. Different credits are allowed for superior and inferior answers. It correlates .73 with the total test and has uniformly high correlations with the other subtests. It is an untimed test.

Diagnostic implications: This is probably the best single test of general intelligence. If a child scores high, he would seem to give evidence of good understanding. If he gives differences rather than similarities asked for, the diagnostician should check further to see if there is a hearing loss.

5. *Vocabulary.* This subtest includes a list of words of increasing difficulty (revised downward in the WISC-R from 40 to 32 words) which the student is to define. The correlation between this subtest and the total test is .85, and it correlates well with most of the other subtests. It is untimed.

Diagnostic implications: This subtest is quite dependent on cultural background. If the student scores low, it may indicate a hearing loss.

6. *Digit Span.* This subtest requires the subject to repeat numbers in series, forward and backward. It correlates poorly with the total test.

Diagnostic implications: This subtest indicates a subject's ability to work under pressure. It seems to be a poor test of general intellectual ability but gives some indication of an individual's ability to perform cognitive tasks under tension.

7. *Picture Completion.* This is the first of the performance subtests. It is a test of the ability of a student to discover important details missing in drawings presented to him. It correlates .63 with the total test. Each picture is exhibited for 15 seconds.

Diagnostic implications: This test indicates the ability of a student to discriminate between important and unimportant details of a picture. A low-ability student in other areas *may* do well if he tends to be very practically oriented or if he is a perfectionist.

8. *Picture Arrangement.* This subtest presents sets of pictures that must be put in logical order to tell a sensible story. The pictures resemble comic strips. Credits are given for both speed and accuracy. There is a .72 correlation with the total test; best correlation is with Similarities and Picture Completion.

Diagnostic implications: Minority groups often do poorly. It is a measure of social intelligence and judgment rooted within the dominant culture. Some low-ability subjects can do fairly well if they come from a strong moral and cultural background.

9. *Block Design.* This is perhaps the best single performance test. It correlates highest of all subtests with the total test, .87, and involves abilities to visualize a solution and to manipulate blocks to reproduce a pattern. It is a timed test.

Diagnostic implications: This test is a good indicator of abstract and analytical thought. Clinicians should watch for the manner in which the student approaches the task (trial and error, etc.) for indicators of motor coordination, insight, and recognition. It does not tend to be affected by emotional factors or practice. Rotation of the patterns and distorted spatial relationships may indicate brain insult. If the subject scores only one low, look for color-blindness.

10. *Object Assembly.* This test consists of formboards which the student assembles like a jigsaw puzzle. Object Assembly correlates well with Block Design and poorly with Digit Span. It is a timed test with credits given for both speed and accuracy.
Diagnostic implications: This test gives insight into a student's ability to perceive and attack a problem. It reveals persistence and reaction to frustration (as do many of the performance tests), and reflects anxiety. It may be culturally biased. It is influenced by practice. If a child scores high, it indicates good general understanding. Mentally deficient students never seem to do well, but mentally retarded students occasionally do well.

11. *Coding.* This is a test for learning new or unfamiliar tasks. The student is asked to associate digits with symbols presented in a series of boxed lines. It correlates best with Digit Span and poorest with Object Assembly.
Diagnostic implications: This test indicates immediate recall and new learning ability. It is affected by tension and anxiety. If the student makes a low score, the diagnostician should check his ability to move efficiently from central to peripheral focus and back. The test may indicate that the student has good imitative ability. It correlates better with reading comprehension.

12. *Mazes.* This is a test of the student's ability to draw a path through a maze puzzle.
Diagnostic implications: This test is an indicator of graphomotor skills and small muscle coordination as well as problem-solving insight. It is not generally viewed as a good test of higher cognitive ability, however.

In considering the diagnostic implications, the teacher should remember that the results on subtest performances are merely indicators and not conclusive diagnostic assessments in and of themselves.

A number of studies with the Wechsler tests have given an interesting comparison of the patterns of subtest scores for poor readers. Although the studies used somewhat different criteria for determining the significance of high and low scores on the subtests, the patterns are rather strikingly similar, as may be seen in Figure 8-1.

Poor readers tend to do comparatively well on the subtests of Comprehension, Picture Completion, Block Design, Picture Arrangement, and Object Assembly. Their performance is mixed in Similarities and Vocabulary, and poor in Information, Arithmetic, Digit Span, and Coding.

Searls (1975) has published an interesting booklet on the interpretation of WISC scores for the reading diagnostician. It contains many helpful suggestions to be gained from the various subtests.

Lateral Dominance   The only type of dominance that has continued to be linked with reading difficulties is handedness. Involved tests designed to determine an individual's preferred eye or foot seem unnecessary. If it is true that the greatest single factor in the relationship between reading achievement and either left- or confused-dominance is obscuring as the student writes (see Chapter

Information	Comprehension	Arithmetic	Similarities	Digit Span	Vocabulary		Picture Completion	Block Design	Picture Arrangement	Object Assembly	Coding
L	H	L	H	L	L	Graham	H	H	H	H	L
L	H	L	-	L	-	Bruce & Burks	H	H	H	H	L
L	-	L	-	L	-	Richardson & Surko	H	-	H	H	L
L	-	L	L	H	H	Altus	H	-	H	H	L
-	-	-	-	-	-	Sheldon & Carton	-	H	-	H	L
L	H	L	H	-	L	Dockrell	-	-	H	-	L
-	-	L	-	L	L	Hirst	H	H	H	H	L
L	H	-	H	L	H	Robeck	H	H	-	H	L
L	-	L	-	L	-	Neville	-	H	H	-	-
L	-	L	-	L	L	McLean	H	-	-	-	L

H = High, or above the mean according to the criteria of the individual study.
L = Low, or below the mean according to the criteria of the individual study.
- = No significant differences found according to the criteria in the individual study.

Figure 8–1. A comparison of WISC subtest patterning for retarded readers.

Three), the diagnostician should observe the student to see whether or not this occurs.

Learning Disabilities   There are particular and peculiar problems in the diagnosis of learning disabilities, as discussed in Chapter Three. The term was originally used to describe a condition or set of conditions within an individual's central nervous system which limited the ability to learn. Specifically excluding low intelligence, emotional disturbance, poor hearing, poor vision, and motor problems, the definition included those students who had "perceptual handicaps, brain injury, minimal brain dysfunction, dyslexia, developmental aphasia, etc." (National Advisory Committee on Handicapped Children, 1968, p. 4).

A thorough review of common learning disabilities tests by Coles (1978) in the *Harvard Educational Review* makes clear the difficulties that face a diagnostician trying to identify learning disabilities defined as a central nervous system dysfunction. The most frequently used tests, according to Coles, include the *Illinois Test of Psycholinguistic Abilities* (ITPA) (Kirk, McCarthy, and Kirk; 1968), the *Bender Visual-Motor Gestalt Test* (1938), the Frostig *Developmental Test of Visual Perception* (1964), the *Wepman Auditory Discrimination Test* (1973), the *Lincoln-Oseretsky Motor Development Scale* (Sloan, 1965), the *Graham-Kendall Memory-for-Designs Test* (1960), and the *Purdue Perceptual-Motor Survey Test*

(Roach and Kephart, 1966). The most crucial test of the effectiveness of these measures would appear to be the ability to discriminate between those students who are learning well and those who are not. By excluding those who are mentally retarded, emotionally disturbed, visually or auditorially handicapped, or who have motor problems, in order to fit the National Advisory Council's definition, it should be possible to use the tests listed above to discriminate between those who are good learners and therefore able to read well and those who are poor learners and therefore unable to read well.

Coles found that the ITPA had only one subtest that appeared to discriminate between good and poor readers, and none of the subtests satisfactorily differentiated between good and poor readers when mental ability was controlled.

The *Bender Test* has accumulated more research than most of the other measures, but it, too, seems to be unable to measure success in learning to read. Interestingly, Ackerman, Peters, and Dykman (1971) found that it also failed to correlate well with neurological deficits as measured by a neurological examination. A sizable body of research indicates that the Frostig *Developmental Test of Visual Perception*, when used beyond the first-grade level, is not a good predictor of reading achievement.

Although the Wepman *Auditory Discrimination Test* is, according to its author, only a test of auditory discrimination and not of learning disabilities, it has been widely used as a test of neurological dysfunction and learning disability. As with the previous tests, research fails to confirm that it can be used to distinguish poor readers from good readers. Coles also finds the *Lincoln-Oseretsky Motor Development Scale*, the *Graham-Kendall Memory for Designs Test*, and the *Purdue Perceptual-Motor Survey Test* lacking in the ability to discriminate good and poor readers and, therefore, lacking in the ability to identify those who would comprise a population of learning-disabled students.

After his exhaustive review, Coles writes:

> Taken as a whole, the tests used in a representative learning-disabilities battery fail to demonstrate that children categorized as learning disabled are neurologically impaired. Some research validating the intent of each test is available, but the predominant finding in the literature suggests that each test fails to correlate with a diagnosis of learning disabilities. The evidence from studies using formal neurological examinations of learning disabled children is especially damaging to the neurological impairment explanation. Surely, if the neurological thesis were to find support anywhere, it would find it in the techniques and science available to neurologists. Unfortunately for those who have held this thesis, studies of borderline symptoms, soft signs, have uniformly failed to contribute to the diagnosis of academic underachievement. (p. 326).

The failure of tests to be able to directly identify those who have a learning disability has forced those in the LD field to turn to what has become known as a "discrepancy" formula. Using the portion in P.L. 94–142, The Education for All Handicapped Children Act, which permits the identification of learning-disabled students as *underachievers* in oral expression, listening, writing, basic reading skills, reading comprehension, mathematical calculation, or mathematical reasoning, most states have developed a process of identification that uses a test of potential and another test to measure achievement. If students have greater potential than their present achievement shows, the discrepancy between the two tests can be used to identify them as learning-disabled. In practice, states and local school districts have usually established slightly more definitive guidelines. In the state of Colorado, for example, the legislature has adopted the following definition:

> A perceptual or communicative disorder is indicated when there is a significant discrepancy between estimated intellectual potential and actual level of performance and is related to basic disorders in learning processes which are not secondary to limited intellectual capacity, visual or auditory sensory impairment, emotional disorders, and/or experiential information. One or more of the following measurable disorders are observed.
> 1.01 (6) (a) Significantly impaired ability in pre-reading and/or reading skills
> 1.01 (6) (b) Significantly impaired ability in reading comprehension
> 1.01 (6) (c) Significantly impaired ability in written language expression, such as problems in handwriting, spelling, sentence structure and written organization
> 1.01 (6) (d) Significantly impaired ability to comprehend, apply and/or retain math concepts

The addition of the term "significant" adds only limited clarification to P.L. 94–142. The diagnostician is left on his own to determine (or more likely, have his school determine) just how much of a discrepancy between achievement and potential is "significant."

The use of a discrepancy approach results from the failure of other instruments to identify processing deficits that clearly distinguish "normal" poor readers from "learning-disabled" poor readers. Legislation and practice in LD assume what seems beyond proof: that if there is a significant discrepancy between an otherwise normal child's achievement and his potential, he *must* be learning-disabled. If the assumption is accepted, there can be little argument with the use of a discrepancy approach to identification. Unfortunately, it is difficult to accept that assumption. There are few who would believe that every such child is learning-disabled. Nevertheless, the definition provides a legal basis for selection of students to enter programs funded by federal and state legislation for learning-disabled students.

Since the basic purpose for identification through a discrepancy approach is programmatic and does not yield diagnostic information useful in planning instruction, there is little reason to administer expensive, time-consuming tests. The time saved can be better used on diagnosis and instruction aimed at helping students become better readers.

Any of a number of good group intelligence tests can be used to indicate mental potential if students can read well enough not to be penalized by them. For those who cannot read well enough to take the group tests, the *Slosson Intelligence Test* or the *Peabody Picture Vocabulary Test* can be administered quickly and easily to arrive at an estimate of potential. If any of the measures above are used, the diagnostician should realize that all the difficulties discussed earlier in this chapter still apply to the measurement of intelligence. The results are not likely to be accurate because poor readers are discriminated against by intelligence measures. The aim of the procedure described is the programmatic identification of students who will be allowed to take part in needed instructional offerings.

The second portion of the identification process is the estimation of achievement in the areas listed in P.L. 94–142 or the related state legislation. Again, it is better to use a shorter group measure for this identification process so that the teacher's time can be saved for more important diagnosis and instruction. There are a number of good achievement tests from which to choose, including the *California Achievement Test*, the *Iowa Test of Basic Skills*, the *Metropolitan Achievement Test*, the *SRA Achievement Series*, and the *Stanford Achievement Test*. Individually administered achievement tests include the *Peabody Individual Achievement Test*, the *Wide Range Achievement Test*, and the *Woodcock-Johnson Psycho-Educational Battery*. The latter claims the added feature of a test of potential within the same battery of tests.

By using group measures, it is possible to complete the legal identification process quickly and begin the instructional program without delay. Though individually administered tests of achievement would seem to be more accurate, there is little reason to believe that that is necessarily so, particularly if the teacher watches the students carefully as they are taking the group test in order to help those who become frustrated and quit trying.

Emotional Maladjustment

Psychoticism.   Formerly, reading teachers seldom worked with students suffering from psychoticism unless they were employed in institutional or "halfway-house" programs. Recent legislation has changed that situation to some extent. In some locations, those who may have encapsulated their psychoticism or who are not considered to be a danger to themselves or to others may no longer be institutionalized and, therefore, are free to enroll in school if they want to do so and are legally permitted to do so by age.

Diagnosis of inhibiting factors should focus on determining a student's ability to profit from instruction in two basic areas: (1) language facility, and (2) ability to concentrate on what they need to learn. Students suffering from childhood schizophrenia or autism often give evidence of communication disorders that interfere with learning to read. Autistic children are also frequently given to emotional outbursts that destroy concentration both for them and for any others in the setting.

Diagnosis seldom consists of formal testing. Teacher observation of children in an instructional setting is usually preferable and a better gauge of the students' ability to learn.

Psychotic students are often more disturbed when they are first introduced to a new situation. Although initial diagnosis is needed, the teacher may want to give such students an opportunity to accommodate to the classroom or learning center for a few days before making a determination of the student's ability to learn to read. Obviously, the student's tractability may be a factor in how long the teacher can delay a decision.

Neuroticism and Emotional Maladjustment.   Diagnosis of inhibiting factors for those who are neurotic or emotionally maladjusted is usually centered on the circumstances that provoke or increase their maladjustment, and the severity of the interference their condition produces in learning to read. Specifically, the teacher needs to know whether reading is associated with the student's condition and, if so, what elements in the reading situation are most disturbing to him. For example, Bert found it difficult to work with a male clinician. Switching him to a female clinician greatly relieved his anxieties and allowed him to make good progress. Greg found it almost intolerable to work with ordinary print materials, so his clinician wrote his reading material on sheets of clear acetate, projecting them onto the wall with an overhead projector. Greg responded well to the approach and began to make progress in reading. June could read light stories, but her reaction to workbook exercises was explosive. When her skills work was individualized and later augmented by single pages torn out of workbooks, she was able to master the attack skills she needed. C. C. avoided formal reading skill instruction by disrupting the entire group. He responded well, first to individualized instruction and later to machine-presented learning.

In each of these situations, the teacher first found that the student's behavior involved reading and was impeding his or her growth in learning to read. Next, the teacher found the specific elements in the reading program which caused the student to be disturbed.

The "instrument of diagnosis" in each case was the direct, probing observation of the teacher. No standardized test is likely to tell the teacher what he wants to know. There are times, however, when a diagnostician may want to make use of a projective technique such as a sentence-completion blank or a semantic differential test to gain insight into the student and his problems. (There are examples of both of these tests in the appendix, and teachers should feel free to adapt either for use in individual situations.)

Sentence-completion tests are free-association tests and have been used for decades in the assessment of personality. Like all personality tests, they are subject to error and are easily affected by temporary variations in mood or circumstances. Anastasi (1968, p. 505) points out that such test responses are influenced by the student's "age, socioeconomic and educational level, regional and cultural background, creativity, and other factors." Used with caution, however, a sentence-completion test can sometimes provide insights into a student's difficulties.

Because the procedure for administration of a sentence-completion test may not be readily available, it is outlined here. The teacher may introduce the test by saying, "I'm going to start some sentences I want you to finish. For example, I might say, 'Swimming is . . . ' and you might finish the sentence by saying something like '. . . a lot of fun.' Do you see what I mean?" If the student seems to understand, each of the "stems" or sentence beginnings should be read; the student should be given time to complete each sentence. It is important that the examiner write the student's responses if the student is a poor speller because otherwise, the student is likely to use only the words he can spell.

As the examiner reads the stems to the student, he should be careful not to give voice or expression signals that will cause the student to change what he would say. Also, as the responses are recorded, the examiner should be careful not to influence the student by reacting in any way to encourage or discourage particular responses.

The first half-dozen responses are less likely to be a measure of the student's feelings than the rest of the test because the student is likely to feel self-conscious and may try to give "acceptable" responses. If the student asks if the responses have to be true, the examiner should say, "They can be if you want to make them true, but they do not need to be." The reason for this response, when it is obvious that it would be more helpful in diagnosis if the responses were true, is that the student is more likely to feel uncomfortable if he thinks the examiner believes what he says is true. He is more likely not to guard his comments if he believes he can disclaim any response by saying that it is not true. Although this is not a textbook in psychology, there is a sense in which anything the student says must be considered a reflection of the individual. Certainly it does not come from anyone else; it comes from within the mind of the student.

But an examiner would be foolish to believe that the surface meaning of each statement was an accurate statement of the student's actions or feelings. An example of this is the use of bland comments. Some students defend against strong feelings by giving unusually bland statements. A trained psychologist, sensing the defensiveness, may be concerned about the student's ability to express normal concerns and may be able to help the student get in touch with his feelings. That is not the role of the reading diagnostician, however.

In trying to identify the emotional factors that may be limiting a student's reading progress, the examiner should go through the completed test to identify those sentences in which unusual or "individual" responses have been made. Interpretations based on sentence-completion tests that are to be used for a reasonably long period of time can be improved if the teacher will keep a record of the responses that have been made, noting the number of customary responses, individual responses, and perhaps even bland responses. This takes a good deal of recordkeeping, however, and makes the final scoring more time-consuming. The examiner should not limit observations to verbal responses. Although the oral response to a certain stem may be customary or bland, signs or emotion or agitation may be exhibited when the student is thinking about the stem. The length of time it takes to respond to a stem can also indicate that the stem may be emotionally loaded.

After going through the individual responses, the examiner should cluster those which seem to reflect similar anxieties. One individual response is seldom noteworthy, but if there are three, four, or five which exhibit a similar concern, the examiner should consider them much more carefully.

Semantic differential tests, like sentence-completion measures, can be useful in indicating personality factors that may affect ability to learn to read. Most semantic differential tests list a number of concepts and beneath each one provide a series of opposing descriptive ratings. In Figure 8–2, for example, the concept is "Reading." In rating that concept, the student would place a check mark at the appropriate point on the seven-stage scale on each of the lines between the bipolar descriptors.

A second way to build a semantic differential scale is to list only one rating for each concept. This approach allows the measurement of many more concepts, with less coverage for each one. (The semantic differential scale found on p. 371 in the appendix follows this form.)

The teacher can quantify the results of the administration of a semantic differential scale by giving each point on the scale a numerical value of from 1 to 7 or by making the center point 0 and having the scale range from positive to negative with the rating points valued as $3, 2, 1, 0, -1, -2, -3$. Records can be kept on results obtained from the administration of a scale to help interpret the relative importance of the various responses.

For pre- and post-test comparisons, the examiner must be aware that attitudes and circumstances surrounding the administration of a semantic differential scale can cause results to change from one administration to the next without reflecting real change within the student. When the semantic differential scale in the appendix was used with a group of high school students who were in a dropout prevention program, the students responded warmly at the beginning of the year to the term, "special reading program," but were less enthusiastic about it at the

Reading

Like	: ___ : ___ : ___ : ___ : ___ :	Hate
Bad	: ___ : ___ : ___ : ___ : ___ :	Good
Interesting	: ___ : ___ : ___ : ___ : ___ :	Dull
Easy	: ___ : ___ : ___ : ___ : ___ :	Hard
Valuable	: ___ : ___ : ___ : ___ : ___ :	Worthless
Slow	: ___ : ___ : ___ : ___ : ___ :	Fast
Unimportant	: ___ : ___ : ___ : ___ : ___ :	Important

Figure 8–2. A Semantic Differential Scale for "Reading"

Note: A complete test would include many more sets of words with accompanying rating scales.

end of the year. In private conversations the students stated that they had been pleased with the novelty of the program as they began but that after having been in the program for several months, some of the newness had worn off; they had reflected that in their response to the scale. Asked if they thought the program was as good now as it had been when they first became a part of it, they responded positively, saying that they thought it was as good as or better than it had been. They noted several improvements and were supportive of the progress that had been made in improving the program. The point is that the semantic differential scale is not sufficiently objective to use as a basis for major decisions, either about a program or—more importantly and more central to diagnosis—about a student and his degree of neuroticism or maladjustment. It, like the sentence-completion test, *can* suggest possibilities or give indications which the diagnostician may follow up through other means.

Vision   There are a number of unusual visual problems that may adversely affect reading ability, as exemplified by the cases of Charles, who had had a recent operation to gain his vision, and Hugh, who burned the retinas of his eyes by looking at the sun. Although diagnosticians should be alert to clues that may lead them to investigate unusual conditions, most visual conditions that may contribute to reading problems are quite common. The first and most frequent is hyperopia or farsightedness—i.e., difficulty seeing near at hand. The second is the lack of oculomotor coordination, particularly exophoria or "wall-eyedness," in which one or both of the eyes turn outward. The third is lack of fusion caused when the visual perception center in the brain cannot fuse a single image from the signals it receives from the two eyes. The fourth condition may be called "cumulative critical visual defect" or, in other words, the combined effect of all the person's visual anomalies which have a negative influence on reading ability. For example, a student may be so mildly farsighted that it would not ordinarily affect his reading, but may have one or two other vision problems which, when combined with the farsightedness, would result in a visual handicap of sufficient severity to create reading difficulties.

Diagnosis of visual difficulties that may interfere with progress in learning to read may begin with teacher observation. Common indicators of visual problems are listed in Figure 8–3.

Formal screening for visual defects has been done through the Snellen Chart since its origination in 1862. The Snellen and a number of other devices similar to it, such as the *American Optical School Vision Screening Test*, the *King Sight Screener*, the *Sloan Chart*, the *School Vision Tester* by Bausch & Lomb, and the *School Vision Tester* by Titmus Optical Company, are all acceptable screening measures for far-point visual acuity. However, they do not effectively identify those who are farsighted or who have problems with fusion or astigmatism unless the visual anomaly is severe (Francis, 1973, pp. 99–110). In the St. Louis Study (Crane, Scobee, Foote, and Green; 1954), which is occasionally cited in defense of the Snellen Chart, the conclusion was drawn that the Snellen was better than any other visual screening procedure against which it was tested, yet the Snellen

Figure 8–3
Visual Screening

Classroom Observation Checklist

Student: _____

I. Indications of possible farsightedness
    _____ Avoids reading; highly distractible while reading
    _____ Holds book far away when reading
    _____ Complains of headaches across forehead and temples after reading
    _____ Squints or grimaces while reading
II. Indications of poor oculomotor coordination
    _____ Turns one or both eyes out, in, or one eye turns up or down
    _____ Closes or covers one eye when reading
    _____ Tilts head while reading
III. Indications of lack of fusion
    _____ Complains of headaches
    _____ Eyes tear when reading
    _____ Blinks frequently while reading
    _____ Loses place or skips words while reading
    _____ Complains of double or blurred vision
    _____ Squints or grimaces while reading
IV. Indications of infection or disease
    _____ Inflamed or encrusted eyelids
    _____ Bloodshot eyes
    _____ Frequent sties
    _____ Rubs eyes frequently
    _____ Eyes continually tear

missed three or four times as many students as the other procedures (Kelley, 1957).

Children often are able to memorize parts of the Snellen Chart while they are waiting to be tested or when they read with a good eye before using their weaker eye. The most serious accusation against the test is that it is a poor measure of the type of reading—near-point—required most crucially in school. Further, when a student passes the Snellen test, he, his parents, and his teachers are likely to feel that there is nothing wrong with his eyesight while in actuality, important visual anomalies have not been screened.

In general, those working in reading clinics in colleges and universities have tended to favor the use of binocular (stereoptic) instruments that can screen students for near-point vision. These can be used in a limited amount of space; the level of illumination is held constant; the test takes a relatively short time to administer; the test cards are not in view of other students before they are to be tested and, therefore, there is limited opportunity for students to memorize the information on the cards; and the instructions for administration are contained in a manual that tends to standardize the test conditions. It is important, however, that the school personnel giving the test should have training in its administration and standards for referral.

The most common binocular instruments are the Keystone Visual Survey Telebinocular, the Ortho-Rater, the New York School Vision Tester (an adaptation of the Ortho-Rater), the Titmus Vision Tester, and two less well-known instruments, the Freeman Protometer (now no longer in production) and the relatively new Johnson Vision Screener which permits self-screening.

Over-referral; that is, referral followed by a clinical examination in which no significant visual deficits are found, is substantially higher for binocular instruments than for Snellen Charts, but the instruments identify elements of vision frequently missed by the Snellen—i.e., farsightedness, fusion, and astigmatism.

Diagnosis of oculomotor coordination problems can sometimes be made by having the student watch the point of a pen or other small object held about 20 inches away from the eyes as the examiner executes a 360-degree circle, watching first one eye and then the other. Afterward, the examiner watches the student's eyes as the pen is moved vertically and horizontally. During this time the examiner should watch the student carefully for difficulty in following the object. Ordinarily, eye movement will be smooth and regular. If there is difficulty at some point, the examiner should go back over that particular portion of the circle or line, because irregularities may be caused by the student's nervousness. The examiner should then move the pen toward the bridge of the student's nose, asking the student to watch it with both eyes as long as he can. Students should normally be able to follow the pen to within about 4 inches of the bridge of the nose before their eyes break away. If they have difficulty at a greater distance than that, there may be an oculomotor weakness precipitant to exophoria. Difficulty tracking the pen in circles and either vertically or horizontally also indicates a possible oculomotor muscle weakness, which should be referred to the school doctor or to other medical personnel. Referrals should always indicate the exact condition for which the student is being referred.

In referring students to an eye doctor, teachers should be aware that some have made a practice of prescribing eye exercises and corrective lenses for many more children than would seem warranted. Although teachers are not in a position to choose particular specialists, if one doctor prescribes the same treatment for virtually every student, this should be noted. It may be necessary to take professional steps to alert those in a position to monitor activities within that profession.

Hearing   As with many of the other factors that may limit ability to improve reading, inadequate hearing may be indicated first by observed clues. Commonly, these include:

1. Inattentiveness and daydreaming
2. Apparent mental slowness
3. Smiling to ward off criticism for not knowing an answer
4. Turning one ear toward the teacher, cupping a hand behind an ear, or sitting in a posture that shows intensity in trying to hear
5. Frequently asking to have directions repeated
6. Frequent colds, sore throats, coughs, and/or runny ears

These symptoms are significantly more common among those with poor hearing, and a teacher observing them should check further to see that they do not signal problems with auditory acuity.

The best means of evaluating a hearing loss is an audiometer test. Most school districts have an audiometer available either in the nurse's office, in a mobile audiometric laboratory, or in the central office. The administration of this test is not difficult, but no one should attempt to give it without first being taught adequately.

For a hearing loss to be considered significant in a reading diagnosis, it should be (1) within the speech range, (2) at least a 20-decibel loss, and (3) a bilateral loss—that is, one involving both ears. The speech range is roughly 100 to 4,000 cycles per second.

Reliable audiometers for school use are produced by Ambco, Beltone, Eckstein Brothers, Grason-Stadler, Maico, and Zenith. Because a hearing loss indicated by an audiometer may be the result of an ear infection or other temporary condition, a student who fails an audiometer test should be retested a month or so later.

Speech   There are three kinds of speech problems that seem to interfere with learning to read: (1) Speech production may be so limited or distorted that it is difficult for the student to make the sounds associated with learning to read; (2) poor speech may give rise to poor self-concept, and the student views himself as unable to learn well; (3) speech "clutter," in which speech is jumbled, hurried, and difficult to understand.

If speech problems appear to have a limiting effect on a student's ability to learn to read, the diagnostician may do initial screening, but usually it is necessary to ask for professional assistance for a proper diagnosis. For the first two conditions given above, speech therapy is usually quite effective. For the third, progress is often slow.

Writing   Although writing and reading have long been considered correlated skills, few people have believed that the ability to write has had any causative relationship with the development of reading skills, or put another way, that poor writing skill has a negative effect on learning to read. Research discussed in Chapter Four indicates that if students obscure what they have written as they write, the lack of visual feedback may result in poorer learning of word analysis skills. Diagnosis of this problem depends on the teacher's ability to observe whether or not the student covers as he writes.

Vitality   Lowered vitality affects alertness and can lessen the chance that students will be able to learn to read effectively. Included in the factors that lower vitality are inadequate sleep, anemia, hypothyroidism, dietary deficiencies, prolonged poor health, and the use of certain legal and illegal drugs and alcohol.

When a student seems to be lethargic, it is sometimes advisable to try to identify problem areas by means of conversation, rather than a formal written interview technique; this latter understandably makes most people uneasy and even evasive in their responses. It is usually much easier to find out about sleep habits, diet, and legal drugs or medications by talking in a relaxed setting. The help of the school nurse may be necessary in screening a student for possible referral for medical conditions and, occasionally, for the use of alcohol and illegal drugs. The detection and treatment for the latter should be placed in the hands of professionals, who are better equipped to diagnose and provide an avenue of help. However, it is frequently the reading or learning-disabilities teacher who initially becomes aware of student problems involving alcohol or drug use. Here, care should be taken to make sure the student is helped rather than harmed, and that there are no unnecessary risks for the teacher and other students.

SUMMARY

In the diagnosis of a student's reading difficulties, it is usually unnecessary to carry out a diagnosis of causative factors. For example, most students are able to improve their reading ability despite the fact that they have had a bad start or that they did not develop reading readiness until relatively late. Some students, however, cannot make good progress in learning to read because of factors that inhibit their ability to profit from reading instruction. In this chapter, we discussed the various conditions that commonly obstruct good reading improvement, as well as diagnostic techniques suggested for their identification.

Diagnosis of inhibiting factors should usually begin with an examination of available information about the student. Clues concerning what may be retarding reading progress may be found in information about a student's prenatal, birth, and early childhood development, or in medical, family, and educational histories. Based on such information, the diagnostician can usually formulate diagnostic questions to guide the investigation.

Areas frequently involved in diagnosis include the student's intellectual functioning, lateral dominance, possible neurological difficulties, learning disabilities, emotional problems, poor vision, inadequate hearing, speech difficulties, lowered vitality, and drug and alcohol problems.

RECOMMENDED READINGS

BOND, G.; TINKER, M.; and WASSON, B. 1979. *Reading difficulties: Their diagnosis and correction.* 4th ed. Englewood Cliffs, N.J.: Prentice-Hall, Chapters 4 and 5.

COLES, G. S. August 1978. The learning-disabilities test battery: Empirical and social issues. *Harvard Educational Review.* 48:313–40.

HARRIS, A. J.; and SIPAY, E. R. 1980. *How to increase reading ability.* 7th. ed. New York: David McKay, Chapters 7, 10, 11, and 12.

NOBLE, E. P., ed. 1978. *Third special report to the U.S. Congress on alcohol and health.* Rockville, Md.: National Institute of Alcohol Abuse and Alcoholism.

RUPLEY, W. H.; and BLAIR, T. R. 1979. *Reading diagnosis and remediation: A primer for classroom and clinic.* Chicago: Rand McNally, Chapters 3 and 4.

SEARLS, E. F. 1975. *How to use WISC scores in reading diagnosis.* Newark, Del.: International Reading Association.

REFERENCES

Ackerman, P. T.; Peters, J. E.; and Dykman, R. A. 1971. Children with specific learning disabilities: Bender Test findings and other signs. *Journal of learning disabilities.* 4: 437–46.

Altus, G. T. A WISC profile for retarded readers. *Journal of consulting psychology* pp. 155–57.

Ammons, R. B. 1948. *Full-range picture vocabulary test.* New York: Psychological Corp.

Anastasi, A. 1968. *Psychological testing.* 3rd. ed. New York: Macmillan.

Bender, L. 1938. *A visual-motor gestalt test and its clinical uses.* Research Monograph no. 3. New York: American Orthopsychiatric Assoc.

———. 1938. *Bender visual-motor gestalt test.* New York: Psychological Corp.

Brown, D. A. 1970. Measuring the reading ability and potential of adult illiterates. In *Measurement and evaluation of reading.* New York: Harcourt Brace Jovanovich, pp. 154–65.

Burks, H. F.; and Bruce, P. 1955. The characteristics of good and poor readers as disclosed by the WISC. *Journal of educational psychology* pp. 488–93.

Coles, G. S. August 1978. The learning-disabilities test battery: Empirical and social issues. *Harvard educational review.* pp. 313–40.

Crane, M. M.; Scobee, R. G.; Foote, F. M.; and Green, E. L. 1954. Screening school children for visual defects. Children's Bureau Publication No. 345. Washington, D.C.: Government Printing Office.

Dockrell, W. B. June 1960. The use of Wechsler Intelligence Scale for children in the diagnosis of retarded readers. *Alberta journal of educational research.* pp. 86–91.

Dunn, L. M. 1965. *Peabody picture vocabulary test.* Circle Pines, Minn.: American Guidance Service.

Francis, L. J. 1973. *The relationship of eye anomalies and reading ability, and an analysis of vision-screening programs.* Unpublished doctoral dissertation, Univ. Northern Colorado.

Frostig, M. 1964. *Developmental test of visual perception.* Chicago: Follett.

Graham, E. E. 1952. Wechsler-Bellevue and WISC Scattergram of unsuccessful readers. *Journal of consulting psychology.* 16: 268–71.

Graham, F.; and Kendall, B. 1960. *Graham-Kendall memory-for-designs tests.* Missoula, Mont.: Psychological Test Specialists.

Harris, A. J.; and Sipay, E. R. 1980. *How to increase reading ability,* 7th ed. New York: Longmans.

Hirst, L. S. 1960. The usefulness of a two-way analysis of WISC subtests in the diagnosis of remedial reading. *Journal of experimental education.* 29: 153–60.

Kawai, A. A.; and Pasamanick, B. 1958. Association of factors of pregnancy with reading disorders of childhood. *Journal of the American medical association* pp. 1420–23.

Kelley, C. R. September 1957. A critical review of the St. Louis visual screening study. *Journal of the American optometric association.* 29: 107–12.

Kirk, S. A.; McCarthy, J. P.; and Kirk, W. D. 1968. *The Illinois test of psycholinguistic abilities.* Rev. ed. Urbana, Ill.: Univ. Illinois Press.

McLean, T. K. 1963. *A comparison of the subtest performance of two groups of retarded readers with like groups of non-retarded readers on the Wechsler Intelligence Scale for Children.* Unpublished doctoral dissertation, Univ. Oregon.

National Advisory Committee on Handicapped Children. January 31, 1968. *Special education for handicapped children.* First Annual Report. Washington, D.C.: U.S. Dept. of Health, Education & Welfare.

Neville, D. 1961. A comparison of WISC patterns of male retarded and nonretarded readers. *Journal of educational research.* 54:194–97.

Noble, E. P., ed. 1978. *Third special report to the U.S. Congress on alcohol and health.* Rockville, Md.: National Institute of Alcohol Abuse and Alcoholism.

Richardson, H. M.; and Surko, E. F. 1955. WISC scores and status in reading and arithmetic of delinquent children. *Journal of genetic psychology.* 89: 251–62.

Roach, C.; and Kephart, N. 1966. *The Purdue perceptual-motor survey test.* Columbus, Ohio: Charles E. Merrill.

Robeck, M. 1960. Subtest patterning of problem readers on the WISC. *California journal of educational research.* 11: 110–15.

Searls, E. F. 1975. How to use WISC scores in reading diagnosis. Newark, Del.: International Reading Assoc.

Sheldon, M. S.; and Carton, J. December 1959. A note on "A WISC profile for retarded readers." *Alberta journal of educational research,* 5: 264–67.

Sloan, W. 1965. *Lincoln-Oseretsky motor development scale.* Los Angeles: Western Psychological Services.

Slosson, R. L. 1963. *Slosson intelligence test,* Monterey, Cal.: Publishers Test Service.

Terman, L.; and Merrill, M. 1960, 1973. *Revised Stanford-Binet intelligence scale.* Boston: Houghton Mifflin.

Wechsler, D. 1974. *Wechsler intelligence scale for children,* Rev. New York: Psychological Corp.

Wepman, J. M. 1973. *Auditory discrimination test.* Chicago: Language Research Assoc.

9

Remedial instruction must proceed from the diagnostic bases discussed in preceding chapters to the placement of students in programs designed to meet their individual needs. Concerns of the teacher include the selection of students, the nature of the program needed by each student, organization for instruction, implementation of good remedial instruction, and the effective use of paraprofessionals.

PRINCIPLES
OF EFFECTIVE
REMEDIATION

A successful instructional program is built on well-prepared and capable teachers. Teachers who have responsibility for student reading improvement should have had courses and supervised experience in the basic concepts of reading, diagnosis, and remediation. The alternative—no professional reading education preparation—tends to result in teachers learning at the expense of the students and, possibly, a failure to develop an adequate foundation for understanding the principles of effective diagnosis and reading instruction.

REFERRAL AND SELECTION

A good remedial reading program must begin with an effective referral and selection process. At the elementary level, teachers are the primary key to identifying those students most in need of assistance. But the principal, and others in the school including the school nurse, assistant principal, librarian, and other teachers should know the route of referral to call a student to the reading teacher's attention. In addition, parents should have the opportunity to meet the teacher charged with the remedial reading program. There should be the opportunity for parents to meet the teacher during parents' visitation night, at parent-teacher nights, and other times during the year. This provides an informal setting in which parents can discuss the problems of their children without the anxiety and fear most feel when they need to make a special trip to school to discuss their child's problems.

Referral slips should be readily available to everyone on the professional staff of the school. One good procedure is to duplicate the slips on bright, light-colored paper (making them easy to identify), cut them into small booklets, and distribute them at least twice a year to all teachers and staff members.

Referral at the secondary school level is much the same as at the elementary except for the important role played by the counseling staff at that level and the fact that students can also play a part in referral. Some students refer themselves; some refer their friends or siblings.

Whether the school is elementary or secondary, a community college, or a correctional or adult learning center program, standardized reading achievement test results can be an important means of identifying poor readers early. Test results at the secondary level and entrance examinations at the college level often indicate 15 to 40 percent of the student population in need of corrective reading instruction.

After the reading teacher has begun to receive the referrals or has ferreted out students who need help by looking through test results, some means of selection must be set up. Figure 9-1 illustrates one means of keeping track of referrals and logging student information. The student's chronological age is entered in the first column, followed by actual grade placement and estimated mental age. As discussed in Chapter Eight, the indication of any realistic mental age is particularly difficult in the case of students who are poor readers. The fact that

Student	Chronological Age	Grade Placement	Estimated Mental Age	Estimated Mental Grade Equivalent	Estimated Reading Grade Achievement	Estimated Reading Lag	Preferred Time for Attendance in Reading Program	Referral Source #1	Referral Source #2	Referral Source #3	Referral Source #4	Notes and Comments	Priority, 1, 2, 3

Figure 9-1. Student Information, Referral, and Selection Form

many poor readers come from backgrounds that differ from the dominant society in terms of language and culture makes it even harder to estimate their intellectual potential. The research of Gerken (1978) and others seem to indicate that if a language other than English is spoken in the home, it is likely to affect measured IQ by an average of ten points or more. The degree to which IQ scores are depressed by poor reading ability, limited English language facility, and lack of familiarity with the dominant culture depends on the severity of each student's limitations. It is undeniable that there will be an adverse effect on IQ scores. The strength of that effect can only be estimated.

The fourth column is for mental grade equivalence, the conversion of the estimated mental age to an equivalent grade designation. For example, students who have not been retained in a grade are usually about 13 years old when they begin eighth grade. Therefore, the grade equivalent of a mental age of 13 years would be roughly eighth grade.

The fifth column is for estimated reading grade equivalence. Although instructional reading level would be preferable here, it is often not obtainable for the initial screening of a large number of students. It is not wise to use instructional reading levels for a few students and standardized reading test scores for the rest when an attempt is being made to compare the students, because the scores will not represent the same levels of ability. Standardized reading-test scores are usually higher than the instructional reading levels obtained from the administration of an informal reading inventory. Since that is the case, when instructional reading levels are not yet available during early screening, it is better to use the same standardized reading achievement test for all the students being screened, listing the reading grade equivalent scores as the estimated reading grade equivalents on the form shown in Figure 9-1.

A special note should be made here of the *Metropolitan Achievement Test* (MAT) (1978) which includes a criterion-referenced reading subtest designed to indicate the instructional reading level. Smith and Beck (1980), in describing the validation research for the MAT, reported exact identification of the instructional reading level only 30 percent of the time. When they allowed a variation of one grade level higher or lower, identification rose to 70 percent.

Clement (1980), in independent research based on a larger sample but limited to fifth-grade level, found that MAT results tended to place poor and average readers approximately one grade level higher than IRI results, and that the MAT tended to place good readers lower than the IRI. She reported that although mean-score differences were not substantial, variation in individual scores made the MAT ineffective in accurately indicating individual student instructional reading levels.

It seems likely that, while the MAT may not be precise in yielding individual instructional reading levels, it may be useful as a screening device, and the results appear to be the closest approximation yet by any standardized reading achievement test, an accomplishment that should not be allowed to slip by without praise.

From a comparison of the student's estimated mental grade equivalence and estimated reading grade achievement, the teacher can derive approximate reading lag—i.e., how far behind the student is in reading ability, keeping his estimated potential in mind. Figure 9-1 makes it possible for the teacher to rank students for inclusion in corrective, remedial, and extreme reading-disability programs on the basis of the severity of their difficulties.

Other columns in Figure 9-1 include spaces in which to indicate preferred times for attendance and who referred the student or the route by which the student came to the attention of the teacher. Next is a space to note the student's needs and the type of instruction best suited for him. Finally, there is a column in which to indicate priority ranking for selection. Figure 9-2 has been filled out to demonstrate the possible uses of the form.

Secondary-school students should be allowed a voice in whether they should enroll in the program. If the program has a good reputation and is not viewed by the students as "dumping ground" for disciplinary problems or undesirable students, almost all those invited to enter the program will elect to do so. When they are allowed to make their own choice about coming into the program, many problems concerning discipline and motivation can be lessened.

OBJECTIVES OF REMEDIAL INSTRUCTION

Greg was referred for reading assistance by his math teacher. Testing showed him to be reading at a beginning fourth-grade level even though he was an eleventh-grader. He worked hard and in less than half a year had increased his reading ability by 1.5 grade levels.

When his math teacher talked with the reading teacher about his success in improving his reading, she seemed less than enthusiastic. She noted that he had been in the reading center for almost half the school year and that she was disappointed he still was not reading at grade level. Probably everyone who has ever worked with poor readers has shared the reading teacher's sense of frustration at that moment.

What *are* reasonable objectives for corrective, remedial, and extreme reading-disability programs? First of all, the closer students are to their grade level, the easier it is to improve their reading ability. A student who appears to have normal intelligence and is a corrective reader will tend to make significantly greater gains than one who has the same capability but is extremely reading-disabled. It is likely that this fact is due in part to the effect extremely poor reading has on a student's self-concept as well as to other factors—those which may not have been identified in the very poor reader's situation but which may be interfering with his growth in reading.

Whatever the cause, the highest predictor of future success in learning to read is a student's past performance in learning to read (Brown, 1970). Those who are corrective readers will often make gains of two grade levels in half a year's time.

Figure 9-2. Student Information, Referral, and Selection Form

Student	Chronological Age	Grade Placement	Estimated Mental Age	Estimated Mental Grade Equivalent	Estimated Reading Grade Achievement	Estimated Reading Lag	Preferred Time for Attendance in Reading Program	Referral Source #1	Referral Source #2	Referral Source #3	Referral Source #4	Notes and Comments	Priority, 1, 2, 3
George B.	14	9	14	9	5.6	3.4	Eng/5th per	Cole Eng	Garcia Guidance			Corrective	1
Joan C.	14	9	12	7	6.4	.6	Eng/3rd per	Brown Eng	Noxie Math	Parent		Corrective	3
Carl D.	15	10	14	9	6.0	3.0	Study-hall 3rd period	Maco Eng	Smith Eng	Butch Vice P		Corrective	1
Bert F.	13	9	15	10	7.9	2.1	Eng/5th per	Student Eng				Corrective	2
Jack F.	15	9	13	8	1.9	6.1	Eng/1st per	Cole Guidance	Parent Cole Guidance	Brown Eng	Bigg SS	Extreme Rdg. Disability	1
Meryl N.	14	9	12	7	4.9	2.1	Eng/3rd per	Garcia Guidance/Josh	Jones Guidance/Josh			Remedial	2
Robert J.	14	9	15	10	3.4	6.6	Eng SS Core/2nd per	Perez Core Guidance	Perez Guidance			Remedial	1
Isidro L.	16	10	15	10-	4.8	5.2	Eng/1st per	self	Guy Assoc			Remedial	1
Carla N.	14	9	14	9	6.3	2.7	Eng/5th per	Costa Eng	Bigg SS	Garcia Guidance		Corrective	1
Joe N.	14	9	12	7	1.8	5.2	Eng/3rd per	Mother Abby	Abby Duo			Extreme Rdg. Disability	2
Roger S.	15	10	13	8	6.6	1.4	Eng/5th per	Brown Eng	Brown Parent			Corrective	2
Pearl S.	14	9	12	7	2.9	4.1	Eng/5th per	Carter Eng	Carter Bigg SS			Remedial? Check	2
Tom T.	14	9	14	8	2.2	5.8	Eng/5th per	Carter Vice P	Carter Eng	Perez Core		Extreme Rdg. Disability	1
Jerry W.	15	9	16	11	5.8	5.2	Eng/1st per	Cole Guidance/math	Noxie Math			Corrective	1

For them, "catching up" can often be possible. For those who are properly classified as remedial readers, gains are smaller; depending on innumerable individual variables, remedial readers can make acceptable-to-good gains ranging from 1.5 to 3.5 grades levels in one year's time. Extremely disabled readers will average even smaller gains. Some will be fortunate to make one grade level increase in a year. Average gains will be in the neighborhood of 1.5 to 2.0 grade levels per year.

In each category, some students will do much better and some will do more poorly depending on the student, the nature of his difficulties, and the support offered by the parents. In addition, the nature of the program, the training and ability of the teacher, the facilities and materials available, and the support for the program among other teachers and the administration will all contribute to the success or failure of the program.

It is important, however, to look at the grade gains from the perspective of the student who has made little or no progress in his reading since he has been in school. If a student has been in school for four years and is reading about as well as a middle first-grader, that means he has gained an average of one-eighth of a year for each year he has been in school. If his gains in a remedial program are about 1.5 grades for his first year of remedial reading instruction, that means his rate of learning has increased an amazing 1200 percent! He is learning twelve times faster than his average before coming into the program.

When John, the left handed young man who was discovered to be obscuring his writing as he wrote, first came to the reading center, he might have been said to have been reading at the 1.2 grade level. A year later, he had made over three years' progress. Treating the data as we did above, we find that he had previously made an infinitesimal .025 of a year gain for each year in school. During his year of remediation, his gains were 120 times greater than his previous annual progress.

Admittedly, such data are dramatic, but they may be used as an antidote for the unwarranted discouragement felt by students, their parents, or their teachers when they have not attained grade-level parity with other students their age in an unreasonably short period of time. Those affected either directly or indirectly by reading programs should understand what reasonable objectives for improvement may be. A good initial grasp of what a reading program can do will result in encouragement rather than disillusionment, and understanding and support for the program.

INDIVIDUALIZING THE REMEDIAL PROGRAM

The larger the discrepancy between students' reading ability and their potential, the greater the need for individualized instruction. "Individualization" does not necessarily mean that instruction will be carried out on a one-to-one basis. It simply means that programs will be planned and conducted to meet individual needs. There are times, of course, when the only way to meet a student's needs is through the individual attention of a teacher working one to one, but, far more frequently, a student can work with other students, or occasionally, work alone for a major portion of the time, with instructional needs filled and good progress made in the individualized program.

The size of the group in which a student should work varies with the degree of his difficulty. Those who may be classified as corrective students usually have enough ability and, therefore, enough independence to work in groups of 16 to 20 students. Individualization for corrective students consists of the provision of instruction and materials needed to meet their needs for the relatively advanced reading skills that separate them from grade-level achievement. They have experienced sufficient success in learning to read to have some self-confidence in their ability to learn, and they read well enough to read directions, work with exercise sheets, and handle other reading tasks necessary to succeed in their program.

Students classified as remedial need considerably more of the teacher's time and attention. Group size usually ranges from three to eight students. When the class has more than that number, students must wait for the teacher to get to them and help them find out what they are to do. Those with extreme reading disabilities frequently must have a teacher–student ratio of 1:1 to 1:3 in order to be successful (Guthrie, Seifert, and Kline, 1978, pp. 2–6).

Another factor in an effective instructional program is its time and duration. Students must have frequent, continual instruction, preferably 45 minutes or so every day for several months if the instruction is to be effective.

Programs in which remedial reading is coupled with special reading taught in content areas seems to be particularly effective. On one occasion, the author experimented with supportive classes in social studies and language arts. Students received one period of remedial or extreme-reading-disability instruction and then were guided into a "core" class in which social studies and language arts were combined in a double period. Gains for those students were approximately 50 percent greater than for students enrolled in the reading instruction groups alone; the latter group averaged 1.46 years gain in 16 weeks, the former, 2.20 years gain in 18 weeks. Forty-six students were enrolled in the core classes, and they were compared with 22 students who were enrolled in the remedial and extreme reading disability classes alone.

Guthrie, Seifert, and Kline (1978, pp. 2–6) corroborate the positions above in their review of research related to remedial reading programs. Although it is difficult to draw exact parallels between the grouping and instructional programs described above and those they reviewed because of the diversity of the programs they examined, they concluded that the duration of instruction and group size are both important. They did not deal with corrective programs but apparently found that for remedial students (whom they did not appear to distinguish from extremely disabled readers), the most effective group size was one teacher for no more than three students.

When students enter an effective reading improvement program, it should be expected that they will make significant gains. This means that placement/grouping should be flexible. A student may start as an extremely disabled reader using an intensive instructional program requiring much individual teacher assistance. Within, say, four months, he could move into a somewhat larger grouping of remedial students in a program in which more independence is both required and fostered. With good progress, it is possible that he would have made the gains necessary to be placed in a corrective program in one or two years. For some students this projection would be optimistic, of course; for others it might even be too slow. But for all students, the teacher must be aware of the need to keep the instructional groupings sufficiently flexible that students may be moved to more challenging placement when it seems indicated.

Generally, remedial readers are assigned to a reading or learning center where they all report on the same starting day and continue throughout the year, with all attending at the same hour each day. An interesting variation provides for one student at a time to be picked up in a remedial or extreme-reading-disabilities program until finally the teacher has added as many students as he thinks he can handle during that period. There are times when a teacher can teach no more than four of five remedial students; at other times, he may be able to handle as many as eight. But if eight are assigned to begin at once, the instructional program will suffer if this proves to be too many, and it is difficult to eliminate students already assigned. By adding students one at a time, the teacher has a chance to "test the water" before adding another student.

INITIATING REMEDIATION

The ultimate aim of reading instruction—developmental or remedial—is to enable students to gain meaning from print. To do so, they must process reading material both in terms of *recognition* of graphic symbols, and the *meaning* of the author.

Remediation cannot be effective if it is divorced from the actual practice of reading. Students must do more than work on isolated reading skills. They must have the opportunity to do regular reading, making an effort to find meaning using syntactic-semantic, visual, and phonemic processes in an intergrated fashion.

The teacher should know each student's functional reading levels, match the student with reading material at an appropriate level of readability and interest, and provide students with *time* to read; the single most important element of successful remedial programs.

However, most remedial students are not able to process materials easily, even when they are given materials at their instructional reading level. The teacher must plan remedial instruction regarding those reading skills found to cause the students difficulty and which deprive them of satisfying and successful reading experience. To ignore skill deficits that are impeding progress, hoping students will learn them on their own, is usually frustrating and unproductive for both the student and teacher.

DEVELOPING INDEPENDENCE

A significant number of poor readers have poor study habits and are unable to assume responsibility for their own instructional programs. It is conceivable that some students have failed to learn to read well because they are poorly organized and dependent on the teacher for guidance and assistance to a far greater degree than other students. At any rate, one of the goals of a remedial reading program should be to develop the ability within each student to work more independently. It is a necessary requisite for moving from extreme reading disability to remedial to corrective reading. Each level requires more independence on the part of students, and if they fail to be more self-directed and self-reliant, their progress will lag.

In learning independence, students must learn to direct their own work with the teacher's guidance. The use of a contract system enables students to select what they are to do on any given day from the work they and the teacher have planned together. A teacher may also use charts or other means by which students can see what work is to be done, make choices, and work on the tasks they have selected in the order they decide. Other means are also effective in developing students' ability to be more self-directing. Whatever approach is used, the remedial or corrective reading teacher should work to have students shoulder more and more responsibility for their own work. Students who daily ask the teacher what is to be done are doing more than just asking a question. They are failing to assume personal responsibility for getting started. If the teacher is the only person responsible for determining what must be done each day, he is fostering dependence. It is far better to provide guidelines, contracts, study units, a weekly outline, individual study plans, listings on the corkboard, or other means by which students may understand what is to be done. Then the teacher can begin to expect, and urge, increasing independence on the part of the student.

Of course, many students are capable of handling their own studies without help but simply prefer to wait for the teacher. In that case, it is less of a matter of teaching students *how* to work independently than it is of *encouraging* them to do so.

USING STUDENT INTEREST

"Reading is a private, individual, and independent process, not a team sport" (Y. Goodman and Burke, 1980, p. 19). Reading should hold the interest of the reader as much as would a private conversation with the author. When reading is uninteresting, the student's personal investment in reading is reduced; his processing of reading material becomes more shallow, as does the richness with which he encodes words and concepts. Lack of interest decreases learning. To attempt to teach using materials students find dull and uninteresting is to court failure with the remedial program.

By using an interest inventory such as that exemplified below, it is usually possible to discover some of the interests of students. Observation of student reading preferences, conversations with individual students, and topics that seem to pique interest in class are all additional means of identifying students' interests.

THE SHIPWRECK

Suppose you've been shipwrecked on a beautiful island. After you get to shore, you find that there is lots of good food and water available. Someone used to live on the island, and they left a nice home that's yours to use. There's even an airstrip. Next to the airstrip is a little hut with a book in it which shows that an airplane comes in about once each month. That means that you only have two weeks to wait to be rescued!

Inside the house, you find several interesting short stories on different subjects. After looking at all of them, you stack them according to how interesting they are to you.

Each of the stories is listed below with its subject and title. On the line after each story, place a number to show whether you think it is interesting. Put a "1" by the story that is most interesting, a "2" by the one that is next most interesting, and so on until you have numbered them all.

The Winning Team (sports group)   _____

Searching for Lost Treasure (adventure)   _____

Let's Go to Hawaii (travel)   _____

Paul Bunyon's Big Blue Ox (tall tales)   _____

Flowers from Joe (romance)   _____

Jokes and Funny Stories (humor)   _____

Call Me "The Animal Doctor" (animals)   _____

Hunting and Fishing Stories
    (sports: individual)   _____

Math Puzzles and Games (math)   _____

Abe Lincoln, Man of Peace (history)   _____

The Story of the Stars (science)   _____

Our Greatest Freedom (social science)   _____

Better Health and Longer Life (health)   _____

Heroes of the Bible (religion)   _____

How to Have a Happy Home (family)   _____

The Law and You (law)   _____

Ways to Improve Your Appearance
    (personal care and appearance)   _____

How to Get a Better Job (jobs)   _____

Cars, Cars, Cars (cars)   _____

More Food for Your Money (shopping)   _____

After identifying interests within the group, a teacher can develop an interest unit to motivate the students to involve themselves more fully in what they are learning. It is unnecessary to build instruction around the topic that most interests each single individual. It is almost always possible to find one or two topics that hold interest for the entire group. One secondary teacher, for example, has developed a well-constructed interest unit on driving. He uses it each year, teaching the vocabulary and reading comprehension involved. It may not be the top choice of each student within the reading groups, but it perennially holds the interest of most of the students in his remedial reading classes for the six weeks or so he uses it each year.

Students' interests should be woven into each element of the instructional program. Their independent reading should be tied to the interest unit or topic. The same should be done for instructional reading. Even skills instruction should involve words or materials taken from or related to the theme of the unit. If, for example, a teacher is working with students on a unit dealing with cars, independent and instructional reading should be woven around materials dealing with cars; if skills work includes the development of a larger basic sight vocabulary, words should be chosen from the area of interest in addition to those that may have been selected from a basic vocabulary list. In this way, the teacher will be able to maintain the thread of interest in all parts of the instructional program, tying the unit together and achieving greater interest, greater involvement, and therefore, greater learning.

One teacher working with a group of remedial students found that they were interested in the opening of spring baseball training camp. Independent reading for the three weeks of the interest unit was taken largely from materials dealing with baseball. The materials included several books and stories at different levels that were taken largely from remedial reading series and individual paperback books, as well as articles from the local newspaper reporting on the spring training camps and rewritten by the teacher and the paraprofessional working with the program. Independent-level reading materials came from the same general sources, with the inclusion of language experience stories written by several of the students and typed for reading by the paraprofessional.

Individual skill development varied, but was composed of such activities as the development of sight recognition vocabulary with some of the words drawn from baseball, the use of baseball terms in learning word attack skills, and so on. A baseball diamond chart was used for part of the reinforcement activities, with the "players" being advanced from one base to another if they were successful in recognizing words, attacking unknown words, or doing whatever was required for that particular activity. Word searches, syllabication games, and so forth included vocabulary drawn from words in the interest unit. The teacher read orally from some of the more difficult material available in the newspapers or sports magazines. Progress was charted on a map which traced the route from spring baseball camps to the home cities of the respective teams. The teacher even obtained the copy of baseball news received by a local radio station. The students used this script to record their own "radio sportscast" on a cassette recorder after they practiced their reading to be sure they could go "on the air" without making too many mistakes and could read the material fluently.

It might seem that such an approach would grow thin very quickly, but that is not usually the case. Students can spend productive hours working on topics they find interesting. It is still necessary to provide material at the students' reading levels, because they will be frustrated and lose interest if materials are too difficult. But if they can read the materials and do the work involved in the interest unit, their level of effort will usually continue at a much higher level than when instruction is simply aimed at rote memorization of skills.

PROVIDING CONSISTENT FEEDBACK

Many errors a student may develop in word recognition occur because consistent correction is lacking. For example, when a student first encounters the words *there* and *where*, he may miscall them. If his teacher provides consistent help in correctly recognizing these words, the student will eventually discriminate between them and recognize them correctly. On the other hand, if the feedback received from the teacher is not consistent, erroneously recognized words may be processed and encoded as correct; a "learned confusion" will be the result.

Learned confusions are common among poor readers. Although the total number of words that are confused would be very large, some examples of frequently confused words are *what-that, this-that, when-then, where-there, those-these,* and *was-saw*.

One way to clarify confusions is to separate the two words and teach them. If *there* and *where* are being confused, the teacher should take one or two minutes each day for a week or so and help the student to learn just one of the two words. The two words should not be put side by side and compared; this will only add to the student's difficulty. (If the student has *not* developed a learned confusion involving the two words, however, it is a perfectly acceptable approach to have him compare them in order to learn to differentiate between them. But not so if he is already confused by them.)

The teacher may put the word *there*, for example, on a word card, use it in a story, have the student write it three times, and have him play with the word.

As soon as the student can respond correctly when he sees the word *there* in print, the teacher should put the word aside. Another word, about which the student is not confused, should then be taught for two or three days, after which the second half of the confused pair should be taught. Teaching a nonconfusing word between the confused pair helps break up any association between the two confused words. If they are taught one after the other, the commonality surrounding their presentation will tend to associate them in the student's mind.

After the word *where* is learned, the teacher should test the student's recognition of the two words as they occur naturally in print, not placed side by side. If they still are confused, they should again be separated and taught individually, although usually they will be learned after one treatment. Occasionally there will be "flashbacks" in which a confused learning will be mastered and then will cause trouble later. When this happens, the teacher should repeat the same process described above. It usually takes significantly less time to master the words the second time.

Of course, the secret in the success of the plan above is that the student is helped to recognize the word consistently. Each time he sees the word, he is helped to recognize it correctly. In any remedial activity, it is important to provide the student with consistent feedback.

LESSON PLANNING

Planning individualized remedial instruction presumes diagnosis but goes beyond it. It is one thing to know the skills a student may be lacking, but quite another to plan how to teach those skills in an order and a manner that will make it possible for the student to learn. Good lesson planning for a remedial or extremely disabled reader involves more than selection of a skill that is to be taught; it involves selection of the skill that should be taught *next*. A poor reader lacks many skills, all of which he needs to learn—eventually. It becomes the responsibility of a capable teacher, removed from the safe guidelines of a curriculum guide or basal reader manual, to determine which skills are more basic in a developmental sense and to marshal his educational forces to help the student learn them.

Objectives   In planning instruction, the teacher should formulate objectives, or expectations, for each period of instruction. An objective may be defined as a statement of a desirable outcome. Objectives are often stated as performance objectives in which the desired student behavior is phrased in measurable terms. The object of instruction is not "to teach" but to have the student learn; therefore, objectives should be stated in terms of what the student is to learn. That means that a teaching objective would not be "to teach the first ten Dolch Basic Sight Vocabulary words"—it would be "to have the student learn the first ten Dolch words."

For an objective to qualify as a measurable performance (or behavioral) objective, the teacher should include (1) the specific behavior to be measured, (2) the conditions under which that behavior will be measured, and (3) the criteria the teacher will accept as evidence that the student has learned that behavior. For example, a performance objective might be stated, "Given the first ten Dolch Basic Sight Vocabulay words (conditions), the student will be able to pronounce nine of them (specific behavior and criterion of mastery)." The teacher can ascertain whether the student has met the objective based on the criterion contained within the performance objective.

There are many times when performance objectives seem to be somewhat artificial, however. In the objective just stated, the criterion is 90 percent performance. Is the instruction and learning a failure if it reaches only 80 percent? Obviously not. The establishment of criteria is arbitrary and, therefore, not always realistic or satisfactory. Performance objectives often are not flexible enough to measure important attitudinal and affective changes. A possible objective of a teacher who is working with a student for the first time is to put the student at ease and establish a good working relationship. It is difficult to put that into a performance objective without using artificial criteria. Since that is the case, many teachers prefer to use a less formal style of objective statement, stating the desired outcome in terms of the student's learning or behavior and attitude, but not trying to quantify each objective. A comparison of the two kinds of statements illustrates the differences.

Performance Objectives With Criteria

1. Given five books at his independent reading level, the student will choose one to read.
2. Given a selected set of words, the student will correctly apply the final silent "e" rule to 90 percent of the words.
3. Given a book dealing with his interests and written at his instructional reading level, the student will demonstrate his enjoyment by ranking the book on an interest scale of 1 to 10.

Objectives Without Performance Criteria

1. The student will select a book to read at his independent reading level.
2. The student will learn to apply the final silent "e" rule.
3. The student will develop reading enjoyment by reading in his areas of interest and at his instructional reading level.

No matter which approach is used, the teacher should have in mind what he wants the student to learn in order to be effective in guiding the student's instructional program.

For planning individualized remedial instruction, the teacher may use a plan book with headings for daily objectives, procedures, materials, and evaluation, as shown in Figure 9–3.

Notice that the "Objective" is brief. The activity is spelled out more fully under "Procedures." The "Materials" list enables the teacher to quickly identify and assemble what the students will need when they come in to do their work. The "Evaluation" is also brief and provides space to make suggestions for any needed changes for future sessions.

Although it takes time to make lesson plans, the benefits are substantial in terms of more significant growth, better instructional activities, higher student interest, and reduced discipline problems.

In preparing lesson plans, the teacher should refer to any observation checklists or "student accounting" sheets as illustrated in Figure 7–2 (page 149) to note

Figure 9-3
A Daily Lesson Plan for a Remedial Reading Program

Objectives	Procedures	Materials	Evaluation
1. To develop greater interest in reading.	2. Bill will read the next 5 pages in *Mr. Popper's Penguins* silently and we will discuss the story.	1. *Mr. Popper's Penguins*	1. Bill is very interested in the story and responded actively in our discussion.
2. To develop better fluency.	2. Bill will read a story in the *Double Action* kit at his instructional reading level. He will read it orally.	2. *Double Action* kit	2. Bill read more fluently today than yesterday. He seems to forget after 3 to 4 minutes and his fluency gets worse.
3. To learn the consonant blends br-, dr-, and pr-.	3. Bill will select words from his reading in the *Double Action* series which begin with the consonant blends br-, dr-, and pr-. He will pronounce them, write them on colored slips of paper, and put them in envelopes labeled br-, dr-, and pr-.	3. Colored slips of paper and envelopes labeled br-, dr-, and pr-.	3. Bill had no difficulty with these. I think his problem with consonant blends is due to incomplete learning at the automatic processing level. Next time I will time him and use flash cards to see if he can get them quickly.

Figure 9–3. A Daily Lesson Plan for a Remedial Reading Program

observations that would be incorporated into the plans. He should also refer to previous lesson-plan evaluations to see that those suggestions are being followed and that there is continuity from week to week.

After beginning instruction, the teacher must be careful that his plans keep pace with the student's growth. It is easy to advance the student too rapidly, and it is equally easy to stay at the same level too long, not challenging the student. The lesson plans must be built on the continued diagnosis and monitoring of student progress. In this regard, groupings should be flexible so that those students who make greatest progress are not held back by those who are unable to progress as rapidly.

The teacher must also be aware of any "snags" in a student's progress. When a student encounters a skill or principle too difficult to master, his progress will slacken, his confidence may be shaken, and he may stop trying. The teacher should be alert to the student's effort and progress and, when something goes wrong, assist the student in overcoming the difficulty. Generally, the teacher must diagnose the problem quickly and break the skill down into simpler elements so the student can handle it more easily.

For example, if the student has difficulty breaking an unfamiliar word into syllables, it may be necessary for the teacher to guide the student to a more basic level. He may need to teach the student (1) what a syllable is, (2) that every syllable has one sounded vowel, (3) that every syllable has a "beat" to it, (4) that the number of beats in a word is the same as the number of syllables in that word, and so on. This will help the student understand the more basic information needed to complete the skill exercise. In planning instruction, the teacher should attempt to program the presentation of the material to provide the student with a good chance for success.

THE REMEDIAL PROGRAM

The earmarks of a good remedial program, and often a program for extremely disabled readers as well, includes a variety of activities to accomplish various purposes. For example, good remedial instruction is generally built around an *interest unit* that has been planned to capitalize on the interests of the students. Also, *independent reading opportunities* must be provided during most reading sessions. Independent-level reading allows a student to automatize word recognition, develop fluency, learn to use context clues in recognizing words, and develop an appreciation and enjoyment of reading. Independent reading should generally be a time to practice silent reading skills.

A third earmark is provision for *instructional-level reading* during each reading session. This is especially important in learning to utilize word analysis skills and adding to the store of previously unfamiliar words a student can recognize.

Although students may read silently during most of their instructional reading, a teacher will find it profitable to ask each student to read orally for 2 or 3 minutes. If the student miscalls a word, the teacher should avoid "verbally bathing" the student with directions about how the word should be attacked. Too many instructions deprive the student of the opportunity to learn to process the word independently. Often all that is necessary is to point to the missed word, saying nothing, and allow the student an opportunity to analyze the word on his own. Too much direction may interfere with the student's own attempts to process the word, and make it difficult for him to experiment with his own strategies.

When students individually read aloud briefly every day or two, the teacher can monitor progress and identify any difficulties. This leads to the fourth earmark of a good program: *practical, applied skills development.* After hearing the student read orally, the teacher can select one or two errors, identify the strategies the student needs to learn, and work with the student at that moment with the application of those strategies to the material at hand. If the student's errors require skills not yet encountered, assuming they are appropriate to learn at this time, the teacher can introduce the student to the principles involved. In this way, the student sees that the skills are not esoteric; they are practical, based on current material and, therefore, of immediate utilitarian value.

Extended skills development should also be related to the actual needs of the student. If a reading-skills workbook is used, it is more effective to tear the workbook pages out and use them as they are needed. Spirit masters and kits with individual cards containing skills-development work should be used selectively, with the student assigned work that relates specifically to immediate skill needs.

Skills development should be a *part* of the reading improvement program, never the total program. A reading program based solely on skills instruction tends to develop students who are good word analyzers but who dislike reading and who are not likely to do well in the areas of comprehension, applied use of context clues, fluency, rate, reading evaluation, appreciation, and enjoyment—all crucial to effective reading.

The fifth earmark of a good remedial reading program is the inclusion of *skill reinforcement activities* such as games, puzzles, and other activities designed to allow students to use the skills with which they have been working for enjoyable ends while practicing them. Reinforcement activities help speed processing and make recognition more nearly automatic. Most reinforcement activities can be used for rewards, but they do more than merely make learning fun (although they may not do that as well). They provide a parallel for the poor reader, through extended time practicing reading skills in a pleasant activity, to that experience which good readers normally receive because they enjoy reading and do a great deal of it.

The sixth earmark of good remedial reading instruction is *oral modeling.* When a teacher reads to poor readers, he demonstrates or "models" what reading should be like so that these students can "experience" good reading. Oral modeling is usually best done when several students rather than just one are listening. Oral reading should be limited in time—to, say, 5 or 10 minutes every few days.

Some students do not respond well to oral modeling by the teacher, but they are few and far between. Students usually respond well to this technique, even when teachers do not have very expressive voices. However, the more communicative teachers are in their reading, the better models they will be.

A seventh earmark of a good program is *progress charting*. A common characteristic of poor readers is that they generally feel that they are unable to learn to read well, and become discouraged. Anything the teacher can do to dramatize their improvement will help to offset this poor self-image.

There are hundreds of ways that progress can be graphically emphasized. One girl chose to add a part to a mobile for every book she read during remediation. Her clinician helped her make the basic structure, and after each book, the student would draw a figure representing the material she had read, cut it out, and hang it from the mobile.

Before long, her mobile began to grow to sizable length, and it attracted the attention of others in the reading center. A reporter from the school paper wrote a story about it. The school librarian, seeing the story, asked if she could hang the mobile in the library for National Book Week. The student agreed, and the mobile was placed on prominent display where it was seen by her parents, grandparents and friends.

Most progress charting fails to attract as much attention as the mobile, but can be just as effective in terms of the encouragement provided for students. Progress charts may consist of graphs, charts, maps—anything that will help students realize they have made gains. One student was allowed to work 5 minutes on a model of a red Model T Ford every time he finished a chapter in the book he was reading. As the Ford took shape, it became concrete evidence of his achievement in the reading program.

For progress charting to be most effective, there should be frequent opportunities for students to indicate their gains. If evaluations that mark progress are done only once a week or so, students will not receive the steady encouragement they get from marking the chart daily.

The charting must be objective, and the teacher should not allow students to mark progress when they have not earned the right to do so. If that happens, the reward will lose its meaning, and the value of progress charting will be lost.

One last earmark of effective remedial instruction is the use of *evaluation*. Achievement should be monitored for the sake of both the teacher and the student. As students enter the program, it is a good idea to record individual performance on one or more measures so that performance at later dates can be compared and achievement noted. If an informal reading inventory is used, it is possible to keep track of students' oral and silent reading rate, the number of word call errors, and reading comprehension for both oral and silent passages. By comparing performance at the end of the semester with that at the beginning, both students and teacher are likely to be encouraged. Progress is usually slow enough that daily gains pass unnoticed. Marks of progress over a long period of time can be gratifying.

There are significant differences between remedial and corrective instructional programs. Groups are larger and general levels of ability are higher for corrective classes. Normal corrective groups may run from sixteen to twenty students, while no more than eight students should be in remedial groups. The larger groups to be found in corrective instruction necessitate the use of group diagnostic reading tests. Although these tests are not as diagnostically accurate as some individual tests, they can be administered to an entire group at once, saving time and effort. The teacher may also make use of a group reading inventory such as that described in Chapter Six to estimate reading levels of the students within a corrective class.

Grouping and classroom management for corrective classes at the secondary level, the one at which most corrective classes exist, can involve certain hazards. Students should never be grouped according to sensitive criteria. The division of students within a class into the subgroups specified to meet particular needs can be self-defeating if students within those groups feel that they have been denigrated by the process. It would be unthinkable for students to be told they have been assigned to a group because they are of lower intelligence. Yet the implications can be almost as bad if they are told that they have been placed in a certain group because their reading comprehension is lower than that of other students in the class.

A less sensitive variable on which students can be divided into groups is reading rate. For some reason, the ability to read faster or slower than someone else seems to arouse few, if any, feelings of personal unworthiness. In speaking to the class, the teacher may want to equate the ability to read rapidly with the abilty to run rapidly, explaining that just as it would not be fair to have the fastest person in the class compete with someone who ran a lot more slowly, it would not be fair for those who read more slowly to be forced to compete wtih those who read more rapidly. Therefore, the teacher may go on, students will be placed in groups that roughly approximate their *rate of comprehension*. This tends to be an acceptable rationale for grouping and seems to meet with few student objections.

Rate of comprehension is an index of reading ability computed by multiplication of the percent of comprehension by the rate in words per minute. For example, if a student received a score of 80 percent correct on the test over the selection, and read at a rate of 200 words per minute, his rate of comprehension would be 80 percent of 200, or $.80 \times 200 = 160$. Rate of comprehension is a better variable to use than simple rate because it identifies the student who skims through the material in order to make a fast reading-rate score but who does not read carefully enough to understand the material.

In order to organize the groupings, the teacher may administer a relatively short (10 minutes or so) reading test measuring students' abilities to read rapidly and understand what they have read. The material should be easy narrative material, and comprehension should be checked with ten questions over the selection. After they finish reading, the students are asked to enter the time it took them to read the selection, after which they answer the questions. Finally, they exchange papers and correct one another's tests. The teacher then has the information needed to make an assessment of each student's rate of comprehension.

The students should then be ranked in order of their rate of comprehension. Their instructional reading levels and any other information such as the results from standardized reading achievement tests may be placed beside their scores. With this information, the students can usually be placed according to their levels of ability. Students who have a higher rate of comprehension than their other scores and instructional reading levels indicate should be moved to a group closer to their level of ability. If the reverse is true, of course, they would be moved to a higher group. On the whole, however, students tend to conform fairly closely to the rank order of their rate of comprehension scores, and grouping can generally be accomplished without injured feelings or lowered self-esteem.

When instruction is individualized and each group of students in a corrective reading class is working on its own program, the first few minutes of the period can be disorderly. Even though the teacher has planned and organized in advance by either posting the work of each group on a bulletin board or providing a student work plan for each group, 5 or 10 minutes may be lost as students gather the material they need for that hour's work. Although the teacher can prepare the student folders in advance for the first group of the day, if there is more than one group using the same materials, it becomes impractical to try to regather the materials and distribute them for the next group of students unless there is a great deal of time between the classes.

A better plan is to appoint a captain for each group to handle the materials needed for that group. The materials can be placed in the individual student folders, distributed to the members of the group, and, when the class is over, collected and returned to the proper places. If there are four groups, only four students are involved in the distribution and collection of materials rather than fifteen to twenty. While the materials are being distributed, the teacher can use the time to involve the rest of the students in other activities.

Some teachers find it difficult to work with two or more groups within the corrective classroom at the same time. While the teacher is working directly with one group, another group may finish what it is doing and may begin to waste time. The teacher must then get the second group back to work quickly so the work of the first group is not interrupted. This necessitates assessing the students' progress quickly, pointing them to their next task if they have finished their first one, or redirecting their attention to the task at hand if they have stalled.

One way to speed such a monitoring process is to include a culminating activity for each task whenever possible. If students must complete a progress chart, fill in answers, write a summary, or complete another terminal activity before the task is considered complete, this enables the teacher to check student progress quickly by looking at the culminating activity for that particular task.

As students make gains, their grouping should reflect their progress. When a corrective reading class first gets underway, the grouping arrangement should have more students toward the lower end of the scale. As students progress, the situation should gradually reverse itself, with more and more students moving to advanced groups.

In initial grouping, some students are likely to be placed higher than they should be. Downward movement, though sometimes necessary in order to have students working at a productive level, can be embarrassing and should be handled in an inconspicuous manner. Even movement to higher groups should be done in a way that will arouse little attention on the part of other students.

In order to lessen the stigma of placement in lower-ability groups, the teacher should utilize vertical as well as horizontal grouping. In vertical grouping, the lower-ability student has an opportunity to work with those who are better readers than he is. Reading tasks can be difficult material or be responsible for work within their ability. The differentiated one-act plays published by Harcourt Brace Jovanovich in its *Echo Plays* kit is an example of the sort of activity that fits nicely into vertical groupings. Some parts are written at an easier level than others, so that students with different reading abilities can take a part in the plays, with all reading at their instructional reading levels.

A corrective reading program should include elements of the good remedial or extreme reading-disabilities program discussed in the previous section: (1) independent reading, (2) instructional reading, (3) work on specific reading-skill deficits, and (4) progress charting. A fifth element, used less frequently, should be occasional modeling of oral reading in which the teacher shares some reading with the class either by reading orally or by having a capable student read for a few minutes.

It can be encouraging to share achievement gains with older students, although the teacher should be careful not to confuse students by using measurement "jargon." Since subtest scores are less reliable than total reading test scores, it is usually better to confine the comparisons of pre-test and post-test differences to total test scores.

PARAPROFESSIONALS

Teacher's aides, paraprofessionals, and tutors have become important additions to the field of education. In general, their role has been to work with individuals or with small groups of students, providing special or additional instruction under the guidance of a trained teacher. Although most paraprofessionals do not look on teaching as a career, they usually have some training in the field of education—either in-service training received as part of their position or pre-service training received before their selection.

Guthrie, Seifert, and Kline (1978, p. 9) have summarized several research studies relating to the effectiveness of teachers, clinicians in training, and older students. They affirm that remedial instruction must apparently be *planned* by people who are "knowledgeable experts in reading" but that others less well trained seem to be effective in implementing the planned instructional program. Paraprofessionals who relate well to the students with whom they will work, if given careful guidance in the planned individualization of the students' reading program, can add strength to reading programs.

SUMMARY

A cornerstone of an effective reading program is the identification and selection process through which the students are added to the program. Referrals should be solicited from teachers, counselors, administrators, parents, and other students. Standardized reading-achievement test results may also be used to help identify those who should be screened for inclusion in the different levels of the reading program of the school.

The objectives of the reading-improvement program should be understood by those involved with the program and also by the teaching staff or the school, the administration, and interested parents and students. The objectives and the program vary with the severity of the students' difficulties, generally requiring more individualization when there is greater limitation of ability. Programs for students who have an extreme reading disability usually cannot accommodate more than three students at a time. Remedial programs can often include up to eight students, and corrective programs, in which the students are somewhat more independent, can usually include a small, classroom-sized group.

Programs that are effective in helping students make significant improvements in their reading ability should meet several times a week and should be long-term. Programs that involve supportive reading instruction in students' content classes tend to be more effective than those in which reading instruction is limited to a remedial class. Remediation should be based on student reading levels and planned to meet reading-skill deficits.

Since improvement depends to some degree on each student's ability to work independently, teachers should work to develop autonomy and initiative. The program should be built around interesting units and should provide feedback and correction so students will learn to recognize their own errors.

Careful lesson planning should include objectives, procedures, materials, and a brief evaluation of each day's work. Earmarks of good remedial instruction should usually include opportunities for independent level reading, instructional level reading, skills instruction, skill reinforcement through the use of activities, some oral modeling by the teacher, and progress charting.

Though corrective reading instruction is different from remedial or extreme reading-disability instruction in size of the groups and in degree of personal instructor involvement needed for progress, there are a number of similarities. Corrective reading classes, like remedial, should provide opportunities for the students to do independent and instruction level reading and skills improvement, and to plot their own progress. They should also have occasional oral modeling by the teacher.

Paraprofessionals have been shown to be effective in carrying out certain aspects of remedial instruction if the instruction has been designed and planned well by a trained professional teacher. A paraprofessional must have some degree of training in order to be competent, and must be able to work under direction.

RECOMMENDED READINGS

Bond, G.; Tinker, M.; and Wasson, B. 1979. *Reading difficulties: Their diagnosis and correction.* Englewood Cliffs, N.J. Prentice-Hall, Chapter 8.

Cheek, M. C.; and Cheek, E. H. 1980. *Diagnostic-prescriptive reading instruction: A guide for classroom teachers.* Dubuque, Ia.: Wm. C. Brown, Chapters 7 and 8.

Harris, L. A. and Smith, C. B. 1980. *Reading instruction: Diagnostic teaching in the classroom.* 3rd ed. New York: Holt, Rinehart & Winston, Chapter 13.

Goodman, Y.; and Burke, C. 1980. *Reading strategies: Focus on comprehension.* New York: Holt, Rinehart & Winston, Chapter 3.

Guthrie, J. T.; Seifert, M; and Kline, L. W. 1978. Clues from research on programs for poor readers. In *What research has to say about reading instruction,* ed. S. J. Samuels. Newark, Del.: International Reading Assoc., pp. 1–12.

REFERENCES

Brown, D. A. 1970. Measuring the reading ability and potential of adult illiterates. In *Measurement and evaluation of reading.* New York: Harcourt Brace Jovanovich, pp. 154–65.

Clement, B. W. 1980. *A comparison of a standardized group reading test and an informal reading inventory in estimating an instructional reading level.* Published doctoral dissertation, Univ. Northern Colorado.

Gerken, K. C. March 1978. Performance of Mexican children on intelligence tests. In *Exceptional children.* 44: 438–43.

Goodman, Y.; and Burke, C. 1980. *Reading strategies: Focus on comprehension.* New York: Holt, Rinehart & Winston.

Guthrie, J. T.; Seifert, M.; and Kline, L. W. 1978. Clues from research on programs for poor readers. In *What research has to say about reading instruction,* ed. S. J. Samuels. Newark, Del.: International Reading Assoc., pp. 1–12.

Smith, W. E.; and Beck, M. D. 1980. Determining instructional reading level with the 1978 Metropolitan Achievement Tests. *The reading teacher.* 34: 313–19.

The students who usually cause a teacher the greatest concern and whose reading abilities are most difficult to improve are the severly disabled readers. Some students have made little progress in reading even after years of school attendance. Skilled, personalized, and intensive instruction, however, can be effective in teaching virtually every student to read. Approaches that have been notably successful with extremely disabled readers are described in this chapter.

INTENSIVE
INSTRUCTIONAL
APPROACHES
FOR
EXTREMELY DISABLED
READERS

Extremely disabled readers need instruction organized to offer the best possible opportunity to improve their reading ability. After experiencing repeated frustration in learning to read, they cannot afford the "luxury" of another attempt that ends in failure. The greatest likelihood of success involves an investment of more teacher time and effort per student, and the use of teachers who have had advanced specialized training.

There are several intensive approaches. The VAKT approach, described below, was first introduced in 1921. More recent methods also have the same objective: to improve reading ability for disabled readers.

VISUAL-AUDITORY-KINESTHETIC-TACTILE (VAKT) APPROACHES

VAKT approaches are unusual in that they employ techniques for learning through muscle movement and touch. *Kinesthesia* is a term given to the sense of position and movement gained through the nerves in the muscles, tendons, and joints. If we hold the hand and arm of another person, making sure his eyes are closed, and move that person's hand in a circle, he can correctly identify the figure because of kinesthetic feedback. Often, in writing or typing, a person realizes he has made an error in spelling before he even looks back at the word. This realization stems from a learned familiarity with the way the muscles of the hand and arm should move to produce that word.

The touch, or *tactile*, sense allows us to make fine discriminations. Given a coin, an adult can almost always identify its denomination, even discriminating between a dime and a penny.

The VAKT approach makes use of the kinesthetic and tactile senses in addition to the visual and auditory senses in teaching individuals to identify words. This technique has an added advantage: it is much more difficult for the student's attention to be diverted when he is concentrating on correctly identifying a word by using all four senses. Sometimes poor readers have a tendency to daydream when they are presumably working to improve their reading. With the VAKT approach, daydreaming is greatly reduced.

Fernald VAKT   Fernald and her associate, H. B. Keller, pioneered the use of the VAKT approach. Their first description of the techniques and results of the approach appeared in 1921 (Fernald and Keller, 1921, pp. 355–77) and was followed later by Fernald's classic work on remediation, *Remedial Techniques in Basic School Subjects* (1943). Fernald described four stages in her approach:

Stage One—Tracing   In Stage One, the teacher writes a word to be learned on a piece of large paper, using a crayon and writing in large letters. The student traces the word, touching it with either one or two fingers and pronouncing the word as a whole or in syllables as he does so. He must pronounce the word as naturally as possible, avoiding a letter-by-letter sounding of the word. The stu-

202

dent traces it until he can write the word on a piece of paper correctly, without looking at the teacher-written word. He then writes the word in a story. This use of the word in context is considered critical. After the story is written, it is typed for later rereading. The student reads the story after it has been typed and then files each new word in a "word file"; this helps him learn the alphabet and learn how to alphabetize.

Stage Two—Writing Without Tracing   At this stage the approach is much the same as in Stage One except that the student does not trace the word. The teacher writes the word, and the student looks at it, reading it to himself. He then writes it without looking at the original copy made by the teacher, saying the word as a whole or by syllables blended together as he writes it. The student again uses the word in writing a story.

Stage Three—Using Print   Here the same procedures are followed as in Stage Two, except that the teacher does not write the word. Instead, the student looks at the word in print, repeats it to himself, and then writes it without looking at the printed word. At this level, the student is allowed to start reading from published materials, choosing any book he likes, and is free to read as much as he wants. The teacher pronounces any words the student does not know. After the student finishes his reading, he looks back at any words he did not know, repeats them to himself, and then writes them. These words are reviewed later to check retention.

Stage Four—Recognizing New Words   During this stage the student is taught to recognize new words by their similarity to familiar words and syllables. The student is encouraged to preread difficult materials, scanning quickly for words that are unfamiliar. In the early levels of this stage, the student pronounces these words and writes them before reading. Later, he pronounces and writes the words judged to be sufficiently important after he has finished his reading. If, during reading, a word is not recognized, the teacher pronounces it for the student, enabling him to maintain the flow of thought and interest in the passage.

Fernald emphasized that (1) the student should never be allowed to look at the original copy of the word while trying to write it; (2) the word should always be written in context after the student learned to recognize it; (3) the teacher should never do the reading for the student; and (4) the student should never be asked to sound out a word.

Amplified Visual-Auditory-Kinesthetic-Tactile Approach   Because of the effectiveness of the VAKT, and because of the need to improve various aspects of the approach, the author has developed the Amplified VAKT that incorporates (1) a screening procedure, (2) more intensive focus on the specific words to be learned, (3) a vocabulary-learning procedure aimed at developing stronger visual and auditory recognition, and (4) an emphasis on student support and encouragement through progress charting.

Screening and Vocabulary Learning.   The teacher asks the student to choose five words he wants to learn to read. They may be any words he likes. The teacher writes them one at a time on 3 by 5 cards with a pen having a broad stroke, and then briefly discusses each word, making sure the student can see the word on the card clearly and right side up during the discussion. As each new word is added, the previous words should be turned over so they cannot be seen.

The teacher then follows the three-level procedure described below:

First Level. The teacher places five word-cards on the table or desk in front of the student so he can see each word. The teacher then pronounces one of the words, asking the student to identify which word it is by pointing to it. If the student is successful, the teacher picks up the card, praises the student while holding the word so it can be seen, and then places the word out of sight. The teacher then pronounces another word and asks the student to identify it.

If the student cannot locate a word, the teacher identifies it for him. If the student confuses the word with one of the other words left on the table, the teacher pronounces both words, indicating which card has which word. The teacher should not coach the student by saying things like, "Look at the way the word ends," or "Look more closely at the beginnings of the word." The teacher's manner and voice should be warm and accepting but not effusive. A minimum of attention should be called to any errors the student makes because this tends to fix the error in his mind. Praise should be extended (in whatever manner the student can accept it) for each correct identification.

As the student identifies the words on the table, the number of cards left becomes smaller and the likelihood of error decreases. If the student fails to identify the last word on the table, the teacher should pronounce it, add one of the word-cards from those out of sight which the student has already recognized, move both cards about, and again ask the student to identify the words, just as above.

After each mistake, the cards are moved, much like the old carnival shell game, in order to help the student save face. The teacher may say something like, "This is the word 'job' and this is the word 'just.' Now let me move these cards around, and we'll see if I can fool you again." The student will invariably follow the movement of the missed word card to its new position on the tabletop very carefully. Rather than confusing the student, moving the cards seems to cause him to focus his attention on the card even more closely—and, in addition, adds a competitive challenge to the task. The process is continued until each of the five words has been correctly identified.

Second Level. The teacher again places all five of the cards in view on the table. This time, however, the teacher simply points to one of the words and asks the student to identify it. If the student correctly pronounces the word, the teacher picks up the card, as before, praises the student with the card in the student's view, and then removes the card. The teacher continues in this fashion until all the word-cards have been correctly recognized and removed.

If the student makes a mistake, the teacher pronounces the word; if the student has miscalled the word by identifying it as one of the words left on the table, the teacher identifies that word as well.

When the student has only one word remaining on the table, the teacher does not need to add another word to it as was done at the last level, because at this level the words are not pronounced as in the previous level. If, however, the student misses the word and the teacher must pronounce it, then another word must be taken from those the student has already recognized and placed back on the table. The cards are then moved around, and the student is asked to identify the words as before.

Third Level. At this level, the teacher holds the cards as a pack in his hand and places them face up, one at a time, in front of the student, allowing the student 1 or 2 seconds to identify each word. As the cards are placed on the table, each new card covers the preceding one. If the student is not able to pronounce the word before it is covered, the teacher stops and helps the student call the word, then picks the word-card up and replaces it in the deck of word-cards, to be attempted a second time.

When the student misses the last card, the teacher must then pick up another card, mix the two of them, and put them one at a time in front of the student again to be recognized.

The keystone to this approach is *success*. The student never finishes without having successfully identified each word three times. The presentation of the word-cards is sequenced from easy to more difficult. Identification is easier if the word is pronounced by the teacher and if all the student must do is to recognize it from among several other cards. The next step is more difficult. The student must call the word himself, taking all the time necessary to compare the indicated word with the other words left on the table. The last step is the most difficult because the student must recognize the word under a time pressure.

After having learned the five words, the student is asked to help compose a story using them. The words are placed before the student, who is told to use each word at least once in a sentence; he may use more than one of the words in a sentence if he wants to do so. It is not necessary to make a complete story. It is much more likely that the student will dictate two or three sentences that are loosely related.

After composing the story, the student is asked to suggest a title and to write his name on the story as author. Each of the five words just learned is then underlined, and the teacher helps the student read the story, pronouncing any of the words with which the student has difficulty. The student is asked to read the underlined words if he can. If he hesitates, or seems unable to call certain words, the teacher should pronounce those words too. The teacher should not try to guide the student into analyzing the words; however, the student may choose to use analysis skills to unlock a word. The story is then typed, to be read the next day.

When the student returns, the teacher should place the five word-cards on the table or desk so that the student can see them as in the first and second levels of the vocabulary-learning procedure, and ask him to identify the words. Instead of picking up the correctly identified words, the teacher leaves them on the tabletop and does not help the student with the words missed. If the student is able to recognize at least four of the five words without help from the teacher, it indicates that the student can learn to read without using the VAKT approach. If the student recognizes fewer than four, it is likely that he will need some sort of an intensive instructional approach such as the VAKT.

Those students who pass the screening may be placed in one of the remedial approaches or one of the higher Amplified VAKT levels. Those who do poorly proceed to the next step in the Amplified VAKT procedure, outlined below.

Amplified VAKT—Tracing   If the screening indicates that the student should use the VAKT approach, the teacher should introduce it by telling him that it is a relatively new and different approach that has been successful with the students who have used it. He may suggest that the student start by building a vocabulary bank containing words he would like to learn to read. The student may want to include the words from the screening session. By using the student's story as a source of unfamiliar words, the teacher has a reservoir of vocabulary known to the student but possibly unfamiliar to him in his reading. The student should select five words from the story which he would like to learn to read. By adding five words to those left over from the screening, he should have between seven and ten words with which to work.

By using the previous day's story, the student is more likely to select words that have higher frequency than if he is simply asked to name five words at random. With the story as a reference, all he has to do is to select them, rather than having to struggle with bringing some words to mind.

As the student selects each new word, the teacher should write it on a 3 by 5 card with a pen that makes a heavy, distinct line. Felt-tip pens, crayons, and many of the newer pens produce a relatively broad stroke. The teacher should talk with the student briefly about each word, keeping the word in view as it is discussed. Here are some examples of what a teacher might say for some specific words:

> *build*—"That's an interesting word. Notice that it has a *u* in it but you don't hear the *u* when you pronounce the word. Listen. 'Build.'. . . Did you have any special reason for wanting to learn this word?"
> *with*—"This is a word we have seen many times. It's one of the 200 or so words that are most frequently used in the English language. Notice that the last two letters go together to make just one sound. Listen to it. 'With.'' . . ."
> *house*—"That's a useful word. It has several letters that are interesting. Notice that it has an *e* at the end that you don't hear when you say the word. Also look at the letters *o* and *u*. They combine to make a sound like 'ow' in 'out.' It's a good word to know. Is there a special reason you decided to learn it?"

The teacher's comments should usually serve to direct the student's attention to the word, noting any peculiarities. The teacher sometimes may ask the student to tell why he wants to learn the word.

For the first few days, no more than five words per day should be added to the deck of words on which the student is working. As he gains more confidence in his ability to learn, the number may be increased. As soon as a word can be recognized after only one tracing, that word should be filed in the student's vocabulary box. Filing should be done alphabetically to help the student learn the alphabet, if he does not already know it, and to learn how to file and locate information in alphabetized listings.

A small metal or plastic file box may be used for the vocabulary bank. Or a box may be constructed easily from corrugated cardboard. Place one of the cards in the middle of a piece of cardboard slightly larger than a sheet of 8½ by 11 inch notebook paper, cut the corners out as shown in Figure 10-1, fold the sides up, and tape them upright with masking tape. A cover can be made by making another box just slightly larger to fit over the smaller box like a cap. Alphabet dividers can be made by the student or purchased.

After the number of word cards reaches fifteen, the teacher should increase the number cautiously, making sure the student does not become discouraged or is unable to handle the larger number with success. It is important that the student choose the words to learn. Self-selection provides more interest and motivation than is the case when the words are selected by the teacher and the student is told to learn them. Even if some of the words the student chooses are uncommon or unimportant, the teacher should allow the student to work with them if he wants to do so. Neither should there be a limit on the length of words chosen, because longer words are sometimes easier to learn than short ones.

After the student has selected the words from the previous day's story, the teacher has written them, and they have been discussed, the teacher is ready to begin the kinesthetic and tactile portion of the program. Placing one of the word cards before the student, the teacher should ask the student to trace the word with his finger, saying the word aloud as he does so. It is important that the stu-

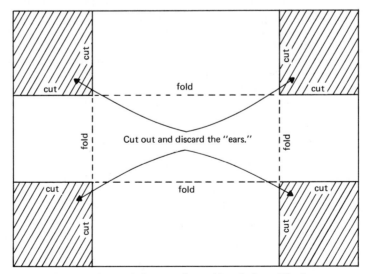

Figure 10-1.   A Pattern for a Vocabulary File Box

dent pronounce the word as he traces it. In pronouncing the word, he should not draw it out unduly or sound it out letter by letter.

Tracing the word while saying it may seem awkward at first, and the teacher may need to demonstrate the process several times, but the student will soon learn how to do it without any difficulty.

Recordkeeping is an important element in the program. Each time the student traces a word, the teacher should place a mark on a record sheet prepared like the one illustrated in Figure 10-2. The record form can be made of butcher paper or tagboard. Across the top of the chart, the teacher should put the date of each session. The words the student chooses to learn should be listed down the left-hand side each day. Under each date, the teacher should record the number of trials necessary for the student to be able to write the word correctly.

The chart should be shared with the student each day. It makes an excellent progress chart. Not only is it a graphic representation of the number of words the student has learned, it also shows the student that he is learning new words with fewer tracing than were necessary when he first began. The chart is an important means of encouragement and an important factor in differentiating successful VAKT programs from those which are not.

The tracing process is relatively simple. It may be summarized as follows:

1. The teacher places the word-card before the student.
2. The student traces the word, using one or two fingers, pronouncing the word as he traces.
3. The teacher records each tracing attempt on the record sheet.
4. After tracing, the teacher removes the word-card from view.
5. The student attempts to write the word on the top line of a strip of notebook paper.
6. The teacher checks to see if the word is correctly spelled.
7. If the word is incorrectly spelled, the teacher folds the word under the strip of paper so that the student cannot see it. This is done to limit the possibility of visual association with the incorrect spelling of the word. The teacher should never urge the student to make corrections on the misspelled word and should avoid critical comments. Continual encouragement of the student is important.
8. The teacher should again place the card before the student.
9. The student should repeat the steps above until he writes the word correctly.
10. When the student writes the word correctly, the teacher should place the word-card alongside the correctly written word and congratulate or reward the student with appropriate verbal praise.
11. If the word has been correctly spelled after the first tracing, the card should be placed alphabetically in the vocabulary file. If it has taken two or more tracings, the card should be kept in the student's working deck.
12. The same process should be followed for each of the other words the student is learning.
13. Words filed in the vocabulary box are reviewed as the student uses them in writing future stories. If he has difficulty with one of the filed words, he may elect to add it to his deck of working cards until he has relearned it. When this is done, the review word is not counted within the limit of new words to be added each day.

Word	10/2	10/3	10/4	10/5	10/6	10/9	10/10	10/11	10/12	10/13	10/16
Hurt	HHt	III	I								
With	HHt IIII	HHt	II	I							
Make	HHt I	II	I								
His	IIII	II	I								
Interested	HHt HHt II	HHt	III	II	I						
Work		HHt I	III	I							
There		HHt II	II	I							
America		HHt IIII	IIII	II	I						
Head		III	I								
Only		HHt	III	I							
Is			II	I							
Do			I								
Reading			HHt	II	I						
Went			HHt I	II	I						
Man			III	I							
Money				IIII	II	I					
Eat				II	I						
Supper				III	II	I					
Was				II	I						
It				I							
The					I						
Like					II	II	I				
Doing					IIII	III	I				
Should					HHt I	IIII	II	I			
Better					IIII	II	II	I			
While						HHt I	III	II	I		
they						IIII	II	II	I		
are						III	I				
Going						IIII	II	I			
Good						II	II	I			
Open							II	I			
Out							I				
Inside							IIII	II	I		
Yesterday							III				
Writing							II	I			
House								II	I	I	
Where								II	II	I	
You								III	I		
Over								II	I		
Use								II	I		
Table									II	II	I
Chair									II	II	I
Room									I		
Pill									I		
Which									III	II	I
Guess										IIII	III
Understand										IIII	II
Window										III	II

Figure 10-2.   A Portion of a VAKT Record Form

209

After the words have been traced, they are presented to the student in the same three levels and in the same manner as in the screening procedure. The student recognizes them (1) as the teacher pronounces them, (2) as the teacher points to them, and (3) as the teacher places them before the student one at a time.

After having identified all the words, the teacher places them so that the student can see and use any of them, together with words from this vocabulary box, in writing the next story. It is unnecessary for him to use all of the deck in the story.

When the student wants to use a word he does not know in the story and when it is not on one of his cards, the teacher should write the word on a card and give it to the student. After writing the story, the student underlines all the words he used from his deck of word-cards, and then reads the story to the teacher or an aide. The teacher should pronounce any words the student cannot recognize on his own. The student should be urged to analyze unfamiliar words at this level.

After reading the story, the student should entitle it and add his name. The story is then typed, and used to begin the next session, in which the student reads the story and selects words from it which he wants to learn to read.

The stories should be gathered into booklets, and the students should be encouraged to reread their previous stories frequently. The repetition is good in developing more automatic word recognition.

There is no accurate way to estimate how long a student may remain at the tracing level. Although Fernald estimated the length of time to be from one to eight months with two months about average, the author's experience at Children's Hospital in Buffalo, New York, and in two different university reading centers, seems to indicate that progress is generally faster when using the Amplified VAKT approach. The length of time in the first level ranges from two to three weeks to as much as six months in rare cases. The average length is about five or six weeks.

Fernald suggested a gradual transition from tracing to the next stage. However, there is some merit in waiting until the student seldom needs more than one or two tracings to write a word correctly and then "promoting" the student to the next level, congratulating him on his progress. It is, after all, a major accomplishment. At the same time, the teacher should point out that tracing is a helpful device which the student may still want to use on occasion.

There are several differences between the Amplified VAKT approach and that of Fernald's. At least five of those differences appear to be of some importance. First, there is much greater control over the words traced in the Amplified VAKT approach. Instead of tracing a great number of different words each day, the student works initially with no more than fifteen. Even after having worked with the approach for three weeks or more, he is unlikely to trace more than two dozen different words each day.

Second, this approach provides follow-up on each word until it is mastered. The same words are kept in a working deck of word-cards until they can be spelled correctly after a first tracing.

Third, recordkeeping helps in following the progress of the student in learning each word and provides consistent encouragement.

Fourth, the use of the three-step vocabulary-learning procedure seems to speed the time it takes a student to master word recognition. It also appears to help the student develop the visual and auditory skills needed in good word recognition.

Fifth, the program is success-oriented and seems to encourage the student to develop greater confidence in his ability to learn to read.

Amplified VAKT—Writing Without Tracing   This stage is much like the previous one, except that the student no longer traces the word unless he has difficulty recognizing it by writing alone.

The student reads his typed story from the previous day and then selects the words he wants to learn to read. The teacher writes them on cards, and the student looks at each word, pronouncing it aloud clearly. The teacher removes the card, and the student tries to write the word on a strip of paper. The teacher marks each attempt on the record sheet just as was done for the tracings at the previous level. Each time the student spells the word incorrectly, the word is folded under the strip of paper, and the process is repeated. If the word is spelled correctly on the first attempt, it is added to the vocabulary box. If it takes two or more trials, it is kept with the rest of the words to be learned.

After writing the words, the student goes through the three-step vocabulary-learning procedures as before. He then writes a story which he reads aloud. It is typed later for rereading during the next session.

At this stage, students may begin to read stories written by other students. If the student is able to complete his VAKT work with time to spare, the teacher may begin to let him read published material at his independent or instructional reading level. It is important, however, that such reading not supersede his VAKT program.

As soon as the student reduces the number of trials necessary to recognize new words to only one or two, he is ready to leave this stage and go into the next.

Amplified VAKT—Language Experience   At this stage the Amplified VAKT approach is no longer strictly for extremely disabled readers. It becomes a modification of the language experience approach for use with remedial readers. Students using this approach may work well in groups of from three to eight instead of the one-to-one instructional grouping. The students screened out of the lower two levels of the Amplified VAKT can often be placed in the program at this level.

Although the students write stories and use a vocabulary file, many other aspects of the approach at this level are different from the previous level. The process, especially with older students, may be initiated by having the teacher lead the group in a short discussion of some topic of interest. Subjects may include current events, school concerns, or any other topics in which the students are interested. Although the time should be limited to about 10 minutes, the teacher should encourage comments from as many students as possible.

The teacher should close the discussion by asking the students to write an "article" about their feelings on the subject, using their vocabulary files to help with words they may not know. If there are words the students want to use which are not in the file, the teacher should write these on slips of paper.

As soon as the students finish their stories, they should proofread them silently, title them, and be sure their names are on them. They should then put their story aside until the teacher can work with individuals for a few minutes. While waiting for the teacher, each student should turn to his learning contract or other study plan to work on other aspects of his remedial program. A contract form such as that shown in Figure 10-3 is one means for developing a student's initiative for assuming responsibility for his own work. With a learning contract, both the teacher and the student agree on the work to be done within a specific period of time, often one week. The teacher should let the student assume as much responsibility as he can handle in determining what he thinks he can accomplish during the period of the contract. After the student and teacher agree on what should be done in all areas of the contract, they each sign it.

In the contract sample in Figure 10-3, under the heading of "Reading on my own" (independent-level reading), the teacher and student might include rereading stories the student had previously written, reading independent-level stories other students have written, or reading published materials at the student's independent reading level. Under "Reading to learn" (instructional-reading level), the student and teacher might list the materials the student is presently writing, harder student-written stories, or published materials at the student's instructional-reading level. Under the contract heading "Building my reading skills," the teacher and student would be likely to include specific reading-skill improvement work such as strategies for the improvement of reading comprehension, word analysis, context clues, and sight vocabulary. "Activities that help me learn" can include games, puzzles, and other activities used to reinforce reading skills.

During the period of the contract, the teacher should take the opportunity to check off those parts of the contract that have been completed. This is more encouraging to the student than doing it all at one time, and it is easier for the teacher, too. At the end of the contract time, the teacher should go through it to see that everything has been done. If something is still incomplete, the teacher should determine why. Sometimes students simply think they can do more than is possible. Sometimes the material is beyond students, and, of course, there are times when the contract is not completed because students have not used their time well. That provides an opportunity to help students learn to plan better.

While a contract should not be used as a whip over the heads of the students, it does provide a mirror that allows them to see their independent efforts more clearly, taking pride in their own strides in initiating and completing tasks. A

Learning Contract	
Reading on My Own:	Reading to Learn:
Building My Reading Skills:	Activities That Help Me Learn:

Agreed to by:_____ This contract will start

_____ on _____

Today is _____ and end _____

Figure 10-3.   A Sample Learning Contract

213

contract also allows the teacher an opportunity to serve as a sounding board as students readjust their next week's work so that they can finish it.

The teacher should avoid the temptation to assume the responsibility for determining the content of the contract. That robs students of the opportunity to develop more independence. The teacher should also be careful not to lecture students who fail to complete work on the contract. There is a natural pressure that arises from the uncompleted work. The teacher should examine the proposed contract with each student, asking questions such as, "Do you think you can complete that much work?" or, if the student seems to be planning too little work in order to have slack time, "Do you think that is all you can do?" The tone should not be critical. The teacher's questions should lead students to think carefully about what they have committed themselves to do and to help them readjust their goals if they are too high or too low. If the goals are reasonable, the questions should lead students to organize their time well.

Not all students work well with contracts and, for that matter, not all teachers find that a contract learning system works well for them. But when teacher and students are amenable to the contract system, it can be a highly productive means of instruction, building work attitudes as well as developing reading ability.

For the Amplified VAKT Language Experience unit, the contract should include reading of published materials as well as student-written materials. It is important that the teacher have available a sizable number of multilevel materials so that each student can read interesting material at his independent and instructional reading levels.

While the students are working on their learning contracts or other lesson plans, the teacher will be able to see the various students and have them read at least a part of their writing aloud. While each student is reading, the teacher should have a clipboard, notepad, ballpoint pen, and a copy of that group's student accounting or observation sheet. As the student reads, the teacher will be able to note the kinds of reading errors the student makes in oral reading. He should generally record the words with which the student has difficulty, pronouncing words for those who are still at the very earliest levels of reading, and helping those who are learning word attack skills by using a pen with retracted point to indicate the words missed. The teacher should not "bathe" the student in suggestions and corrections but should let the penpoint "do the talking." A quiet indication of the word or words that have been missed allows students the opportunity to go back to the word, analyze it themselves, and try to call the word correctly.

After the student has finished reading, the teacher should take a few minutes to go over the words missed during reading. If there are examples of the skill work the student has been doing, these are especially good to include. The teacher ought not to try to teach, or even review, more than two rules per session, however. And the rules should be taught only in application. Isolated rules of word analysis are never as effective as applying the principle directly to actual reading materials.

The stories should be gathered into "books" of ten to twenty articles and placed on easily accessible shelves so that students who have written them can take pride in them and reread them, and other students also may read them. Covers may be made inexpensively from construction paper, or the "books" may be slipped into ready-made clear or tinted plastic covers.

VAKT—Phonic Variations   Approaches such as the Orton (1976), Gillingham-Stillman (1966), and Slingerland (1974) methods have the students first learn the letters and their sounds, then write the letters, trace them, and perhaps finally "write" them in the air. The Hegge-Kirk-Kirk (1955) "grapho-vocal" method also uses a strong phonic approach augmented by VAKT.

Other approaches make use of VAKT only as an occasional supplement. Monroe (1932) advocated the use of tracing for students having difficulty with certain words in her strong phonics-based approach as early as the late 1920s. Today it is a relatively common practice to use the VAKT for a short time with students who are not making progress in another approach or to help students with some of the more difficult words.

Augmented Tracing   In this approach students are asked to trace words in sand, corn meal, salt, or some other granular substance placed in a shallow tray. The purpose is to increase tactile sensitivity, giving the word richer encoding than if the student had traced the word only on the smooth surface of a card. Some teachers use augmented tracing as an additional step after tracing the word on a card, while others substitute augmented tracing for card tracing.

Another way of augmenting the tactile qualities of a word is by using flocked or felt letters, by using sand glued to the letters, or by using three-dimensional letters punched out of plastic or cardboard.

The value of augmentation is, so far, a matter of individual judgment. There has been little research to prove its value, although those who use various kinds of augmentation are steadfast in their belief that it is helpful.

INTENSIVE PHONIC APPROACHES

Intensive phonics instruction is a popular approach for use with extremely disabled readers. Criticisms of the approach indicate that it is tedious and boring, that it is based on repetitious drill, that it requires a rigid structure demanding much teacher preparation, that it lacks interesting and educational content, and that it promotes a monotonous word-by-word type of reading. Nevertheless, there are many cases in which learners have made good progress using the approach.

There are a number of programs which utilize a VAKT approach as part of their method. Some, such as the Slingerland approach, are sufficiently complicated to require special teacher training.

The Monroe approach, although one of the oldest, is a good example of an intensive phonics approach. Still quite usable, it can be learned directly from Monroe's textbook (1932). In general, an intensive phonics approach follows the sequence of phonic skills development described in Chapter Two, and involves lightly brushing up those skills in which students have relative competence and emphasizing skill areas in which they need attention.

IMPRESS METHOD

The impress, or "neurological" impress, method was originally described by R. G. Heckleman in 1962 and was explained further in an article in *Academic Therapy* (Heckleman, 1969, pp. 277–82). The approach initially resulted from a personal experiment with a seriously disabled reader. Heckleman clarified the procedures and conducted a six-week study of the approach with twenty-four students in Merced County, California.

In the impress method, the teacher sits to the side of and slightly behind the student. They both look at the same book, and the teacher indicates the words as he and the student simultaneously read the passage aloud. As they read, the teacher speaks into the ear of the student, providing ongoing simultaneous "feedback" of what is being read. There is no previous preparation of the reading material except that it is to be material which the student has expressed an interest in reading; it should be at a level which the student would find possible to read. Initially, the teacher should read more loudly and a bit faster than the student. After the student begins to gather more confidence and ability, the teacher takes a more reserved position in the reading, letting the student lead out. When the student begins to falter or slow down, the teacher should be more assertive, taking the lead and increasing volume.

Heckleman does not maintain that the impress method is *the* way to improve reading abilities, but suggests it may be used as an adjunct to other programs. He suggests that 15 minutes per day is generally sufficient for optimal benefits.

Some limited additional research has indicated that the method is generally successful with older extremely disabled readers when conducted on a one-to-one basis for 15 minutes each day. The approach has not proved to be as successful when it has been used with better readers, when there have been larger intervals between readings, or when the teacher's portion of the reading is taped (Hollingsworth, 1970, pp. 114, 187).

There seem to be several strengths in the impress method. It maintains the attention of the student; it provides for constant correction while reading; it provides the repetition necessary to develop automatic word recognition; it provides a good model of oral reading for the student to emulate; and it makes the student read more. Since the teacher is to read faster than the student ordinarily reads on his own, it also tends to increase reading rate to some extent, although rate is not a great concern for extremely disabled readers.

There are also some objections to the approach. The method is time-consuming, requiring the teacher to work one on one with the student; which also increases the expense of the program. The physical position the teacher must maintain is somewhat awkward and tends to become tiring after a time.

Although Hollingsworth (1970) concluded from his research that the impress method required the "personal involvement" of the teacher with the student rather than using tape recordings in order to be successful, Jordan (1967) reported success in a study in which the student read aloud while listening to a cassette recording selected from a library of multilevel materials. He theorized that the earphones reduced outside interference and increased the reader's attention to the material and instruction. He reported good gains from use of this method.

It seems likely that the impress method has received less attention than it may deserve. That may be partially due to its original, somewhat misleading name, the "neurological impress method." The approach is no more "neurological" than any other approach and does nothing to affect a student's neurological functioning in any unusual way. All learning involves neurological processing, and those who learn by the impress method use that processing no differently than those who may learn to read by the language experience or any other approach.

The impress method may be used with extremely disabled readers, but not at the very beginning levels. It can be used more effectively with students who have developed at least a small basic sight vocabulary. It would be interesting to see if research would support the need to position the teacher behind and to the side of the student, speaking directly into the student's ear. It is possible that this aspect of the method may be found to be unnecessary. At any rate, the method, even with the objections to its use, is an effective approach for extremely disabled readers at a certain stage of development, provided it is used by a teacher who is comfortable with its use and with students who accept it.

LINGUISTIC SATURATION APPROACH

One of the newest and yet one of the oldest approaches is the linguistic saturation method. Few people have not listened to a preschool child "read" a book he has memorized. He knows the words so well that if an adult reader miscalls one of them, the child can—and usually does—correct the reader immediately. Of course, the child does not "read" the story in the true sense of the word. He has simply gone over the story so many times that he knows it word for word.

Linguistic saturation resembles that "approach." It also bears a resemblance to the impress method and may involve elements of the language experience approach. In linguistic saturation, students go through material so many times that they virtually memorize it.

The first step in the approach is quite similar to language experience and is used for the most seriously disabled readers. The teacher initiates instruction by using the procedures discussed in the Amplified VAKT Language Experience section described earlier in this chapter. After a topic has been introduced and briefly discussed by the members of the group, the students write what they want about the topic, receiving the assistance of the teacher with words they cannot spell but want to use in their stories. They title and sign their stories, and read them to the teacher or aide, who then has them typed for the next session.

During the next session, the students read their stories again. They then select five words they want to learn from the story. If there are not that many unknown words in the story, students may suggest other words. The teacher then uses the three-stage vocabulary-learning procedure, presenting the cards just as explained in the screening procedure at the beginning of the Amplified VAKT approach.

The stories are kept in a binder, and the students read them on a practice cassette until they know every word and can read with normal expression and fluency. As soon as they can do this, they can produce a finished recording of the story. Both the finished recording and the "book" of the writings are kept together on an accessible shelf so they may be read and heard by others. In addition, in some programs it is possible for students to take the finished book and recording home to share with their family.

As to students begin the practice process, they read the story themselves until they feel ready to make a trial recording. The teacher helps with any words they cannot recognize. They then record their first (typed) story onto a cassette and play it back, listening through earphones as they read. If they find errors, they are free to correct them. When they believe they have recorded the story perfectly, they and the teacher listen together to the story. If there are no word call errors and the fluency is satisfactory, the students are ready to make the finished recording.

Then they are given a second cassette, on which they record the story. Sometimes students become frustrated by their inability to record error-free material; in this case the teacher should remind them that even the best readers make mistakes. The teacher may want to share the fact that those who record television and radio commercials often have to rerecord them dozens of times before they make a recording they think is just right. A student should not let mistakes, or "fluffs," as professional readers call them, discourage him. The only thing to be concerned about is that the finished tape is correct. Students may go back over their tapes any number of times in order to eliminate word call errors. Every time an error is found and reread, the word is being processed deeply and encoded richly.

Students are usually willing and able to go back over their own writing many times. By rereading a story ten to fifteen times, they become able to "read" it well. The first story is generally the most difficult. After the finished recording of the first story has been made less time is needed to master the stories that follow.

While students practice the first story, preparing to make a finished recording, they are not only adding a new story to their collections almost every day but also adding new words to their vocabulary-learning cards. As each new story—usually half a page or less when typed—is added to the collection of readings, students go over them, too. Rarely will the combined length of the stories be such that students are unable to rehearse them all and also complete other activities within a 40- or 50-minute period of time.

An alternate activity that provides occasional variety is having two or three students write a radio play, which they prepare in much the same way as their stories, reading and recording it on a cassette. Simple sound effects can be added to provide a professional touch. Most libraries have speech and theater handbooks which list possible sound effects that are simple to produce yet which add a satisfying dimension. For example, the sound of a crackling fire or a rainstorm can be made by slowly crumpling a piece of paper next to a microphone. Sound-effects records also can be used. They are usually available in larger music stores or theater arts supply houses.

A developmentally more difficult level of the linguistic saturation approach involves students reading from printed material. Each student chooses a story or book that is only slightly below the frustration level. The process is basically the same as with the lower-level linguistic saturation approach, beginning with the student and teacher reading aloud simultaneously. The student then works to prepare a trial tape, proofing it until it is correct. After the teacher approves, the student prepares a "finished" recording.

In short, the linguistic saturation approach seeks to teach students normal reading behavior through multiple exposures to the same material, building familiarity with good reading patterns, helping him to develop automatic word recognition skills, instilling a sense of confidence, and promoting interest in reading through use of the student's own language and syntax at the first stage and later through use of interesting published material. Moreover, the use of recordings helps to limit the amount of individual teacher time necessary and also adds interest and prestige to the student's learning situation.

The first person with whom the author used this approach could consistently recognize only about twenty words. He began by writing ten stories and, although it took nearly a month before they were all recorded, the improvement in his attitude was remarkable. It took over three months before he was able to record his first story from published material. But before the end of the year, he no longer needed the approach nor the recorder, and was making satisfactory improvement in his reading abilities.

A few students are initially reluctant. Some of them believe that they will not be able to succeed, and continual encouragement is necessary. However, these students usually become more enthusiastic when they have completed their first book.

Chomsky (1978) has used a similar approach with good success. She does not begin at the language experience level, and she suggests that her approach be used with students who are retarded in reading by one or two years and lack flu-

Table 10-1

Intensive Reading Instruction Summary Sheet

Approach	Lowest Ability Level of Students for Whom Approach Is Appropriate	Skill Development of Students for Whom Appropriate	Emphasis of Approach	Cognitive Domains Principally Affected
VAKT and Amplified VAKT	Pre-primer, non-readers, lowest level of reading development	Extremely limited basic sight vocabulary and word analysis skills.	Meaning. Reading integrated with language.	Syntactic-semantic, phonemic, visual, kinesthetic (motor), tactile
VAKT—Language Experience	Primer	Some basic sight vocabulary, limited word analysis skills.	Meaning. Reading integrated with language.	Syntactic-semantic, visual, kinesthetic (motor)
VAKT—Phonics	Primer	Some basic sight vocabulary, limited word analysis skills. Do not use with those for whom English is second language.	Skills with some meaning. Reading integrated with some language	Phonemic, Kinesthetic (motor), tactile, syntactic-semantic, visual

Augmented Tracing (supplementary to other approaches)	Pre-primer, non-readers, lowest level of reading development	Extremely limited basic sight vocabulary and word analysis skills.	Dependent on the approach it is used to supplement.	Kinesthetic (motor), tactile, visual, phonemic
Intensive Phonics	1² reader, upper first-grade reading development	Basic sight vocabulary, limited word analysis skills. Do not use with those for whom English is a second language.	Skills. Reading as a word analysis process.	Phonemic
Impress Method	2² reader, Mid- to upper second-grade reading development	Basic sight vocabulary, some word analysis skills.	Syntax. Reading as oral language.	Syntactic, visual
Linguistic Saturation Approach	Primer	Some basic sight vocabulary, limited word analysis skills.	Syntax, fluency, and meaning.	Syntactic-semantic, visual

ency but have developed initial word attack skills. Her description of her approach is interesting and contains several case studies of students with whom she has worked.

SUMMARY

Approaches for extremely disabled readers include such intensive methods as the Fernald VAKT; the Amplified VAKT; the VAKT with intensive phonic programs; the use of augmented tracing in which the student is asked to trace words in sand, cornmeal, salt, or some other granular substance; intensive phonics programs; the impress method; and the linguistic saturation approach. All require significant personal attention from the teacher but are effective in overcoming the reading difficulties of very poor readers. Care should be taken to match the approach with the student, taking into account level of reading development, interests, and preferences for learning.

Table 10-1 on pp. 220–221 outlines the lowest ability levels of students for whom the various intensive instructional approaches should be used, the skill development profile of students who might benefit from the approaches, the primary emphases of the approaches, and the cognitive domains principally affected by them.

RECOMMENDED READINGS

Bond, G.; Tinker, M.; and Wasson B. 1979. *Reading difficulties: Their diagnosis and correction.* 4th ed. Englewood Cliffs, N.J.: Prentice-Hall, Chapter 11.

Chomsky, C. 1978. When you still can't read in third grade: After decoding, what? In *What research has to say about reading instruction,* ed. S. J. Samuels. Newark, Del.: International Reading Assoc., pp. 13–20.

Fernald, G. M. 1943. *Remedial techniques in basic school subjects.* New York: McGraw-Hill, Chapter 5.

Harris, A. J.; and Sipay, E. R. 1980. *How to increase reading ability.* 7th ed. New York: Longman, Chapter 15.

REFERENCES

Brown, D. A; and Newman, A. 1968. *A literacy program for adult city-core illiterates.* Final Report on U.S. Office of Education. Research Grant No. OEG-1-7-061136-0385. Buffalo: State University of New York at Buffalo.

Chall, J. 1978. A decade of research on reading and learning disabilities. In *What research has to say about reading instruction,* ed. S. J. Samuels. Newark Del.: International Reading Assoc., p. 40.

Chomsky, C. 1978. When you still can't read in third grade: After decoding, what? In *What research has to say about reading instruction,* ed. S. J. Samuels. Newark, Del.: International Reading Assoc., pp. 13–30.

Fernald, G. M. 1943. *Remedial techniques in basic school subjects.* New York: McGraw-Hill.

Fernald, G. M.; and Keller, H. B. 1921. The effect of kinaesthetic factors in the development of word recognition in the case of non-readers. *Journal of Educational Research* pp. 355–77.

Flatt, E. A. October 1969. The influence of individualized eye-span training on effective reading rate. *Journal of Reading* p. 12.

Gillingham, S. and Stillman, B. 1966. *Remedial training for children with specific difficulty in reading, spelling, and penmanship.* 7th ed. Cambridge, Mass.: Educators Publishing Service.

Heckleman, R. G. 1962. *A neurological impress method of reading instruction.* Merced, Cal.: Merced County Schools Office.

———. 1969 A Neurological impress method of reading instruction. *Academic Therapy* pp. 277–82.

Hegge, T.; Kirk, S; and Kirk, W. 1955. *Remedial reading drills.* Ann Arbor, Mich.: George Wehr Publishing.

Hollingsworth, P. M. November 1970. An experiment with the impress method of teaching reading. *Reading Teacher* 31: 112–14, 187.

Jordan, W. C. Summer 1967. Prime-O-Tec: The new reading model. *Academic Therapy* 2: 248–50.

Monroe, M. 1932. *Children who cannot read.* Chicago: Univ. Chicago Press.

Orton, J. L. 1976. *A guide to teaching phonetics.* Cambridge, Mass.: Educators Publishing Service.

Slingerland, B. H. 1974. *A multi-sensory approach to language arts for specific learning disability children.* Cambridge, Mass.: Educators Publishing Service.

Weaver, P. 1978. *Research within reach.* St. Louis: Research & Development Interpretation Service, and Washington, D.C.: National Institute of Education.

11

Some of the approaches presented in the previous chapter for extremely disabled readers may be modified for use with remedial and occasionally even corrective readers. In addition, however, there are several approaches discussed in this chapter which, although not providing the individualization required by extremely disabled readers, are quite effective for remedial students. These remedial approaches, in turn, can be modified for use with students in corrective programs.

Corrective instruction is often formulated from an eclectic base and uses various organizational patterns including cross-classroom and cross-grade grouping, learning centers, and resource rooms. In addition to adaptations of approaches used with remedial students, corrective reading instruction frequently includes diagnostic-prescriptive instruction that utilizes kits and other packaged programs and machine-presented instruction.

REMEDIAL AND CORRECTIVE PROGRAMS

While intensive instructional approaches are used principally for those students with the most severe reading difficulties, they have obvious applications to instruction for remedial and even corrective students as well. The upper stages of both the Fernald and Amplified VAKT approaches are effective means of remediating students who have the ability to work in groups of from three to eight students, a group size usually associated with remedial rather than extreme reading disability instruction. The impress method, linguistic saturation, and even intensive phonics instruction have all been tried with students above the level of the extremely disabled reader with success.

The line of division, then, between the methods used for remedial and extremely disabled readers depends not so much on what can be used with the remedial students but with what can be effective with the poorest readers. Although a modified basal approach, language experience approach, individualized reading, and some other methods can be useful in working with remedial readers, they are not usually as effective for extremely disabled students, who generally need more intensive reading instruction.

At this point, then, let us look at additional approaches that can be used with remedial readers.

Modified Basal Approach   Most elementary developmental reading programs use one of the basal series as their primary structure. There are significant differences between some of the various series. The scope and sequence of skills is usually different. Sometimes even the names by which the skills are called may be different. In developing a remedial program based on a reading series, the teacher should choose one that the student did not use in earlier grades and one that is not currently in use in the lower grades in that school. The latter precaution decreases the possibility that younger children in the student's family may be reading from materials he may recognize. It is usually embarrassing for a seventh-grader, for example, to find that he is reading from the same book as a third-grade sibling.

Basal series generally present a well-organized development of reading skills, providing stories and expository readings, skill-development activities, a wealth of suggested reading lessons, and usually supplementary materials such as filmstrips, spirit masters, workbooks, and other enrichment materials. A modified basal approach used as a remedial approach usually has no lack of material for instruction. The theory of instruction is "Let's just start all over again, and this time we'll do it right."

A modified basal approach has some disadvantages. First, the stories, illustrations, and accompanying material have been prepared for children on a grade level below that of the remedial student. While it is possible to use basal materials a year or two lower without insulting the older student, greater discrepancies tend to magnify the fact that the remedial student is "behind" and working on a par with those two or more years his junior. This often creates serious attitudinal problems.

A second difficulty is the "Swiss-cheese effect" most remedial readers have in their skill development. Remedial students are unlikely to be a *tabula rasa*, a blank slate, on which the teacher may begin to inscribe reading skills beginning with the most primary and leading to the most complex. Remedial readers usually have a scattering of skills which they have learned during the years they have been in school. Yet these skills are usually unpredictable. Students may have some skills that surprise the teacher, and lack others they might be expected to know. As a result, a program based on the thorough scope and sequence of skills in a basal series tends to waste time because of possible unnecessary review of skills the student already has in the process of getting to those skills he needs to learn.

In general, a modified basal approach ought not to be used with older students, and even when it is used with younger students, it should be used selectively. The skills that need attention should be identified, and the portions of the series that are most concerned with those skills should be used.

Reading Management Systems   In recognition of the "Swiss-cheese effect," many teachers have utilized testing and tracking systems to maximize the time and attention given to each student's needs and to minimize the time spent teaching what students already know. Developing a lengthy list of objectives, the designers of a number of commercial programs have produced criterion-referenced tests (CRTs) to assess student abilities related to the objectives, have coded instructional materials to the objectives, and have created continuous progress charts to map students' gains in achieving program objectives. Management systems are an attempt to help the teacher handle the logistics involved in teaching the various aspects of reading in an appropriately sequenced order.

Management systems are relatively new, yet they are being used widely in both developmental and remedial programs. Despite their pervasiveness, there is virtually no independent research dealing with their effectiveness. Probably their increasing popularity can be traced to their obvious appeal in making the most of every minute of reading instruction and the concern for accountability. By using a management system, teachers and administrators can keep track of instructional needs, efforts, and gains, and can present test results as evidence of the program's benefits for each student.

There are two kinds of management systems: those whose objectives are coded to a specific set of instructional materials and those that are presumably compatible with a wide variety of reading instructional materials. These latter systems are sometimes used as the entire remedial reading program. More often, they are viewed as the basic skills-development portion of a broader program. A number of commercial programs are available, but frequently management systems can be obtained through state departments of education. Larger school districts often develop their own.

Objections to the use of management systems as a remedial approach include, first, that their creators too frequently view reading as the mastery of a number of isolated skills. Most of the instructional time involves exercises aimed at learning those skills rather than creating interest in reading, developing comprehension of what the author is communicating, and helping the student to use reading to solve problems, learn subject matter, generate ideas, or interact with the author's imagination. Reading is often equated with the completion of exercise sheets. No student ever wanted to learn to read so that he could syllabify a list of words or complete an exercise dealing with consonant blends.

The second objection concerns the method by which management systems indicate assumed mastery of the various objectives. After a student has passed a criterion-referenced test, a notation is made or a hole is punched in the student's skills card, and it is presumed that, once having learned the skill, he will not forget it in the future. Unfortunately, most students—remedial readers included—often require many "masteries" before a skill is retrievable consistently over a long period of time.

A third objection is the tendency of some management systems to, in a sense, reduce the reading teacher to a test administrator and recordkeeper, leaving little time to teach the students. Although this is more likely to be true for larger classes and for developmental reading classes, it is also frequently true for remedial classes as well. The machinery of the system can become so time-consuming that it defeats one of the purposes for which it was created: providing more time to teach the student.

Linguistic Approach   Linguistics is the study of language, and only recently have linguists turned their attention to the area of reading and reading improvement. In actuality, there is no "linguistic approach," since all reading relates to language. Therefore, all reading approaches are linguistic approaches in that sense. However, there have been certain materials produced for reading instruction which emphasize the patterns of language, and these have been identified as linguistic approaches.

Linguistic approaches control the introduction of word structures, beginning with simple sentences in which certain patterns are employed, such as:

The man ran to the tan van.

Such patterns are intended to teach students that the words are alike except for the initial letter or phoneme and that, therefore, the words can be identified by distinguishing between these various phonemes.

Next, the simple patterns are intermingled so that the student will learn to distinguish between the patterns. For example, the student might work with the following words:

can man ran cat tan mat sat fan fat

In general, irregular words are taught as sight words, and students are asked to discriminate only between regular word forms. The progression of patterns is carefully mapped, and students encounter increasingly difficult patterns as they advance. Repetition allows students to master the various patterns.

Among the objections to linguistic materials is that the beginning portions are often stilted and uninteresting. The words introduced often lack interest or importance to the student. Reading is viewed as a word recognition process rather than as an effort after meaning. Interestingly, although the approach described above is commonly labeled a "linguistic approach," some of the most severe critics of the method are other linguists. Many linguists prefer to emphasize the importance of the author's message in reading (Wardhaugh, 1969).

Programmed Approach   Originally, programmed reading materials were designed to be used with learning machines. Students read only one frame at a time, made a response when requested, and proceeded to the next frame of instruction.

Today most programmed materials are available in workbook form. The basic construction is the same, however; students are supposed to work one frame at a time, making responses as required, and then move on to the next frame to check answers or receive instructions. Many of the workbooks use a "slider," a slip of cardboard with which students can cover the correct responses as they check their own responses. This allows students to receive immediate feedback on their work before continuing to the next frame.

Programmed approaches are frequently used in remedial programs because (1) they allow students to move at their own rate, (2) students feel a sense of accomplishment as they move through the program, and (3) students can work on different materials at their individual levels easily.

Most programmed reading materials use a linguistic reading philosophy. They proceed on a well-organized sequence of skills from simple to more complex patterns.

Objections to programmed reading relate to specific material and content as well as to the basic plan of organization. Since most programmed reading material follows a linguistic style, the objections to that approach are shared by programmed reading. Criticisms of the basic organization of the approach include observations that students become bored with the approach rather quickly, particularly if it is used as a total program rather than as a supplement to another remedial approach. Many students ignore the proper use of the slider, simply preferring to copy the right answers rather than to do the work themselves. While it is true that students proceed at their own individual rates, every student must climb the same ladder of skills with the same number of steps. Although testing can eliminate some of the ladders the students climb, once they have begun, most workbook programmed materials allow little flexibility for skipping over certain elements or dealing more fully with others. Programmed reading is basically geared to reading very small segments at a time and does not seem to prepare students for the longer kinds of reading normally encountered. Comprehension skills are limited to whatever can fit comfortably within a frame, neglecting the development of many other kinds of comprehension. Programmed reading does not lend itself well to differences in individual tastes, critical reading, or interest in reading everyday materials.

Despite its drawbacks, programmed reading has been effective for many students. One specific advantage of the approach is the feeling of success it engenders. It is sometimes added to another reading approach just because it is a good confidence-builder. Students can see daily indications of gains. Remedial students universally lack faith in their ability to improve their reading skills, and the frame-by-frame progress that is part of programmed materials can help them develop greater confidence in their ability to learn.

Modified Alphabet Approaches   The twenty-six letters in our alphabet may be used to represent some forty-six different sounds. Modified alphabet approaches are designed to simplify the beginning or remedial reader's task by establishing a one-to-one relationship between sound and symbol. UNIFON, the Initial Teaching Alphabet (i/t/a), and *Words in Color* are among the various approaches that have been used to accomplish this aim. Presumably, each of them can be used with any approach because they really represent different ways of presenting sounds. The proponents of each modified alphabet approach, however, have been forced to prepare materials using their own variation, and the materials produced have often become confused with the approach.

The Initial Teaching Alphabet, or i/t/a, as it is more commonly known, was originally identified as the Augmented Roman Alphabet. It seeks to regularize the spelling of words through modified alphabetic characters, with each of forty-four distinctive graphemes representing a phoneme. UNIFON uses forty different characters, all capitals, for the different phonemes. *Words in Color* uses color to signal different sounds.

The advantage of modified alphabet approaches is that remedial readers are able to quickly learn to read more conceptually advanced material because they do not have to deal with the complex analysis involved in using regular English print. Difficulties seem to be greater in using this approach with remedial readers than with developmental readers at first-grade level. First of all, the longer a student has dealt with traditional spelling and type, the more difficulty he seems to have with a new system of print. Adults taught to read using i/t/a explain that when they look at an i/t/a symbol, they transliterate into the traditional alphabet forms with which they were more familiar in order to recognize the letter sound. For example, a student looks at the character used for the long *e* sound in i/t/a, then associates it with the letter *e* as it is printed in traditional orthography to identify it and recognize the sound it represents. They then ascribe that sound to the i/t/a character (Brown and Newman, 1968).

Secondary concerns associated with the use of modified alphabet approaches deal with the difficulty in obtaining materials printed in the various characters and in learning to write using the modified alphabet. In addition, when students make the transition, as they must, from the modified alphabet to traditional print, they tend to have some degree of difficulty and often have problems learning the word analysis skills they bypassed when they used a system having a one-to-one sound–letter association.

Language Experience Approach   The language experience approach has already been discussed to some extent in connection with the Amplified VAKT approach used with extremely disabled readers. The approach is built on the language and the experiences of the student and has been a popular approach to adapt for use with remedial readers, including those who come from different cultural and language backgrounds.

Ordinarily, students begin by dictating a story to the teacher, although they are led to write their own stories as soon as possible. They develop a vocabulary file and build collections of their stories, which they frequently bind and place on a shelf to be shared with other students; finally they graduate into reading published writings. At this last stage, the approach may be blended into an Individualized Reading approach (capitalized to emphasize the difference between Individualized Reading as a specific reading approach and "individualized reading" meaning the individualization of reading instruction).

An advantage of the language experience approach is that it is based on the language of the remedial student, avoiding the possibility that the student may be unfamiliar with the language and vocabulary in the reading material from which he may be asked to read. Reading comes to be viewed as part of communication, and the student is more likely to understand that good reading involves comprehension and interaction with the author and not just word recognition. The language experience approach also tends to enhance the individual's self-worth because it places a value on his thoughts and writing.

The teacher must monitor individual students' development of reading skills closely to make sure they are receiving the skill instruction they may need. This means the teacher must be knowledgeable in reading instruction.

Individualized Reading   In the Individualized Reading approach (again using capitals to emphasize the difference between Individualized Reading as an approach and "individualized reading," meaning the individualization of reading instruction that should be a goal of any reading approach), almost all reading is done from books and other reading materials which students themselves select. They then confer with the teacher concerning their reading. Skill instruction, not originally a part of the approach, is now generally carried out as an adjunct.

When the Individualized Reading approach is used with remedial students, the teacher should make certain that the students choose their reading materials from selections available at their instructional or independent reading levels. Unlike students who have succeeded in reading, remedial students have a tendency to select materials that are too difficult for them to read.

In order to use the Individualized Reading approach, there should be a number of materials available at the various levels. Further, the teacher must be familiar with the materials in order to help the students find subjects of interest to them. Then, as students are ready to make their next selections, the teacher can direct them to materials that (1) are likely to be of interest and (2) are of appropriate difficulty.

The books in the reading center can be grouped according to their readability on different shelves. Reading difficulty can be indicated by a line marked horizontally on the spine of each book, with the distance of the line from the bottom indicating the readability level. In this way it is possible to tell readability quickly. Also, errant titles can be quickly spotted and placed where they belong.

It is useful to duplicate lists of books available in the reading center by levels of reading difficulty, placing the lists in a looseleaf notebook. Each student is assigned one of the duplicated lists for his own record, underlining books from the list as he selects them to read and crossing them off after he has finished them.

When a student is ready to select a different title, he is directed to the shelf holding the materials at his instructional reading level. After making a decision, he looks at his list of titles in the notebook, draws a red line under the title of the book he has chosen, adds the title to his learning contract, and begins reading.

After the student has read the book, the teacher initials the student's contract, and the student crosses off the title of the book in the notebook. If he starts the book but decides that he is not interested in it, he discusses it with his teacher and makes the change in his contract. He may be allowed to circle the title in the notebook but not to cross out the title. This procedure serves as a silent spur to encourage a good selection of the books the student decides to read and further encourages him to complete those he checks out.

When students are ready to move to a higher level of difficulty, their notebooks serve as a good progress chart. The teacher may point out to the student that he is now ready to try any of the books listed at the new level and that books below that level are now classed as "easy reading" books for him—books that could be read just for fun. Many students will purposely select titles at the lower levels from time to time just to enjoy less challenging materials.

Student–teacher conferences are an essential part of the Individualized Reading approach. The teacher and student sit together and discuss the books read, reading progress, and reading interests. The conferences are important in maintaining remedial students' interest.

If a contract system is not used with students in the individualized approach, some other means of charting progress should be kept. One of the disadvantages of the Individualized Reading approach is that skill development may tend to be haphazard, and good recordkeeping will lessen that possibility. This approach also demands that the teacher be well-prepared in reading education and understand the developmental scope and sequence of reading skills.

Skills instruction should be a regular part of each student's program. When Individualized Reading is used with remedial groupings of three to eight students, the teacher should place students together who have similar skill instruction needs, teaching them in small groups rather than individually whenever possible.

Advantages of this approach when used with remedial students are that it capitalizes on students' reading interests, the reading is more representative of the sort of reading students are normally expected to do, and the student–teacher conferences provide the teacher with an opportunity to become familiar with each student and his reading abilities. It forms a good basis for the most effective kind of diagnostic-prescriptive instruction, in which the teacher is able to chart the student's learning from an intimate knowledge of the student's strengths and weaknesses.

Eclectic Approach   It is likely that the most common approach in use with remedial students is an eclectic approach in which the students are taught by whatever means seem most suited to their individual needs. While some students respond well to one approach, it may not work well with other students at all.

An eclectic approach need not be composed of all possible approaches, methods, techniques, and variations. A teacher may choose two or three approaches that provide broad-range remedial instruction—that is, instruction that can afford a basis for teaching almost any aspect of reading such as sight word recognition, word analysis skills, use of context clues, comprehension, fluency, and so on. With these broad-range approaches as a base, the teacher may add two or three variations that are essentially supplementary methods to be used compatibly with one or more of the broad-range approaches. Then, if an approach seems to fail with a student, the teacher can select another. If one part of the second approach seems ineffective, the teacher can delete that portion and use a compatible supplementary method to teach the skills needed.

When Gilbert first attended the reading center, his clinician placed him in a remedial language experience approach. For some reason, the approach was ineffective with him, so the clinician substituted Individualized Reading. Gilbert responded well, but he needed more work with the development of automatic sight vocabulary and certain word attack skills. The three-level vocabulary teaching procedure described in Chapter Ten was used to meet the first need and a diagnostic-prescriptive approach was used for the second.

CORRECTIVE PROGRAMS

The remedial approaches discussed in the preceding section may be modified for use with corrective students. Because corrective readers are more capable and more independent than those who are remedial, they are able to work in larger groupings. Therefore, remedial approaches should be adapted to the larger group instructional settings typical of corrective instruction; or a system of student contracts or recordkeeping can be used that will allow the teacher to keep track of the larger number of students.

Corrective programs are usually built on an eclectic base and make use of organizational patterns designed to limit the diversity of ability levels within groups of corrective students or to organize instruction in a way that will meet that diversity effectively. Common organizational patterns include cross-classroom and cross-grade grouping and the use of learning centers and resource rooms.

In addition to using modifications of remedial approaches, corrective programs often use reading kits, packaged approaches, and machine-presented instruction.

Cross-Classroom Grouping   One pattern of organization designed to provide instruction for larger groups of students is cross-class grouping, in which several classes at the same grade level have reading instruction at the same time. Those with higher reading ability may receive advanced reading instruction, those in the middle-ability groups receive developmental reading instruction, and corrective and sometimes remedial students go to separate teachers to accommodate their reading needs. Such an organizational plan would work with any approach, of course, although it is more common to see it used with a modified basal, language experience, or Individualized Reading approach.

An advantage of cross-classroom grouping is that the range of abilities is narrower than that with which a teacher must deal in the regular classroom. A companion disadvantage is the tendency for teachers to think that since the range has been narrowed, the students are similar in abilities—this is not true. Students need the attention of a well-prepared reading teacher who understands how to conduct classroom diagnosis of students' reading problems and knows how to plan and implement effective corrective teaching.

Cross-Grade Grouping   This type of organization is sometimes referred to as the "Joplin Plan" and is similar to cross-class grouping in that students go to the classrooms of other teachers to receive reading instruction. If, for example, the plan were put into effect in a school having two classrooms each at grade levels four, five and six, each of the six teachers involved would be assigned to teach one of the following: one advanced group of students reading at seventh- and eighth-grade levels, one at sixth-grade, one at fifth-grade, one at fourth-grade, and one at third-grade, and one at the first- and second-grade levels. The students assigned to the classes would be drawn from all three grade levels so that the remedial group at the first- and second-grade levels would probably include some sixth-graders as well as fourth- and fifth-graders. Grouping students together from different age levels for corrective or remedial instruction can often cause difficulties because the older students feel they have been denigrated.

Learning Center   A relatively new means for providing remedial and corrective instruction is through the use of school learning centers or reading resource rooms. The reading specialist stationed in the center has a good supply of diagnostic and instructional materials which may be used in the learning center or in the classroom where he works with students who are poor readers but who do not need the individualized attention required for remedial or extremely reading-disabled students.

The advantages to having a resource teacher who can work with students in the regular classroom is that students are spared the embarrassment of having to be placed in another class. In addition, it is more economical to equip one resource room with the materials necessary to do a good job of teaching reading than it is to provide reading materials for every classroom in the school. Obvious disadvantages include the logistical problems of transporting materials to different classrooms. If a resource teacher is teaching in a room some distance from the learning center, it is not handy to go back to the learning center for materials needed on the spur of the moment.

Diagnostic-Prescriptive Approach In addition to the modified basal, language experience, and Individualized Reading approaches, which can be adapted for use with corrective readers, the diagnostic-prescriptive or management system approach described earlier has also been used widely as a corrective approach. Criterion-referenced tests coded to behavioral objectives are used to identify student reading needs; students work individually or in small groups with materials keyed to the objectives, and then are retested later to assess mastery. Objections to the approach are much the same as those expressed for use at the remedial level, but at the corrective level, even greater care must be given to see that the approach does not become too mechanistic. Reading must not be allowed to degenerate into "word-solving" but must excite the students to want to read. Nevertheless, at the corrective level, it is necessary to have some sort of organized diagnostic and prescriptive plan and to be able to track student progress. Management systems and diagnostic-prescriptive instruction focus on doing just that, and if they are used with good judgment, they can be an effective adjunct to a good corrective program.

Kits and Packaged Programs A number of publishers have prepared kits for use in corrective reading programs. Most kits provide multilevel materials of general interest, placement tests to indicate an appropriate starting level for each student, a teacher's manual to guide in the use of the kit and provide brief diagnostic suggestions, and answer keys so the students can check their own work. Progress charts are usually available also; these are helpful in letting the teacher evaluate the students' gains and in encouraging students by dramatizing their gains.

Although they are not generally useful for remedial students, kits can be a useful addition to a corrective program. The structure of the program is laid out in the teacher's manual, which is helpful for teachers who have little preparation for handling a reading program. The kits encourage student independence and provide some degree of success by starting students at an easy reading level. On the other hand, kits usually fall short of providing either a full spectrum of reading tasks or a complete reading development program. Most of the materials in kits tend to be limited to pamphlets or booklets, and most do not provide much in basic skills instruction. Neither of these limitations should rule them out as a useful supplement to a program, but either objection should caution against viewing a packaged program as a total corrective reading program.

A number of published kits contain collections of high-interest low-vocabulary stories, some with excellent appeal to corrective readers. Although the kits do not offer a full reading program, their attractiveness can be a major asset to corrective reading instruction.

Machine-Presented Instruction   The first reading machines were controlled-exposure devices that flashed an image which the reader tried to recognize or that exposed connected discourse at a predetermined rate of speed, segment by segment. The first are called *tachistoscopes* and the second are usually called *controlled readers.* A third mechanical device, often called a *pacer,* is usually placed over regular reading material. A descending shutter or beam of light forces the student to read fast enough to keep pace with the machine.

There are commercially produced hand-held tachistoscopes with word-cards that can be slipped into them. The shutters are generally spring-operated. Other tachistoscopes project an image on a screen and can be used with an entire group of students at one time. They are more expensive than individual hand-held tachistoscopes and are less flexible because they use the same words or images for everyone in the group. Smaller projectors can be purchased for individual work, but when the cost is multiplied by the number of students who might be using them at one time, the expense becomes a consideration.

There seems little advantage in using anything other than words or phrases in a tachistoscope. The carryover from using geometric forms or numbers seems to have little value in terms of improving reading ability (Flatt, 1969).

The most crucial question related to the use of tachistoscopes, of course, is whether or not they are effective in improving reading ability. Two values seem apparent. In programs for poor readers, a tachistoscope is a glamorized flash card. Although fluency is a concern of teachers working with poor readers, "speed reading" in the usual sense is not. Trying to force very poor readers to read rapidly only results in causing them to make their usual basic reading mistakes at a faster rate. First, they need to develop a firm foundation in the basic skills. After that, they can work to improve their ability to read rapidly. For the poor reader, a tachistoscope should be used for the same purpose as flash cards: to help in learning to recognize specific words. Used this way, there is no question that it can be used effectively with remedial readers.

If, on the other hand, the tachistoscope is used to present words from a previously developed list, which frequently contains words that are too difficult or that are not relevant to the student's reading improvement program, the student will almost certainly gain more from flash cards—which he can use to master the words he needs. In addition, if the tachistoscope is used to flash words at rapid rates of speed, not giving the poor reader time to recognize individual words, it will be ineffective because he will not have time to react to and process words efficiently. Such a practice will cause the student to become discouraged with his ability to learn.

The second apparent advantage is student motivation. Mechanical devices like the tachistoscope tend to arouse interest on the part of learners. They usually like to learn to manipulate the tachistoscope and enjoy the challenge of the device if the teacher allows them to expose the words at a rate that will permit success. Since they are being challenged to recognize words during a relatively brief exposure, they are likely to concentrate on the task more than with the untimed exposure of a flash card. Students can also generally learn to work with the tachistoscope independently, checking themselves on the words they are to learn and freeing the teacher to do other things.

Relative to the first point above, teacher-made tachistoscopes (see Chapter Twelve) have certain advantages over commercially produced models. Although blank inserts are available for commercial tachistoscopes, it is more difficult to write the words on them than on the word cards that fit into a hand-made tachistoscope. In addition, students often learn the order in which words are presented and rely on that for cues in recognizing words. With a teacher-made tachistoscope, the words are presented one at a time, and their order can be continually changed. However, commercially available models are often more attractive, at least initially. Students can make their own tachistoscopes—they enjoy doing this, and they are more likely to be motivated to use their own creation than one made commercially.

Studies dealing with the effectiveness of the tachistoscope have usually dealt with reading-rate improvement rather than with its use as a glorified flash card. While those studies have generally found tachistoscopic training to be of questionable value for rate training, it seems much more likely that its use as a flash-card device can be of greater value.

The second mechanical reading device, the controlled reader, is designed to control the rate at which the reader may see material. A story may be projected on a screen in phrases, or a moving illuminated slot may be passed over the story seen on a screen, allowing the student to see a limited portion of the story at a time and controlling the speed with which the student may read.

When used in corrective reading instruction, controlled readers should be used only with those students who have a problem with repetitions while reading and who need to improve their mechanical reading rhythm. This device should be employed for a relatively small percentage of time, should be set *below* the student's ordinarily fastest reading rate, and should always be followed by having the student read in a normal fashion from regular reading materials.

Lemuel came into the reading center as a corrective reader. Although his reading skills were basically sound, he had great difficulty maintaining a satisfactory reading rhythm, continually repeating himself as he read. Lemuel would read the sentence

When Karbel came into the village, all the children stopped their play and stared.

in a repetitive, hesitating manner: "When . . . When Karbel . . . When Karbel came . . . came into the village . . . When Karbel came into the village . . . ."

He was placed in material at an independent level on a controlled reader, the reading rate was turned down so he could keep pace with it, and he was asked to read with the rate controller for 10 minutes a day. After he had finished, he read from ordinary reading material for several minutes. The program frustrated him at first. He objected to being unable to reread what he had already read " to see if I read it right." He was persuaded to endure the frustration and continue with the program, and he eventually overcame his need to review his reading as he had done before. When he read from ordinary material without rate control, he repeated words much more than under controlled reading, but his general performance improved notably. After six weeks, the number of repetitions had been cut by over 70 percent when he read ordinary materials.

There are several objections to the use of a controlled reader. First, it is not a natural way to read. Reading is done from a screen rather than from a book or other print materials. It prevents regressions when a student is trying to fit a word into the context in order to define it or to recognize it. It is often misused to produce rate improvement when a student should be working on more fundamental reading skills. The exposure of the reading material is inexorable and does not allow students to practice the normal and necessary flexibility in rate which allows them to read some portions rapidly, others slowly. Purchase of the equipment is initially expensive. Unless the classroom is equipped with carrels or other means of obscuring the screens from view, the projection of words on the screens can distract other students in the room. Some students are bothered by the presentation of the material illuminated by a slot moving back and forth across the screen. Occasionally, students complain of eye irritation and headaches after using a controlled reading machine.

A program administrator intending to invest in rate controllers for use in a corrective reading program should weigh the objections against the benefits in initially increased motivation and interest and the tendency to reduce regressions for some students in the program.

A third machine designed to improve reading ability is the reading pacer. In reality a variation of a controlled reader, it works directly over ordinary printed material. A beam of light is directed onto the material, or a shutter or blind descends over the material at a controlled rate of speed. In order to keep up with the light or keep ahead of the descending shutter, students must read at the predetermined speed.

Although reading pacers are capable of helping students increase reading rate, their use in a corrective program is limited. There is some motivational value, but with the exception of those corrective readers at the high school and community college level, that alone is not likely to be sufficient reason for investing in the machines. For upper-level programs, where rate improvement may be a consideration even in corrective programs, pacers may have more value. Even here, other techniques have been shown to be just as effective in improving reading rate, and the other means of rate improvement are not as expensive and are more like ordinary reading in nature, an important consideration affecting transfer of training to situations outside the reading class. When students learn to improve their rate by using a pacer, they may grow to depend on it. Because they do not use a pacer ordinarily when they read at home, in the library, or in their other classes, they may learn to read one way with the pacer and another way under more normal reading conditions. A review of the objections to the use of the controlled reader, however, shows that a pacer escapes some of the criticisms leveled at rate controllers that use a projected image on a screen.

Later developments in machine-presented instruction have tended to be more promising for corrective reading. Teaching machines use sequentially organized programmed material calling for the student to read a segment or frame and respond to it. The machine provides immediate feedback to the student who, depending on his answer, proceeds to the next higher step in the sequence or, if his response is incorrect, receives elaborative instruction to develop further understanding. This latter technique is called "branching." The reservations earlier noted relative to programmed reading instruction apply to teaching machines, from which programmed instruction came. However, it is not as easy to look at the answers with a teaching machine as it is with programmed reading material. Students can still "con" the machine by deliberately selecting the various possible answers without trying to think through their answers. The machine is unable to differentiate between those answers which have been produced by insight and understanding and those produced by chance and experimentation.

Another drawback to the use of the teaching machine is that it is impossible to enclose the totality of reading in a machine with a series of program cards. The machine's scope is too small. Trying to learn to read well enough to enjoy a novel or study a textbook on biology does not logically fall within the domain of a segmented, frame-by-frame, programmed approach that uses a teaching machine. Teaching machines must necessarily be used in a supportive role in a broad-range approach if the intent of the program is to be fully rounded.

It is possible, however, that the earlier use of teaching machines for reading instruction was only a first step in producing more sophisticated instructional approaches. Realizing the limitations of teaching machines, Atkinson and Fletcher (1972), among others, experimented with computer-assisted instruction. The greater capacity of computers has opened broader horizons for branching instruction. The recent development of compact semiportable computers able to support a number of individual student stations has greatly increased the use of computers for reading instruction. Rhyan and Miller (1980) at Kansas City, Kansas, Community College, have demonstrated the use of such a system for corrective adult learners and, as technology improves and costs continue to go down, there is good reason to believe that computerized reading instruction will become a common tool of the reading teacher at all levels and in all areas of reading instruction.

Computer-assisted instruction uses a tube similar to that on a television set on which can be shown pictures and print. Animation is possible as needed. The student can interact with the program through a keyboard like that of a typewriter. Directions and instruction can be given visually and/or auditorially. In addition, the computer can branch for additional instruction if a student fails to respond correctly, or it can skip frames or segments if the student already seems to have an understanding of certain portions of the program. Student errors can be recorded so that the student is helped to learn the concept at a particular point in time, with the recorded concept repeated later to make certain the comprehension has been retained. If the student responds incorrectly when the concept is presented the second time, the program can branch for further review.

Difficulties with computer-assisted instruction include the initial costs (although these are decreasing), teacher apprehension in using the equipment, difficulty of repair when there are breakdowns, and the inability of the computer to discern when students are using the program properly to learn and when they are faking their way through without learning.

Most computer-assisted instruction up to this date has been supplementary to more broadly based reading programs. Present equipment seems more suited to instruction in word analysis and other basic reading skills. Furthermore, certain kinds of reading can be taught more logically by ordinary reading materials. Though it is possible to teach dictionary skills by computer, they are more easily taught by using dictionaries, for example.

The capacity of a computer is inadequate to include all the branching that might possibly be needed to meet every student's needs in a total reading program—at least at this time. Advances in computer technology are being made rapidly, however, and no one can pretend to see the impact computers will have on reading instruction in the years to come.

Innovators have introduced various kinds of viewers for reading instruction. Film loops, or "concept loops," present illustrated stories or project reading material onto a small screen. The students go through introductory instruction and then do most of the reading for themselves.

Another type of viewer resembles a small television set. Still pictures are projected onto the screens from within the machine. The students are guided through much of the work, reading stories and making responses on worksheets that accompany the pictures. Their responses can then be reviewed as they listen and watch the viewer. Although branching is limited, the programs have good initial motivation and appeal, and they often allow corrective readers to make acceptable gains. Unfortunately, some are not well-programmed or properly paced and are incomplete in skill development presentation. Still, the appeal of the approach is generally high, particulary while the program is still novel to the students.

It is imperative that those who produce and those who use machine-presented approaches understand the vital role played by the teacher in reading instruction. During one study of adult illiteracy, students were asked to tell why they liked or disliked a particular machine-presented program that had been used with them. They expressed a strong preference for programs that provided more teacher contact, saying that they disliked the programmed machine approach because it meant that "the teacher never has time to work with us." The personal contact with a teacher was important to them (Brown and Newman, 1968).

There is some teaching equipment that the corrective teacher should have by all means. Cassette recorders and cassette players are invaluable. Videotape recorders and playback units, though expensive, can be used in a number of ways in reading instruction. Cameras that can produce developed pictures in a few seconds are excellent motivators and have several applications in a corrective or remedial class. Students can place a prepared card on a track in a voice-recording and playback unit such as the *Language Master* and see the word and hear it pronounced at the same time. They can even record their own pronunciation of the word and compare it with the pronunciation pre-recorded on the card.

Advances in machine-presented reading instruction encourage the hope that such instruction will become more useful for poor readers in the future. While present instruction can be profitably supplemented by some of the machines discussed above, machines will continue to be less important to good reading instruction than the teacher. Machines may, however, enable teachers to do a better job.

SUMMARY

Remedial students are less dependent on the teacher than extremely disabled readers and therefore are able to use some of the intensive instructional approaches ordinarily used with extremely poor readers; they are able to use a number of additional approaches as well. Among those which can be adapted for use with remedial readers are the modified basal, language experience, Individualized Reading, and management system, as well as the linguistic, programmed, and modified alphabet approaches. The eclectic approach, which combines the best from the various approaches to meet the needs of individual students, is probably the most widely used of all.

Corrective instruction often utilizes adaptations of remedial approaches. Such programs are frequently eclectic, organized under such varied patterns as cross-classroom or cross-grade grouping and learning centers or resource rooms. In addition to adapted remedial programs of reading instruction, corrective programs commonly make use of diagnostic-prescriptive instruction involving the use of reading kits, packaged programs, and machine-presented instruction. Among the latter, computer-assisted instruction has made the greatest gains within the last few years.

RECOMMENDED READINGS

CHEEK, M. C.; and CHEEK, E. H. 1980. *Diagnostic-prescriptive reading instruction: A guide for classroom teachers*. Dubuque, Ia.: Wm. C. Brown, Chapter 8.

HARRIS, A. J.; and SIPAY, E. R. *How to increase reading ability*. 7th ed. New York: David McKay, Chapter 3.

HARRIS, L. A.; and SMITH, C. B. 1980. *Reading instruction: Diagnostic teaching in the classroom*. 3rd ed. New York: Holt, Rinehart & Winston, Chapter 12.

HEILMAN, A. W. 1977. *Principles and practices of teaching reading*. 4th ed. Columbus, Ohio: Charles E. Merrill, Chapter 4.

RANSOM, G. A. 1978. *Preparing to teach reading*. Boston: Little, Brown, Chapters 4, 5, and 7.

RUPLEY, W. H.; and BLAIR, T. R. 1979. *Reading diagnosis and remediation: A primer for classroom and clinic*. Chicago: Rand McNally, Chapter 14.

REFERENCES

Atkinson, R. C.; and Fletcher, J. D. January 1972. Teaching children to read with a computer. *The Reading Teacher* 25: 319–27.

Brown, D. A.; and Newman, A. 1968. *A literacy program for adult city-core illiterates*. Final Report on U.S. Office of Education Research Grant No. OEG-1-7-061136-0385. Buffalo: State Univ. New York at Buffalo.

Flatt, E. A. October 1969. *The influence of individualized eye-span training with digits on effective reading rate*. Unpublished doctoral dissertation, Univ. Connecticut.

Rhyan, D.; and Miller, P. October 30–31 1980. Demonstration of computer-assisted instruction at Kansas City, Kansas, Community College, Kansas State Right-to-Read Seminar/Workshop, Butler County Community College, Eldorado, Kansas.

Wardhaugh, R. 1969. Is the linguistic approach an improvement in reading instruction? In *Current issues in reading*, ed. N. B. Smith. Newark, Del.: International Reading Assoc.; pp. 254–67.

12

The reading approaches and methods suggested in Chapters Ten and Eleven provide sufficient breadth to serve as an instructional framework for virtually all students. Still, there are many techniques and activities, too limited to be called either approaches or methods, that can provide immediate interest and produce improvement in reading skills. A number of these are described in this chapter.

TEACHING BASIC READING SKILLS:
Readiness, Sight Recognition, Word Analysis, and Fluency and Rate

In teaching poor readers, the teacher should organize instruction to accommodate the "earmarks of good remediation" discussed in Chapter Nine. These include developing interest units which provide opportunities for (1) independent reading, (2) instructional reading, (3) skill development, (4) oral modeling by the teacher, (5) skill reinforcement activities, and (6) progress charting. These elements usually can be integrated easily into the intensive instructional approaches generally used for extremely disabled readers. In the case of remedial and especially corrective students, for whom instruction tends to be less rigidly prescribed and more eclectic in nature, the teacher must plan more carefully to include these six elements.

In planning skills instruction, many teachers use a *directed reading activity* (DRA) format. The directed reading activity has the following basic steps:

1. *Preparation.* The teacher should provide an ample supply of multilevel reading materials related to a carefully selected interest theme for the DRA. Enough material should be available that all students will be able to read at their own independent or instructional reading levels. The teacher should identify reading skills to be developed as indicated by student diagnostic profiles, and material should be prepared with which to teach them.
2. *Motivation.* A significant effort should be made to interest the students in the theme of the DRA. Visual aids, recordings, role-playing techniques, dramatizations, discussions, and other means of creating interest may be employed. Unfamiliar vocabulary and concepts should be explained.
3. *Selection of Material.* The teacher should make it possible for all students to select materials at their individual instructional levels dealing with the topic. The students should be able to select the material quickly and easily.
4. *Opportunity to Read.* The students should be afforded time to read much or all of the material during that period.
5. *Culminating Activity.* After reading, the students should participate in an activity in line with the theme of the DRA and a natural outome of the DRA. For example, if the theme has been "famous ghost stories," the activity might be to write or tell a short ghost story, either original or adapted from the one read.
6. *Skill Application.* The group should complete the skill-development activities planned by the teacher to meet their needs as indicated by their diagnostic profiles.
7. *Projection.* The students should be challenged to do further reading related to the topic. They should be helped to find sources of additional reading materials.

The reading approaches outlined in Chapters Ten and Eleven generally have the breadth and flexibility to meet individual needs for basic skill instruction. Those students needing to improve their sight vocabulary, for example, would receive emphasis on aspects of the approach which would support that development; those needing to improve their comprehension would receive different emphases, all within the framework of the approach being used.

However, a teacher often has to supplement an approach with techniques or activities specifically aimed at the improvement of one or more basic skills because the student's skill deficits cannot be remediated completely by the ordinary instruction within an approach. This chapter presents activities for the development of specific reading skills from which the teacher may choose those needed to supplement the basic reading approach being used.

In selecting an activity to supplement an approach, the teacher should be sure that the activity and the approach are compatible. If, for example, the primary approach being used is programmed reading, it would be unwise to select an activity emphasizing phonic analysis, because programmed reading and phonic analysis are based on different, somewhat antagonistic theories of reading instruction.

The activities are grouped under headings that correspond to the basic reading skills in the "Diagnostic Model of Reading Behavior" which appears in Chapter Two. The techniques and activities described should be modified by the teacher as needed so they will fit different levels of development and different instructional settings.

READING READINESS

There are at least four subdivisions of reading readiness of concern to the reading teacher. These include inadequate visual discrimination, poor auditory discrimination, inability to concentrate or "focus" on a task at hand well enough to learn effectively, and impoverished language background. Although the activities are divided under the different headings, an activity will frequently be useful in developing more than one skill.

Visual Discrimination   Visual discrimination is the ability to differentiate meaningfully between visual forms. Relative to reading, it has been found that the most effective means of improving visual discrimination is through instruction using word and letter forms rather than gross visual forms or equally fine forms unrelated to reading.

Although visual discrimination is not usually a concern for the reading teacher who works with middle elementary and older students, it can be a problem when working with younger and, occasionally, older students. The following activities are useful in developing visual discrimination.

Match Me   For this activity, four sets of cards, ten to a set, are prepared. All four sets have the same words, but printed in four different sizes. The word *boy*, for example, would be printed four times—in large letters on one card, slightly smaller on a second card, still smaller on a third card, and smallest of all on the last card. The words within each set are also varied so that not all the large-print words appear in one set. The four sets can be differentiated by means of different colors or numbering on the back.

The activity works best with four players, but fewer can play if four players are unavailable. The sets of cards are shuffled separately and one of the sets is then given to each player face down in a pile in front of him. A "pitcher" is chosen who begins the activity by turning up his top card and saying, "Match me." Each of the other players turns over the top card. If one of them matches the pitcher's card, he says, "I match" and claims the pitcher's card. If two or three players match the pitcher's card, the first one to say "I match" can claim the pitcher's card and the other cards as well. Matches do not count unless they match the pitcher's card.

After making a match, the player puts his cards aside to count up at the end of the game. As soon as all ten cards have been shown, each player counts the number of matched cards, the sets are separated, shuffled, and one set is given to each player. The next player is named the pitcher, and the process is repeated until every player has served as pitcher once. The total number of cards matched is counted, and the game is over.

Younger children often enjoy this activity without being greatly concerned about who has won and who has lost. For older students the game can be made more challenging by the use of words that are more similar in appearance. It should be noted that it is unnecessary for the student to be able to read the word, but only to be able to tell whether the words are alike.

Match Me (for one or two players)   A variation of the activity above can be played with the same cards. One set is spread out face up on the table while the student keeps his set in front of him face down. He turns over one word at a time and matches it with one of the cards on the table. If two play this variation, each one takes a turn until all the cards are matched. There is no "winner" in this variation. If only one student plays, someone should check the cards after the student has finished.

Center Match   This game is for two, three, or four players and uses forty-eight 3 × 5 cards. The same word is written on each of four cards until a dozen words have been used. The cards are shuffled and equally divided among the players and a pile in the middle of the table. If, for example, there were three players, each player would receive twelve cards, and twelve more would be placed in the center. If there is an uneven number, the extra cards are placed in the center. The stack of cards in the center is placed face up so that only the top card can be identified. The cards for each player are placed face down in front of each student.

The first player turns his top word-card over. If it matches the card on top of the center pile, he can pick up both cards and start a new pile face up on the table so that everyone can see it. If his word-card does not match the word on the center pile, he must take his card off the top and place it underneath his card pile, leaving a new word to be turned over when it is his turn again.

The next player, the student to the first player's left, may see if his top word-card matches the word-card on the center pile. If it does not, he may play his word card on top of the other player's new match pile on the table if his word matches the words in that pile. If he cannot match either word, he places his top card underneath his word pile. Play continues until someone is able to get rid of all his word cards by matching them with the other cards on the table. Again, it should be noted that it is unnecessary for the student to be able to read or pronounce the word. Since this is an activity to develop visual discrimination, all that is needed is to match the words correctly.

Big Letter, Little Letter   This activity should not be used until the students have become familiar with the letters, the letter names, and both capital and lowercase forms of the letters. On pieces of tagboard approximately 5 × 8 inches print a large uppercase letter at the top and the lowercase form of the same letter at the bottom. Do this with several letters. Then cut the tops and bottoms apart, using a distinctive cutting line so that no two of the cards have the same pattern of cutting line separating them. If more than one set of cards is made, use a different-colored felt-tip pen for each set so they may be quickly sorted into the different sets. The student takes a set and matches the capital letter with its lowercase form. If he is correct, the two pieces will fit together. Younger students enjoy this activity, and the teacher may want to laminate the cards to protect them from wear.

Jigsaw Words   This is an individual activity in which the student tries to fit together a jigsaw puzzle which the teacher has made from a word written on a piece of tagboard approximately 9 × 13 and then glued to a piece of corrugated cardboard trimmed to the same size. The teacher then cuts each word-card into about a dozen pieces, trying to include a portion of the word on each part of the puzzle. The puzzle pieces should be kept in labeled plastic bags large enough to store them without bending them. When the student works with the puzzles, different words may occasionally be mixed together, so it is a good idea to use different colors for each word. The words should be made with broad strokes so the student can identify the lines easily.

Domino Words   Make the dominoes by drawing a line that divides 3 × 5 cards in half. Choose ten words for the student to discriminate. If the words are numbered from 1 to 10, each word would be coupled with itself and with each other word by following the plan below:

1:1									
1:2	2:2								
1:3	2:3	3:3							
1:4	2:4	3:4	4:4						
1:5	2.5	3:5	4:5	5:5					
1:6	2:6	3:6	4:6	5:6	6:6				
1:7	2:7	3:7	4:7	5:7	6:7	7:7			
1:8	2:8	3:8	4:8	5:8	6:8	7:8	8:8		
1:9	2:9	3:9	4:9	5:9	6:9	7:9	8:9	9:9	
1:10	2:10	3:10	4:10	5:10	6:10	7:10	8:10	9:10	10:10

For 1:1 above, the teacher will write word #1 on both ends of the first card. For 1:2, the teacher will write word #1 on one end and word #2 on the other, and so on.

As many as six students may play. The dominoes are turned face down and mixed. Each student draws six dominoes. The first one to draw a double domino (a domino having the same word on both ends) starts the game. He places his domino in the middle of the table. The student to his left takes the next turn. He may play if he has a word that will match the domino in the middle. Just as in regular dominoes, he must place the ends that match together. If a student does not have a word that will match one of those on the end of the lines of dominoes on the table, he must draw until he has one he can play. The first player to play all his dominoes wins. If everyone still has at least one domino but no one can play, and there are no more dominoes to draw, the one with the fewest dominoes left is the winner.

Auditory discrimination   Auditory discrimination is the ability to differentiate between sounds. Although the ability to hear is necessary before it is possible to discriminate, hearing acuity and auditory discrimination are not the same. A person may be able to hear the words *pet* and *bet* and be unable to discriminate between them. Auditory discrimination is usually more difficult for a person who speaks English as a second language. For those who are trying to learn English, certain words are difficult to discriminate between; for example, *leaf* and *leave*, *pin* and *pen*, and *full* and *fool* are so similar in sound that students must develop keen discrimination before they can differentiate between them. The following remedial activities help develop auditory discrimination.

Sound-Alikes   Three paddles are made for each student by gluing wooden stir sticks to 3-inch circles of colored construction paper. Each paddle is numbered 1, 2, or 3 on both sides; each number is a different color. Each student places his three paddles on the desk or table in front of him.

The teacher reads sets of three words, two of which have the same beginning sound. The students are to listen carefully to all three words as the teacher reads them. The teacher then says, "Get set . . . go," and the students raise the paddle representing the number of the word that sounds different. If a student raises his paddle before the teacher says "go," he is declared "offside" and does not receive points for that round.

Each student who correctly identifies the word that is different receives 10 points. Each game consists of 100 points. If a student begins to watch the responses of others before making his response, the teacher may impose a time limit. This may be done by saying, ". . . and the word is _____," naming the word. If the student does not raise his paddle before the teacher pronounces the word, his response is not counted. For example, the teacher may say, "I want you to show me which word *begins* with a different sound. Listen—fall . . . big . . . ball. Get set . . . go! (pause) and the word is . . . fall." The teacher would then award 10 points to everyone lifting paddle #1.

The same activity can be used for ending and rhyming sounds, although they are more difficult.

Going to California   The teacher announces, "I am going to California, and I'm taking my _____," naming something beginning with a letter-sound he wants students to learn to discriminate. If the letter is *t*, for example, he might say, "I'm going to California, and I'm taking my *tent*." The next player repeats what the teacher has said and adds something beginning with the same initial sound that he is going to take. He might say, "I'm going to California, and I'm taking my *tent* and *towel*." Each student in turn repeats everything the person before him said, adding his own item to the list until someone fails to remember everything on the list in correct order and breaks the chain. The teacher then selects a new letter-sound and begins again.

The teacher may want to make it easier for younger students by simply having the student say only the name of the one item he is "taking to California" instead of naming all the items everyone has named. This activity can be varied by using common ending and rhyming sounds, but the teacher should be sure the sound is known to the students.

Fractured Fables   The teacher takes a common story, fairy tale, or nursery rhyme and selects words within it whose letter-sounds can be changed to produce a different word. The teacher then reads the story slowly and distinctly, allowing the students to interrupt when they hear a word that sounds wrong. They tell the teacher which word is wrong and how the word should sound. The teacher then reads on until they stop him again.

For example, the nursery rhyme "Little Bo Peep" could be changed to read

> Little Bo *Beep* has lost her *shape*
> And doesn't know where to find them.
> *Leaf* them alone, and they'll come home
> Wagging their *tells* behind them.

Shopping Bag   Pictures clipped from advertisements of various items that can be purchased in a grocery store are glued to 3 × 5 cards. One student gives them out so each student has several cards. The teacher, and afterward a student "shopper," says, "I want to buy something that begins with the sound of *b* as in *boy*" (or any letter plus a key word). Each student deposits his picture card in the teacher's shopping bag, and the teacher calls for another letter until all the cards have been gathered.

Rhyming Pictures   The teacher prepares a large sheet of oaktag by gluing a number of pictures on it. Holding the pictures so that everyone can see them, the teacher says, "I'm thinking of a picture that rhymes with 'bat.' Which picture do you think it is?" Most students enjoy making the charts used in this activity; this not only helps the teacher but provides a good learning activity in itself.

Initially the teacher may want to have students respond verbally. Later, the pictures can be numbered, and the students can write the number of the picture they select. Answers are checked and each student is helped to understand the correct identification.

Attention   Many poor readers have difficulty concentrating on what they should be learning. Since it is unlikely that students can learn to be effective readers unless they can give their attention to what the teacher is trying to teach, it is important to help them develop that ability.

There are many things a teacher can do to help students learn to concentrate. The teacher should stand relatively close (perhaps within 5 or 6 feet) to students having difficulty concentrating. He should try to be active and vital, varying his speech in tone, rate, volume, and quality. He should learn the names of the students as quickly as possible and call them by name. He should use multiple-response techniques, employ visual aids, and provide frequent changes of pace during instruction. This can be partially achieved by using materials with emotional appeal—excitement, humor, tenderness, and courage—as well as content value. The learning environment should be bright and cheerful without being gaudy or distracting. Heating, cooling, ventilation, noise control, and lighting should be such that they contribute to the student's concentration. The following activities will help develop attention.

Concentration   This activity calls for the use of ten pairs of matched word-cards. If the game is used by nonreaders, pictures or letters may be substituted for words.

The pairs should not be identifiable from the back. The cards are shuffled and turned face down on the table. As each student plays, he selects two cards and turns them up. If they match, the student may keep them and play again. If not, they must be turned face down again, and the next student plays. The player who captures the most pairs is the winner.

Words likely to be confused such as *what* and *that*, *where* and *there*, *was* and *saw*, and *when* and *then* may be included among the matched pairs (two *whats* and two *thats*, for example) to sharpen visual discrimination as well as to develop concentration ability.

Student Authors   The teacher should select an interesting story to read to a relatively small group seated together. Reading the story in a lively manner, the teacher stops at each important juncture. He then asks the students what they think might happen next. After everyone has guessed, he continues the story to find out what the author has written. Then the teacher asks the students what they think would have been the best way to have written that portion of the story and asks them to explain why.

Simon Says   The leader, standing in front of the group, gives directions to do various things, usually preceded by the phrase "Simon says." Each student follows the directions unless the leader does *not* say "Simon says." If he does what the leader says to do in that case, he is out of the game.

For example, the leader may say, "Put your hands on your knees." (No one should do so.) The leader says, "Simon says, 'Put your hands on your knees,'" (Everyone should put their hands on their knees.) The leader says, "Put your hands behind your back.'" (Everyone should do so.) The leader says, "Put your hands over your head.'" (No one should do so.) Each time someone makes a mistake, either by doing something when not given the cue "Simon says" or by not doing the action when the leader gives the cue, he drops out until the next game.

A variation for younger children is to have the ones who make a mistake move one place to the left in the line of students each time they do so. This allows them to continue to play.

Language Base   Many students who speak a different language in their homes or who come from homes where they do not develop a strong language facility, have difficulty learning to read. When this is the case, the teacher must use various means of encouraging them to be involved in the use of language by providing opportunities for them to discuss, interact with others, listen, and raise questions to develop a better language background.

Although nothing is better for the improvement of oral language skills than the exercise of that language with peers and with the teacher, some activities can help to foster language growth by providing opportunities for language participation. Some activities that have proved useful are included below.

Continued Stories   The teacher tells the beginning of a story, and then, after 2 or 3 minutes, he "passes it on" to another member of the group. That student adds to the story for about 2 minutes and then, in turn, passes it on to another student. The activity continues in this manner until everyone has had a chance to tell a portion of the story. After the first time, the teacher can lead the group in trying to construct nearly impossible conditions for the characters in the story before passing it on, forcing the next person to contrive some sort of fantastic rescue in order to save them and tell the next part of the narrative.

In the Bag   The teacher gathers a bag full of all kinds of items, and the same general format is followed as in the activity above. This time, however, the person who is talking must first reach into the bag, pull out some sort of object, and weave it into the story in a logical way. The last person to draw something from the bag must conclude the story.

Tell Me a Story   Students are given a title and told that they have 5 minutes to make up a story which they can then record on a cassette recorder. Absurd titles like, *The Fish Who Couldn't Swim, Why the Elephant Stepped on My Car, The Mountain Made of Bubblegum,* or *The Golden Snowflake* can sometimes stir the imagination. A timer should be used to stop the story-teller after about 5 minutes.

After all members of the group have recorded their stories on tape, the group listens to them. After each story, a few minutes is allowed for discussion. Remarks should be kept on a positive plane.

Buddies   This game requires two or more teams of students. The teams should have no more than three or four members. Each team has a captain. The team members have 5 minutes in which to learn as many things as possible that they have in common with one another. They may include facts from their background such as the places they were born, places they have gone, where they have lived, what they like to eat, the kinds of music they like, and so on. They cannot include such things as physical characteristics common to all, such as having eyes or noses, but they can include having variable things like brown eyes, freckles, blonde hair, etc. The team discovering the greatest number of similarities within the time limit is the winner.

· *Word Stories*   The teacher starts by giving the first word in a sentence; then each student follows, adding one word. The teacher writes down the words as they are given, and a story is developed, word by word and sentence by sentence. As soon as the story is completed, the teacher reads it back to the group. This provides a good opportunity to further group cooperation as well as to develop an understanding of language structure.

Tell It Like It Is   The teacher provides a picture with a number of objects in it. No one is allowed to see the picture before the game starts. Then the first player looks at it, puts it back face down on the table, and tries to describe one of the objects he saw without naming the object. He then chooses someone to guess the object. If the student succeeds, he becomes the next person to look and describe an object. If not, the teacher asks the student to name the object and appoints someone else to be "it."

AUTOMATIC SIGHT RECOGNITION VOCABULARY

The development of an automatic sight vocabulary is an important first step in building word analysis skills and later in becoming a fluent, effective reader. The most important single activity that contributes to the development of a sight vocabulary is wide reading at the independent reading level. If students (1) become interested in reading, (2) are given the opportunity to read, and (3) read materials at their own independent level, they are likely to develop a good automatic sight recognition vocabulary.

Many poor readers have found reading to be so difficult that it is not easy to interest them in reading just for enjoyment. They must be helped to develop a sight vocabulary by means of other motivation. Once they have begun to make progress in building a sight vocabulary, their reading improves, and they may find reading easier and more fun. In order to arrive at that point, however, it is often profitable for them to use flash cards. The three-level vocabulary-learning procedure discussed in Chapter Ten is an excellent method for working with flash cards. For younger students, it can be helpful to label objects in the room to develop sight vocabulary.

In addition to these techniques, there are a number of activities described below which can help increase students' immediate sight vocabulary.

Tachistoscopes   A tachistoscope is a device that allows the reader to attempt to recognize a word or other visual stimulus during a relatively brief exposure. Usually the rate of exposure is controlled and predetermined. Hand-held tachistoscopes are little more than flash cards with a shutter. A teacher-made tachistoscope can be made, as shown in Figure 12–1, at little or no cost. The procedure is simple. A window is cut in a piece of cardboard as shown in Step 1. On the back of a notepad, cut a piece approximately 8½ × 5 inches and make the window about 5/8 × 2¼ inches (different measurements may be used to suit the teacher). For the second step, cut a shutter with a handle shaped as seen in Figure 12–1. The bottom of the shutter should be approximately 3 inches across, with a

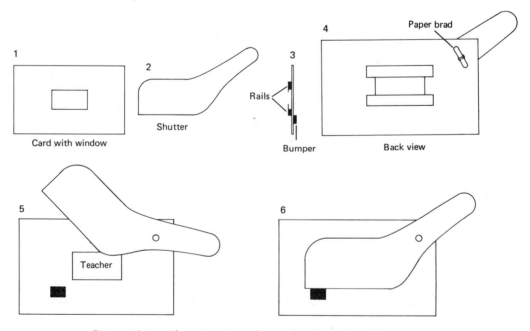

Figure 12–1.   The steps in making a hand-made tachistoscope

height of 2 inches. The handle should be long enough to extend 1½ inches or more beyond the edge of the card when it is mounted in place.

For step three, fasten a "bumper" to the front of the tachistoscope as shown. It may be made by gluing squares of ½ × 1-inch cardboard together. Two rails to hold the word cards in place should be made of two or three strips of cardboard with one slightly wider piece being added last to form a lip. The rails may be glued in place. As seen from the back, the rails are slightly longer than the window. This is Step 4. For Step 5, fix the shutter to the front of the tachistoscope with a paper brad so that when it is raised by pushing down on the handle the word can be seen clearly. The shutter should be worked up and down several times until it is possible to flip the handle with a finger and have the shutter open and close easily. When the shutter is closed, it rests on the bumper, obscuring the word, as seen in the diagram in Step 6.

The word-cards to use in the tachistoscope are about the size of business cards. They can be slipped between the rails while the shutter is closed. While the student is looking at the front of the tachistoscope, the shutter handle is flipped, exposing the word briefly, and the student attempts to recognize the word. The length of time cannot be accurately controlled, but that does not appear to be of any great importance. The student should be able to see the word for a long enough period of time to recognize it but not long enough to try to sound it out.

Race   Draw an oval track on a large piece of tagboard, dividing it off into 100 spaces. Some of the spaces may be used for penalties or rewards. The words the students are working on are divided into those worth one space, those worth two spaces, and those worth three spaces. This may be done on the basis of known difficulty or through division by word length, with words that are three letters or shorter being worth one space, words of four or five letters worth two spaces, and words longer than five letters worth three spaces.

Each student may select words of his choice from the pile. If, for example, he sees a penalty space ahead, he will want to avoid it by choosing a word that will award the number of spaces that will keep him out of the penalty space. If he correctly pronounces the word, he moves ahead the appropriate number of spaces. If he misses the word, he goes back one space. If he goes back one space and someone else is already on that space, he must "slide" back to the last penalty space and take whatever that penalty is. If, when he gets the word right, he moves forward to a space that is already occupied, the person already on that space is moved *forward* to the next penalty space and must do whatever is indicated by that space. The markers for the players can be any number of things, but small plastic animals or figures make good ones.

Scrambled Words   Make duplicate lists of scrambled words, one list for each player. If there are several students in the group, they may work as teams, or one student may do the first word, the second the next word, and so on. The first student, or team, to unscramble all the words is the winner.

Baseball   Write words the students are trying to learn to recognize on flash cards. Draw the outline of a baseball diamond on the chalkboard or on a large piece of tagboard. Then divide the students into two teams. The pitcher for the first team selects a word to show the batter of the second team. If the batter calls the word correctly, he advances to first base. If he does not, the word goes to a member of the other team who tries to "field" the ball by reading it correctly. If he succeeds, the batter is out. If he "muffs" it by not reading it correctly, it is called a strike, and the batter gets another chance to hit another pitch. Generally, only two strikes should be allowed per player rather than the traditional three because three strikes prolongs the game unduly.

Tic Tac Toe   This is a game for two people. The teacher makes up several Tic Tac Toe diagrams but adds different vocabulary words on the diagrams. Before the student can mark an X or O, he must correctly pronounce the word on the diagram where he wants to place his mark. Whoever makes the first complete line of marks wins the game. See the diagrams below.

this	on	there
able	use	over
yes	him	they

when	our	which
even	top	ear
went	help	no

ever	too	seek
with	put	now
hope	gone	seem

Head of the Table   The students are seated on one, two, or three sides of the table with the teacher seated on the fourth side. Each student has his own pile of vocabulary words placed face down between him and the teacher, and within easy reach of the teacher. The teacher shows the top card of each student's word pile to that student. The card should be seen for about a second. If the student correctly identifies the card, he remains seated where he is, but if he fails to do so, he moves to the foot of the table. The object of the game is to get to the head of the table.

The Missing Card   Students work in pairs for this activity. Using the vocabulary cards each student is trying to learn, place three of them face up on the table. The student has 10 seconds to look at them and then must close his eyes or look away. The second student takes one of the cards and moves the other two into different positions on the table. The student looks at the two remaining cards and tries to identify the one that is missing.

An alternative to this activity is to have the student write the missing word. If he merely identifies it, he receives 1 point; if he can write the word correctly, he receives 3 points. The students exchange roles after twenty trials, and the one who has the most points wins.

Add-a-Word The teacher should draw the "face" and tail of a caterpillar on an 8-inch oval of colored construction paper for each student. Every time the student masters a new sight vocabulary word, it is printed on another oval the same size and placed between the head and tail of the caterpillar, building its body. The sizes can be made smaller if space is a consideration.

Football Two students may play this game, or two teams of two or three students each. Each student divides the words he is trying to learn into three piles in order of difficulty. A fourth pile can be made by the teacher of words the student would start to learn next. A football field is drawn on a large piece of tagboard or borrowed from the numerous football-game boards one may find in thrift stores and second-hand shops. A cardboard football can be used for a marker.

The first player "kicks off" to the other by trying to read words from the fourth pile. If he cannot recognize the word, the ball is put in play by his opponent on the 50-yard line. If he reads it correctly, the ball goes another 10 yards to his opponent's 40-yard line. He then tries to read another word from that pile. Each time he reads correctly, the ball goes another 10 yards until finally the ball comes to rest on his opponent's goal line, where the other player takes over.

That player may select from any of the word piles in front of him. If he chooses a word from the first (easiest) pile, he gains 2 yards. If he chooses from the second, he gains 4 yards, and from the third, he gains 6. If he wants to pass, he may pass for 6 yards by reading a card from his third pile, for 10 yards by reading one card from the fourth pile, or 20 yards by reading two words—both correctly—from the fourth pile. If he decides to punt, he does so by reading words from the fourth pile in much the same way as on a kickoff. The punt travels 15 yards even if the student misses the word. For each word correct from pile four, the student advances the ball an additional 10 yards. If he is within the 50-yard line, he may convert a field goal by reading one word from the fourth pile for every 10 yards away from the end zone to the nearest 10 yards. For example, if the student were on the 36-yard line, he would have to consider it the same as from the 40-yard line.

Scoring is done by advancing the ball into the opponent's end zone, for 6 points. The extra point can be scored by correct recognition of the first word from the third pile.

Although this game takes some preparation, it is an effective means of teaching sight vocabulary words and will meet with considerable interest.

WORD ANALYSIS

The ability to analyze and recognize words includes the use of phonic and structural clues and the ability to blend the separate word elements together to make a word the student can recognize. More advanced readers tend to recognize words using larger elements than beginning readers.

The major purpose behind teaching word attack skills is to help students develop independent word recognition abilities. The student who develops good word attack and good use of context cues will usually become a competent reader. Self-reliance does not always come automatically, however. The teacher should work to help students exercise their independence in analyzing unfamiliar words. Students should be allowed time to attempt to analyze the words they meet; if the teacher rushes to pronounce the word or interferes with a student's thoughts by talking to him while he is trying to concentrate on unlocking a word, the student will come to rely on the teacher to "solve" the words for him.

The teacher should also encourage flexibility in attacking new words. When students have difficulty in analyzing a word, the teacher may be able to point out that giving letters a different sound or putting the accent in a different place will help "solve" the word.

Phonic Attack Skills   Phonic analysis is based on the relationship between a letter or letters and the sound or sounds they produce, and sometimes is abbreviated to "sound-symbol relationship." There is no question that "phonics" is an important means of identifying words, but not every poor reader needs phonic instruction. Some have already learned how to use phonics in analyzing words, and some few may be at such a low level of development that they are not yet able to relate letters and their sounds. Some of the approaches discussed in Chapters Ten and Eleven made little use of formal phonics instruction, although that does not necessarily mean that students using these approaches do not learn to associate letters with their sounds. Most VAKT approaches, for example, make little use of formal phonics at the first two levels. Linguistic approaches do not use specific phonics instruction either, although both VAKT and linguistic approaches develop the equivalent of practical, applied phonics through their own methods. In the linguistic approach, for example, students become familiar with and learn to recognize words having similarly sounded groups of letters or phonemes. In VAKT, though students are not usually instructed or permitted to "sound out" the words they are tracing or writing, they nonetheless learn to associate the letters they see with the sounds of the word.

There is a significant difference between applied phonics and the memorization of phonic principles. Each teacher has had a student who is able to recite a number of phonic generalizations but who is unable to apply them. It is obviously of limited value to know the "rule" but to be unable to use that rule in recognizing an unfamiliar word. Even in those approaches in which a significant amount of time is spent in teaching phonic principles, correct application should always weigh much more heavily than the ability to recite the rule.

The application of phonic principles can be taught to poor readers in a manner that causes them more difficulty than it provides assistance. In general, in working with poor readers, the teacher should include only those phonic principles which the student needs and which have wide applicability. The student probably will already know some rules, which he has learned either directly or indirectly, and he may be unable to grasp others just as yet.

There is a temptation to try to push the poor reader to "catch up" by teaching him a number of different rules one right after the other. The teacher needs to remember that poor readers are often confused and discouraged about their analysis abilities, and it is better to have them learn slowly and successfully than to try to have them learn so quickly that they fail again. By teaching a group of remedial readers several principles in one week, the teacher may cause even more confusion than existed before. By limiting principles to one, two, or three widely applicable and necessary rules, the teacher may succeed in having students learn both the rules and their practical application, *and* give students a sense of pride in their accomplishment.

Phonic principles should never be taught in isolation. They should be taught directly related to the words the students are reading. If it is difficult to find a word or words which exemplify a rule, it seems likely that the principle ought not to be taught, at least at the students' present level of development.

In teaching phonic principles, the teacher should help students understand that few rules apply all the time. If one principle does not help in recognizing a word, they should try another. Students should learn that almost all rules have exceptions. It is sometimes helpful to include an exception to a rule along with examples in which the rule applies. This helps the student develop flexibility in application of phonic principles.

After introducing a phonic principle and helping the student see how it may be applied, the teacher may want to arrange for the student to use it in applied practice. There are a number of sources of practice materials, and these should be screened on at least two bases: (1) to see that they are coordinated with the basic approach being used with the student and (2) to see that they are not trying to teach too many rules at the same time.

The best way to teach phonic analysis is by pointing out its application to students as they are reading. Let's say that a student is reading to the teacher, who is using a notepad to jot down the words with which the student is having difficulty. As soon as the student has finished reading, the teacher should take time to go over some of the words that might have been more easily recognized by correct application of one or two phonic rules. This enables the student to learn the *application* of the rule at his point of need. This is not a lengthy process, and it is very profitable.

Structural Analysis   Unlike phonic analysis, structural analysis is the identification of words through the analysis of meaningful elements. In general, the structural elements are larger than phonic elements and are encountered at a developmentally later date. The major exceptions to this rule are inflectional changes and compound words, both part of structural analysis and both taught relatively early. Root words, prefixes, and suffixes are taught later.

It is as important in structural analysis as in phonic analysis that instruction be fitted to the needs of the student. It is all too common for teachers to obtain lists of the most commonly used root words and affixes and teach them to all their poor readers without assessing the students' needs or readiness to learn.

Blending   The need to teach poor readers to blend individual word parts together in order to arrive at a meaningful word is sometimes overlooked. There are several points that will help the teacher do a good job in developing good blending skills in students. First, letter-sounds should be taught as part of words rather than as isolated sounds; this reduces the tendency to produce artificial syllables. The student learns to associate the sound of the letter *b* as the beginning sound in the word *boy* rather than as the "b-uh." In the latter case, the student's sounding of the *book* is likely to be segmented into "b-uh-ook" instead of "book."

Second, the students should be encouraged to consider the context in conjunction with their word analysis. They should be taught to read beyond the word, then back up a few words before the unfamiliar word and try to fit it into context, making it sound natural.

Third, students should be taught—if they have trouble quickly identifying a word—to repeat the syllables first slowly, then more quickly as they try to put the word together. They should be careful as they increase their pace not to drop one or more of the syllables. If they do so, they should repeat the process over again, saying the word slowly enough to be sure they are pronouncing all parts of the word.

The teacher should be aware that as students begin to get reasonably close to the correct pronunciation of the word, they may suddenly gain insight and make the "leap to recognition." It is unnecessary for the student to sound out the word perfectly in order to recognize it. Apparently the auditory perceptual centers can accommodate a certain degree of ambiguity just as the visual perceptual centers can. Although it varies with each person, as the student is able to make a general approximation of the word, he is able to make the leap to recognition and to pronounce the word.

It has been pointed out many times that the memorization of rules of syllabication is not useful in the recognition of words; this finding is a corollary to a similar finding that the memorization of phonic principles is not helpful for word recognition. However, just as the application of phonic analysis is an important ingredient in good word recognition, so the *application* of syllabication is helpful to the poor reader. The reading teacher is unlikely to be concerned about whether students break the words they are attacking at precisely the "correct" places. What the teacher really wants from students is the courage to try to break the word into manageable parts and to try to put it back together again. Surely, it does not matter whether the student breaks the word *different* by separating it into *dif-fer-ent, diff-er-ent, dif-fe-rent,* or some other way, as long as he can blend the individual parts—syllables—together again in a way that enables him to correctly recognize and pronounce the word.

The activities below are adaptable in teaching most facets of word analysis skills, including phonic and structural analysis and blending.

The Longest Word   This activity is particularly good to use with older students. As mentioned previously, secondary students tend to be especially sensitive to some aspects of instruction dealing with word analysis skills. It is deadly to try to work with a senior high school student on phonic analysis, asking him to respond to the sound of the letter *b* as in *boy*. Even if he does not know the sound of the letter *b*, he is still likely to feel that such an approach is demeaning and insulting. "The Longest Word" is not demeaning.

The teacher tells the students that he is going to teach them the longest word in the English language that is not a medical or technical word. (In actuality, the word has been dropped from recent unabridged dictionaries—what a loss!) He then writes the word *honorificabilitudinatatibus*, meaning honorableness, on the board.

He should *not* tell them that the word will be easy for them to learn to pronounce. If he indicates to them that they should have no difficulty in learning to say and read the word, it will take away the sense of achievement they will feel when they master it. Instead, he should tell them that it is a hard word—after all, it *is* the longest word in the English language which is not part of a specialized vocabulary—and that they probably do not know anyone outside the class who will be able to pronounce it. They will be able to learn the word because the teacher will show them some special techniques that will help them. By this time, the teacher should have their undivided attention.

The first principle is that with long, very difficult words, the reader should break the word into syllables starting from the right of the word and working forward, repeating the syllables left to right as he does so. For example, with the word on the board, the last syllable in the word is *-bus*. The student should pronounce that syllable, *-bus*, with the teacher.

Some of the students will not know what a syllable is, and most of them will not know how to identify it. The teacher should demonstrate that *-bus* has only one "beat" by tapping his finger on top of the desk as he says the word. By contrast, he may ask, "How many syllables does the word *cotton* have?" tapping his finger for each of the two syllables. He should illustrate by this method that the number of beats in a word is the same as the number of syllables in the word.

Next, he should point out that although some syllables have no consonant sounds, they all have one sounded vowel sound. He should ask what the vowels are and put them on the board. He may point out that sometimes it takes more than one vowel to produce one sounded vowel sound and that at other times vowels are silent. He may use a word such as *course* as an example, showing that there are three vowels in the word, two of them combining to make the single vowel sound, and the final vowel being silent. *Course* has three vowels but only one vowel sound and has only one syllable.

Returning to the word on the board, the teacher helps the students work their way through the word, breaking off syllables from the end of the word. The student would read them

```
        -bus
       -i-bus
     -tat-i-bus
    -a-tat-i-bus
  -in-a-tat-i-bus
 -tud-in-a-tat-i-bus
-i-tud-in-a-tat-i-bus
```

and so on until the entire word has been repeated. By starting with the ending portions first, the student develops greater familiarity with that portion of the word. Generally, when trying to read a lengthy word, the student attempts it from the beginning, and each time he falters, he begins from the first of the word again. This has the effect of providing great practice with the beginning word parts but little or no practice with the ending. As a result, when he tries to pronounce a new word he sees in print, he tends to "bog down" as he reads farther into the word. By starting with more practice on ending word parts, he has an excellent chance of overcoming this problem.

In addition, the first part of most words is often easier for the reader than the middle and latter parts. The first two or three syllables of *honorificabilitudinatatibus* are easier and more familiar to the reader than the last two or three syllables, for example. It makes sense to spend more time practicing the parts of the word that are more difficult.

The teacher should always have the students repeat the word with each added syllable. With the addition of each new syllable, there is an opportunity to teach or, more likely, to review some element of word analysis. Using the word as a springboard, the teacher can point out different vowel sounds, the schwa sound (the "uh" sound given many unaccented syllable vowels), the use of stress or accent, the importance of flexibility, the role of roots, and other elements helpful in good word analysis. If more than one or two of these are unfamiliar to the students, the teacher must be careful to limit the concepts to those they can grasp at one time.

By the end of half an hour or so the teacher can teach the class to read and pronounce the longest nontechnical word in English, but, more importantly, he will have had the attention of the students in reviewing much about word analysis skills and will have demonstrated the value of breaking a word into syllables in order to master it.

Changeover   Students are divided into two teams. The teacher writes the same word on the top line of a sheet of paper for each team. Below the word, ten lines should be numbered. Each student on the team changes the word by making a letter change. The change must result in a real word. The next student, in turn, changes the last student's word, and play continues until the tenth change has been made. The teacher then goes back through the changes with the entire group to see that all words have been real words and that not more than one letter has been changed on each line. The first team to make all ten changes correctly is the winner.

The game can be changed by allowing only beginning, ending, or vowel changes, but the teacher must choose the tipoff word carefully in that case to be sure that there are enough variations to allow the needed changes.

Word Puzzles   The teacher makes up a number of cards with a vowel in the middle of the card and consonants around the edge of the card, as in the illustration.

The student tries to make as many words as he can from the letters on the card by going from one square to any other square, touching it. For example, in the illustration a person could start in the middle with the letter *a* and go to *n* on the adjacent square. He could also start with *b*, go to *a*, then to *n*, and finally to *d*; all these are adjacent to one another. He could not, however, start with *t*, go to *a*, then to *r*, and jump to *p* to spell *tarp*. It is permissible to move vertically, horizontally, or diagonally. After leaving a square, it is permissible to return to the same square.

As soon as the student has made as many words as he can, he should turn the card over and check his word list against the words others have made. If he finds that he has made one or more words that others have not found, he should add them to the list on the back. Cards may also be made using consonant digraphs, double vowels, and so on.

Word Runs   The teacher prepares a set of cards with one letter on each card. The number of word cards for each letter should be as follows:

a = 7, b = 2, c = 3, d = 2, e = 9, f = 2, g = 2, h = 4, i = 7, j = 1, k = 3, l = 4, m = 3, n = 3, o = 7, p = 2, q = 1, r = 4, s = 5, t = 4, u = 5, v = 1, w = 2, x = 1, y = 3, z = 1.

Each student is given five cards, and the rest are placed face down in a pile in the middle of the table. Each student plays in turn by drawing one card from the top of the center pile, making a word from his cards, if possible, and laying it down in front of him. If he cannot play, he passes to the next player without doing anything other than taking the card from the center pile. In order to lay his cards down, a player must be able to pronounce the word. If he mispronounces it, he must hold the word in his hand until his next turn.

As soon as a player has laid down all the cards in his hand, scores are counted. A player receives 1 point for each letter card he has been able to lay down. A point is taken off for each card he has left in his hand.

Grab   The teacher prepares a set of cards in groups of four. Each group has some element of word attack in common. For example, a set of cards could be made of these seven groups:

brake	crook	drink	free	grow	pretty	track
broke	crow	drag	from	green	pride	tree
brim	crank	drop	fresh	grass	prize	trim
broom	crab	draw	front	grab	price	truck

Within each group, four cards would be made with each word rotating at the top. For example, with the *br-* group the cards would be

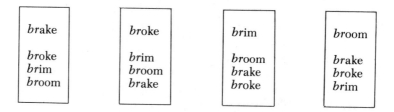

The object of the game is to have the student collect all four cards in each group in his hand and then lay them down on the table. Each student in turn asks any other player for one of the cards he needs in order to make a "book" of four related cards. He calls for the card by the word at the top. The three words below only indicate the other cards in the group. If the other player has the card, he must surrender it to the player who called for it. That player may then call again for another card, continuing to call as long as he is successful. As soon as he calls for a word from a player who does not have that word, his turn is finished, and the next player can call.

As soon as one player has laid all his cards down, the game is over. Scores are counted with 4 points for each book of four cards a player has been able to lay down.

Crazy Otto   The teacher should prepare a set of forty cards in groups of four, with each group having a rhyming ending, plus four more cards called "Crazy Otto's." Beginning sounds of the forty regular cards must all be different within the groups of four, but among groups they should be repeated. For example, two of the ten groups of cards might be

ring	*rake*
sing	*sake*
wing	*wake*
sting	*bake*

"Crazy Otto" cards should have the words "Crazy Otto" printed on them, and they may be illustrated.

Each student receives five cards, and the remainder are placed face down in the middle of the table. The first student starts by playing a card face up in the middle of the table and pronouncing the word. If he does not do so correctly, he must pick the card up and hold it in his hand until his next turn. The next student must play a card on top of the first student's card. It must either have the same ending or the same beginning sound. He must pronounce the word correctly as he places the card on the pile or pick it up and replace it in his hand until his next turn.

If a student has one of the four "Crazy Otto" cards in his hand or if he draws it from the pile, he can use it in place of one of the correct cards. If a "Crazy Otto" is played, the next student is free to play any card on the pile he wants.

If a player does not have a rhyming card, a card with the same initial sound, or a "Crazy Otto," he must draw from the pile that has been placed face down in the middle of the table, adding to his hand until he finds a card he can play. The winner is the player who gets rid of all the cards in his hand first.

Phonic Baseball   Draw an outline of a baseball diamond on the chalkboard or on a large piece of tagboard. Write a word on each base. Divide the group into two teams. The first batter must name a word that begins with the same sound as the word on home plate. In order to keep running, he must pronounce a word beginning with the same sound of the word on first, then second, and finally third base. If he succeeds in naming a word correctly for third base, he scores one run. If he cannot name a correct word at some point, he is out. Players cannot use words that have been used by previous players. As soon as there are three outs on a side, the side is retired, and the other team comes to bat. After each inning, the words on the four bases are changed.

Shuffleboard   Cover the top of a table with a piece of butcher paper marked at one end with areas similar to those on a shuffleboard layout. Instead of using numbers, however, each area should have a grapheme written in it. Graphemes may be chosen from initial consonants, consonant blends, short vowel sounds, or any letter-sound association. Each player tries to slide a checker from the opposite end of the table onto one of the areas. He then receives 1 point for each word he can name that has that sound in it, up to a maximum of 5 points.

Match Up   The teacher prepares two sets of cards. The first set contains sixteen cards, four each for the suffixes *-ness*, *-ful*, *-less*, and *-ly*. Sixteen root words are placed in the other pile. These include words such as *kind, hope, help, friend, cheer, sweet, mean, care, sad, glad, harm, quick, need, thank, hate,* and *good*.

The cards for the root words are divided among the players. The suffix pile is placed in the middle of the table. The first player takes the top card from the suffix pile. If he can add it to one of the root words in his hand, he lays them down in front of him. If he cannot, he replaces the card under the others in the suffix pile, and the next player takes his turn. The player to lay all his cards down is the winner.

Word Builder   The teacher should make identical sets of cards for as many students as are likely to play the game, usually from two to six. There are three different kinds of cards in each set—prefixes, suffixes, and root words. The prefixes may include *dis-, un-, pre-, re-, im-, in-, per-,* and so on. Suffixes could include *-ed, -d, -ness, -ing, -ment, -ly, -able, -less,* and *-est,* among others. Any number of root words could be selected for inclusion.

The cards are divided among the students, and the first player places a root word on the table in the center. The next player can add to the word by playing a prefix or suffix next to the root word or may put another root word on the table. Play continues in this manner, with players being able to add to roots or play a root from their hand, but they are not allowed to play a prefix or suffix unless it is attached to a word to make a real word. If a player cannot play, he passes, and the next student takes his turn. The first player to play all the cards from his hand is the winner.

Word Wheels   The teacher may make word wheels by cutting out two complete circles, one slightly larger that the other. Words are printed around from the center to the outer edge. A small window is cut in the smaller circle through which the words can be seen when the smaller circle is laid over the larger one. A prefix is printed just in front of the opening. The two wheels are then fastened together with a paper brad, and the student can move the window from word to word, adding the prefix and thus making a new word. The wheels are illustrated below.

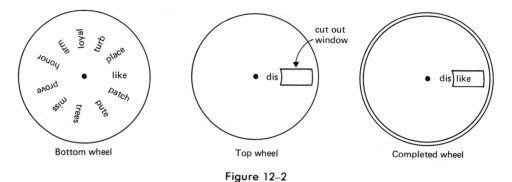

Bottom wheel   Top wheel   Completed wheel

Figure 12–2

A similar device can be made for suffixes. The suffix is placed just beyond the window rather than in front of it.

CONTEXT CLUES

Context clues are useful to the readers in identifying unfamiliar words and in defining words whose meaning in the passage are unknown. A student may know the word *crochet* when he hears it, but its appearance in print may be unfamiliar to him. Using the context, it is possible for him to identify the word in the sentence, "She decided to crochet a beautiful scarf for the bureau." He would likely have mispronounced the word without the context, but with it, he can identify the word.

The second use of context clues is to define a word or words which the student may be able to pronounce but does not understand. Without the context, it is impossible to know the meaning of the word *coast*, for example. The context in the sentences, "I went to the coast" and "He can coast downhill" makes the meaning of the word clear.

Although the context will amplify the meaning of most words, context alone is inadequate to identify or define many words in a passage. For example, in the sentence, "She wore a _____ coat" the context does not provide sufficient information to indicate whether she wore a *red* coat, a *heavy* coat, a *fur* coat or some other sort of coat. There are almost limitless possibilities. Perhaps because of this uncertainty, some students do not make good use of context clues. They have not learned to anticipate the next word or phrase and are more limited as readers because they do not do so.

Instruction in the use of context clues should usually include the use of the initial letter of the word. Students should be helped by their teachers to "guess" what the next word might be in reading. When a student is having difficulty with a word, the teacher should pointedly include the use of the context, where it is helpful, in determining what the word may be.

There are a number of skill-development materials that have been produced to lead students to use context clues. But before these materials are used, it is usually beneficial (1) to help students clearly understand how the context can help, (2) to assist students in applying context clues in dealing with words they encounter in their reading, (3) to work to make their word recognition of most words automatic, and (4) to develop some degree of fluency in students' reading. Readers who do not know anything about the use of context, have never used context, struggle with a number of words in their reading, and read in a nonfluent, word-by-word fashion, will have difficulty learning to use context clues.

The level of the material students are reading may also work to their advantage or to their disadvantage. For the best development of skilled use of context, the reader should have frequent exposure to reading independent-level material.

As with the improvement of most reading skills, one of the best means for improving a reader's use of context clues is wide reading in conjunction with the above instruction. Although slow, analytic, word-by-word readers have the greatest difficulty in learning to use context, practice provided through wide reading coupled with direct instruction aimed at developing understanding and fluency can be effective.

There are fewer activities that can be aimed at the development of skills in using context clues, but some that have been helpful are described below.

Riddles   The teacher collects or prepares a number of riddles, writing each one on a card and including only the initial letter of the answer. For example, "I am tall and have snow on me. I am a m_____." "I grow on trees. I am red and good to eat. I am an a_____." "I can write and I can erase. I am a p_____." "I am the biggest wild animal in America. I am the A_____ br_____ bear."

After students have become slightly familiar with the riddles, the teacher may want to have them time themselves going through the cards to see if they can improve on their last performance.

Lost Treasure   The teacher gives a student the directions to find a long-lost treasure. Unfortunately, some of the words have been smudged. The student must try to fill in all the missing words so that he can find the treasure.

> I hid three thousand g_____ pieces in a secret hiding pl_____. To find it, you have to find the dead tr_____ at the north end of Dead Man's Pond. Go straight up the h_____ until you come to a r_____ as high as your h_____. Turn w_____ and pace off 25 st_____. You will be at the f_____ of an old oak tr_____. Look straight up. Three f_____ above you you will see the sk_____ of an old buffalo. Cl_____ up the tree and sight through the two eye h_____. You will see the mouth of a small c_____ about half a mile away. The treasure is b_____ two feet deep in the fl_____ of the cave.

Other descriptions are similarly easy to make and may include directions to various places, directions on how to make things, and so on.

Extra   The teacher prepares a set of cards with a sentence on each. In each sentence is a word that makes no sense. As the students go through them, they identify the word that does not make sense, checking their answers against the answer on the back of each card. Each student can go through, checking the time it takes him to do the cards, or teams of students can compete with other teams, with the first student handing his card to the next student on his team as soon as he finishes it. The winning team is the one on which all members have read the cards correctly first. For each mistake, the team is penalized 15 seconds.

What Is It?   The teacher must prepare cards ahead of time that will fit various categories in the game. The students try to "beat the clock" by naming as many words within a category as they can in 60 seconds. The teacher allows each student to choose a category from among those for which he has sets of cards. Examples are colors, foods, animals, things to do in school, and so on. While one student watches the clock, the teacher shows the contestant one card at a time in his chosen category. If, for example, the student chooses colors as a category, the teacher might show him a card on which is printed [wh_____]. As soon as the student says "white," the teacher shows him another card on which is printed [y_____]. After each correct response, the teacher gives the student another card to identify.

Some categories need more context clues. "Things to do in school," for example, would require a lead-in sentence by the teacher. The first card could read, [Go to the library to r_____]. The next might be [Eat your l_____ at noon].

I'll Paint a Picture   The students sit in a group facing one another. The teacher (or first player) says, "I see something." The rest ask, "What do you see?" and the teacher replies, "I'll paint you a picture." Then he describes what he has seen. For example, he might say, "It is blue, brown, and green." If the students cannot guess or if they guess incorrectly, he continues to describe what he has seen until they guess correctly.

Phony Fairy Tales   The teacher should rewrite a popular fairy tale, changing names and characters to make it foolish. Little Red Riding Hood may become Small Green Walking Cape, the Big Bad Wolf may become the Big Bad Kitten, and so on. The written story should be duplicated and given to the students. They are to cross out the "phonies" and insert the correct names.

FLUENCY AND RATE

Fluency and rate are treated together because those activities which tend to influence the development of better fluency also lay a foundation for the later development of rate. Rate improvement, in the ordinary sense of the term, is not a major concern for the extremely disabled, remedial, or corrective reader. The development of fluency *is* a concern for even the most seriously disabled reader because it reflects the fact that reading is part of communication—that reading should "sound like talk written down," to use a cliché common to most reading educators.

Fluency   Fluency is a mystery to some students. Reading has never made sense to them. It has never communicated anything to them. For them, reading is a burdensome, boring, tiring "decoding" process in which they must puzzle out word after word much as they might try to solve a seemingly endless parade of braintwisters. The diagnosis and remediation of poor readers is probably the single most interesting area in the field of education, but surely one of the most incredibly wearying jobs in education must be listening to a disabled reader as he reads in a slow, halting, word-by-word manner. If that is true, just think how bored the reader must be. Everything he reads is read in that manner. While good readers pick up reading material and make it come alive as they read, the poor reader, in a nonfluent manner, *endures* reading, decoding one word after another with his eye on the clock, hoping for an end to his ordeal.

Fluency in reading signals that communication has come and that reading has become more than word-solving. Where the words once were dead symbols, they have now become alive. Where they once were only isolated word "puzzles," they now have become the means through which interesting people tell the reader fascinating stories, impart useful information, and instruct him in the "wisdom of God and of man."

Instruction in fluency should first be modeled by those who already read well. The strong aversion to oral reading in the classroom has its roots in the practices of some teachers half a century ago who thought reading could best be taught simply by reading to students. This caused many teachers to stop reading aloud to their students altogether. Many students have no models other than the teacher who can show them how good reading ought to sound. When the teacher never reads aloud or only reads briefly and infrequently, students often lack anyone from whom they may learn that reading ought to communicate the thoughts of the author just as if he were talking.

There are limits that should be observed in oral reading. It reaches a point of diminishing returns if the teacher reads too long or too frequently. Oral reading can be most beneficial when it is used to whet the appetite of the listeners—not to "while away the hours."

If oral reading is important in developmental reading, it is equally important for poor readers involved in special programs of reading improvement. The teacher should look for opportunities to share oral reading with students who are nonfluent readers. Although listening to recordings can be helpful, it is important for the student to *see* the reader as well as to hear him. When a poor reader sees the teacher read, hears his voice, and watches his expressions as he reads, there can be no denying that reading is for "real people."

The amount of oral reading in a poor reader's individualized educational program should be limited, but if he lacks fluency, it should be included. It can and should be arranged in an informal manner, especially for older students. The teacher may bring in something he has selected as interesting to the students and simply share it. It should not be so long that it requires a significant amount of time to read. A passage that lasts only 2 minutes can be as effective as something that might take 10 or 15 minutes, and frequently, it can be *more* effective without sacrificing valuable instructional time.

Although oral modeling is basic to the development of fluent reading, it is not the only factor. Direct instruction is generally needed for poor readers. The teacher may ask a nonfluent reader to read a sentence just as though he were simply speaking it. In the process of reading it in this fashion, the teacher may point out that fluent reading clusters words into thought units with slight pauses between the clusters. The important words are emphasized and the less important words within each cluster or thought unit are touched lightly. In the sentence "*Bill* went to the *store* to *buy* a *loaf* of *bread*," the *underlined* words receive greater emphasis than the rest. The sentence might be presented graphically as

B i l l wentoth' *s t o r e* t'b *u y* al *o a f* ab *r e a d.*

Some words are barely brushed by the tongue. Others not only receive greater emphasis, they are stretched out to consume more time. This is one of the reasons that good fluency can lead to improved reading rates. The rapid reader learns to give lighter emphasis to less important words while a poor reader tends to give them all equal emphasis.

After a student has begun to grasp the concept of fluent reading, he should practice what he has learned. The teacher may find great interest in the use of cassette recorders in recording and replaying a student's reading. Students often are willing to record short radio plays on a cassette. The experience is a good one for students working to overcome poor fluency in their reading. Other activities that are useful in improving fluency are described below.

Flash Phrases   The teacher prepares a set of phrase cards that may be shown to the student one at a time for a second or less. The student learns to read the entire phrase quickly and as a thought unit. A tachistoscope may be used, as described earlier in this chapter, and students may work in pairs to master their phrases.

An alternative is to flash short questions to a small group of students. Instead of reading the phrases, they answer the question, indicating that they have understood the question.

Story Box   The teacher can make a viewer from a small box about the size of a children's shoe box. If a slit is cut in the top and bottom, a strip of paper can be inserted from the bottom and out through the top. Another slit is cut in the front of the box wide enough so that the story written on the strip of paper can be seen one line at a time. Words should not be divided at the end of a line, and thought units should be completed on each line rather than being divided.

The student is able to read the story through the slit in the front of the box by pulling the strip of paper out the top of the box.

News Editor   Have the student read a news story and then mark off the thought units by dividing the sentences with slash marks. He then should try to read the story, recording it on a cassette recorder, following the markings he has made in the news story.

Marking Thoughts   The teacher distributes copies of a short story to the group and then reads while they follow along silently. As he pauses for emphasis, the students make a slash mark on their duplicated copy of the story. The students are then paired off, and the partners take turns reading the story, dividing it into thought units and emphasizing words as the teacher has done. When they have finished, the total group may discuss where they might have read it differently from the teacher.

Critic The student reads a story at his independent reading level, recording it on a cassette tape. He then listens to his reading and makes notes on where he could have read better. Next, he shows his suggestions to the teacher or an aide and tries again. He may record several times, critiquing his reading after each trial. He may erase any of his readings except the first one. When he is satisfied that he has done a good job, he and the teacher listen to his first performance and then his final reading. The improvement is usually encouraging to the student.

Characters After students have read a story and are familiar with the characters and the plot, have them select a character in the story and tell how they think the character might have felt in the story. After several characters have been discussed, have each student locate and read the speeches of their selected character which suggest the feeling they have expressed. This is a good activity for older poor readers.

Team Reading Type a story, double-spaced, with one or two thought units on each line. Number the lines in sequence and distribute them in order to each student so that the story can be read phrase by phrase in regular rotation. In a group of five students, for example, the lines, by number, would be distributed as follows:

Student A	Student B	Student C	Student D	Student E
line 1	line 2	line 3	line 4	line 5
line 6	line 7	line 8	line 9	line 10
line 11	line 12	line 13	line 14	line 15
line 16	line 17	line 18	line 19	line 20

The students try to read the story as if only one person were doing the reading. After several practice trials, they then record their attempt on a cassette recorder. Students usually enjoy this activity, and it gives them an opportunity to read in thought units and to try to make their reading sound communicative.

Trickery The teacher tells each member of a group of students to select a sentence to read and then to silently think of another sentence he could say without reading. Then, without telling the students the purpose beforehand, the teacher takes each one to a part of the room away from the group, preferably sheltered by a bookcase or screen, and allows them to record both sentences, one being read and the other spoken without reading. After everyone has recorded, the cassette is placed where the entire group can hear. As each recording is heard, the students try to guess which sentence was read and which was spoken. The activity is enjoyable and conveys the point that good oral reading should be indistinguishable from speech.

Rate   Even though rate improvement is not usually a primary concern for the poor reader, it may be a problem for some corrective readers at the senior high school level. Whenever rate improvement is an objective of the instructional program, it should be related to comprehension, to the reader's purpose, and to flexibility.

Rate without comprehension is of no value. Some poor readers "go through" material, simply turning pages and glancing at the print. To call them good fast readers who lack comprehension would be foolish. Someone who "reads" but does not understand what he has read is no more a good reader than a person who "listens" but does not understand what he hears is a good listener.

Comprehension varies with the purpose of the reader. If the reader only wants to grasp the main idea of a passage, he should not read the material intensively as if he were going to make a detailed report. Since the level of comprehension is limited to the main idea, he can increase his reading speed and settle for a less thorough mastery of the material. Students frequently are unaware that there can or should be any difference in the way they approach their reading based on what they want or need from the material. When poor readers were compared with good readers in a study by the author, it was found that good readers varied their rate in accordance with their purposes, but poor readers made no logical or effective adjustment in their rate (Brown, 1964).

Flexibility is also a concern. A good rapid reader should also have the ability to slow his rate and increase his comprehension whenever he needs to do so. Inflexibility in rate will result in the reader going too fast when he should not, or too slowly when a faster rate would produce more efficient results. Training students to vary their rate necessitates moving them from one purpose to another and letting them exercise conscious effort to adjust their rate to fit their purpose. A student may be given a short time to overview a chapter or to gather the main idea of a passage and then be given more difficult material which he must understand in detail. Such material might include complex paragraphs, mathematics or science puzzles, directions, and so on. Other activities designed to improve reading rate are described below.

Graphing   Students are encouraged to choose a book from which to read and chart their progress in rate improvement. They should read a similar amount each day—say five full pages—and record their results on a graph by entering the time it takes them to read their daily selection. This activity provides a good way to use charting to improve rate without forcing readers to watch a clock at the same time they are reading. By placing a mark at the end of the reading selection for the day, students are able to give their full attention to their reading until they come to the mark, when they stop, note the elapsed time, and mark their graph.

Rate and Power   The teacher should find a selection which the entire group can read without difficulty. Short-answer questions based on immediately preceding content should be spaced throughout the reading selection. For example, the first question may be answered after reading only one-tenth of the selection, another after reading two-tenths, another after three-tenths, and so on.

The group is divided into two equal teams. The teacher tells the teams when they may begin and allows them to continue reading for a limited amount of time, usually just long enough for the fastest readers to finish. They then put away their reading passages and answer the questions. Points are awarded to each team for the number of correct answers given by each team.

This activity places equal emphasis on both rate and comprehension. Repeated once a week or so, it enables students to learn to read rapidly when it is possible for them to do so with good comprehension and to slow their rate when they have greater difficulty understanding what they read. The activity can also be based on individual rather than on team performance.

Limited Independent Reading   Although independent-level reading is usually good for rate improvement, some students continue to read more slowly than they need to unless there is some sort of an incentive given them to finish more quickly. One subtle incentive exists in limited independent reading. Students are provided with interesting materials from which they may choose. They are not allowed to take the materials out of the room, but are allowed to read as much of it as they can for 5 minutes each day, after which they are stopped. This can often be the last 5 minutes of the period. The spur for the students to find out what is going to happen in the story creates a subtle pressure to read as much as possible before the time elapses and they must put the book aside.

RECOMMENDED READINGS

DALE, E.; and O'ROURKE, J.; 1971, *Techniques of teaching vocabulary.* Palo Alto, Cal.: Field Educational Publications.

HARRIS, A. J., and SIPAY, E. R., 1980. *How to increase reading ability.* 7th ed. New York: Longman, pp. 434–46.

MALLETT, J. J., 1975. *Classroom reading games activities kit.* West Nyack, N.Y.: Center for Applied Research in Education.

PLATTS, M. E.; MARGUERITE, R.; and SHUMAKER, E., 1960. *Spice.* Stevensville, Mich.: Educational Service.

Spache, E. B. 1976. *Reading activities for child involvement.* Boston: Allyn & Bacon.

Wagner, G.; Hosier, M.; and Cesinger, J.; 1972. *Word power games.* Riverside, N.J.: Teachers Publishing (Macmillan).

REFERENCES

Brown, D. A., 1964. *The effect of selected purposes on the oculo-motor behavior and comprehension of third and seventh grade students of fifth grade reading ability.* Unpublished doctoral dissertation, Eugene, Oregon: University of Oregon.

13

Specific strategies and activities for the improvement of higher cognitive reading skills are discussed in this chapter. Although most wide-range reading approaches are sufficiently flexible to encompass the teaching of all the basic reading skills, there are many times when additional techniques or games can be used to enrich, enliven, and emphasize instruction in some specific area. The activities in this chapter are to be used as supplemental to and congruent with the basic reading approach being used with the students. Care should always be taken to select supplementary activities that do not violate the philosophy and nature of the basic reading approach being used.

IMPROVING HIGHER COGNITIVE READING SKILLS: Comprehension, Locational and Study Skills, and Reaction

The basic reading skills discussed in the previous chapter are all part of the virtually automatic processing of an effective reader. In this chapter, however, we will deal with the ultimate business of reading: understanding and reacting to the author's message. We shall examine specific means of improving these higher-level reading skills.

COMPREHENSION

Comprehension may be divided into four basic categories. As seen in the Diagnostic Model of Reading Behavior in Chapter Two, these categories include vocabulary meaning, understanding details, understanding general significance or the main idea, and the ability to imply or infer meaning when the meaning is not explicitly stated.

Vocabulary Meaning   To help students understand the vocabulary they meet in their reading, it is helpful for the teacher to use oral language that will allow students to develop a familiarity with the terms they will read.

If students have a limited English vocabulary, it is necessary to help them improve language facility as they work to improve their reading. A language base should be laid for the reading the student will do. Most reading instruction is based on the assumption that students have had years of immersion in the language they will be learning to read. When this is not true, the teacher should attempt to provide means by which students can develop a larger language base. (See the section on language development in Chapter Twelve.)

Even if students have a good background in the language they will be reading, comprehension of specific vocabulary can still be a problem. To overcome both general and specific vocabulary deficits, poor readers need to develop a lifetime interest in words. When most poor readers find a word they do not know, they ignore it, hoping for a miracle of comprehension of the passage without understanding the vocabulary upon which the passage has been built.

The teacher may use a number of activities to interest students in words and word meanings. Through the use of dictionaries explaining word origins, interesting words may be highlighted to pique student curiosity. Students may be asked to bring in unusual words which can be placed on the bulletin boards or, as one teacher did, placed on one wall of the room. In this case, when a student brought a word in, the teacher used a felt-tip pen to put it on a piece of construction paper, folded a small piece of masking tape sticky side out, and stuck the paper to the wall with the masking tape on the back of the piece of construction paper. Eventually a major portion of the wall was covered by words. The larger the collection, the more interest was expressed by the students.

An activity that can create a great deal of interest in words is to have students collect the words they would like to learn. They are given time within the class hour in the reading center to look up their words and use them in a sentence.

Another activity is to use a bulletin board on which jokes about words are collected. They may be cartoons (best) or any other sort of humor dealing with word meanings. There are several comic strips which frequently focus attention on one aspect or another of vocabulary.

The teacher may model the use of a few larger words, using them in discussions with the class and explaining them by using appositional phrases to define them. For example, he may say, "The legislative, or *lawmaking*, branch of the government . . . " "When the crowd began to congregate, or *gather*, he . . . " or "He decided he could alleviate, or *ease*, the situation by . . . " The teacher should try to make the inclusion of vocabulary at or above the level of the students a habit, and he should be equally careful to include these brief explanations. This can and should be done without condescension and can be accomplished with a minimal loss of time. By doing this, the teacher can develop student familiarity with a more challenging level of language. With the teacher as a model, students can be led to adopt vocabulary terms they would not otherwise have chosen. Even those who do not use the vocabulary themselves will understand the terms better and feel more comfortable with them.

A study of root words and affixes can be helpful to students doing poorly in reading mathematics, science, and social studies. By learning the meaning of roots and affixes, students can often anticipate—although not always accurately predict—possible word meanings from word structure. It is usually helpful to point out the interplay between the use of word structure to identify meaning and the use of context.

Various other activities to develop reading vocabulary are listed below.

Promulgating Esoteric Cerebration   For corrective students seated in a circle, the teacher serves as recorder as the first student starts a sentence by giving a word that can be the first word in a sentence. The next student adds a word, and each student around the circle adds a word until a logical sentence is made. The teacher may write the words on the board or on a large piece of newsprint. The students try to work in as many polysyllabic words as they can. Individual scores can be kept by giving a point for each letter in the word a student suggests. Scores are not usually necessary, however, to maintain interest. The structure of the sentences is usually enough to keep the students involved in the activity.

Crazy Stories   The teacher collects the following from the students. Each student can supply all the items asked, or the students may take turns giving suggestions.

1. The name of a person	*8. A time of day*
2. A place	*9. Another person's name*
3. A sad occurrence	*10. A place to hide*
4. A means of transportation	*11. An activity*
5. A liquid	*12. An adverb*
6. A period of time	*13. A question*
7. Another place	*14. An answer*

One of the students, or the teacher, then reads the following story, fitting in the names etc., numbered above.

(#1) left (#2) because (#3). He/she left by riding a (#4). Unfortunately, all they gave him/her was (#5) and the trip lasted (#6). Arriving at his/her destination, (#7), at (#8), he/she decided to look for (#9). He/she finally found him/her in (#10) (#11). (#9) looked at (#1) (#12), and asked, "(#13)." (#1) replied, "(#14.)"

News Stories   Using old newspapers, each student cuts out any picture he wants and, using words cut from other stories, composes a new story to fit below the picture. An interesting alternative is to take a large ad and recompose it by using words cut from other ads. Another variation is to make up an entirely new ad using pictures and words cut from the ads in a newspaper.

Vocabulary Cards   The teacher provides each student with twenty cards about the size of business cards. They then make their own vocabulary card pack by taking a piece of simulated leather plastic 4 × 8¼ inches long and creasing 2 inches from each end. This can be either glued with a fine bead of glue at each end of the pocket or, if the students want to do so and arts and crafts leather-working tools are available, they may lace the ends. The two pockets may be folded together, and the vocabulary cards can be put in each of the pockets. Definitions may be put in one side with a sentence using the word, and the word appears in the other side. The students can review their vocabulary words, taking them with them in the packets.

Pieces O' Eight   The teacher or a student writes fifteen or twenty vocabulary words on the board. The students each divide a piece of paper into eight different sections by drawing lines across it. Then they select any eight of the words on the board, writing one word in each of the eight squares on their sheet of paper. The teacher gives a definition for one of the words on the board. Students who have that word circle it. The teacher then gives a definition for the next word and so on, until one player has all eight words circled. The first player to do so wins, signaling that he has won by saying, "Pieces O' Eight."
    After a player indicates that he has won, the leader checks the player's answers to see that he was correct in circling his words. If the student has made a mistake, the game continues until another player says, "Pieces O' Eight."

Mystery Words   One player in the group starts the game by saying, "I'm thinking of a word. It means about the same as *large*." The next person in the group guesses what the word is. If he is wrong, the rest of the players take turns trying to identify the mystery word. The one who finally suggests the correct word is the winner and becomes the next person to think of a mystery word.

Crossword Puzzles   The teacher can find simple crosswords found in children's game books, or make simplified crossword puzzles in which only a few words cross one another. If the words the students hope to learn include *pursuit, honesty, justice, freedom, liberty, life,* and *democracy,* for example, a simple puzzle interweaving the words may be constructed, as in the example below.

Across:

1. America's form of government
2. Opposite of bondage
3. Not dead

Down:

4. Fairness
5. Going after something
6. Not cheating
7. Able to do as you want

```
                              [6.]h       [7.]f
              [1.]d  e  m  o    c     r  a  c  y
      [4.]j              n        e
         u              e        e
         s       [5.]p  s        d
         t          u  t        o
[2.]l i  b  e  r  t  y    ■ m
      c          s    ■      ■
      e          u
         ■ [3.]l i  f  e    ■
                  t
```

Categories The teacher prepares a set of cards with words representing different categories. At a simple level, several words may be included representing colors, several may include shapes, some may deal with the body, and still others may represent sizes. Using those categories, the teacher distributes the words as follows:

Colors	Shapes	Body	Sizes
orange	round	abdomen	small
blue	oval	forearm	enormous
aqua	square	wrist	little
emerald	rectangle	knee	gigantic
yellow	oblong	finger	normal

The cards are mixed together, and students time themselves to see how quickly they can identify the categories and sort the various cards into the right list. There are literally hundreds, if not thousands, of different categories, and the only limitation to this activity is the time it takes to make the different sets of cards.

Understanding Details   Noting and organizing detailed information is essential to success in many kinds of reading. Readers who have difficulty with details often have problems reading and following directions, understanding sequence, and identifying pertinent information or discriminating between important and unimportant facts. There are a number of activities that are helpful for the poor reader who has difficulties with detailed information.

The Pressman's Hat   Those who work in the pressrooms for newspapers make a hat out of two full sheets of newspaper folded together in a special way. The directions for making a pressman's hat provide an excellent exercise for following directions. All that is needed is some newspaper and a copy of the directions below.

To construct a pressman's hat:

1. Place two full-page sections of newspaper on the floor.
2. Fold the top left corner of the two papers held together to the centerfold line, forming a triangle.
3. Do the same with the top right corner, forming a peak at the top.
4. Fold the bottom edge of the top sheet of newspaper so that it touches the bottom of the triangle, and crease it.
5. Now fold the same section again, making a hat band.
6. Turn the hat over.
7. Fold the right edge, overlapping the centerfold line 1 inch.
8. Do the same with the left side edge.
9. Fold the lower right corner, making a triangle that touches the bottom of the hat band.
10. Do the same with the left-hand corner.
11. Fold this new triangle above the hat band.
12. Fold the top of it down and tuck it under the hat band.
13. Fold the peak down to the bottom of the hat band and tuck it inside the hat band.
14. Holding the hat, open it wide, and flatten out the top.
15. Fold the peaks down toward the bottom of the hat.
16. Crease the top edge and tuck the ends into the hat band.
17. You are now holding a genuine pressman's hat!

Odd Sentences   The teacher should prepare cards with paragraphs containing one sentence that does not belong with the rest of the paragraph. If possible, the cards should be laminated. If not, they may be fastened inside an acetate folder or a piece of acetate may be cut and taped over the card.

As students read the paragraphs, they mark out the sentence that does not belong, using a water-soluble pen. After the work is checked, the mark can be removed with a damp cloth. Examples of the kinds of paragraphs include the following:

Billy was very happy. He had never ridden a horse before. He waited for the man to bring the horse to the gate. As the horse came closer, Billy's eyes got very big. The horse was much bigger than he had thought it would be. Billy's favorite food was ice cream.

When Marsh pulled on his boots, he had no idea what he would find outside the door. The moaning had been going on ever since he had awakened, and no telling how long before that. He wrestled into his jacket and grabbed his rain slicker and rain hat. He fumbled in the dark for his rifle. The sun shone so brightly he could hardly see. He opened the door cautiously, and peered out, straining his eyes in the direction of the sounds to see if he could make out the form of an object in the eerie half-light of the moon.

On those paragraphs that give a student difficulty, the teacher may want to help the student see which sentence is discrepant and why.

As I Was Saying   The teacher or an aide can take sentences out of old workbooks or other disposable materials and cut the sentences in two. Five sentences—ten halves—are put into an envelope. Students can then take an envelope, empty the sentence halves, and try to arrange them so that they make sense.

It is important to cut the sentences uniformly so that the students cannot match them up simply by looking at the sizes of the pieces.

Reporter   The teacher should prepare file folders with a newspaper article glued to the right side of the folder and a dittoed worksheet paper-clipped to the left side. Care should be taken to see (1) that the news story is at the student's instructional level or below and (2) that the information asked for on the dittoed sheet is contained in the article.

Each student should put his name and the headline of the article on his worksheet and then fill in the newspaper writer's *Who? What? Where? When? Why?* and *How?* The worksheet should provide space for the student to fill in that information. The teacher may need to elaborate on the single-word questions by telling the students that *Who?* asks about the people involved in the story, *What?* asks the students to tell what happened in sequential order, *Where?* asks where the event took place, *When?* asks the time it happened, *Why?* asks for any reasons behind the event, and *How?* asks about special circumstances that should be included to explain how the event happened.

TV Writer   The teacher reads a short, action-filled story to the group. Each student then draws a scene from an assigned section of the story. (Older students can profit from discussing the story and deciding themselves on which scenes should be portrayed.) The pictures all should be the same size and should be small enough to fit inside a half-gallon milk carton. After the scenes have been drawn, they should be taped together to make the "film." Extra sheets should be used to give the title and to publicize the credits for the show. Blank paper should be added to each end so the "film" can be threaded through the viewer.

The back of a half-gallon milk carton should be cut out so the students can reach inside to thread the film. A viewing frame, just the size of the pictures, should be cut in the front of the carton. Plastic drinking straws are used to pierce the carton from side to side just below and just above the viewing window. If the plastic straws are unavailable or if the students are young and pull too hard to use the plastic straws, pencils can be used instead. The film should be threaded between the straw and the front of the carton, up past the viewing window, under the second straw, and out the back.

The students can move the story from scene to scene by pulling gently on the top end of the strip of paper, and they can either tell themselves the story or record it on a cassette player to be replayed as they view the "film."

Pantomime   Students can be asked to pantomime a story they have just read. Sometimes this can be done with another student reading the story as the players enact the scenes.

Just the Facts   The teacher introduces a short story or poem, asking each student to note as many of the facts or important features of the story as possible. After the story, each student is asked in turn to tell one fact, continuing until all the facts have been given.

In a variation of this activity, the story can be recorded on a cassette tape, then replayed individually, with the students noting the facts. They then take the story or an answer key and check their notes.

Describe That Person   Students each choose one character from a story the group has read and write a description which they then record on a cassette tape. An answer key is made that provides the names of each character they have tried to describe on the tape. The students then listen to the tape using headphones and try to identify the person being described. They write their answers and then compare them with the answer key. After everyone has had a chance, the teacher may go over the answers with the students.

Cause and Effect   The teacher writes ten cards giving causes and ten cards listing logical results of those causes. Students, working in pairs or singly, try to match the causes with the results. Examples of some of the cards would include the following:

Causes	Effects
The day was hot.	*Bob pulled off his shirt.*
Janie hit the ball with all her might.	*She scored a home run.*
Phyllis lost her purse.	*She couldn't pay the bill.*
Sam combed his hair.	*Sam looked neat.*

Main Idea   The ability to understand the main idea of a passage seems rather strongly related to the ability to retrieve academic information. Virtually every

reading-study formula and every approach to improve comprehension and retention of content material includes an emphasis on finding out the general significance of a selection. Retrieval is enhanced if details are meaningfully attached to
some central theme. Good readers and good students seem generally to approach
an assignment by trying to see how it fits into the larger picture before trying to
master the separate facts and details.

If understanding the main idea is as important as it appears, students who have
difficulty with comprehension should be helped to develop ability to identify the
main thought in passages. The reading teacher can work to this end no matter on
what level the student is working.

As noted in Chapter Ten in the description of approaches for extremely disabled readers, students even at that level should be asked to title their stories
because a good title must be based on some grasp of the general significance of the
story. The teacher should include questions such as, "What is this story mostly
about?" as he discusses materials a student has read. Captioning pictures and cartoons leads students to consider general significance. Other activities include
those below.

Crossed Captions   Captions that would be reasonable to use with a set of ten
cartoons are mixed and put under the "wrong" pictures. The student must decide
which captions should go with which cartoon.

Illustrations   Some students profit from illustrating a major principle within a
passage. The procedure can also be turned around. The students can "read" a
picture that illustrates a story or an article and be asked to tell as much as they
can about the story from the illustration.

Outlining   For students having difficulty finding the main idea, the teacher
may use a series of short selections, and provide a brief outline for each selection.
For the first passage, one statement in the outline is deleted, and the student must
complete the outline by adding what would appear to be the missing portion. The
next selection has two statements missing; the third has three missing; and so on.
The student must complete the last passage totally on his own. It is important
that the selections be short and well-organized so they can be rather easily outlined. This activity should be spread over several days; otherwise, students may
find it very difficult.

If students have difficulty with the exercise, determine whether the selections
are at the proper instructional reading level for the students using them. If they
still have problems, provide more than one selection at each step and shorten the
selections. The activity is very effective.

Project-a-Title   Paragraphs and titles are placed on separate acetates. The
teacher keeps the paragraphs and hands out the separate titles to the students in
the group. The paragraphs are shown with an overhead projector, and the
students are given time to read them. As soon as they finish reading a selection,

the teacher asks, "Who has the title for the paragraph?" If more than one student thinks he has it, have them both put their titles on the overhead, and let them suggest why they think their titles would fit the selection. (There may be occasions when two titles will fit equally well.) The group then makes a selection, and they go to the next paragraph.

The Very Idea   The teacher selects a number of interesting passages to read to the group. The students listen and decide what the main idea is for each passage, writing it down on a piece of paper. After reading all the selections, the students share their main idea for each selection.

Key Words   The teacher puts a story on the chalkboard so everyone in the group can see it. The students read the story and then go back through it sentence by sentence, trying to identify the most important two or three words in each sentence. The teacher then goes through the story with them and erases all the words except the words the students agree are most important. The students then decide how they might summarize the main ideas of the selection by using the key words they have identified.

"Hunting Lines in the Jumble"   The teacher prepares packets of sentences by typing a short story or anecdote, with each sentence on a separate line. Several additional lines are also prepared with sentences that do not belong in the story. Three "titles" are also provided, one that fits the story and two that do not.

The students go "Hunting Lines in the Jumble" by finding and arranging the sentences in proper order to tell the story. They give each story the proper title and put aside the extraneous sentences and titles.

A quick scoring "key" can be made by simply including a copy of the original story. There are times when a different sentence order will tell the story just as well, and sometimes the teacher may inadvertently include "extra" sentences that may be seen as fitting into the story. Although care should be taken to avoid that, when it happens those sentences should be credited as long as they make good sense.

News Show   Each student is allowed to select a story from the newspaper which he then pantomimes. As one student portrays the story, the others search the paper for the story being enacted. The first one to find the story is allowed to act out his story next.

Inference   The ability to infer is involved in much humor, poetry, and fiction. Inference allows readers to understand the characters in a story or a play and may allow them to understand why a character says or does certain things. In dramatics, when a person develops the ability to infer within a particular play, he is said to begin to "feel the part."

Inference allows the reader to anticipate what is coming next. In that sense, inference is a part of all good fluent reading. It indicates that the reader is thinking with the author, sometimes looking forward to the next word or two, and at other times, anticipating what the author is likely to say several pages later.

In helping students develop the ability to infer, the teacher may begin by reading a story aloud, then posing questions that make the students put themselves in the place of characters in the story. The question "How do you think he felt when he saw his last avenue of escape destroyed?" causes the student to consider the predicament in a personal way. Sometimes the teacher may need to exaggerate the situation to some extent for the student to begin to realize that words in print are more than marks on paper; that they represent the lives, thoughts, and feelings of people. The development of inferential ability can often be aided through oral modeling (reading) by the teacher. By sharing gripping, touching, or humorous passages, the teacher may engender greater ability to imply or infer. This can be increased by stopping at crucial points and asking students having difficulty with inference what they think is likely to happen next. Inference may also be developed using the following activities.

Reviewing the Situation The teacher may find or write descriptions of various situations involving predicaments or problems which usually arouse relatively strong emotional reactions and which may involve a difficult decision. Good sources include human-interest stories from the daily papers, from national news magazines, and from the numerous school newspapers and news magazines. These "situations" can be placed in a small, attractively decorated cardboard box with an opening just large enough to allow the student to reach in and remove one of the papers.

Either the teacher or a student may read the situation to the group, and the students are encouraged to discuss it for a few minutes. They then write how they think the characters felt, and, if a decision was to have been made, they explain what they think that decision should have been. After they have written their comments, they should be allowed to share them with the other students in the group.

This activity works well with the language experience approach used as a remedial approach for older students.

What's Happening? The teacher prepares a set of cards, each containing three or four statements which lead to a logical conclusion. Students may read through them and write what they think could be concluded from the statements. Answers should be kept in a separate place rather than being written on the back side of the card. (It is too tempting for the student to glance at the back of the card instead of working out his own conclusion.)

Examples of sets of statements include the following:

1. The crowd began to fill the stadium.
2. The warm autumn afternoon was decorated with green and yellow pom-poms and the uniforms of the players.

3. The loudspeakers crackled as they announced the officials.
4. The band struck up a lively march.
   WHAT'S HAPPENING HERE?

1. The flowers arrived just at six o'clock.
2. Linda's formal was pink and white.
3. Jim arrived with Bill and Trudy.
4. Mom took everyone's picture before they started off.
   WHAT'S HAPPENING HERE?

Detective Stories The teacher writes or collects short passages describing scenes or activities and puts them on cards. A student can then read them and answer the prepared questions to be answered by inference from the passage. Examples are:

When Deb climbed out, her hair was an absolute mess! Having fallen in without her cap, her hair had responded by turning into something that looked like blonde steel wool. She lay down on a lounge, letting the sun dry and warm her.
Questions:

1. Where was Deb?
2. What had happened to her?
3. What was the temperature of the water?
4. What sort of day was it?
5. What season was it likely to have been?

Marge packed the chicken, and Paul and Mary filled and iced the jugs. Mom found an old tablecloth and paper plates, while Sue sliced cheese and Dad spread mayonnaise on the bread.
Questions:

1. What were they probably going to do?
2. What were Dad and Sue making?
3. What do you think they will likely do with the tablecloth?
4. What time of year do you think it probably was?
5. Do you think the chicken was cooked or not? If you think it was cooked, do you think it was baked, stewed, or fried? Why?

LOCATIONAL AND STUDY SKILLS

The most basic locational and study skill is the ability to utilize the alphabet to locate information. Not only the dictionary, but virtually every index and filing system makes some use of alphabetizing as a key to gain information. Although it is unnecessary for a student to memorize the alphabet in order to read, the ability to alphabetize is certainly essential to using reading to find information.

Related to alphabetizing, but carried far beyond it, is the ability to make use of the library or media center. Classification of reading materials by area and author often confuses poor readers, making it difficult to locate the materials they need even if they are able to read them after they have found them.

Much map and globe instruction lacks practical application in today's world of weather tracking and satellite views of major portions of the globe. The most common map in use today is a weather map. It is seen far more frequently than the various types of maps commonly used in geography instruction in schools, yet is seldom mentioned in the standard curriculum. The weather maps now in use are much more sophisticated than they were a short time ago, involving outlines of state, provincial, and national boundaries superimposed over live scenes from satellites showing the actual movement of the weather. The watcher is expected to recognize geopolitical entities by their outlines, an ability that is likely to be far beyond the ken of poor readers.

Locational and study skills also include the appropriate use of schedules, menus, the "yellow pages" in telephone directories, want ads and business advertising in newspapers, and such things as traffic direction signs.

Instruction to help students handle these functional reading tasks may begin within the walls of the learning center but must go beyond them in order to be completely effective. Color slides taken within a grocery store, library, or bank can help to bring functional reading into the reading center. Field trips and visits by representatives of various businesses, and institutions can make the instruction even more useful. Activities that can help to develop certain locational and study skills are listed below.

Alphabet   This game requires seventy-eight cards. One letter of the alphabet is written on each card, and each letter is written on three cards, totaling seventy-eight cards. A card holder for each player can be made from a piece of tagboard cut 4 × 9 inches and folded lengthwise in the middle. Then six slanted or "herringbone" notches should be cut part of the way through the folded piece of paper from the folded side. The notches should be narrow enough to hold cards placed in them. The notches should be evenly spaced. The tagboard strip should then be opened slightly and placed on the table or desk with the notches up.

Each player draws six cards in turn from the stack of seventy-eight cards (with cards shuffled and placed face down). The first card drawn *must* go in the notch farthest from the player, the second is placed in the next farthest, and so on until the sixth card drawn occupies the slot closest to the player. Play is then ready to begin. The top card on the stack in the middle is turned over and placed beside the draw pile face up. The first player may then either draw one card from the draw pile or take one card from the pile beside the draw pile (discard pile). He may exchange the card selected for any of the cards in his card holder in order eventually to have all the cards in the holder in alphabetical order. The first one to accomplish that objective is the winner.

An important and interesting variation is the use of words in place of letters. Three words beginning with each letter of the alphabet are included in the deck of word cards. The object is eventually to have all the words in the card holder listed in alphabetical order. The activity can be made even more sophisticated by choosing words that are differentiated by the third, fourth, or fifth letters in the word. This activity is not only an effective teaching game but highly enjoyable as well. As sets of cards are made, they should be laminated so that they will last longer without replacement.

Before and After   The letters of the alphabet are put on 3 X 5 file cards cut in two to make cards that measure 3 X 2½ inches. Students time themselves with a stop watch if possible as they withdraw one card at a time from a small box or bag in which the cards have been mixed. They write the letter drawn plus the letter that goes before it and the letter that comes after it in alphabetical order. They go through the entire set of cards in this manner, stop the watch, and put down their time. They then go back through their work to find any mistakes they have made. They should then enter their time and number of errors on two different simple graphs as shown in the examples below.

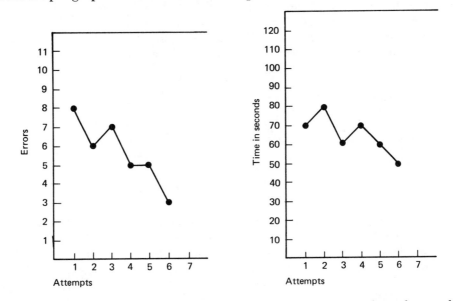

This teaches the use of graphs in an applied situation that the student understands.

Dictionary Scavenger Hunt   A number of different bits of information that may be found in a dictionary are listed on a dittoed sheet for each student in the group. Each one then uses his dictionary to locate the needed information. A key may be used to check answers, or students may pair off to compare their answers by having the first student to finish check his answers with the second, the third with the fourth, and so on.

Library Scavenger Hunt   As a variation on the above activity, the teacher lists information requiring the use of various sources within the library or media center. Students work alone until the last 10 minutes of the period, when they may help one another.

Textbook Scavenger Hunt   Another variation involves the use of a textbook from social studies or science. The book should be chosen at a reading level within the grasp of the students in the group. The dittoed sheet should require information to be gathered from the index; the table of contents; the listing of tables, charts and graphs; maps; time lines, tables of weights and measures; and so on. The students should work on their own to find the information requested. After they have finished, the teacher should ask the students for the information they have found, allowing them to check their answers and clarifying any questions they may have.

What Is It?   Students are given a listing of words drawn from three or four different categories. Using their dictionaries, they look up the words and decide how they are to be categorized. This may be done as an individual activity or, more enjoyably, in pairs. An example might be a combined listing of dogs, birds, flowers, and fish, as shown below.

sturgeon	*Afghan*	*macaw*	*aster*
geranium	*dahlia*	*heron*	*Dalmatian*
ray	*gar*	*Samoyed*	*puffin*
chrysanthemum	*malamute*	*mackerel*	*pointer*
chow	*cormorant*	*grouse*	*nasturtium*
tern	*hibiscus*	*tarpon*	*Airedale*
fuchsia	*grebe*	*Pomeranian*	*grouper*
pike	*mynah*	*poinsettia*	*skate*

Catalogue   Catalogues should be obtained from bicycle shops, stores, seed companies, etc. together with a number of order blanks. If the order blanks cannot be obtained, they may be duplicated and run off in sufficient quantity for use. The students are given a project such as laying out a garden and ordering the number of seeds they would need to plant the garden. They then must learn how to use the index to locate the seeds they need. With catalogues from a large department store, the project can be planning clothes and equipment for a camping trip, outfitting a backyard play area, and so on. One teacher brought an old bicycle into the classroom. He told a group of students that he wanted them to find out what was wrong with the bicycle and to use the catalogues he had provided for them to order the parts needed to overhaul it.

Mapping It   The students are provided with maps of the area obtained from the local chamber of commerce or county government agency. Each student is then given a list of places he is to find on the map. He may start at the school or learning center, trace his way to the library, find where he could buy a hamburger, go to the park where he could eat it, go to a grocery store, and so on. Maps can sometimes be placed on tables with a large sheet of acetate over them so that the students can trace their routes with a water-based pen; the acetate can then be erased for use by others.

Taking a Trip   Using maps obtained by writing to one of the major oil companies, the students plan a trip from their present location to some other area of interest to them. Working in groups of two or three, they consult the weather maps in the daily papers to see what sort of weather they may expect when they arrive at their destination and the conditions they can expect on their way. They calculate the amount of time it is likely to take, the cost of the trip including overnight stops, food, gas and oil, spending money along the way, and clothing.

Taking a Bus   Using a bus schedule and road maps, the students figure out how they will go from their home town to some other destination. They must find out (1) when their bus will leave, (2) when it will arrive at the destination, (3) how many changes they will have to make before they arrive at their destination, (4) how long their layovers will be, and (5) what sort of bus they will be riding on.

Tour Guide   As an addition to the activity above, the students choose places along the route the bus will take to visit. Each student will look up everything he can about one of the places and will share this information as though he were a tour guide. If he prefers, the information may be recorded on a cassette tape and played back to the entire group.

News Columns   Working with the group, the teacher labels a large piece of tagboard with headings representing the different parts of a daily paper: front-page news, editorials, society, sports, and comic sections, want ads, and so on. The teacher then takes randomly selected short items from different sections of the paper and asks each student to place it under the proper heading. After placement, the other members of the group are free to agree or disagree, and the teacher is able to correct any mistakes made.

REACTION

Reaction is the highest level of reading behavior. When they react to material, readers are adding themselves to what the author has written, and critically evaluating, appreciating, and/or enjoying what they read. Reaction is seldom attained without guidance. We learn to appreciate the artistry of beautiful writing style by being led to it through those who appreciate and can help us to see the sensitivity of the author expressed in the fine use of his words. We learn to be more critical, and less gullible, by watching and listening to those who read with care, pointing out pitfalls along the way. And we often learn to enjoy reading because our parents, teachers, or friends enjoyed it and passed their enjoyment along to us.

Although it is possible to teach many word analysis skills almost mechanically, students learn to react to their reading by watching and listening to those who model reaction for them. To teach reading appreciation, the teacher must discuss what he and his students have read, sharing with them as much as they can digest of what he has come to enjoy and appreciate in the writings of various authors. In a sense, appreciation is better "caught than taught."

Critical evaluation and assessment may appear to be taught more directly, but it is likely that it will be a seldom-used reading tool unless the student grasps the *attitude* of critical reading from his teacher as well as the *techniques* of critical reading that may be learned from a textbook.

Enjoyment is probably the most important of all. People read most of the time because they *enjoy* reading. Although a person may read this textbook because the reading has been assigned, it is likely that usually he reads because he likes to read. It is also more than likely that if a person is a good reader it is largely because he has read a great deal, practicing the skills needed, not for the sake of practice but because he enjoys reading. If every student could be made to *enjoy* reading, the number of corrective, remedial, and extremely disabled readers would virtually disappear. They would climb over all the obstacles that lay in their way in order to read—if it were enjoyable to them.

How can a teacher develop reaction? Besides modeling and sharing and discussing—all the most important steps that can be taken—there are several activities which are profitable.

Maybe Yes—Maybe No   To help students develop a sense of the difference between fact and fiction, have them react to a story they have read, looking at various portions of it to tell where the author may have exaggerated to make a point, where he was completely factual, where he expressed his opinion, where he says something that is not at all possible, and where his statements are intended only for humor and are not to be taken seriously.

True and False   The teacher may put a series of statements on a set of cards, one statement per card. Students should then sort the cards, putting those which are likely statements of fact in one pile and those which are matters of opinion in another. Another student may check them or the teacher may discuss any cards with any student who has a question. Examples of the kinds of statements on the cards might include the following:

1. The sun rises in the east.
2. Snow melts in the summer sun.
3. My mother is the best cook in town.
4. Everyone should jog.
5. Winter is more fun than summer.

Tele-Fact?   The teacher should gather a number of statements from television programs and advertising, some of them true and some not. Each statement or claim should be put on a separate card. After an initial discussion, establish that many things seen and heard on television are not necessarily true. Mix the cards, and then give each student the opportunity to take one of them from the pile and tell whether he thinks the statement is true or false. Encourage the students to raise questions.

Tell It Like It Is   In working with a corrective class, the teacher may have a group read the same story and then tell what parts were enjoyed the most. Afterward, let the students select a passage from the part they liked and read it in a manner that expresses the feeling in the part. Sometimes the same part may be read differently by different students, representing various interpretations of the passage. This can lead to worthwhile discussion.

Ham   Taking a passage that has varied emotional overtones and a good deal of conversation in it, have boys read the girls' parts and vice versa. It is not only entertaining to have them trade roles, it serves as a good vehicle to show the effect on a story when the style and presentation of the characters are changed.

A variation is to have the students change the voices of the characters from what they would expect, making a bully speak softly, the timid person aggressive, and so on. This activity reaches its limits quickly, but for 5 or 10 minutes it makes a good point.

Double Stories   Find two versions of the same stories and have the students read them both to compare the different versions. It is relatively easy to find different versions of stories like *Cinderella, The Gingerbread Boy, Jack and the Beanstalk,* and folk tales such as *Paul Bunyan* or *Pecos Bill* by looking in children's anthologies, old basal readers, or inexpensive children's stories found in bookstores.

After the two versions have been read, have the students explain how the stories differ and why they might have been written differently.

Silhouette Theater   Although the preparations for this activity are somewhat elaborate, the students generally find it quite enjoyable. A sheet is strung across a corner of the reading center, and a light is placed behind it so that those who stand behind a curtain will cast their shadow on it. Plan most action to take place near the middle of the screen to minimize distortion.

As one set of students reads a play or a story, alternating story sections, another set of students enacts the events taking place in the story so that the audience can see the silhouettes. Several rehearsals are necessary before this can be done effectively, but the activity provides an excellent reason for needing to read and interpret different characters for both the readers and the actors.

What If You Were . . .   After reading a story, have the student or students answer questions such as, "What if you had been the hero in this story? How do you think you would have felt? What if you were the victim in this story?" Many students are better able to project themselves into situations than they are simply to state their own feelings.

Puppet Talk   Younger students often respond positively to the use of puppets to explain why they liked or disliked stories, what they thought was wrong with a story, or even to re-enact a portion of the story. There are a number of "Muppet"-style puppets available that are enjoyable to younger children, but other puppets will also work well.

Time Machine   When reading stories that take place in an earlier time, ask students to project themselves backward through the "time machine" to that time and place. Have them describe what they think it would have been like then. For older students, who often respond well to this technique, ask them to do some parallel reading about the particular era before they describe their impressions and then have them do so as though they were actually there, recording their descriptions on a cassette recorder.

RECOMMENDED READINGS

DALE, E.; and O'ROURKE, J. 1971. *Techniques of teaching vocabulary*. Palo Alto, Cal.: Field Educational Publications.

EKWALL, E. E. 1976. *Diagnosis and remediation of the disabled reader*. Boston: Allyn & Bacon, pp. 143–54.

HARRIS, A. J.; and SIPAY, E. R. 1980. *How to increase reading ability*. 7th ed. New York: David McKay, Chapter 17.

MALLETT, J. J. 1975. *Classroom reading games activities kit*. West Nyack, N.Y.: Center for Applied Research in Education.

PLATTS, M. E. 1970. *Anchor: A handbook of vocabulary discovery techniques for the classroom teacher*. Stevensville, Mich.: Educational Services.

WAGNER, G.; and HOSIER, M. 1970. *Strengthening reading skills with educational games*. Riverside, N.J.: Teachers Publishing (Macmillan).

REFERENCES

Brown, D. A. 1964. *The effect of selected purposes on the oculo-motor behavior and comprehension of third and seventh grade students of fifth grade reading ability*. Unpublished doctoral dissertation, Univ. Oregon.

The success of any special reading program depends most crucially on those who teach it. Because that is so, it becomes too easy to consign program management to a level of comparative unimportance. This is unfortunate because, although good organization cannot compensate for poor instruction, bad organization and bad management can make it difficult to provide good instruction. Since good instruction and good management are so interdependent, it is important that we look at the earmarks of good organization and management.

ORGANIZATION
AND MANAGEMENT
OF READING PROGRAMS

Whether initiating a special reading program or working to improve one that is already established, a person hoping to understand the organizational management of an effective program may need to look at a number of different elements, including:

Working with a task force
Conducting a needs assessment
Developing program objectives
Scheduling
Selecting students
Securing professional staff members
Working with the administration
Working with other teachers
Finding materials
Evaluating the program

In addition, there may be special concerns about programs for community colleges, adult basic education centers, and correctional learning programs.

Reading-improvement programs usually are begun as a response to someone's *active* concern for poor readers. As that concern is shared with the administration and/or teachers, enough interest is aroused to do something about the problem. Often, capitalizing on the availability of governmental funds, formal steps may be taken to initiate a program to improve the reading skills of poor readers. Although there may be any number of ways to organize successful programs, the steps that follow are effective and have been utilized widely, being generally the same as those espoused by the United States Department of Education through programs such as its Right-to-Read and Basic Skills efforts.

TASK FORCE

One of the first steps in organizing a reading program can be the development of a task force composed of those who are concerned about the improvement of reading skills. Since the establishment of a special reading program usually originates from within the professional staff, the task force should certainly include at least one administrator and several teachers. But others also should be included. Something to be learned from the success of the learning-disabilities movement is that parents are willing and able to contribute their time and effort to worthwhile causes such as improving the instruction of their children. Although they should not be expected to deal effectively with diagnosis, prescription, and instruction, they can provide valuable support within the community and worthwhile advice toward program objectives, and can be an effective sounding board facilitating communication between the school and the community. An effort should be made to include at least two parents with children in the program. Another parent or community leader may also be added.

In selecting a task force, commitment is an important consideration. To be an effective member of the group, the individual must attend meetings of the task force.

The task force should not be allowed to become too large. Eight to twelve members is usually a manageable group. In larger groups some members feel reluctant to express themselves. Individual members feel less important in larger groups.

The principal should indicate the purpose of the task force at the beginning of the first meeting. A permanent chairperson and recorder should be selected, and a suitable time for meetings should be discussed and set.

Capable leadership is important. The principal of the school is often the one the group looks to as the logical chairperson, and there are times when that individual should chair the task force. However, there are times when the principal can be more effective serving as a member of the group and assisting someone else in chairing the task force.

The secretary of the task force should include the names of the members in news releases, and their names should be included in the school announcements.

NEEDS ASSESSMENT

Needs assessments for reading-improvement programs have become commonplace in some states, and there may be little need for the task force to do more than locate information made available by some previous needs assessment. In most areas, however, the task force will find that, though there is general agreement on the need for a reading improvement program, specific data on the extent of the needs are lacking. When this is the case, one of the first actions of the task force should be to carry out a needs assessment.

A form such as that shown in Table 14–1 will help guide the task force members as they attempt to determine the reading deficits, if any, at each grade level. The data to fill in the first portions of the form can usually be obtained from test scores that are already available. Every area of reading skills should not necessarily be filled in. Other reading skills such as reading enjoyment, for example, may be included in the form.

In determining how each skill should be marked, the task force member assigned to gather the information should first find the mean performance on that skill as indicated by a suitable standardized reading test. The difference between the mean student performance and the test norms for that skill should be determined, and the *difference* entered on the scale.

Scores and differences *may* be expressed in terms of grade equivalence, but for greatest accuracy, means should be calculated in standard scores. The difference between the test norm and the mean performance of the students for each skill should be marked on the chart.

Obviously, standard scores and grade equivalent scores should not be marked

1. Total number of students in grade _____
2. Overall student performance in skill areas, when compared with national norms, shows the following achievement:

	Below			Above	
	− 2.0	− 1.0	0.0	+ 1.0	+ 2.0
A. Sight Vocabulary	:	:	:	:	:
B. Word Analysis	:	:	:	:	:
C. Context Clues	:	:	:	:	:
D. Comprehension					
1. Vocabulary	:	:	:	:	:
2. Details	:	:	:	:	:
3. Main Idea	:	:	:	:	:
4. Inference	:	:	:	:	
E. Locational and Study Skills	:	:	:	:	:
F. Rate	:	:	:	:	:
G. Critical Reading/ Evaluation	:	:	:	:	:

3. Total number of corrective readers _____
4. Total number of remedial readers _____
5. Total number of extremely disabled readers _____

Figure 14–1.   Reading Needs Assessment for Grade _____

on the same chart, and the chart should indicate which measure is being used.

Numbers 3, 4, and 5 below the chart in Table 14–1 should be filled in next. Using the definitions described in Chapter Five, the number of students at each level should be identified and listed on the form. At the very lowest levels in school, it is likely that only extremely disabled readers and remedial readers should be included. By the time students have entered fourth grade, however, information on the number of corrective readers can be entered. The task force is now able to see the general status of reading performance as reflected by the tested achievement of the students in the school.

OBJECTIVES

Having completed the needs assessment survey, the task force is better able to determine the objectives of the program. It is likely that the task force primarily will use instructional objectives—that is, objectives that relate directly to hoped-for achievement. It is possible, however, that they may also consider program objectives—objectives related to the functioning of the program.

The task force members may decide that reading instruction should be instituted for extremely disabled readers (program objective), and that the students entered in that program shall make an average gain of no less than 2.0 grade equivalents for each year of instruction (instructional objective). They may decide that greatest priority should be given to the improvement of comprehension and reading enjoyment for corrective students (instructional objective), but if that objective means the initiation of a new program for corrective readers, the objective is also a program objective.

As objectives are set, it is necessary to consider how their accomplishment will be assessed. Reading enjoyment, for example, may possibly be estimated by the number of books being checked out of the school library after one year in comparison with those checked out the previous year; or it may be checked by a student questionnaire or checklist attempting to assess the students' attitude toward their reading or asking the students whether they are checking out and reading more books than they did a year ago. Comparisons, to be meaningful, should be based on comparable students at comparable levels.

SCHEDULING

Guthrie, Seifert, and Kline (1978) cite research indicating that significant gains were achieved by programs involving special reading instruction for 45 minutes of instruction per week. Longer durations of instruction apparently produced stronger gains after remedial instruction was ended. The research cited—Lovell, Johnson, and Platt (1962); Cashden and Pumfrey (1969); and Pearlman and Pearlman (1970)—all deals with younger children, and does not include regular instruction in the reading assistance the children received. It ought not to be concluded, as has been done in some quarters, that 45 minutes of remediation per week is *all* the reading instruction the students received, nor that that limited amount of reading instruction is sufficient to produce the reading growth poor readers need. These conclusions were not drawn by the original researchers nor by those who summarized their research.

When effective reading instruction is being carried on in the regular classroom, remediation may be viewed as adjunct instruction, and the students involved may show significant gains with relatively little help from the special reading teacher. The more severely handicapped the students and the older they are, the less likely it is that regular classroom instruction will be sufficient and the more likely students are to need daily remedial reading help.

Scheduling is somewhat simpler at the elementary level than at the secondary level. Since there is less departmentalization, it is easier for the teacher who has the reading students most of the time to arrange classwork so that they can receive special instruction, whether in their own classroom or in another location, and still carry on regular classroom activities to whatever extent they are able.

It seems ironic that as poor readers are advanced to higher grades they usually develop even greater needs for remedial reading instruction and often have greater difficulty fitting it into a suitable schedule. The difference in the organization for instruction at the upper levels makes it difficult to assign secondary students to any schedule that involves less than a full class period for reading assistance each day. Although there are exceptions, scheduling a poor reader for remedial reading instruction only two or three times a week causes a number of problems for everyone involved. Both teachers and students become confused concerning which day the students may be scheduled. This is especially true when the student is scheduled for instruction every other day and goes on Monday, Wednesday, and Friday one week and Tuesday and Thursday the next. Secondary students often take advantage of the confusion by not reporting to their assigned classes. Teachers become concerned that the students cannot possibly cope with class instruction when they are there only half the time, and students often blame their poor work and uncompleted assignments on the fact that they have missed class so often.

If the reading periods are shorter than the regular class period—a device frequently used to ensure that students are counted for roll and that they hear announcements and assignments—they tend to disrupt the class by coming and going at odd intervals. The reading teacher often has to cope with students who do not show up because the classroom teacher or student forgot, the student wanted to stay in class to see "the end of the film we started on Friday," or says, "We're doing something important today!" The result is that the classroom teacher, the reading teacher, and the students often become confused, resentful, and sometimes uncooperative when using a part-time schedule.

Instruction by a reading specialist in the regular classroom does not cause the disruption of movement to another room, but it often has its own sort of distraction, especially when the work is with remedial or extremely disabled students or older students. The level of instruction necessary for those who are seriously behind in their reading may attract the attention of other students in the regular classroom and cause the poor reader to be ridiculed or shamed by those who notice. Corrective readers at the lower levels are less conspicuous and often may be instructed in the regular classroom. At the upper levels, however, even corrective readers may occasionally be denigrated if they are taught in the same room with average and above-average readers.

In short, scheduling should be planned so it will not detract from the instructional programs of other teachers and should provide students with enough reading instruction to make good gains.

STUDENT SELECTION

There are special guidelines for the selection of students in many of the governmental programs, but where there are no specific regulations to be followed, a selection process may include (1) a review of standardized test results to identify those whose reading achievement is significantly low, (2) referrals by teachers and counselors, (3) referrals by parents, and (4) at the upper levels, referrals by students referring either themselves or their friends.

A referral summary sheet such as that shown in Figure 14–1 is a helpful means for collecting information to be used interviewing and testing students for possible inclusion in the program. The reading referral forms (Figure 14–2) should be distributed to teachers and counselors. They provide a written record of the referral, giving information on the best time to schedule an initial diagnostic interview.

TEACHER INVOLVEMENT

The relationship between the special reading program and the other important aspects of instruction in the school often comes down to the relationship between the reading teacher(s) and the rest of the staff. Teachers should be involved by their representation on the reading task force, by referring their students for help, and by informal communication between themselves and the reading teacher. *Brief* objective reports on the progress of the reading program through faculty announcements or during a teachers' meeting can keep the teaching staff up to date, but such communication can be as dangerous as it is beneficial. If reports are too long or delay those hoping to get away from the teachers' meeting, they may be received negatively. If the reports are too glowing, they may be viewed as suspect. If not glowing enough, some will question the "validity of the program."

The acceptance of the program by the staff frequently rests on less formal communication. The opportunities for such communication should not be left to chance. Reading teachers should plan to arrive a little early and leave a little late for teachers' meetings. They should avoid the appearance of belonging to a clique by purposely varying those with whom they spend time—eating lunch with different groups of teachers from time to time, for example. They should make it a point to attend faculty get-togethers, to work with teacher committees outside their own area, and to spend a few minutes in the teachers' lounge—all places where other teachers can get to know the reading teachers, talk with them, and get to understand the reading program.

It goes without saying that because of the extreme importance of the reading program, reading teachers' behavior should be attractive. They should be quick to listen, slow to criticize.

Reading teachers can often magnify their efforts by volunteering to help with textbook selection committees, doing demonstration teaching, assisting curriculum committees, helping set up workshops on activities and techniques for improving reading comprehension and locational and study skills, and so on. The more the teaching staff has contact with the reading program through the reading teachers, the better will be their understanding and support.

Many teachers will become interested in the reading program, and, after a time, there will be opportunities for reading teachers to "export" good reading in-

Figure 14-2. Referral Summary Form

Student Names	Grade	C. A.	Original Referral Source	Other Referral Sources: Tchr Tchr Cslr Prnt Stud					Stndzd Rdg Test Scores Voc. Comp Ttl			Learning Potential	Lag	Corrective, Remedial, or Ex. Rdg. Dis.?

```
┌─────────────────────────────────────────────────────────────┐
│                   Reading Referral Form                       │
│                                                               │
│  Student's name:  _____    │
│                                                               │
│  Nature of reading difficulty:  _____      │
│                                                               │
│  _____ │
│                                                               │
│  _____ │
│                                                               │
│  _____ │
│                                                               │
│  Best hour/period for interview:   _____     │
│                                                               │
│  Room:  _____                                           │
│                                                               │
│  Date of this referral:  _____     │
│                                                               │
│  By:  _____  │
│                                                               │
└─────────────────────────────────────────────────────────────┘
```

Figure 14–3. Reading Referral Form

struction by working with classroom teachers who want to improve their students' reading ability. Generally, they want to improve their own reading instruction, or they want to help specific students. When this happens, the school will begin to impact the reading of all its students.

On the other hand, reading teachers should not be discouraged by the likelihood that some teachers may be disinterested, not wanting to become involved in the reading program. Reading teachers are wiser to work with those who *want* help rather than forcing themselves on those who do not. They should be careful not to ostracize those who do not seek them out, and also protect those who want to improve their reading instruction. If a reading teacher begins to talk to others about shortcomings he may have observed, his effectiveness will soon be finished.

Those who are concerned about the reading problems of their students and enthused about the possibilities for improving their reading instruction will tend to be successful, and their success will be attractive to others who may initially have been less interested.

Reading teachers may often be in a position to help plan a staff development program in the area of reading improvement. Different states and provinces have different avenues of professional training available, but in general, assistance can be obtained through the reading departments in colleges or universities in the area, the state department of education, neighboring school districts with successful programs and good leadership, professional organizations such as state reading councils, publishers' representatives, professional consultants, and in some cases, professional leaders from more removed locations.

In contacting a college or university to seek a consultant, the school district is expected to cover expenses and provide a reasonable honorarium. The honorarium is seldom large enough to be a deterrent to obtaining the best services.

Before the consultant arrives, the goals and objectives of the visit(s) should be clearly understood by the arrangements committee and the consultant. Provisions should be made for the consultant to become acquainted with the school before program revisions are suggested, and should allow for at least one (preferably three or four) return visits. The committee should be careful about hiring three or four consultants on a round-robin basis—arriving, speaking, departing, and never seen again. Positive change in teaching ideas and performance seldom is achieved in this fashion. Change usually requires more interaction between the teachers and the consultant.

In order to simplify arrangements for visiting consultants, a form, illustrated in Figure 14-3, can be used. This form should be kept by the person who chairs the arrangements committee.

READING SPECIALIST

The person selected to direct the reading program should have training in both developmental and remedial reading instruction as well as supervised practicum experiences in working with poor readers. Additional coursework should include reading instruction in content fields, children's or adolescent literature, and internship programs. Professional preparation seems to be an important criterion for determining those who are responsible for administering effective reading improvement programs (Guthrie, Seifert, and Kline, 1978).

In addition, reading specialists or reading teachers should have had experience in a regular classroom teaching situation. This will not only enable them to understand the poor reader's difficulties better, it will also provide greater credibility in the eyes of the rest of the staff. If such professionals have never taught in a normal classroom, some will view their suggestions as less likely to be workable, since they have never tried to apply them themselves as classroom teachers.

Finally, effective reading teachers should be able to work well with the other members of the teaching staff. Reading programs frequently fail because the reading teachers are seen as isolated from the rest of the school, receiving special privileges that allow them to work with small groups of students, not required to assume hall duty, lunchroom duty, or otherwise failing to share in any of the onorous chores that befall fellow teachers. It does not take long for such percep-

```
Consultant:_____

Office address:_____    Home:_____

_____    _____

_____    _____

Phone: (___)_____    Phone: (___)_____

Dates for visit:_____    Calendar cleared by_____

Objectives for the visit:_____

_____

_____

Vita_____ and picture_____ received.  Copy sent to the

person who will introduce consultant (if the consultant

is to give talk)_____

Persons in charge of advertising:

   Newspaper:_____ School announcements:_____

   Letters sent to participants:_____

   Other:_____

Agenda:_____    _____

   _____    _____

   _____    _____

   _____    _____
```

Figure 14–4. Consultant Arrangement Form (*continued*)

(Figure 14–4 continued)

Topic(s):_____

_____

_____

Introductions by:_____

_____

Materials to duplicate: received____reproduced____by____

AV needs:_____by_____

Personal arrangements:

    Arrival date____hour____flight____location_____

    Departure date____hour____flight____location_____

    Person assigned to meet consultant:_____

    Person assigned to escort consultant to point of

    departure:_____

    Housing at:_____Confirmed by:_____

    Local travel arrangements:_____

    _____handled by:_____

Payment to be handled by:_____

(Figure 14–4 *continued*)

```
    Receipts          Needed     Received:     Amounts:

      Travel          _____    _____    _____

      Local travel    _____    _____    _____

      Parking         _____    _____    _____

      Meals           _____    _____    _____

      Housing         _____    _____    _____

      Misc.           _____    _____    _____
                                               _____
                      TOTAL................    _____

  Honorarium.............................    _____

Processed and mailed by:_____

   Total Expenses:_____  date:_____

   Total Honorarium:_____  date:_____
```

tions to cause the teaching staff to pull away from the reading teacher and the reading program. Effective reading teachers do well to involve themselves in the activities ordinarily required of teachers in school, and should seek to maintain identity within the teaching staff.

MATERIALS

Commercially Produced Materials   In reviewing reading programs at all levels, it is apparent that one of the earmarks of an effective program is a good supply of reading materials. There are a number of materials published especially for use in remedial and corrective reading programs. It is dangerous to list publishers of materials because of the changing nature of the field; moreover, it is easy to overlook some good publications. It is difficult to maintain a current listing of publishers and their publications because new materials are constantly being produced, old companies merge and change their names, some companies go out of business, and new companies begin to offer reading materials for the first time. Some writers of professional texts have tried to list every publisher that has entries in the field of reading, resulting in a plethora of references providing little usable information regarding the quality of the entries listed.

There are certain publishers who have produced materials of exceptional quality whose publications should be mentioned for the sake of the reading teacher looking for good reading materials. Therefore, with apologies in advance to those who may have produced good materials that have been inadvertently overlooked, the following listing of publishers and publications is presented. The materials listed have been found to be useful in working with corrective and remedial students at various levels.

Publisher	Material	Readability	Interest
Addison-Wesley Publishing Co. Jacob Way Reading, MA 01867	Morgan Bay Mysteries	2–5	4–10
	Checkered Flag Series	2–5	5–12
	Deep Sea Adventure Series	2–5	4–10
	Reading Development Kits	2–10	Adult
Allyn & Bacon 470 Atlantic Ave. Boston, MA 02210	Breakthrough	1–8	6–12
Barnell Loft, Ltd. 111 South Centre Ave. Rockville Centre, NY 11571	Specific Skill Series	1–10	1–Adult
Benefic Press 1900 N. Narragansett Chicago, IL 60639	Dan Frontier Series	pp–3	2–7
	Emergency Series	2–4	2–10
	Sports Mysteries	2–4	5–12
Bowmar/Noble Publishers, Inc. 4563 Colorado Blvd. Los Angeles, CA 90039	Play the Game Series	3–6	5–12
	Search Books	3–6	5–12
	Young Adventures Series	4–6	5–12
Continental Press, Inc. Elizabethtown, PA 17022	Continental Press Materials	1–10	1–adult
Fearon Pitman Publishers 6 Davis Dr. Belmont, CA 94002	Jim Hunter Series	1–4	6–adult
	Pacemaker True Adventures	2–3	5–12
	Pacemaker Classics (adapted classics)	2–3	5–12
	Specter	3–4	5–adult
	Space Police	3–4	5–10
	Galaxy 5	3–4	5–12
	American West	4–5	4–10
Garrard Publishing Co. 107 Cherry St. New Canaan, CT 06840	Basic Vocabulary Books	2	3–6
	Discovery Books	2–4	3–7
	Indians	3–4	3–6
	Junior Science Books	3–4	3–6

Publisher	Material	Readability	Interest
Garrard Publishing Co. (*continued*)	Good Earth Books	3–4	3–7
	Folklore of the World	3–4	3–10
	Pleasure Reading Books (adapted classics)	4–5	4–8
Globe Book Co., Inc. 50 W. 23rd St. New York, NY 10010	Adapted Classics	4–8	4–adult
Harcourt Brace Jovanovich, Inc. 757 Third Ave. New York, NY 10017	Plays for Echo Reading	3–6	3–7
Jamestown Publishers P.O. Box 6743 Providence, RI 02904	Jamestown Classics (adapted classics)	4–6	6–adult
Lyons & Carnahan (Rand McNally & Co.) P.O. Box 7600 Chicago, IL 60680	Phonics We Use Workbooks	1–6	1–10
Macmillan Publishing Co., Inc. 866 Third Ave. New York, NY 10022	Macmillan Reading Spectrum	1–8	1–10
Prentice-Hall, Inc. Englewood Cliffs, NJ 07632	Be a Better Reader Series	3–8	3–adult
Random House, Inc. 201 E. 50th St. New York, NY 10022	Landmark Books	4–7	5–8
	All about Books	4–7	5–9
Reader's Digest Educational Div. Pleasantville, NY 10570	Reading Skill Builders (four series: original, new, advanced, and adult)	1–9	4–adult
Scholastic Magazines and Book Services, Inc. 50 W. 44th St. New York, NY 10036	Individualized Reading (several paperback "libraries")	3–10	3–adult
	Action kits (three)	2–6	4–12
Science Research Associates, Inc. N. Wacker Dr. Chicago, IL 60606	SRA Reading Laboratories	1–adult	1–adult
	SRA Pilot Libraries	1–9	3–12
Webster	Everyreader Series (adapted classics)	4–5	5–12
Xerox Education Publications 245 Long Hill Rd. Middletown, CT 06457	Pal Paperback Series	2–6	6–12

What to Do When "There's No Money in the Budget!"   One of the more frustrating situations a reading teacher may face is realizing a need for more reading materials but finding that "there is no money in the budget." When that occurs, there are several options that may produce results.

1. Teachers should scour the storerooms in their school and, if possible, central office storerooms and storerooms of other schools in the district. One teacher who followed this suggestion found one used multilevel reading kit and two other kits that had hardly been used. She also found the previous year's issues of some high-interest, low-ability news magazines with articles, stories, and plays that were quite usable. In addition, she found some old Reader's Digest Reading Skill Builders that were in good condition.

2. Teachers should check "thrift" stores such as Disabled American Veterans, Salvation Army, and others that carry used paperback books. It is often possible to buy a number of usable books for very little money.

3. If there is a paperback distributor in the area, teachers may contact the company, explain the situation, and ask if it is possible to obtain copies of selected paperbacks that have not sold and have had the front covers torn off for return to the publisher for refund.

4. Teachers can develop a system to interest students in donating books. One procedure that works well is to explain to the students the need for books and ask for contributions. A number of gummed labels can be printed, reading, "This Award is in Appreciation for the Gift of This Book to the Reading Center Library by _____." For each book accepted, a label should be filled out with the name of the donor and placed inside the front cover of the book. For those students who bring in more than, say, ten books in the course of the year, a printed Award of Appreciation can be given at an assembly at the end of the school year. Printers and many stationers carry forms adaptable for this purpose.

5. Parent–Teacher groups, civic groups, service clubs, and fraternal groups often look for projects each year. Reading teachers can often receive a positive response to a request to help purchase materials for the reading center. One teacher was invited to address a local Lions' Club regarding the new secondary reading program. At the close of his comments, he pointed out the need for several materials the program did not have. The group later invited him back and presented him with some of the materials. Incidentally, the materials were labeled with the name of the donor organization in appreciation for the club's support.

6. As high-interest, low-ability magazines and papers come to the school, the teacher may ask to be the last to receive them (if they are passed from room to room). That way, the reading teacher can keep them for use anytime in the future. The teacher may elect to remove particularly useful stories, articles, or plays from the magazines and "bind" them in construction paper. An interesting title cover can be made by reproducing the title and illustration taken from the story and gluing it to the front. These separate stories and articles can be filed according to readability levels for use with students at their correct instructional reading level.

7. Teachers should check with the librarian. Some of the material in school libraries is

not kept for binding. For example, three copies of some of the children's magazines may be ordered, but only one would later be bound for permanent placement in the library. The other two would normally be discarded. By asking the librarian to keep those materials which are deemed useful, reading teachers can begin to build a store of magazines for use in the reading center, or can go through them to find puzzles, games, stories, and articles that can be kept and used.

8. Teachers may ask the central office for information regarding the whereabouts of lower-grade-level textbooks that are no longer used. Although they are often burned, it may be possible to save them, tear them apart, and use portions that may be valuable in the reading program, binding them between sheets of construction paper.

9. If the situation is known early enough in the school year or in the summer, reading teachers may contact teachers who have retired or resigned the previous spring to see if they have materials they would be willing to donate.

10. Finally, reading teachers should prepare in advance for incidental money that may become available during the course of the year. Special program funds sometimes become available at the end of the budget year, for example. If reading teachers have made a list of materials they need together with ordering information, when announcement of the funds is made to the teaching staff, they can make reading needs known quickly and easily.

EVALUATION AND REPORTING

The purpose of reporting is to let others know about aspects of the program that are of interest to them. It may be appropriate to give an annual report to the principal of the school regarding the program's progress, and other reports to individual teachers about the progress of certain of their students, but these two types of reports would have different content because the interest of the people who read them would be different. It is equally important to report only what needs to be known rather than including information that serves little useful purpose for the reader. In general, the shorter the report, the more likely it is to be read by those who have a responsibility to use it. A report of thirty pages outlining the case history of a poor reader and making suggestions for improved instruction is much more likely to remain unread than is a five-page report.

Reporting to Administrators   Those charged with the responsibility to oversee the reading program should be given an annual report evaluating its success and addressing its weaknesses. It should be balanced with both objective measures and subjective observations. While it is important to let the principal or school board know that the mean gain for students in the program was 2.4 years, it is equally important that they hear the results of the program in human terms. Tell them briefly how specific students have benefited from the program.

Results should not be compared with the gains ordinarily made by developmental readers but with the gains the students in the program had made before they entered the program. If the average reading gain per year before coming into the program was .5 of a year, a gain of 1.25 of a year in one school year is two-and-one-half times greater than before and lets the administrator see what is really happening through the program. Such a statement is more realistic than saying that the students gained "a little over a year" or ".25 of a year above the average gain."

Reporting required by federal programs often stipulates that certain data be supplied relative to the program within the school. To be sure of honest and accurate reports, it is sometimes wise to review the results with someone having expertise in the area of measurement. A telephone call may save later embarrassment.

In one situation, an elementary principal was disturbed by test results showing that what he had believed to be an excellent reading program had produced results little better than the regular reading program that had been used the previous year. After he discussed the results, he found that during the year the new program had been in operation, a spring building boom had brought a number of new children into the school just in time to be tested. Those results were included with the rest of the students' scores, and the gains were only average. When the new students' scores were deleted, the results were as good as the principal had hoped for.

Reporting to Teachers   Teachers are often interested in a summary of the gains students make in the reading programs; such information can be reported personally to those who are most interested, or shared in a teachers' meeting or in faculty announcements. It should not be reported in announcements that go to the student body, because even though the results are positive, sharing them with the bulk of the students may lead to misinterpretation.

Clinical or Case Study Reporting   When a formal diagnostic case report is made, usually as part of a clinical experience, it should be written with care to be as objective as possible. Formal style should be followed, and it should be brief and to the point. Although there are many different formats for formal reports, in general they call for information that identifies the student and his parents, teachers, and others who may be involved with that student's reading difficulties; a section describing the reason for referral; and other sections dealing with the student's background, behavior during the clinical experience, a summary of test results, and analysis and diagnosis.

One format, adapted from the *Reading Center Manual* (Glaser and Brown, 1979), is included below.

Diagnostic Case Report

Name:

Date of Report:

Birthdate:

C.A.:

School:

Teacher:

Parent or
Guardian:

Address:

Phone:

Grade:

Referral Source:

Examiner or
Clinician:

Report to: 1. Referral source
2. School (c/o principal, counselor, teacher; marked "Attn_____")
3. Parents (may receive an oral or written summary)
4. Original to Reading Center files

I. *Reason for Referral:* This should be brief, indicating the person, persons, or agency who referred the student, and the reason why he was referred to the Reading Center.

II. *Background Information:* This section should be concise without ignoring important information. Sources of information should be indicated. The following areas may be among those considered:

1. Physical factors
   appearance, health, physical disabilities, vision, hearing, etc.
2. Social factors
   peer relationships, cultural factors, language background and facility, etc.
3. Educational factors
   initial reading readiness, onset of reading difficulties, grades, teacher–student relationships, etc.
4. Psychological factors
   emotional adjustment, attitude, self-concept, attention span, dependency, need for encouragement, willingness to attempt activities, intelligence, etc.
5. Family factors
   parent–child relationships, husband–wife relationships, sibling relationships, role in the family, etc.
6. Other factors

III. *Behavior during Diagnostic and/or Instructional Sessions:* This section should contain the clinician's observations of the student's behavior within the diagnostic or instructional setting in regard to factors such as the following:

1. Rapport between the student and the staff
2. Student appearance and reactions
3. Student level of effort and manner of response to the clinician (labored, hesitant, bored, etc.)
4. Specific instances of unusual or notable behavior such as responses to failure or frustration, or reactions to testing
5. Validity of the test results

IV. *Summary of Test Results:*

Ability	Test Title	Test Score	Comments
Reading:			
Independent Reading Level			
Instructional Reading Level			
Frustrational Reading Level			
Automatic Sight Vocabulary			
Word Analysis			
1.			
2.			
3.			
4.			
Context Clues			
Comprehension			
1. Vocabulary			
2. Details			
3. Main Idea			
4. Inference			
Fluency			
Rate			
Physical Measures:			
Vision			
Hearing			
Psychological:			
Personality			
Learning Rate			

V. *Analysis and Diagnosis:*

1. The severity and the classification of the student's reading difficulty, e.g. "He is five years below his general level of ability and would be classified as a remedial reader."
2. The factors that contribute to his reading difficulty.
3. A summary of the student's reading skill weaknesses.
4. A summary of the student's strengths to be utilized in developing the prescribed program of instruction.

VI. *Recommendations:*

1. Referral for specialized help or diagnosis, such as referral for a hearing or vision examination.
2. Instruction
   A. The purpose or goal of the instructional program.
   B. The general structure of the program; that is, those who would be involved, where the instruction would be conducted, and what form it would take.
   C. Correction of problems that interfere with the student's chances for success in learning, such as finding a quiet place for study at home, counseling for the family, etc.
   D. Specific instructional suggestions. This should relate to the reading-skill weaknesses noted in V. 3. above, and should contain suggestions for both an overall approach and specific techniques.

Signed _____
(clinician or examiner)

VII. *Bibliography of tests and suggested materials:*
VIII. *Attachments:* This may include checklists of difficulty, handouts or brochures on treatment, booklists, etc.

SUMMARY

Most reading programs can benefit from the advice and assistance of a task force composed of professionals and laypeople interested in improving reading in the school. A needs assessment enables the task force and the reading specialist to determine the most pressing needs and to plan how to meet those needs. A planned program for reading improvement requires program objectives, staff involvement, care in scheduling and student selection, and well-prepared, experienced reading-teacher staff able to work well with other members of the staff. A good selection of materials is an important element in a good program, and short budgets often require creativity in obtaining the necessary materials. Communications and reporting results of the program help to insure that the program will receive continued support.

RECOMMENDED READINGS

AARON, I.; BINGHAM, A.; BROWN, D.; HUNT, J.; KNIGHT, C.; MOORE, B.; RANSOM, P.; and THRASHER, J. 1982. *Principals' reading leadership program.* (Eight segments.) Right to Read-Basic Skills. U.S. Office of Education.

Brown, D. A. 1979. *Organizing and managing a literacy program: A handbook for adult programs.* USOE. Washington, D.C.: U.S. Government Printing Office

Ekwall, E. E. 1976. *Diagnosis and remediation of the disabled reader.* Boston: Allyn & Bacon, Chapters 13, 14, and 15.

Harris, L. A.; and Smith, C. B. *Reading instruction: Diagnostic teaching in the classroom.* 3rd ed. New York: Holt, Rinehart & Winston, Chapters 15 and 16.

Rupley, W. H.; and Blair, T. R. 1979. *Reading diagnosis and remediation: A primer for classroom and clinic.* Chicago: Rand McNally. Chapters 14, 17, and 18.

REFERENCES

Cashden, A.; and Pumfrey, P. D. 1969. Some effects of the remedial teaching of reading. *Educational Research* 11: 138–142.

Glaser, N. A.; and Brown, D. A. 1979. *Reading center manual.* Greeley, Col.: Basic Education Trade House.

Guthrie, J. T.; Seifert, M.; and Kline, L. W. 1978. Clues from research on programs for poor readers. In *What research has to say about reading instruction,* ed. S.J. Samuels. Newark, Del: International Reading Assoc. pp. 1–12.

Lovell, K.; Johnson, E.; and Platt, D. A. 1962. Summary of a study of the reading ages of children who had been given remedial teaching. *British Journal of Educational Psychology.* 32: 66–71.

Pearlman, E.; and Pearlman, R. 1970. The effect of remedial reading training in a private clinic. *Academic Therapy* 5: 298–304.

APPENDIX

Student Interview and Record Form

READING LEVELS

	PP	P	1^2	2^1	2^2	3^1	3^2	4	5	6	7	8	9	10	11	12	C^o	L
Sight Word Recognition Level																		
Independent Reading Level																		
Instructional Reading Level																		
Frustration Reading Level																		
Listening Comprehension Level																		
Oral Reading Rate and Fluency																		
Silent Reading Rate																		
Word Attack Skills—Criterion Referenced Tests																		

Name: _____
Date: _____ Birthdate: _____ Age: _____
School: _____
School Address: _____

School Telephone: _____ Grade: _____
Teacher: _____
Report to: _____
Parent/Guardian: _____
Address: _____

Telephone: _____
Business Telephone: _____ Ext. _____
Diagnostician: _____
Diagnostician's Title: _____
Diagnostic Agency: _____
Agency Address: _____

Agency Telephone: _____ Ext. _____
Diagnostic Summary: _____

DIAGNOSTIC READING TEST BATTERY
Don A. Brown

University of Northern Colorado

Basic Education Trade House, P. O. Box 3102, Greeley, Colorado 80631

316

2

BACKGROUND INFORMATION

1. Reason for referral: _____

_____

2. Physical factors such as health, vision, hearing, speech, and pertinent physical disabilities:

_____

_____

3. Social factors such as peer relationships, cultural differences, and economic deprivation:

_____

_____

4. Educational history including beginning reading difficulties, previous diagnoses and remedial instruction, general performance in school, and relationships with teachers:

_____

_____

_____

_____

5. Psychological factors such as emotional problems, attitude, self-concept, attention span, dependency, need for encouragement, willingness to attempt activities, and intelligence:

_____

_____

_____

6. Family factors such as parent-child relationships, sibling relationships, educational background of the parents, attitudes and interests of the family related to education, and the interest of various family members in reading:

_____

_____

_____

_____

BEHAVIOR DURING DIAGNOSTIC SESSIONS

1. Rapport with the diagnostician including level of effort, and manner of responses:

_____

_____

2. Reactions during the diagnostic session(s) to the diagnostician, to the testing situation, and to success and failure situations:

_____

_____

_____

_____

317

DIAGNOSTIC READING TEST BATTERY*

I. WORD RECOGNITION TEST

Select a starting list at a level which will be easy for the student. Have the student read the first five words on the list. If he makes no errors, have him move to the next higher list. If a student makes one mistake in the first five words, have him read all ten words on the list. If he makes more than one error in the first five words have him move to an easier list.

After finding an appropriate starting level, continue having the student read the words on progressively more difficult lists until he reaches the highest list on which he makes no more than one error in ten words. In order to make certain he could not have gone further, it is usually good to let the student read until he has made two or more errors in two consecutive lists. As the student reads, his errors should be recorded for later analysis regarding the word attack strategies he uses on isolated words, that is, without the help which may be derived from using context clues.

After identifying the highest level at which the student makes no more than one error, turn to the informal reading inventory passages and begin with a selection one level below that level.

* The *Diagnostic Reading Test Battery* is available to the reader, who can use the ideas presented without having to make his own IRI or set of criterion-referenced tests. The reader is free to duplicate copies of the tests, although no one may duplicate them for sale or profit. If the reader prefers to use the test in its published form, it may be purchased from the Basic Education Trade House, P.O. Box 3102, Greeley, Colorado 80633.

318

Pre-Primer

and   _____
big   _____
go   _____
has   _____
you   _____
is   _____
can   _____
the   _____
here   _____
to   _____

Primer

am   _____
came   _____
give   _____
man   _____
help   _____
went   _____
see   _____
that   _____
way   _____
yes   _____

1^2

ask   _____
called   _____
thank   _____
after   _____
better   _____
with   _____
night   _____
walked   _____
never   _____
under   _____

2^1

large   _____
few   _____
which   _____
family   _____
kitchen   _____
raining   _____
should   _____
answered   _____
sentence   _____
turned   _____

2^2

write   _____
smiled   _____
newspaper   _____
ground   _____
covering   _____
build   _____
finish   _____
machine   _____
carefully   _____
welcome   _____

3^1

person   _____
each   _____
sorry   _____
unless   _____
modern   _____
followed   _____
direction   _____
arithmetic   _____
doesn't   _____
safety   _____

3²

argument   _____
blanket   _____
depend   _____
frightened   _____
gentle   _____
settle   _____
continue   _____
charge   _____
beautiful   _____

4

journey   _____
approaching   _____
business   _____
blizzard   _____
length   _____
successful   _____
pronounce   _____
nervous   _____
automobile   _____

5

giant   _____
acquainted   _____
detective   _____
equipment   _____
chemistry   _____
scraped   _____
straggling   _____
thermostat   _____
preparation   _____

6

curiosity   _____
barometer   _____
efficiently   _____
bough   _____
legislature   _____
instinct   _____
ounces   _____
patiently   _____
twine   _____
wring   _____

7

auburn   _____
consensus   _____
evaluate   _____
contemptuous   _____
domination   _____
croft   _____
undaunted   _____
dissension   _____
tourniquet   _____
mutation   _____

8

ascribe   _____
beneficent   _____
discretion   _____
paranoid   _____
baptize   _____
aquarium   _____
envision   _____
context   _____
voluminous   _____
prosecute   _____

9

absolution	_____
consolation	_____
chastize	_____
fusion	_____
juvenile	_____
revival	_____
conscription	_____
revulsion	_____
corporate	_____
monoxide	_____

10

assumption	_____
conjugate	_____
monotheistic	_____
predilection	_____
procrastinate	_____
trapezoid	_____
incarceration	_____
strobe	_____
tangential	_____
zeppelin	_____

12

absentia	_____
contamination	_____
claustrophobia	_____
viscera	_____
morgue	_____
clandestine	_____
proselyte	_____
convolution	_____
absurd	_____
crochet	_____

College-Adult

alleviate	_____
avaricious	_____
indict	_____
glycerine	_____
plethora	_____
superfluous	_____
placate	_____
chrysalis	_____
polygamy	_____
misanthropy	_____

SUMMARY:

Level	Errors	Level	Errors
PP	_____	5	_____
P	_____	6	_____
1^2	_____	7	_____
2^1	_____	8	_____
2^2	_____	9	_____
3^1	_____	10	_____
3^2	_____	12	_____
4	_____	Coll-Ad	_____

Highest level at which the reader makes no more than one error in 10 words: _____

II. ORAL INFORMAL READING INVENTORY

Oral Reading Checklist

READINESS
_____ *Visual discrimination*
_____ *Auditory discrimination*
_____ *Language base*
_____ *Attention*
_____ *Left-to-right progression*
_____ *Holding book, turning pages*
_____ _____

SIGHT VOCABULARY
_____ *Size of sight vocabulary*
_____ *Speed of recognition*
_____ *Accuracy of recognition*
_____ _____

WORD ATTACK
_____ *Initial consonants*
_____ *Digraphs*
_____ *Consonant blends*
_____ *Silent letters*
_____ *Word endings*

_____ *Long vowel sounds*
_____ *Short vowel sounds*
_____ *Diphthongs*
_____ *Compound words*
_____ *Syllabication*
_____ _____
_____ _____

CONTEXT CLUES
_____ *Word recognition*
_____ *Word meaning*

COMPREHENSION
_____ *Details*
_____ *Vocabulary*
_____ *Main idea*
_____ *Inference*
_____ _____

RATE AND FLUENCY
_____ *Fluent oral reading*
_____ *Silent reading rate*

322

Table 1

Functional reading levels indicated by word call and comprehension errors in oral reading

	Good man (PP)	Jan (P)	Fire (1²)	Blizzard (2¹)	Whales (2²)	Longhorn (3¹)	Coal (3²)	Vikings (4)	Strongest nation (5)	Menche's Cone (6)	Shrew (7)	Niagara (8)	Radium (10)	Michelangelo (12)	Physical differences (College)
Independent Reading Level															
Word Call Errors	0-1	0-1	0-2	0-2	0-3	0-3	0-4	0-3	0-4	0-3	0-3	0-3	0-3	0-3	0-3
Comprehension Errors	0	0	0-1	0-1	0-1	0-1	0-1	0-1	0-1	0-1	0-1	0-1	0-1	0-1	0-1
Instructional Reading Level															
Word Call Errors	2-3	2-3	3-4	3-6	4-8	4-8	5-9	4-8	4-7	5-9	4-8	4-8	4-7	4-8	4-8
Comprehension Errors	1	1	2	2	2	2	2	2	2	2	2	2	2	2	2
Frustration Reading Level															
Word Call Errors	4+	4+	7+	10+	15+	15+	18+	15+	14+	17+	14+	14+	14+	16+	15+
Comprehension Errors	2+	2+	4+	4+	4+	4+	4+	4+	4+	4+	4+	4+	4+	4+	4+

A GOOD MAN [Pre-primer]

The dog was cold. A man saw him. "Come here," he said. "Come with me. We will go home."

The dog went with the man. His home was warm. The man was nice. The dog liked him.

Time: _____ Errors: _____ Comprehension: _____

_____1. What was wrong with the dog?
_____2. Who saw the dog?
_____3. Where did the dog go?
_____4. What would be another good title for the story?

JAN   [Primer]

The rain was over. The sun was warm. It was a pretty day. Jan and two girls walked to school. They all talked. It was fun. It was a nice day to go to school.

Time: _____ Errors: _____ Comprehension: _____

_____1. What kind of day was it?
_____2. How many girls walked with Jan?
_____3. Where were they going?
_____4. Make up your own title for this story.

THE FIRE [1²]

No one thought anything was wrong. The lights blinked once or twice. Then a low roaring sound could be heard. Bill looked up from his book and saw the light outside the window. "Dad!" he yelled. "The house is on fire!" The light from the fire shone through the window. Everyone ran to get out the front door. The firemen came quickly. They worked fast and were able to save most of the house.

Time: _____ Errors: _____ Comprehension: _____

_____1. What was Bill doing before the fire?
_____2. What sound did they first hear?
_____3. Who noticed the fire first?
_____4. Where did everyone go to get out of the house?
_____5. Who came to help?
_____6. How much of the house were they able to save?
_____7. What is the main idea of this story?
_____8. What would be another good title for this story?

THE BLIZZARD [2¹]

Before the blizzard, the day had been warm. Although it was winter, it seemed like spring. Just before night, the wind began to blow. Soon it was so strong it began to tip over trash cans. People began to hurry home.

Then the snow came. It snowed for five days without stopping. Out on the plains, ranchers couldn't get out to feed their cattle. Drifts were so high that the cattle couldn't move. They huddled together with their backs to the wind. It was days before some of them could be fed. Many died before help came.

Time: _____ Errors: _____ Comprehension: _____

_____1. What kind of day had it been before the storm?
_____2. What time of day was it when the storm began?
_____3. How strong was the wind?
_____4. What did people do when the wind began to blow?
_____5. How long did it snow?
_____6. Why did so many cattle die?
_____7. What is the main idea of this story?
_____8. Make up another title for this story.

WHALES   [2²]

Blue whales are the biggest animals that ever lived. Like most of the large whales, blue whales have no teeth. But it isn't hard for them to find food. They just open their mouths as they swim along. In this way, they catch hundreds of very small sea animals. They let the water out but keep the food in their mouths.

Whales may look like fish, but they aren't. They can't stay down under the water all the time like fish. If they can't come up to the top of the water once in awhile, they will drown! They are not cold like fish. Their bodies are warm like ours. They are also much smarter than fish. They are even able to talk to one another. People have been trying to understand what they say. Maybe some day we will be able to talk with whales!

Time: _____ Errors: _____ Comprehension: _____

_____1. What is the biggest animal that ever lived?
_____2. How do blue whales find food?
_____3. What kind of food do they eat?
_____4. What will happen if a whale stays under water a very long time?
_____5. How are whales different from fish?
_____6. In what way are they like fish?
_____7. What is the main idea of this story?
_____8. What would be another good title for this story?

LONGHORN CATTLE [3¹]

Years ago most cattle were raised in Texas. People didn't think cows could stand the cold winters up north. The cattle they raised were called "longhorns." They were thin and had long, sharp horns. Their meat was not as good as the meat we buy today. But they were strong enough to walk hundreds of miles. Ranchers had to drive them a long way to get them to a place where they could ship them to market.

There aren't many longhorns around now. Today we raise cattle in every state. We haul cattle to market by truck or train. We don't need strong, tough cattle that can stand long cattle drives.

About the only time we see longhorns now is on TV or in a movie. Some of them are on ranches or even in zoos. They are kept to let us see what they looked like.

Time: _____ Errors: _____ Comprehension: _____

_____1. Which state used to raise most of our cattle?
_____2. Why weren't cattle raised up north?
_____3. What were the cattle called?
_____4. What were they like?
_____5. Where are cattle raised now?
_____6. Where can longhorns be seen now?
_____7. What are two ways today's cattle are different from longhorns?
_____8. What is the main idea of this story?

COAL   [3²]

When people first tried to sell coal, no one would buy it. They thought it was just black rocks. Coal looks like rock, but it isn't. Coal comes from trees and other plants that lived ages ago. At first, the plants were part of a swampy jungle. After they died or the wind blew them over, they began to decay. More plants took their place. These plants also died and added to the growing layer of decaying vegetable matter.

As the earth and its climate changed, these hot steaming forests could not live. The swamps became dry land. Rivers washed dirt, sand, and rock over the layers of dead plants. Wind covered it with dust and sand. Finally, it lay buried under tons of rock and soil which pressed it so hard it became coal.

Time: _____ Errors: _____ Comprehension: _____

_____1. Why wouldn't people buy coal at first?
_____2. What does coal come from?
_____3. Where did the trees and plants live?
_____4. What happened to the jungles?
_____5. How were the dead plants covered?
_____6. What caused the dead plant matter to become coal?
_____7. How is coal different from rocks?
_____8. What is the main idea of this story?

VIKINGS [4]

Long ago, the Vikings were the best sailors on the sea. Five hundred years before Columbus, they sailed the ocean without maps or a compass. They told directions by the sun and stars. They used the constellations to guess their location. They could even tell how far they were from land by observing the birds and watching things floating by in the water.

Their ships had one large square sail and sixteen oars. The sail was brightly striped. They used the oars when they were near land or when there was no wind. Their ships were constructed with great care. The builders knew the strengths of each kind of wood, and they used exactly the right wood for each part. The bow was usually shaped like a dragon's head and the stern like a dragon's tail. Each vessel was a work of art.

Time: _____ Errors: _____ Comprehension: _____

_____1. What were the Vikings best known for?
_____2. What did they use to tell directions?
_____3. What sort of sail did they use?
_____4. When did they use their oars?
_____5. What knowledge did the builders use to make good ships?
_____6. How did they decorate the bow and stern of a ship?
_____7. How could they tell whether they were near land by watching birds or things floating in the water?
_____8. What would be another good title for this story?

THE STRONGEST NATION [5]

As we left the little Arab village, we felt the heat close in on us. We were headed across a desert so barren that no living thing could be seen for miles. Our jeeps had no road to follow; only a glimpse of a winding trail here or there to let us know we were on the right path. It was a sight I'll never forget, seeing those two jeeps slowly tracking across the endless dunes.

Toward night, we reached our goal. Mounds of earth dotted the area. Under each mound was the unearthed remains of temples, palaces, and other buildings of an ancient people. In the distance, we could see workers digging at a site. It did not seem possible that we were standing on what had once been the heart of the strongest nation in the world!

Time: _____ Errors: _____ Comprehension: _____

_____1. What sort of country were they in?
_____2. How did they know which way to go?
_____3. What did they use for transportation?
_____4. When did they arrive at their destination?
_____5. What was under the mounds of earth?
_____6. What were the workers doing?
_____7. What had once stood at this place?
_____8. What would be another title for this story?

MENCHES' CONE [6]

One day in 1904, Charles Menches and his girl friend visited the World's Fair in St. Louis. At one of the booths, Charles saw a bouquet of beautiful red roses. He decided to buy them for his girl. At another booth, he saw some ice cream. At that time, ice cream was sold only to be eaten in dishes or as an "ice cream sandwich," with the ice cream placed between two wafers. Charles bought her an ice cream sandwich.

As they began walking away, Charles noticed that water was dripping from the stems of the roses. He took one of the wafers and formed it into a cone and placed the rose stems in it to keep the water from getting on his girl's dress. It worked so well that he took the other wafer and made another cone. In this one, he placed the ice cream. And that's how Charles Menches became the inventor of one of America's favorite treats, the ice cream cone.

Time: _____ Errors: _____ Comprehension: _____

_____1. Where were Charles and his girl?

_____2. What sort of flowers did Charles buy?

_____3. What did he buy his girl to eat?

_____4. Why did he make the first cone?

_____5. What did he make the cone from?

_____6. What did he put in the second cone?

_____7. What kind of person do you think Charles Menches was? What does this story tell about him that makes you think so?

_____8. What is the main idea of this story?

THE SHREW [7]

If you were asked to name the most ferocious animal in the world, you'd probably think of a lion, tiger, Alaskan brown bear, polar bear, or perhaps even a rhinoceros. While all those are notable for their ferocity, none of them is comparable to the little mouse-like shrew. It attacks and devours animals several times its size.

A teacher once accidentally placed a shrew in a cage with a white rat. The shrew instantly reared on its hind legs, let out a squeal of rage, and attacked as the entire class watched in amazement. The shrew moved so fast it was impossible to follow him. He stormed all over the rat, biting, slashing, and overpowering it. The next morning, the shrew had totally consumed the rat. Even the bones were gone. The cage was empty except for the shrew, licking its lips and looking around for another rat.

Time: _____ Errors: _____ Comprehension: _____

_____1. What is the most ferocious animal in the world?
_____2. How big is the shrew?
_____3. What size animals will the shrew attack?
_____4. What animal did the shrew attack in this story?
_____5. How did the shrew act when it saw the rat?
_____6. What did the shrew do to the rat?
_____7. Why do you think you would be less afraid of a shrew than you would be of a tiger?
_____8. What would be another good title for this story?

NIAGARA   [8]

Water plunging over Niagara Falls is atomized into a fine silvery spray, moving those who see it for the first time to stand in awestruck wonder. The continuous thundering of the falls caused the Iroquois Indians to name it Niagara, "Thunder of Waters."

An interesting aspect of the falls is that it moves upstream at a rate of about five feet a year. Piece by piece, chunks of rock break off as the water tears away at the lip of the falls. Now and then a larger section of rock breaks free, and bystanders are treated to an unusual crashing sound and a quaking of the earth. By tracing the movement of the falls upstream to its starting point, we can estimate the length of time it has been flowing. Present calculations indicate that Niagara began to flow at the end of the last Ice Age, about ten thousand years ago.

Time: _____ Errors: _____ Comprehension: _____

_____1. Who were the ones who named Niagara Falls?
_____2. Why did they call it "Niagara"?
_____3. How fast are the falls moving upstream?
_____4. What causes it to move upstream?
_____5. What happens when larger pieces break off?
_____6. How long ago did the falls begin flowing?
_____7. How are they able to estimate how long ago the falls began to flow?
_____8. What is one of the two main ideas in this passage?

RADIUM   [10]

When Marie and Pierre Curie discovered radium in the latter part of the nineteenth century, they had little idea how hazardous the element could be. Even forty years later, people working with radium took no steps to protect themselves. Girls using radium as an ingredient in paint for painting clock dials which would glow in the dark shaped the tips of their brushes with their lips. They soon became ill and died from the radioactive substance.

Today those who work with radium wear protective clothing and work from behind thick shields of lead, water, or concrete. Geiger counters and other devices monitor any escaping radiation. Still, because radiation is invisible as well as deadly, its use must be closely supervised. It is extremely useful in treating cancer, but used carelessly, it would be more dangerous than even that dread disease.

Time: _____ Errors: _____ Comprehension: _____

_____1. Who discovered radium?
_____2. When was it discovered?
_____3. What was startling about the way radium was handled for many years after its discovery?
_____4. What happened to the girls who were painting clock dials?
_____5. What materials are used to shield people from radiation?
_____6. What disease is radium useful in treating?
_____7. What do we know about radium which wasn't known by the Curies?
_____8. What would be another good title for this story?

MICHELANGELO   [12]

The mention of the name Michelangelo brings to mind his brilliance in sculpture and painting. Not content with ordinary artistic observation, he dissected human bodies in order to represent muscle structure more accurately. A person of strongest dedication, he spent four years painting the vault of the Sistine Chapel as a young man in his thirties.

An interesting addition to that story, however, is that he had been paid in advance not only to paint the ceiling, which he did, but the wall behind the altar. Unfortunately, he spent the money but kept deferring the enormous task until he was in his sixties. Michelangelo describes himself as "ill and suffering greatly" as he began the sixty-foot-high painting entitled "The Last Judgement." It took him almost every day for five years to complete the masterpiece, working with only his assistant, who applied wet plaster to the wall on which Michelangelo created his magnificent painting.

Time: _____ Errors: _____ Comprehension: _____

_____1. In which two areas of artistic ability did Michelangelo excel?
_____2. To what lengths did he go to understand muscle structure?
_____3. What are two examples of his dedication?
_____4. How old was he when he painted "The Last Judgement"?
_____5. Who helped him with this task?
_____6. How long did it take to complete this task?
_____7. What personal characteristic of Michelangelo's is most important in this story?
_____8. What is the main idea in this passage?

PHYSICAL DIFFERENCES   [College]

Computer analysis of differences between athletes in the various track events has yielded interesting confirmation of theories long held by many coaches and physiologists. The studies have involved the resources of many areas. The results have tended to indicate that middle-distance runners have long legs while those who run the marathon have relatively short legs. Peculiarly enough, sprinters also tend to have shorter limbs than intermediate-distance runners.

An analysis of the research data indicates that the variances seem to arise from growth patterns of muscular individuals who attain maturation and cease growth slightly earlier than others. This earlier maturity deprives the limbs of further increments of growth to a greater extent than it does the torso. The end result of such a growth pattern appears to be the greater endurance needed for distance running and the greater strength and quickness needed for the sprints.

Time: _____ Errors: _____ Comprehension: _____

_____1. What does this passage describe as a subject of computer analysis?
_____2. Whose theories have been confirmed by this study?
_____3. What have been the results relative to middle-distance runners?
_____4. What were the results concerning marathon runners?
_____5. What results were reported regarding sprinters?
_____6. What growth pattern differences contributed to the results?
_____7. Why should the finding that sprinters have shorter legs than intermediate runners seem strange?
_____8. What would be a better title for this passage?

24

Table 2
Analysis of miscues and errors

Passage level	Word	Error or miscue	Was it a substitution?	Was it a mispronunciation?	Was it a transposition of words?	Was it an omission?	Was it an addition?	Was it a block?	Was it due to dialect?	Did it maintain meaning?	Did it fit the syntactic structure?	Did it resemble the word in print?	Did it sound much like the word in print?	Did the reader self-correct?

339

25

Table 3
Reading grade levels indicated by oral reading rate with comprehension of seventy-five percent or higher

Reading level indicated by reading time	Good Man (PP)	Jan (P)	Fire (1^2)	Blizzard (2^1)	Whales (2^2)	Longhorns (3^1)	Coal (3^2)	Vikings (4)	Strongest Nation (5)	Menches' Cone (6)	Shrew (7) *
PP	1:20– 1:40	1:15– 1:35	2:15– 2:50	2:45– 3:10	3:25– 4:00						
P	1:05– 1:19	:58– 1:14	1:50– 2:14	2:15– 2:44	3:00– 3:24						
1^2	:52– 1:04	:48– :57	1:35– 1:49	1:55– 2:14	2:40– 2:59						
2^1	:35– :51	:34– :47	1:10– 1:34	1:20– 1:54	1:55– 2:39	2:15– 2:50					
2^2	:20– :34	:18– :33	:45– 1:09	1:00– 1:19	1:25– 1:54	1:40– 2:14					
3^1					1:00– 1:24	1:05– 1:39	1:55– 2:40	2:05– 2:40			
3^2						:55– 1:04	1:35– 1:54	1:40– 2:04			
4						:48– :54	1:10– 1:34	1:15– 1:39	1:30– 2:05	1:50– 2:30	1:40– 2:20
5							:50– 1:09	1:00– 1:14	1:10– 1:29	1:25– 1:49	1:20– 1:39
6*								:50– :59	:45– 1:09	:55– 1:24	:50– 1:19

* Performance at the 6th grade level represents attainment of competence in oral reading rate. Performance standards for oral reading rate are not listed for passages above 7th grade difficulty.

III. SILENT INFORMAL READING INVENTORY

Silent Reading Checklist

_____ *Lip movements*	_____ *Vocalization*
_____ *Pointing to words while reading*	_____ *Needs assistance with words*

SILENT READING PASSAGES

THE RACE [PP]

Sue liked to run. She was fast. One day there was a race. "I will win," she said. All the girls ran. Sue ran fast. But she did not win. One girl ran faster.

Time:_____ Comprehension:_____

_____1. What did Sue like to do?
_____2. How did Sue run?
_____3. How well did Sue do in the race?
_____4. What would be another good name for this story?

341

LUNCH TIME   [P]

The bell rang. Bob stopped his work. "It is time for lunch," he said. He was glad. He liked to eat. "Good food makes me happy," he said. "I want something to eat."

Time:_____ Comprehension:_____

_____1. How did Bob know it was time for lunch?
_____2. How did he feel?
_____3. How does good food make Bob feel?
_____4. What is this story mostly about?

SHARK! [1²]

A man was swimming under water. He saw some fish go by him very fast. Then he saw a big fish chasing them. He didn't wait. He knew it was a shark. He swam quickly to the top of the water. His friends pulled him into the boat. He was glad he was not a shark's lunch!

Time:_____ Comprehension:_____

_____1. What was the man doing?
_____2. What did he see that scared him?
_____3. What did he do?
_____4. What would be another good name for this story?

THE SAIL TRAIN   [2¹]

Years ago a man thought he had a good idea. He built a new kind of train. It ran without an engine. It looked like a boat because it used a sail to make it go. But it didn't run on water. It ran on rails. It worked very well if the wind was right. But when the wind was wrong, the people had to wait. If they tried to sail against the wind, they just went backward. People became tired of the sail train. They could never be sure if it was going to work or not.

Time:_____ Comprehension:_____

_____1. What did the man build?
_____2. How could it move without an engine?
_____3. What did it run on?
_____4. When did it work best?
_____5. What was wrong with the idea?
_____6. Why didn't the people like it?
_____7. If sails work all right for a boat, why don't they work well for a train on land?
_____8. What is the main idea of this story?

BEES   [2²]

Bees have many different jobs in their lifetime. At first, young worker bees clean their hives. When it is cold, they have to keep the younger ones warm. When it gets too hot, they fan them with their wings.

Later, they have a different job. They make a special food called "royal jelly." They feed this to the younger ones. They also feed it to their queen.

Next, they make wax. They use it to build the honey comb. During this time, some of them work as police. They protect the hive from outsiders.

Their last job is looking for food. They leave the hive in search of flowers. When a bee finds some good flowers, she tells the others. She tells them the kind of flower she has found and how far away it is. Then the other bees eat just enough food to get to the flowers and back home. They never take more than they need to do their work.

Time:_____ Comprehension:_____

_____1. What do young bees do when the weather is hot?
_____2. What do they do with the "royal jelly"?
_____3. What do they use to build the honey comb?
_____4. What is the last job they have?
_____5. What two things does a bee tell the other bees when she finds good flowers?
_____6. How much food do the bees take with them?
_____7. What word would you use to decribe the bees in this story?
_____8. What would be another good title for this story?

DINOSAURS   [3¹]

Long ago, dinosaurs lived in many parts of the world. Some of them were small, much like the lizards we see today. Others were big. Some were as large as a house. They were so big they could eat as much in one day as you eat in a year.

Even though they were so large, their brains were small. A huge dinosaur might have a brain smaller than a baseball!

Dinosaurs fought by using their jaws, teeth, and claws. They were protected by their thick skins. Then other animals began to come along with larger brains. They could think better than the dinosaurs. Soon the dinosaurs died off. Today only small, fast lizards are left. They remind us of the monsters which ruled the world years ago.

Time:_____ Comprehension:_____

_____1. How big were some of the dinosaurs?
_____2. How much could they eat in one day?
_____3. What size were some of their brains?
_____4. How were dinosaurs protected?
_____5. How were newer animals that began to come along different from the dinosaurs?
_____6. What is still alive today that reminds us of dinosaurs?
_____7. What does the writer seem to think happened to the dinosaurs?
_____8. What is the main idea of this story?

DEATH VALLEY   [3²]

Death Valley is the hottest place in North America. During the Gold Rush of 1849, many people nearly died there. They thought it was a safe shortcut to the mining camps. Once they started across it, they found that the water was no good, and the heat was so bad it could drive a person crazy. Some of them barely made it out of the valley.

Death Valley is 140 miles long and from 4 to 16 miles wide. It has all sorts of unusual formations. One of the most interesting is the "Race Track." It's a dry lake bed. As you first see it, it looks like a huge saucer. The sand of the lake bed is as flat as if someone had leveled it. On one side of the lake bed are some big boulders. They are called the "Skating Rocks." Behind each rock is a long track left by the rock when it moves. Everyone knows the rocks have been moving, but no one knows how or why they move.

Time:_____   Comprehension:_____

_____1. What is the hottest place in North America?
_____2. Why did people go through Death Valley during the Gold Rush?
_____3. What two things were hard on those who tried to cross the valley?
_____4. What is the Race Track?
_____5. What's behind each of the Skating Rocks?
_____6. What has caused the track?
_____7. Why are they called Skating Rocks?
_____8. What would be another good title for this story?

DANIEL BOONE   [4]

When Boone was a boy, he lived in a cabin beside the woods. He always wondered about the forest. No one seemed to know what was in it or what lay beyond it. Little Daniel made up his mind to find out. So when he was old enough, he went into the woods to learn what he could. By watching what the animals eat, he found out which plants were good for food. He became a good tracker and a fine hunter. He was soon able to live on what he gathered and hunted.

It wasn't long before people came to Boone to find out about the woods. He told them that he had found a beautiful place over the mountains in what the Indians called "Kentucky." It had lots of water, good land to farm, and deer and other animals for meat. Many people asked him to show them the way. Boone organized a wagon train and led them. When they got to Kentucky, they named their new town in his honor. They called it "Boonesborough."

Time:_____ Comprehension:_____

_____1. Where did Boone live as a boy?
_____2. How did he learn which plants were good to eat?
_____3. What did the Indians call the place Boone had found?
_____4. What kind of things did Kentucky have that made it a desirable place
          to live?
_____5. What did people ask Boone to do?
_____6. What did they call their new town?
_____7. Why did people ask Boone to lead them rather than go on their own?
_____8. What would be another good name for this story?

PETROLEUM   [5]

Man first began to use oil over 5000 years ago. They found where it seeped out of the earth and used it to patch boats and baskets, to build roads, and as a glue to hold things together. Sometimes they used oil as a medicine.

Thousands of years later, petroleum was still used as a medicine. Then, about 1830, people began to use it in their lamps. In thirty years, people were using so much kerosene, made from oil, that they had to drill for oil. In forty years, production had risen to sixty-four million barrels of oil a year. Almost all of it was used in lamps.

Now we make many products from oil. We use much more oil in one day than the whole world produced in an entire year in 1900.

Time:_____   Comprehension:_____

_____1. How long ago did man first start using petroleum?
_____2. Name three things they used it for.
_____3. What product, made from oil, did they use in their lamps?
_____4. When demand increased, what did they have to do to find enough oil?
_____5. What did people use most of their oil for in 1900?
_____6. Compared with 1900, how much oil do we use now?
_____7. Why has oil production increased so much since 1900?
_____8. What is the main idea of this passage?

ICEBERGS   [6]

Can you imagine taking a drink of water that had fallen from the clouds fifty thousand years ago? That's happening in some places today. It comes from using icebergs as a source of water.

Some of the snow in the arctic north never has a chance to melt. In Greenland, for example, snow has collected year after year for centuries. Snow falling in mountain valleys forms glaciers. Some of the compacted snow in glaciers has been found to be fifty thousand years old. The weight of the glaciers forces them down the mountains and out to the sea like a slow-moving river of ice.

After the glacier reaches the coast, the edge breaks off into the sea. About 16,000 glaciers are formed this way each year. Large glaciers can be towed to desert areas to provide for drinking and farming. Some day you may be in a place where part of the drinking water is thousands of years old!

Time:_____ Comprehension:_____

_____1. How old is some of the snow found in glaciers in Greenland?
_____2. How are glaciers formed?
_____3. How do glaciers get from the mountains to the sea?
_____4. How are icebergs made?
_____5. How can they be moved to desert areas?
_____6. How are they used there?
_____7. Would drinking water that is thousands of years old be good to drink? Why do you think so?
_____8. What would be another good title for this story?

THE UNIVERSE   [7]

If you look into a clear night sky, you can see so few of the many stars that it would be like trying to see the entire ocean by opening your eyes under water. There are about as many stars in the universe as there are grains of sand on all the seashores in the world. In the Milky Way alone there are one hundred billion stars, and the Milky Way is only one of many galaxies in the universe.

But the real meaning of "one hundred billion" is almost beyond us. In order to understand the number better, first imagine that each star is the size of a ping pong ball. Then imagine clearing and leveling an entire city block. If you were to put a three-foot fence around it and fill it to the very top, it would hold about a billion ping pong balls. To enclose the same number of balls as there are stars in the Milky Way would take one hundred blocks fenced and filled that way!

Time:_____ Comprehension:_____

_____1. How many stars can you see on a clear night?
_____2. How many stars are there in the Milky Way?
_____3. What is the Milky Way?
_____4. How many ping pong balls would fit in a city block three feet high?
_____5. How many blocks like that would it take to hold enough ping pong balls to equal the number of stars in the Milky Way?
_____6. What comparison does the writer make between sand and stars?
_____7. Why does the passage ask you to imagine the number of ping pong balls in a city block?
_____8. What is the main idea of this story?

THE TOP OF THE WORLD   [8]

As Hillary and Tenzing started the final leg of their ascent up Mount Everest, they could only breathe by using their oxygen tanks. At one point, they had to cling to the rocks in front of them for what seemed an interminable period of time as the wind tore at them relentlessly, trying to snatch them away from the mountain and hurl them into the abyss below.

Eventually, they accomplished the final ridge before the top. The blowing snow obscured almost everything. It was impossible to repress the memory of an earlier climber who had last been seen almost at the top but who had disappeared into the wind-driven snow, never to be seen again.

They fought their way forward blindly, chipping footholes in the snow, taking one step at a time. And suddenly, almost before they were prepared for it, they were there. They had succeeded. They had made it to the top. In what seemed like an unreal dreamlike world, they had become the first men to ascend to the lofty heights of the highest mountain in the world!

Time:_____ Comprehension:_____

_____1. How many men were climbing the final leg of the trip?
_____2. How were they able to breathe?
_____3. What conditions made it difficult to climb?
_____4. What had happened to the person on a previous trip who had almost made it to the top?
_____5. Why was the mountain they were climbing so well known?
_____6. What was the name of the mountain they climbed?
_____7. What record do Hillary and Tenzing hold?
_____8. What is the main idea of this story?

THE OLYMPIC GAMES [10]

When the Olympic Games were originally begun in the Greek city of Olympus, deep religious significance was attached to them. The Greeks felt that men could best honor their god Zeus by developing their mind and their body. Therefore, for twelve centuries, each four years as the games would begin, a sacred truce was declared, all warfare ceased, and all eyes turned on the athletes to honor them for their physical abilities.

As Rome replaced Greece as the dominant political and military power in the world, the games began to decline. When the Roman emperor Nero ruled Rome, he entered and won every event because the athletes were afraid to defeat him. This was so ridiculous that the games lost prestige, and winning lacked the meaning it had once held. Eventually, loss of prestige and the brawling among athletes caused the games to be stopped. Fifteen centuries later, after archeologists began to dig up the ruins of Olympia, interest was renewed, and the modern Olympic Games were begun.

Time:_____ Comprehension:_____

_____1. Where were the Olympic Games originally held?
_____2. How did the Greeks feel they should honor their god Zeus?
_____3. For how many centuries did the original Olympic Games continue?
_____4. What unusual observance marked the games each four years?
_____5. What did Nero do?
_____6. How did this harm the Olympics?
_____7. What is meant by the phrase, "winning lacked the meaning it had once held."
_____8. Why did archeological diggings create new interest in the games?

LEIF ERICSON'S VINLAND   [12]

Ancient Norse sagas tell us that Leif Ericson was probably the first European to set foot on the North American continent when he landed at a place he called "Vinland." Speculation on the reliability of the sagas prompted an interesting test in 1893. A group of men constructed a replica of an old Norse ship complete with dragon's head bow, woolen sails, and lashed planking. They then succeeded in sailing it across the perilous North Atlantic from Norway to Newfoundland, proving the possibility that Norsemen could have made such a voyage.

Then, in 1963, the remains of an old Viking colony were found not far from a remote fishing village on the northwest tip of Newfoundland. Two years later, an old map, scientifically dated about 1440 AD, was discovered which showed the outline of the area described by the old sagas, and which contained notations indicating a visit by Leif Ericson. These findings seem to leave little doubt that Ericson discovered America.

Time:_____ Comprehension:_____

_____1. Who is the person the sagas say landed on North America?

_____2. What did he call his discovery?

_____3. How was the possibility tested that he could have sailed so far?

_____4. Where were the remains of the old Viking colony discoverd?

_____5. Why was the old map so important?

_____6. How old was the map?

_____7. Why was Ericson's discovery of America less important than that of Columbus?

_____8. The map was made 450 years after Ericson's discovery. What does that imply concerning the Vikings' knowledge of his findings?

CONFLICT   [College]

Conflict is at the root of much mental illness. Simply stated, conflict derives from equally strong drives in two mutually exclusive directions. A person caught between two equally attractive or equally repulsive goal-objects will experience conflict. A hungry dog, for example, placed half-way between stacks of T-bone steaks, according to theory, will die a frustrated death, being unable to resolve his conflict and make a choice. Although such an illustration hardly accounts for all the possible factors which could enter into a dog's eventual decision, it does underscore, through exaggeration, the power involved in conflict. In actual practice, conflict is less often the result of inability to resolve a drive for two clearly apparent goals and more likely to involve opposing desires of a less obvious nature within an individual. Possibly because the source of conflict is often veiled, it becomes more difficult to gain insight regarding the cause of the conflict and may require expert psychological help in its analysis.

Time:_____ Comprehension:_____

_____1. What lies at the root of much mental illness?
_____2. What produces conflict?
_____3. What would be the effect on the degree of conflict if two goal-objects were not equally attractive?
_____4. What is the "clearly apparent" drive involved in the illustration?
_____5. What is an example of an internal goal of a "less obvious nature"?
_____6. What professional field specializes in the analysis of problems concerning conflict?
_____7. If a miser who could not swim was in a sinking rowboat with a ton of gold bars far from shore, would he experience conflict? Why?
_____8. How does the proverb, "You cannot have your cake and eat it, too" relate to this passage?

Table 4
Reading grade levels indicated by silent reading rate with comprehension of seventy-five percent or higher

Silent reading time for each passage

Reading level indicated by reading time	Race PP	Lunch time P	Shack 1²	Sail train 2¹	Bees 2²	Dinosaurs 3¹	Death Valley 3²
PP	1:03–1:13	1:08–1:20	2:00–2:20				
P	:49–1:02	:43–1:07	1:35–1:59	1:50–2:19			
1²	:40– :48	:30– :43	1:15–1:34	1:35–1:49			
2¹	:28– :39	:25– :29	:55–1:14	1:15–1:34	2:40–3:10	2:15–2:45	3:10–3:55
2²			:40– :54	1:00–1:14	1:40–2:39	1:30–2:14	2:15–3:09
3¹				:40– :59	1:10–1:39	1:10–1:29	1:50–2:14
3²				:30– :39	:50–1:09	1:00–1:09	1:30–1:49
4						:50– :59	1:20–1:29
5							
6							
7							
8							
9							
10							
11							
12							
College							

Boone	Petroleum	Icebergs	The universe	The top of the world	The Olympic Games	Leif Ericson's Vinland	Conflict College
4	5	6	7	8	10	12	College
1:45–2:25							
1:30–1:44	1:08–1:20						
1:20–1:29	1:00–1:07	1:14–1:22					
1:10–1:19	:53– :59	1:06–1:13	1:10–1:18				
	:47– :52	:58–1:05	1:04–1:09	1:07–1:14			
		:50– :57	:57–1:03	1:00–1:06	:56–1:04		
			:47– :56	:52– :59	:50– :55		
			:42– :46	:46– :51	:44– :49	:44– :49	
				:39– :45	:39– :43	:39– :43	:40– :46
					:35– :38	:34– :38	:36– :39
					:30– :34	:29– :35	:31– :35
					:23– :29	:22– :28	:22– :30

357

IV. CRITERION REFERENCED TESTS OF WORD ATTACK SKILLS

Summary Chart

Skill	Score Range	Mastery	Mastery
Visual Discrimination of Letters	0:1:2:3:4:5:6:7:8:9:10:11:12:13:14:15:16:17:	Mastery	18:19:20
Visual Discrimination of Words	0:1:2:3:4:5:6:7:8:9:10:11:12:13:14:15:16:17:	Mastery	18:19:20
Auditory Discrimination of Word Beginnings	0 : 1 : 2 : 3 : 4 : 5 : 6 : 7 : 8 :	Mastery	9 : 10
Auditory Discrimination of Word Endings	0 : 1 : 2 : 3 : 4 : 5 : 6 : 7 : 8 :	Mastery	9 : 10
Spoken Context with Initial Letters	0 : 1 : 2 : 3 : 4 : 5 : 6 : 7 : 8 :	Mastery	9 : 10
Initial Sight Vocabulary	0:1:2:3:4:5:6:7:8:9:10:11:12:13:14:15:16:17:	Mastery	18:19:20
Initial Consonant Sounds	0:1:2:3:4:5:6:7:8:9:10:11:12:13:14:15:16:17:	Mastery	18:19:20
Final Consonant Sounds	0 : 1 : 2 : 3 : 4 : 5 : 6 : 7 : 8 :	Mastery	9 : 10
Consonant Blends	0 : 1 : 2 : 3 : 4 : 5 : 6 : 7 : 8 :	Mastery	9 : 10
Consonant Digraphs	0 : 1 : 2 : 3 : 4 : 5 : 6 :	Mastery	7 : 8
Long and Short Vowel Sounds	0:1:2:3:4:5:6:7:8:9:10:11:12:13:14:15:16:17:	Mastery	18:19:20
Final Silent "e"	0 : 1 : 2 : 3 : 4 : 5 : 6 : 7 : 8 :	Mastery	9 : 10
"r" Controlled Vowels	0 : 1 : 2 : 3 : 4 : 5 : 6 : 7 : 8 :	Mastery	9 : 10
"l" and "w" Controlled Vowels	0 : 1 : 2 : 3 : 4 : 5 : 6 : 7 : 8 :	Mastery	9 : 10
Vowel Digraphs	0 : 1 : 2 : 3 : 4 : 5 : 6 : 7 : 8 :	Mastery	9 : 10
Hard and Soft "c" and "g"	0 : 1 : 2 : 3 : 4 : 5 : 6 : 7 : 8 :	Mastery	9 : 10
Diphthongs	0 : 1 : 2 : 3 : 4 : 5 : 6 : 7 : 8 :	Mastery	9 : 10
Open First Syllable	0 : 1 : 2 : 3 : 4 : 5 : 6 : 7 : 8 :	Mastery	9 : 10
Closed First Syllable	0 : 1 : 2 : 3 : 4 : 5 : 6 : 7 : 8 :	Mastery	9 : 10

358

DIRECTIONS TO THE TEACHER: The criterion for mastery is a successful completion rate or 90 percent or higher for each of the following subtests. In each subtest, only the crucial letter or combination of letters is counted in judging the student's response. In other words, in a test of a student's ability to correctly pronounce the long vowel in the word *pate*, the student's response would be correct if he pronounced it as "tape" because even though he had mispronounced the word, he would have correctly identified the long "a" sound which is the crucial task in the subtest. If there are two words in an item, the student must pronounce the crucial element in both words correctly in order to receive credit for the item. The approximate reading level of expected mastery is indicated in parentheses after each subtest title. Reading approaches differ in the level at which mastery may be expected, and the reading levels indicated may be modified to correspond more closely to the sequence of skill development expected in any specific approach.

Visual Discrimination of Letters (Reading Readiness Level)
Directions to the student: "Circle the letter on each line that looks different."

1.	P	R	P	P		11.	x	z	z	z
2.	E	E	E	F		12.	a	a	o	a
3.	G	C	C	C		13.	l	l	i	l
4.	L	J	J	J		14.	n	n	u	n
5.	W	M	W	W		15.	a	a	a	s
6.	O	O	Q	O		16.	e	c	c	c
7.	l	l	l	l		17.	n	h	n	n
8.	i	i	j	i		18.	n	n	n	m
9.	y	x	y	y		19.	p	b	p	p
10.	t	t	t	f		20.	d	d	d	b

Score: _____

Visual Discrimination of Words (Reading Readiness)
Directions to the student: "On each line circle the word that looks different."

1.	one	one	anyone	one
2.	of	to	of	of
3.	mom	mom	wow	mom
4.	bus	bus	sub	bus
5.	top	top	top	pot
6.	big	dig	big	big
7.	cat	cat	eat	cat
8.	hut	hut	hut	nut

359

9.	took	took	took	look
10.	sometime	someone	someone	someone
11.	just	jump	just	just
12.	land	land	lamp	land
13.	harp	hard	hard	hard
14.	think	think	thing	think
15.	bum	bun	bun	bun
16.	church	chuck	church	church
17.	bag	bag	bang	bag
18.	shrink	shrink	shrink	shrank
19.	closet	closet	closest	closet
20.	shock	shack	shock	shock

Score: _____

Auditory Discrimination of Word Beginnings (Reading Readiness)
Directions to the student: "Listen carefully to each of these sets of three words. After each set, tell me which word does not have the same sound at the beginning as the other two words." (Repeat the directions for each of the first four sets of words.)

1. bad, dog, big	5. rough, pack, rope	9. just, yes, yell
2. hat, hit, wig	6. name, not, some	10. fix, same, four
3. cat, for, car	7. get, visit, gone	
4. lit, mug, love	8. kid, to, kite	

Score: _____

Auditory Discrimination of Word Endings (Reading Readiness)
Directions to the student: "Listen carefully to each of these sets of three words. After each set tell me which of the three words does not have an ending sound that rhymes with the other two words." (Repeat the directions for each of the first four sets of words.)

1. hand, sand, bat	5. it, ran, man	9. hot, will, hill
2. and, tall, small	6. had, ham, bad	10. big, man, pig
3. hat, call, rat	7. hit, say, day	
4. bed, can, red	8. set, fan, met	

Score: _____

Spoken Context with Initial Letters (Reading Readiness)
Directions to the teacher: Read the story aloud to the student, pausing before the blank at the end of each sentence. On the right side of the story, point to the letter

which corresponds to the blank. After the student suggests a word, record his response and continue the story.

Directions to the student: "Listen carefully as I read a story to you. Some words have been left out of the story. When I come to the end of the sentence where one of the words has been left out, I will stop and point to the letter which goes at the beginning of that word. Tell me the word you think has been left out. The word must make sense in the story, and it must start with the letter I point to."

THE STORM

The wind kept blowing, and snow began to f_____.
I put on a warm cap and buttoned my c_____. I had
never seen it so c_____! I opened the
d_____. The wind was so strong, it blew the door
out of my h_____! I opened the door again, and this
time I pushed very h_____. I went out and closed the
door behind m_____. It was snowing so hard I could
hardly s_____. I was glad my coat was
w_____. It kept out the snow and the
w _____.

: 1. f _____
: 2. c _____
: 3. c _____
: 4. d _____
: 5. h _____
: 6. h _____
: 7. m_____
: 8. s _____
: 9. w_____
:10. w_____

1. fall, 2. coat, 3. cold, 4. door, 5. hand(s), 6. hard,
7. me, 8. see, 9. warm, 10. wind.

Score: _____

Directions to the student: "From this point on in the test, read each of the following words to me."

Initial Sight Vocabulary (1² Level)

1. big	6. have	11. may	16. see
2. can	7. he	12. me	17. she
3. come	8. is	13. not	18. the
4. find	9. like	14. said	19. we
5. good	10. look	15. saw	20. you

Score: _____

Initial Consonant Sounds (1² Level)

1. best bend	6. hunt help	11. note nine	16. will want
2. cot cab	7. job jam	12. pit punt	17. yell yet
3. dog done	8. kind kite	13. rest rock	18. zip zero
4. fast found	9. long luck	14. tell test	19. ship shall
5. gone goat	10. much most	15. very visit	20. this them

Score: _____

Final Consonant Sounds (1² Level)

1.	rob grab	4.	fill bell	7.	map tip	10.	fit mat
2.	hid mad	5.	ham dim	8.	car for		
3.	park took	6.	plan win	9.	mess yes		

Score: _____

Consonant Blends (2¹ Level)

1.	blink black	4.	grab grim	7.	snap snow	10.	from frame
2.	class clam	5.	skin skip	8.	swing swap		
3.	flat flame	6.	slam slip	9.	trap trail		

Score: _____

Consonant Digraphs (2¹ Level)

1.	chin chap	4.	what which	7.	white when
2.	ship shall	5.	church chip	8.	thin thimble
3.	think thud	6.	shot should		

Score: _____ (Mastery = 7 correct)

Long and Short Vowel Sounds (2² Level)

1.	wait	6.	top	11.	why	16.	feet
2.	send	7.	way	12.	fuse	17.	coat
3.	got	8.	mitt	13.	get	18.	use
4.	at	9.	cup	14.	fish	19.	day
5.	bite	10.	pet	15.	punt	20.	soak

Scoré: _____

Final Silent "e" (2² Level)

1.	sate	4.	mace	7.	rifle	10.	bide
2.	bane	5.	kale	8.	mute		
3.	rile	6.	sage	9.	pate		

Score: _____

"r" Controlled Vowels (2² Level)

1.	mar	4.	snarl	7.	cur	10.	mirth
2.	per	5.	bird	8.	hurl		
3.	burr	6.	whorl	9.	terse		

Score: _____

"l" and "w" Controlled Vowels (3¹ Level)

1. mall	4. mull	7. haw	10. hull
2. vellum	5. nil	8. balkan	
3. taw	6. bellum	9. rill	

Score: _____

Vowel Digraphs (3¹ Level)

1. mead	4. peel	7. fie	10. due
2. taint	5. doat	8. deem	
3. oaf	6. doe	9. aim	

Score: _____

Hard and Soft "c" and "g" (3¹ Level)

1. cape	4. central	7. recede	10. goblet
2. cite	5. ingest	8. regale	
3. general	6. becalm	9. cull	

Score: _____

Diphthongs (3¹ Level)

1. moil	4. ouch	7. rouse	10. aught
2. coy	5. rout	8. doily	
3. tout	6. coil	9. pause	

Score: _____

Open First Syllable (3² Level)

1. bogus	4. minor	7. saber	10. wager
2. cable	5. labor	8. solar	
3. focus	6. piper	9. vital	

Score: _____

Closed First Syllable (3² Level)

1. batten	4. totter	7. lubber	10. segment
2. cobble	5. witty	8. festoon	
3. motley	6. kelvin	9. gambol	

Score: _____

TEST THAT'S NOT A TEST

The T–NAT is a series of reading passages of increasing difficulty designed to be used as an initial screening test. It indicates an instructional reading level based on oral reading ability using the criteria developed for informal reading inventories.

Because the T–NAT is suggested for use in identifying a level for initial instructional placement, all appearance of a formal testing situation is to be avoided. There is no need for score sheets, stop watches, clipboards, or any of the other usual indicators that the student is being tested.

As in any testing situation, the examiner should try to put the student at ease as much as possible before introducing the T–NAT. The first card should be chosen at a level the examiner feels the student can handle with ease. If he underestimates the difficulty of the passage and the student has significant difficulty reading it, the examiner should stop the student, reassure him, and drop to an easier level without waiting for the student to finish the card if he can do so without embarrassing the student.

The student should proceed through the cards of increasing difficulty until the highest level is found in which the number of his reading errors does not exceed the *number of the card.* Sometimes it is advisable to try the next more difficult passage even though the student has exceeded the permissable number of errors on the last card he has read. If the student is then successful on the more difficult level, he is given credit for the easier level also and is permitted to continue the test.

The T–NAT has been specifically designed so that the number in the upper right-hand corner of each card not only represents its place in the series of cards but also indicates the *grade level* and the *highest number of errors permitted* in passing the card. If the reader makes more errors than the number on the card, he has not passed the level of reading represented on that card. For example, if a person reads passage 1 with no mistakes, passage 2 with 1 mistake, passage 3 with 3 mistakes, and passage 4 with 6 mistakes, it would indicate that he can read material as hard as third grade level (passage 3), but would have difficulty reading fourth grade material (passage 4). These levels are listed below:

Passage Number	Grade Level Difficulty	Permissable Errors
1	1	1
2	2	2
3	3	3
4	4	4
5	5	5
6	6	6
7	7	7
8	8	8

When a card is presented to a student, the examiner should say, "Let me have you read this story to me so we can find the best (class/group/materials) for you to work in." The examiner should assure the student that he will help the student if he needs assistance. If the student begins to read silently, he should be reminded to read aloud. The student should not be allowed to pre-read the passages silently before oral reading.

It is important that the examiner be familiar with the paragraphs and that he not give any indication that he is counting errors. It is a simple matter for the examiner to tally the errors on his fingers, out of sight of the student.

Errors   The only errors which are counted in determining the correct instructional levels are the following:

1. Mispronounced words. Part or all of the word may be mispronounced. Dialectic pronunciations should not be counted as mispronunciations. A mispronounced word resembles the correct word in sound, appearance, or both. The word *horse* mispronounced as "house" would be an example.
2. Substituted words. A substituted word has little similarity to the correct word. The substitution of "pony" for the word *horse*, for example.
3. Omitted words. One error is counted for each word deleted.
4. Added words. One error is counted for each time words are added even though two or more words may have been added at a time.
5. Pronounced words. One error is counted for each word pronounced for the reader. The examiner should wait five seconds before pronouncing a word on which the reader has blocked.
6. Transposed word order. One error is counted for each time a reader transposes the order of words in a sentence. An example of transposed word order is reading "He can" for *Can he.*

1.

HOME

It was raining. I saw a little wet dog ouside. "Come in, boy," I said. "My home is your home."

2.

AIRPLANES

I went up in an airplane once. After a while, I looked down and saw the ground a mile below. It gave me a funny feeling. But everything went all right. And after we landed, I wanted to fly again.

3.

THUNDERSTORM

It was hot. Nobody was moving in the little park across the street. The ground lay dry and cracking from the sun's heat. Then just an edge of thunder clouds began to show over the tops of the trees. Slowly the sky began to fill with them. Thunder and lightning moved closer, and then the cool rain washed the land.

4.

TELEVISION

Some people say they don't like television, but I do. I enjoy most of the programs I see. Some of them are exciting, and others teach you about different people, places, and things.

I guess I'd have to admit that there are times when it's easy for me to sit in front of our TV set and do nothing else. And there are evenings when no good shows are on. You've got to use your head and choose what's best.

5.

BIG ED

Ed is the biggest, finest man I ever saw. He isn't just big, he's *enormous!* I remember him standing in the middle of the floor in my room, putting both hands on the ceiling and lifting it at least six inches!

Last Tuesday, he saw a little old lady whose car had run into the gutter. There was no way she was going to be able to drive it back up onto the street. Ed lifted the front end and swung it up on the road. He went to the back, put his shoulder behind the car, and pushed it out.

9.

LA SALLE

La Salle discovered and named the great Louisiana Territory. He was the first to travel the length of the Mississippi River. Because of his explorations, France was able to claim the Mississippi Valley as her own.

La Salle was born in France of rich parents. He sailed to Canada when he was only 23 years old. At first he tried farming but soon lost interest. The stories of fur trappers and Indians from the West excited him. They told him of a broad river in the West that led south to the sea. Selling his farm, he gathered some brave men and began to search for this great river. Its discovery and exploration took all the rest of his life.

7.

THE NETHERLANDS

The name *Netherlands* means "lowlands," and from their earliest history the Dutch have battled the sea for the coastal lowlands near the sea. It has been a long struggle and a battle they have frequently lost. Many times they have freed land from the sea only to see storms, wind, and tides reclaim it.

But in 1932, they began to defeat their old enemy, the sea. They built a dam across a narrow neck of the Zuider Zee and began to pump out the sea water. They were interrupted by World War II when, in order to stop the invading German army, they flooded thousands of acres of premium farmland with salt water.

After peace had returned, the Dutch fell to work again and not only regained the land they had lost but cleared more than they had had before.

·8

AQUATIC INSECTS

There are nearly a million kinds of insects, and only a few thousand of these are able to live in liquids. However, these few are surprising in their ability to live in harsh environments. Some are able to live in salt water, others live in hot springs, and at least one is able to survive in crude oil.

Aquatic insects have developed different means for adapting to their hostile surroundings. Some capture air and take it with them as they go about their business under water. One of them is able to digest petroleum, a fact that amazes those working on problems of oil pollution. Still others are able to drink salt water and can make fresh water for their use from it. If we could learn the process by which they do this, it is possible that we could produce all the fresh water drier parts of the world need by making fresh water from the sea.

Directions for Using the Fry Readability Graph (See pp. 370 for graph.)

1. Select three 100 word passages from the reading material. Do not choose introductory or summarizing passages. Try to select passages which are representative of the reading material. For example, if the material is largely expository, do not select a sample that is dialogue. In the 100 words, do not include proper nouns of difficulty above the general level of the passage. For example, in a passage that is roughly of fifth grade difficulty, count words such as *Bill* or *America* but not *Americus Vespucius*.
2. Count the number of sentences in each 100-word passage, estimating the length of the fraction of the last sentence to the nearest one-tenth.
3. Count the total number of syllables in each 100 word passage.
4. Find the average number of syllables and sentences per 100 words.
5. On the graph plot the average number of syllables and the average number of sentences per 100 words. The curved line is the line of increasing difficulty. The gray areas indicate invalid results. The perpendicular lines mark off the grade level designations.
6. Add one year to the difficulty of materials which have been translated from another language or which were written before 1900.*

* Adapted from "Fry's Readability Graph: Clarification, Validity, and Extension to Level 17," by Edward Fry, *Journal of Reading*, December, 1977.

Fry Readability Graph

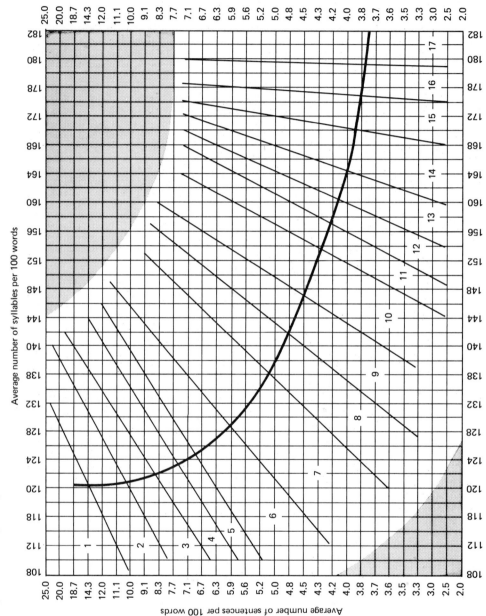

Average number of syllables per 100 words

Average number of sentences per 100 words

Semantic Differential Scale

The following are statements of opposites. Check the point on the scale
which best represents your feelings in regard to each of them.

Example:

A.   <u>School</u>
Like   _____:_____:_____:_____:_____:_____:_____   Hate

1.   Schoolwork
Easy   _____:_____:_____:_____:_____:_____:_____   Hard

                                      Teachers
Friendly   _____:_____:_____:_____:_____:_____:_____   Unfriendly

                                  Making Friends
Easy   _____:_____:_____:_____:_____:_____:_____   Hard

                                  My Appearance
Good   _____:_____:_____:_____:_____:_____:_____   Bad

                                  Other People
Like me   _____:_____:_____:_____:_____:_____:_____   Don't like me

                                  Missing School
Like   _____:_____:_____:_____:_____:_____:_____   Don't like

                                     Reading
Like   _____:_____:_____:_____:_____:_____:_____   Hate

                               My Sense of Humor
Good   _____:_____:_____:_____:_____:_____:_____   Bad

                                   My Future
Good   _____:_____:_____:_____:_____:_____:_____   Bad

                                       TV
Interesting   _____:_____:_____:_____:_____:_____:_____   Dull

                                  Reading Class
Fun   _____:_____:_____:_____:_____:_____:_____   Boring

371

(continued)

My Brother

Nice   ____:____:____:____:____:____:____   Mean

My Character

Ambitious   ____:____:____:____:____:____:____   Lazy

My Sister

Like   ____:____:____:____:____:____:____   Don't like

My Body

Like   ____:____:____:____:____:____:____   Don't like

Food

Good   ____:____:____:____:____:____:____   Bad

Night

Good   ____:____:____:____:____:____:____   Bad

Sleep

Like   ____:____:____:____:____:____:____   Don't like

Reading

Important   ____:____:____:____:____:____:____   Unimportant

School

Interesting   ____:____:____:____:____:____:____   Uninteresting

My Character

Honest   ____:____:____:____:____:____:____   Phoney

My Personality

Likeable   ____:____:____:____:____:____:____   Not likeable

My Friends

Good   ____:____:____:____:____:____:____   Bad

Math

Easy   ____:____:____:____:____:____:____   Hard

Special Reading Program

Like   ____:____:____:____:____:____:____   Hate

SENTENCE COMPLETION FORM

Name: _____

Directions: Complete each of the following sentences.

1. Summer is _____
2. When I watch television I _____
3. My favorite game _____
4. When it rains I _____
5. When I was younger I used to _____
6. When my hands are dirty I _____
7. My schoolwork is _____
8. The thing I would like best is to _____
9. I feel that money _____
10. If I could do anything today I'd _____
11. I think my future will be _____
12. Spelling is _____
13. Going to church _____
14. Reading is _____
15. When my feelings are hurt I _____
16. Friends _____
17. I would like to show _____
18. My home is_____
19. My clothes _____
20. Laws and rules are _____
21. My biggest worry is _____
22. I am afraid that_____
23. I think boys _____
24. I sleep _____
25. My dreams _____
26. The thing that scares me most _____

27. When I read I _____

28. Fighting is _____

29. My mother _____

30. There are times when I _____

31. I think that eating is _____

32. When I look in the mirror I _____

33. My imagination _____

34. To me God is _____

35. My mind is _____

36. One thing I would change about me is _____

37. I feel that my father _____

38. It bothers me that _____

39. Our family _____

40. I don't feel well _____

41. I think girls _____

42. If I could paint a picture it would be _____

43. My eyes _____

44. Earning a living _____

45. My health _____

46. My worst habit is _____

47. My stomach _____

48. My looks _____

49. When it is dark _____

50. My childhood _____

51. I have trouble understanding why I _____

52. I wish I had _____

53. Death _____

54. One thing about love, I think that _____

55. The thing I'm proudest of is _____

56. When I work on my reading I _____

57. When people take their own lives _____

58. My brother_____

59. I feel upset about _____

60. Other people _____

61. I think most people worry about _____

62. My body is _____

63. Teachers are usually_____

64. Taking tests _____

65. I would like to read about _____

66. My head _____

67. The thing that bothers me about school is _____

68. I am ashamed when I think about _____

69. My sister_____

70. My teacher_____

71. I was embarrassed _____

72. My face _____

73. I feel hurt when _____

74. The nicest thing that ever happened to me was _____

75. I like _____

Names and addresses of companies that publish materials for use in reading.

Addison-Wesley Publishing Co.
2725 Sand Hill Road
Menlo Park, CA 94025

Allyn and Bacon, Inc.
Rockleigh Industrial Park
Rockleigh, NJ 07647

Barnell Loft Ltd.
958 Church St.
Baldwin, NY 11510

Basic Education Trade House
P.O. Box 3102
Greeley, CO 80633

Benefic Press
10300 West Roosevelt Road
Westchester, IL 60153

Continental Press, Inc.
520 East Bainbridge St.
Elizabethtown, PA 17022

Doubleday and Co., Inc.
277 Park Avenue
New York, NY 10017

Fearon Publishers
6 Davis Drive
Belmonte, CA 94002

Field Educational Publications, Inc.
2400 Hanover St.
Palo Alto, CA 94304

Garrard Publishing Co.
1607 North Market St.
Champaign, IL 61820

Ginn and Co.
191 Spring St.
Lexington, MA 02173

Globe Book Co.
175 Fifth Avenue
New York, NY 10010

E. M. Hale and Co.
1201 South Hastings Way
Eau Claire, WI 54701

Harcourt, Brace, Jovanovich
757 Third Avenue
New York, NY 10017

Harper and Row, Inc.
10 East 53rd St.
New York, NY 10022

Jamestown Publishers
P.O. Box 6743
Providence, RI 02904

Kenworthy Educational Service, Inc.
P.O. Box 3031, 138 Allen St.
Buffalo, NY 14205

Lyons and Carnahan, Inc.
407 East 25th St.
Chicago, IL 60616

The Macmillan Publishing Co.
866 Third Avenue
New York, NY 10022

Charles E. Merrill Publishing Co.
1300 Alum Creek Drive
Columbus, Ohio 43216

Prentice-Hall, Inc.
Englewood Cliffs, NJ 07632

Random House
201 East 50th St.
New York, NY 10022

Reader's Digest Services, Inc.
Educational Division
Pleasantville, NY 10570

Scholastic Magazines and Book Services
50 West 44 St.
New York, NY 10036

Scott, Foresman, and Co.
1900 East Lake Avenue
Glenview, IL 60025

Science Research Associates, Inc.
259 East Erie St.
Chicago, IL 60611

Steck-Vaughn Company
Box 2028
Austin, TX 78767

Webster Division of McGraw-Hill
  Book Company
1221 Avenue of the Americas
New York, NY 10020

Xerox Educational Publications
Education Center
Columbus, Ohio 43216

INDEX

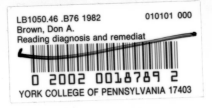